If the Rains
Don't Cleanse

If the Rains
Don't Cleanse

Ben Patrick Johnson

HAVENHURST BOOKS
LOS ANGELES

Also by Ben Patrick Johnson:
In and Out in Hollywood
Third and Heaven
One Size Fits All

Havenhurst Books, Los Angeles 90046
© 2009 by Havenhurst Books
All rights reserved. Published 2009
Printed in the United States of America
14 13 12 11 10 09   5 4 3 2 1
ISBN 978-0-9822853-0-5   0-9822853-0-2
Johnson, Ben Patrick.
If the rains don't cleanse.

To my mother and father, for living extraordinary lives in the service of humankind. With apologies to history, I've taken liberties here and there with time and events, creating some characters and modifying real-life figures to enhance the storytelling. But at its core, the joy and pain on these pages is more real than I, as a writer, could ever hope to invent. Thanks to both of them for the many hours of recorded interviews, answering my umpteen questions, and for patience with my lousy grasp of African tonal language.

I used to wake up in the night in cold sweats, terrified that my parents would die before I had a chance to express how much I admire them both. It was only when I began working on this book that my nightmares went away.

Los Angeles
February 2009

Acknowledgments

IT'S HARD TO BELIEVE that fourteen years have passed between my conceiving this book and the completion of its final draft. Along the way, many people had a role in its inspiration, research, development, and production.

I wish to acknowledge Joseph Conrad for taking English readers to the heart of darkness over a century ago, give thanks to the great Chinua Achebe for laying the literary foundation for modern Africa, thank Isak Dinesen and Beryl Markham for flying west with the night and foreseeing the end of colonialism, and salute Barbara Kingsolver for showing that a story about crazy missionaries can indeed find a wide audience.

Thanks to my parents for seemingly endless hours of recorded interviews and to fellow missionary Ben Hobgood for language and cultural notes.

Thank you to Claudia Cross and Mike Lubin who championed this project at the William Morris Agency early in its life, to agent Alison Picard for bringing four (and counting) of my novels to fruition, to fellow writers Loki Jordan and Gali Kronenberg for their unflinching feedback, to my creative brother Charles Randolph-Wright for tireless advocacy and living-room readings. Credit is due Chris Freeman for superb instincts and a sense of humor, to Johnathan Wilber at Houghton Mifflin Harcourt for bringing the book that swingin' Chicago style, and to Christopher Rice for keeping the literary bar high and putting up with my teasing in the gym.

Finally, thanks to Aubrey Hooks, U.S. Ambassador to the Ivory Coast, for his service to humankind and passion on the subject matter and to West Hollywood Mayor Honorable John Duran for setting an example of how to live out loud yet with dignity.

One

My name is Eva Marie Dunagan.

In two weeks, I will be twenty-seven years old.

The Disciples of Christ Missions board has sent me here. I want to do what is right.

In my pocket are a soiled handkerchief, the case for my tortoise-shell sunglasses, a tattered spiral notebook full of Lonkundo language phrases, and a letter that arrived yesterday from my mother.

I am deep in the interior of the African continent, a stone's throw from the equator. I thought, growing up in Oklahoma City during the Great Depression, that I knew something about heat and despair. My mother raised me in a two-room apartment as the dust bowl swept misery across the parched soil of the panhandle. We scraped for pennies and nickels, improvising poverty-line comfort by sucking on chips of ice and cooling ourselves with funeral home paper fans. But never in those years did I experience anything like this.

In the middle of the day, it is too hot here to think clearly. The air shimmers as it hangs over ragged grass. It is too humid for marital relations, not that there is enough privacy for that anyhow. At noon, my head hurts from the sunlight. It burns my blue eyes. Night brings a brief respite, the simmering jungle cooling as shadows grow long. But with dawn, the temperature rises. It may not be any hotter in Congo than during the dog days of an Oklahoma summer, but back home, summer passes. Here, the heat and humidity are relentless, giving in only twice a year for a short rainy season. Right now, I crave rain.

My husband, Richard, and I have been in Africa for eight weeks and are halfway through our missionary orientation. For four years we trained for this, and now there are days I wonder why. Whatever could my purpose be in this world, which is so thoroughly not my own? I was resolute about coming here, as bullheaded as I am about everything I do. I brace against the strangeness.

The Africans we see are dirty and half-naked, their skin running with sweat. Many have tattoos, like war wounds, on their cheeks and foreheads. Some wear their teeth chipped down to little points. I remind myself each day not to pass judgment simply because of their primitive appearance. I have been trained not to judge.

I sit next to Richard in the back of a battered pickup truck, jostling along a rutted path through thick green foliage that threatens to grow across the narrow road and block our way. I read in a book on Congolese geography that such overgrowth happens quickly. After a rainy season and some powerful equatorial sun, the men have to go out and clear the road with Bulgarian machetes on a weekly basis. The governor requires it, like a tax.

It is not far to our destination, and we are full of the Holy Spirit, though today's business promises to be ghoulish. We are being taken for a day trip to the local leper colony. It is part of our training.

I had nightmares about it last night. I lay beneath mosquito netting, watching the glowing wick of the kerosene lantern that hangs from the rafters. A breeze catches the lamp sometimes, and shadows shift on the walls. I hear creatures calling in the jungle, and it makes me shiver despite the heat. Last night, faces of the dying were standing around my bed. They walked toward me, sad and determined. There were withered old women and bright-eyed babies with no idea that, with or without the Lord, they would soon be gone from this earth. The women wheezed and whispered and reached for me with wilted fingers.

I awoke with a start. Richard slept soundly beside me.

This morning Martha Stubbins, the wiry, gray-haired nurse in charge of medical care on the Disciples of Christ mission where we are staying, gives us a ride. She runs the leper colony, delivers babies on the mission, and in between, practices dentistry, powering her diamond-tipped drill with the treadle of an old Singer sewing machine.

It is just ten-thirty, but the temperature already has risen to thirty-seven degrees centigrade. In the oppressive humidity, clothes hold no crease, straight hair no curl. I look at myself in the cracked side mirror of the pickup. I wear a broad-brimmed hat to shield my face from the sun. The straw of the hat matches the color of the long skirt and cotton blouse, which I made myself from a mail-order pattern. In the mirror, I see dark circles of sweat in the fabric under my arms. I sigh and take a swig of water from the canvas-wrapped canteen beside me.

I learned very quickly that it is futile to put on makeup in Congo. On the morning after we arrived, I fixed up my face with lipstick and eyebrow pencil, trying to feel pretty after a long, most unglamorous trip. Within minutes, the lipstick melted into the cracks of my skin and the eyebrow pencil ran into my eyes. Now I just stay clean and am content not to have dust caked in the folds of my elbows and knees.

We jostle alongside the Tshuapa River, one of countless tributaries to the Congo. Down the embankment, there is a Disciples of Christ minister and half a dozen shirtless Africans standing waist deep in the river with their arms raised and palms turned to the sky. The water looks like day-old coffee. The minister is speaking to the group.

"Another baptism," Martha says, pointing. She always is terse, always instructing.

"We've performed over four hundred this year," she boasts. "Bringing 'em over to the side of the righteous. Before we got here, things were pretty bad. Raw open ulcers. The African men had bunches of wives; they beat 'em good when they felt like it, too. Worshipped little pieces of wood instead of God, had slaves. There were cannibals, all the worst that you've heard."

As the truck draws closer to the algae-covered rocks that line the river, I hear the group belting out "O Happy Day" in Lonkundo, their native tongue. I smile to myself. The music reminds me of home. I miss my home.

A few of the missionaries at Mondombe have made little flower gardens in front of their houses, set off from the dirt path by stones they have carried up from the river. I like the little gardens. They are familiar sights and smells in this otherwise strange place. Beyond that, the landscape here is devoid of anything that blooms. The colors that meet my eyes as we sputter along are overwhelmingly green and orange-brown, the palette of leaves and soil. I always imagined the jungle would be more vibrant.

My jaw tightens as we near the edge of the leper colony. There is a palpable feeling of death in the air, so thick that I think I can smell it. I remember my dream from last night.

Martha's truck lurches to a stop on the thick razor grass. She pulls the hand brake aggressively. It ratchets tight. At first, what lies before us looks to be a typical African village, interchangeable with any we have seen. A dozen packed-mud huts are arranged in two straight lines, one row on either side of a central path. The huts are modest in their construction, with mangy thatch roofs made from palm fronds. At the end of the path is a makeshift clinic, distinguished from the others by its corrugated-iron roof, leopard spotted with rust.

Martha marches ahead of us, medical bag tucked sternly under her arm like a riding crop. Richard and I move closer to the buildings, walking between two of the mud huts, toward the center of the village. We hear a yelp, then a little boy appears around the corner and comes running up to greet us, grinning and flailing his skinny arms. Without intending to, I turn away, unprepared for the sight. He has no nose, just two holes in his face surrounded by decaying flesh.

"It's okay, Eva," Richard promises. His Tennessee tenor is sweet but has the familiar hollowness I have heard in my own voice when saying something purely because I ought to.

I brace myself. Of course it's okay. I am prepared for this. I turn to the little boy again. He stops ten feet in front of us, cocks his head to one side and looks at me curiously. After a moment's hesitation, he offers me a gap-toothed smile and a gentle wave. The boy is missing two fingertips. I try to smile back, but something is wrong with my mouth. After what is surely a miserable grimace, I look down at the dirt. I must do better than this.

"This is Mbende," Martha tells us, walking toward the boy. "His father died two months ago, right about the time you arrived here in Congo, but he's recovering." Martha looks around the compound like a mother bird counting her chicks, squinting and shielding her eyes from the sun.

"Come on, then," she says curtly, gesturing to the medical hut. "It's part of your orientation."

Little Mbende waves goodbye.

For the rest of the morning, we follow Martha on her rounds, dispensing antibiotic sulfa and compassion to all who will receive it. At first, I am afraid to touch the lepers, squeamish at the sight of their molding-potato flesh, but Martha assures me it is safe. I cannot catch what they have. At one point, I stop for a moment and ask myself, is it leprosy of which I am most afraid, or desperation?

There are a hundred, perhaps a hundred and fifty, lepers in the camp. Those who are able to care for themselves tend to those who have lost such facility. A number of the younger men hew out logs to make clumsy-looking wooden river canoes, which they sell to healthy natives in the nearby villages. The lepers also build their own mud-and-palm-thatch huts, though I cannot imagine how the buildings stand up to the rainy season, about which we have been amply warned.

Richard and I are just beginning to learn the Lonkundo language, so our ability to communicate is limited. Today, however, we do not need words to understand the Africans. The lepers' deep-set stares tell their stories in the universal language of pain.

Several times, I have to stop and sit, collecting my wits before I can continue. I cannot imagine myself in these people's condition, lying around a fire at the center of the village in the thick tropical heat, slowly rotting. Maybe Jesus is exactly the hope they need. But hope for what? For salvation? A heaven where they have arms and legs that work, where they will once again embrace loved ones lost to malaria, to rot, to the wrong end of a machete?

Some of the lepers have fans made from elephant tails, which they use to shoo flies off their festering wounds. The fans appear to be their only possessions. I know the notion is ghastly, but I am struck by how much the wrinkled, amputated elephant tails look like an extension of the lepers' own decaying arms.

Again, they smile at me. How is it they can do that and I cannot return the simple gesture? I may have Jesus to sell them, but these natives already have something I do not even understand.

We go back to the truck to eat our lunch, though I have little appetite. I spread a dishtowel on the hood of the truck and fix sandwiches from a can of horsemeat I packed this morning. Martha brought ripe bananas and guava. I watch as she spits seeds on the ground. I put mine in my handkerchief and empty them into the brush after we have finished eating. As we trail Martha on her afternoon rounds, I take a long look at Richard's face. I don't understand how he can be so cool. I pull him aside.

"Why have you been so quiet?" I ask.

Richard squints and looks out across the compound. An old native woman, still graced with the attachment of all her body parts, watches suspiciously from the shade of a doorway.

"I reckon I'm just trying to do what we're here for," he says at last, wiping the sweat and dust from his brow with a handkerchief. Yes, this is what we are here for. Still, this is nowhere I have ever been, and my heart doesn't know what to do with what I am beholding.

Richard is a year younger than I am. Sometimes it seems as though we are even further apart than that. Then again, there are times when he acts as though he is the older brother I never had. I never will be able to understand men and what makes them behave the way they do.

We have been married for three years now, and I do not know whether how we get along is the way married people should. I can only speculate, as my real father left us when I was two years old. When my mother finally remarried, it was to a bachelor nine years her elder, a man who withdrew for days at a time. I have never really felt I know him.

"I just . . . I can't rightly imagine what God has in mind, making his creatures so pitiable," I say. "Why would you want to go on living?"

Richard surveys the camp, silent and still. Children laugh and scamper across the ground, raising a cloud of dirt in their wake. A man with his decaying arm in a sling ambles through the dust, waving the cloud from his nostrils with his good hand.

"Well, now, then," Richard says slowly, pursing his lips. "The Lord gives us great strength, each of us and each of them." He nods toward the lepers. "It's our duty to persevere, not to surrender. If Martha got all weak kneed like you-no offense-nothing would get done around here. There'd be no one to minister to these . . . whaddya call . . . to the sick and dying."

I look at the miserable congregation before us.

At the equator, the sun sets at precisely six every evening. As the afternoon sun begins to give way to shadow, the heat relents. It does that each day, like a fever breaking after a bout of influenza. Martha takes a swig from my canteen, drawing the back of her hand across her mouth to dry her lips. I watch and think about how ungraceful her gestures are. During my tenure in Congo, will

I, too, lose what little bit of refinement my mother worked so hard to teach me? Growing up as poor as I did, I did not have the privilege of white gloves and fancy tea parties, the way young Southern women do in the books and movies, but Mother always taught me to comport myself in a respectable, ladylike manner.

Martha packs up her things to go. We stand with her in the medical shed as she fills out requisition forms for more sulfa, more bandages. She walks to the food hut and checks the lepers' supply of palm nuts. The oil from the bright orange nuts sustains them, as does manioc root. These are staples of the Nkundu diet, which are sometimes supplemented with fresh meat and other delicacies. Here at the leper camp, the manioc is all they ever have. It is not a regime that I would want to endure.

I trail Martha as she counts the palm-nut clusters, writing numbers on her typewritten form.

"How do you do it?" I ask quietly.

Martha looks at me without any trace of emotion.

"Why are you here?" she asks me after a pause.

I stammer an inconclusive reply and feel my cheeks flush with embarrassment. A moment passes before Martha speaks again.

"I just do," she says at last. "It's not like I imagined it would be. There is no preparation they can give you for this. I waited awhile before bringing you and Richard here because I wanted to be sure you were ready."

I nod as though I am right along with her on this point.

"Years ago, when I first got here," she continues, "we didn't have sulfa to treat these people. All we could do was dab on some chaulmoogra oil, bandage them up, and say a prayer. Now, at least, we can give them a shred of hope. You'll see that hope on their faces, if you look for it. Tell me that it's not worth it, being here."

She glances at me for a moment, as a trace of a smile appears on her lips. Then she looks back out at the lepers, their skin leathery from years in fierce sun, shooing away flies, waiting to die, waiting to be cured, waiting for a miracle from the Christ the missionaries have promised them.

"Come on," she says. "When you get your permanent assignment, there's no telling what you'll encounter, but pray to God it's no more desperate than this."

I feel so green.

Martha tucks her clipboard under the arm of her sweat-stained uniform, turning and walking back to the medical shed. I don't follow her immediately, instead reaching down and picking up a fat, pumpkin-color palm nut. I notice its surface is smooth, shiny, and surprisingly cool as I roll it back and forth in my hands. A boy, older and less disfigured than the one who greeted us on our arrival, walks up to where Richard stands leaning against the doorway of Martha's shed. The boy holds a wooden carving he has made. It is a statuette of a man, maybe five inches tall. The boy hands it to Richard reverently, as if it were an offering placed on the altar in church. When Richard takes the fetish and shows it to Martha, the young African grins.

All day, the lepers have ogled us, but I have been dismissing it. I realize now that we must appear wealthy to them. They are the poorest of the poor, starving but for a bit of manioc and the good will of others, ostracized by their families and former neighbors, owning nothing but elephant-tail fans and yards of the frayed, dirty cloth that comforts them at night. Compared to them, we live like royalty, with tailored shirts and stylish plastic eyeglass frames. We have sturdy shoes on our feet and a truck to navigate the gravel roads, albeit precariously. Most of all, we have five digits securely attached to each hand and each foot and the narrow Caucasoid noses of power firmly planted on our faces.

AS WE RETURN TO THE MISSION, a steamboat arrives, rusted and weary from the half-century it has spent negotiating the Congo's swirling channels, and moors at the bank of the river. The boat could use a coat of paint and, most probably, a good deal of mechanical repair. Its native officers have put up a gangway and are beginning a procession, unloading crates and drums to the bank.

Off to one side, stands a tall, rigid African man observing the goings-on with an air of aristocratic impartiality. He is somewhere in his thirties, although his dark sunglasses obscure my view of his face. He wears white trousers and a crisp, long-sleeved white shirt. Acne scars roughen his cheeks and a sour expression draws his mouth tight.

"Is that the boat captain?" I ask Martha, as Richard heads back up the hill to clean up for dinner.

"No, the captain's an old man. This one," Martha says, pointing at the man, "he's up from Bolenge, where you'll be heading once you finish your orientation. You may end up working with him—he's a teacher, too."

"If he's from Bolenge, what's he doing up here?" I ask.

"Waiting on a package he ordered from Brussels and collecting a bride's dowry for someone in his family," Martha says, turning to lift a big canvas bag of medical supplies from the back of the truck. "It's a tricky negotiation they go through, with the dowry, I mean. If you ask me, it's a lot easier just to have the girl's father pay for the wedding the way we do."

I watch more boxes come off the boat.

"What do they use for the dowry? I mean, how do they pay?"

The white-clad man crosses his arms and growls something in Lonkundo at one of the boat officers. The officer either does not hear or is ignoring him.

"He'll probably negotiate some brass spears, anklets maybe, a copper rod or two," Martha says. "Most of these people don't put a lot of faith in paper money. Wouldn't do them much good, to tell you the truth. Got nowhere to spend it."

"I see."

"If you're so curious, why don't you go talk to him?" she suggests.

I demur. I don't want to admit it, but as I look at the man, the sternness of his manner intimidates me.

"Go on," Martha urges me. "He speaks good French. I talked him up for a few minutes this morning."

"All right," I say.

Reluctantly, I cross through the thick grass of the riverbank to where the white-clad African stands.

"Bonjour, Monsieur," I say tentatively as I approach him.

The man turns and very slowly looks me up and down without answering. Then he grins. "Bonjour, Mademoiselle," he says succinctly, taking a toothpick from its resting place upon his lip.

"C'est Madame," I correct him, surprised at his presumption.

With a smirk and a casual wave of the back of his hand, he dismisses the distinction I have drawn.

"To me, it's all the same." There comes a sly hint of a smile. He is flirting with me. I feel myself blush.

"I . . . I . . . understand you're from Bolenge?" I continue in French.

"I am one of the important men of Bolenge, yes. And, white woman, you are a missionary. A new one."

"Yes, it's true. How did you know?"

"It is in the way you carry yourself. You do not yet know the ways of the jungle. It is apparent when you approach."

"Well, I—"

"It is of no concern. For I shall teach you what you need to know." He winks.

This man has a lot of gall.

"Thank you, really," I say as coolly as I can, "but I've had lots of classes, my husband and I have. I . . . we're doing very well on our own, and I . . . I just came over to ask you about the dowry you're collecting and to tell you that we're teachers, and we're going to be stationed at Bolenge, so I thought—"

"What is your name?" he asks.

"Dunagan. Madame Dunagan."

"And I am Joseph Boale. You will hear talk of me. I have no more time for your idle conversations now. I will see you on the Bolenge mission when you arrive."

I wait for him to tell me goodbye. Instead, he turns his back to me and walks toward the boat, where a parcel, presumably his, is being precariously maneuvered down the gangway.

EVENING COMES.

The hours that follow dusk are the most pleasant time of day in Congo. The heat breaks. Insects sing in the distance. Monkeys chatter about the day's events from tree to tree. Tonight, I have changed clothes, trading the dusty things I wore to the leper colony for the button-up cotton pajamas and heavy shirt in which I will sleep. Martha's houseboy cooks dinner for us tonight, setting bowls of soup and crusty bread on the table in her wood-and-brick house. After endless seasons of being chewed to a hollow honeycomb by termites, one leg of her wooden table is precipitously shorter than the others, so as Martha sits down, she reaches instinctively to shove an upturned tuna-fish can under the offending limb.

We say grace and lay our napkins in our laps. Just as I take my first bite, Martha stands abruptly, looking with alarm toward the window.

"Oh, mercy," she whispers, reaching up and cupping her hand behind the wick of the lamp overhead. With a quick breath, she blows out the fire.

I look to see what startled her so. A cloud of some kind of insects moves toward us in the twilight. They come in through the open window, thousands of them. Martha dashes into the humble back room, lighting the lamp and picking up a cut glass perfume atomizer. She sprays the air of the little room liberally, and the smell of lavender reaches us quickly. I swat insects out of my face, but most of the cloud is moving toward Martha. She hurries out of the little room and comes back to the table.

"Flying ants," she explains, catching her breath and adjusting her spectacles set askew in the rush. "They come by from time to time."

In short order, the bugs have all but left the room where we sit, drawn to the perfume and light of the other part of the house. I look down, dumbfounded, at a pair of ant wings floating in my soup.

"Here, let me strain it for you," Martha says, taking my bowl.

I look at Richard, who raises his eyebrows in comical dismay.

Martha returns, exhaling loudly and setting my bowl back in front of me.

"Part of your orientation!" she says with an air of finality.

NOW, AS I SIT, I can hear the Tshuapa River rolling by the Mondombe mission, another gurgling tributary making its way to the mighty Congo. It flows all day and all night, bringing me blissfully peaceful sleep. I rest my eyes as Richard listens to a seventy-eight of Fred Waring and his Pennsylvanians on a hand-crank phonograph borrowed from the mission.

When the record has finished, Richard comes over and sits beside me.

"You're listening to it again," he says.

"Huh?"

"The river. The water. You get a particular look on your face when you're listening to it. You had that look about you a lot while we were coming here."

The boat trip from the capital Léopoldville to the Mondombe mission was slow, and I was anxious. We spent day after day sunning and reading aboard the General Winston, a proud old steamboat with three decks tiered like a big-city wedding cake. The Missions board booked us a cabin in the first-class section, as Europeans simply do not travel in steerage. It was a cooler ride for us on the top deck than for the Africans, deep in the belly of the boat, for we received the questionable benefit of the breeze constantly blowing across the river.

Those below us were forced to contend with the insects that swarm at the surface of the water. At day's end, the millions of mosquitoes formed such a thick cloud that they would appear as a sort of shivery fog. Hippos trumpeted on either side of the boat, outraged at being disturbed. The poorest natives were allowed to tether flat barges to the sides of riverboats. One of the African officers on the General Winston told us that he does not bother keeping a head count of those in steerage or on the barges. Sometimes there are casualties from malaria, and the bodies of the dead are disposed of in the river.

"However, it's been over six months since we lost a passenger," he boasted, leaning against the panel of knobs and wheels that control the boat.

The officer held a dish of fried grubs, slick with palm oil, picking one up and biting into it. Oil dripped on his chin, which he wiped with the back of his sleeve. The officer extended the dish to offer us a larva. I declined.

As we made our way up the five-mile-wide Congo River, natives in hollowed-out-log canoes pulled away from docks and paddled alongside us, hawking food and earthen cooking pots to the passengers on the lowest deck. Crowds of natives formed at the bank. At first, I assumed they were waiting for the boat to arrive to bring them something—a parcel, a loved one—but we moved past each crowd without stopping. I realized after a time that it was the sheer spectacle of the boat's passage that drew them. We served as entertainment. The Africans stood watching in the clearings, bare breasted and tattooed, shading their eyes from the powerful sun, hopping with excitement and waving as we passed.

"White man! Mondele!" they called to us in Lingala, the language spoken along the river.

Richard went out on deck and snapped their pictures with his Argus. We waved back at the natives, and they clapped their hands as though our very acknowledgment was worthy of applause.

As the second day of our trip drew to a close, I began to feel distinctly dirty. The officer asked Richard and me whether we would like to bathe. We accepted. For ten francs, we had the privilege of using the bath in his cabin. It was the only bath on the boat that worked. I stood in the chipped porcelain stall and lifted a bucket of river water over my head, squinting tightly as the wet-ness stung my eyes. The water was warm, drawn from the Congo's tepid current. It shared the weak-coffee color of the Tshuapa's water but was thick like mulled cider and smelled lived in." As eager as I was for the dousing, I could not wait to be finished and dry myself with a towel.

The General Winston slowed to a crawl each evening, pulling in closer to shore, for there was no light in the sky but the thinnest slice of moon to guide our way. Under such conditions, the surface of the Congo River becomes glassy, its undisturbed width stretch-ing as far as the eye could see.

Each evening of our trip, Richard would turn down the sheets of the bunk in our hot, stuffy little cabin, kiss me good night, and crawl into bed. I sat up, writing in my diary by the glow of a wall-mounted kerosene lantern. Around each of us hung a gauzy drap-ery of mosquito netting. Again and again, we have been instructed to keep it tucked tightly under our mattress to ward off malaria as we sleep.

When the third day wound down, the captain drew the boat quite close to the shore, explaining on his public-address micro-phone that there were devil's currents ahead in the deeper channels of the river. As we got closer to the shore, I became excited. For the first time I could distinctly hear the sound of the jungle at night, buzzing and humming, cawing and quarreling in the darkness. This was what a circus midway would sound like if it could whisper. In-termittently, there came the screeching of Kulokoko birds—huge, gangly things that should live in nightmares instead of trees.

Out on deck, some of the other passengers giggled and chatted in the moonlight, sipping liquor, playing cards, and singing bawdy folk songs in French and Lingala. Sometimes their cigarette smoke drifted into our porthole and made my nose itch. Where I come from, cigarette smoking is looked upon as a vice that puts you just one step closer to sin.

I LAY BETWEEN THE THREADBARE SHEETS and closed my eyes. There was a high-pitched buzzing sound near me. Somehow, a mosquito had gotten past the netting. I sat up and—thwack!—I smacked the palm of my hand against the wall. The netting shuddered. Richard stirred and opened his eyes, looking up at me in confusion.

"It's okay. Go back to sleep," I whispered, and he did.

13

I looked at the spot where I hit the wall, and there was a mangled mosquito. There also was, next to the bug, a tiny smear of red against the whitewash. Apparently, I had struck a little too late. The light from my lantern flickered, and, as I shook the tin base of the lamp, the flame went out. There was no more kerosene.

I lay still, thinking about the millions of creatures God has put on this earth, each making its own way, scraping and struggling to survive. Then I wondered what an Oklahoma girl was doing in the middle of a big, dark night on the Congo River. I have come a great distance to find a patch of peace.

RICHARD BLOWS OUT THE FLAME in the lamp that lights our borrowed room. In the darkness I see the faces of the lepers again, this time from memory rather than imagination. I stare into their dark eyes and try to see the hope of which Martha spoke so optimistically.

Dear God, I pray, protect these people. Give them relief from the scourge that has beset their bodies, and free them to Your service, as You have both freed and charged me to serve.

Having finished my prayer, I kiss Richard good night and head to our mosquito-netted bed. I see the arrogant man from the boat, who repeats his pronouncement from this afternoon: "I have no more time for your idle conversations now."

In the dark, I stick out my tongue at him.

I counted one hundred fifty-four little red sandfly bites on my limbs and shoulders last week. But now, after wearing long cotton socks and long sleeves and being diligent with the mosquito netting, I am down to seventy-four. I'll get the hang of this yet.

Two

I HAVE THIS TERRIFYING FEELING that if I stop moving, I will cease to exist. I will break apart into a thousand pieces or simply dissolve.

The first time I felt the panic was when I was a little girl. I am now a young woman, and it still chases me. Sometimes it is barely there. Sometimes it is a shadow loping gently after my every step. Once in a while it threatens to consume me. I fight back with all I have, though sometimes my methods are unusual.

My Zonta Club sister Esther convinced me to go to a party on Friday night. I should have known not to. I had a miserable time. I am not quite sure what I was expecting, but Esther made it sound fun. Then again, Esther makes everything sound fun. In any case, I did not plan to end up standing by myself in a corner, sipping 7 Up punch, and looking through leather-bound volumes in a girls'-club library in Enid, Oklahoma. I was valedictorian of Phillips University last year, but no one at the party paid me particular mind. I suspect other things make them tick. Maybe that is part of why I have never fit in.

This autumn marks my first year of graduate seminary at Phillips, and I am restless to begin making my mark in the world. It is not as though I have been a social hermit the last four years. I have dated a little. I have gone out. I started seeing boys soon after I arrived here. I went out with Norm, then Bud, then Timothy. At least, I think Timothy was third. Actually, I have been trying to let the particulars slip from memory. None of the well-scrubbed young men I dated as an undergraduate ever seemed meant for my life ahead. Now, I am simply too occupied with schoolwork to bother much with romance. Hence, as Esther would say, my current predicament.

I study all day every day, cramming for Greek-language and Old Testament quizzes until dawn. I dull pencils and gray typewriter ribbons, polishing term papers on religious education and Plato and the Babylonian captivity. I take pride in being an A student. My church and family expect it of me for all they have done to get me here. Ultimately, I expect it of myself. I would be ashamed to open my transcript and see a B. Getting a B would mean that I was average. I think of being average and shudder, the specter of mediocrity almost too much to bear.

Still, when Friday nights come around, I look at my textbooks with remorse, whispering a silent promise in their direction before heading off to the lavatory to fix myself up. I consider most of this ritual rather unnecessary and quaint, but there remains in my head the danger of ending up an old maid or imperfectly married like my mother.

It is a ritual: I set my hair in pins, laying brushes and my few cosmetics out on the counter, vying for mirror space with the other girls in my dormitory. I have a matching sweater and skirt, bought with saved-up toot money my mother sent me. A girlfriend, usually Esther, zips me up. I hook a costume gold chain behind my neck, pull on bobby socks and loafers, and I am set for the evening. If I am seeing a young man, then Norm or Bud or whoever will pick me up, and we will go to the game or perhaps out to the Varsity Shop afterwards, and that is about the extent of it. I usually am back in the girls' dormitory by ten. If I am not dating someone, I go to the movies with Esther, in which case I am home even earlier. It is not so very different from high school, really, except the dorm mother and not my stepfather sets the curfew.

I have gone on like this for four years—studying, setting my hair pins, dating, falling in and out of small-time romance, writing letters home, opening letters of commendation from the dean, darning the holes in my moth-eaten Zonta jacket.

I KNOCK ON ESTHER'S DOOR. It is eight o'clock on Sunday morning. I know it's early to stop by, but Esther should be up for chapel soon anyhow.

"Whoever it is, you may go to hell," Esther mumbles from behind the closed door.

"It's me, and you're lucky it is," I whisper, hoping no one else heard her blasphemy.

"Come back in a week. My hangover should be gone by then."

"Don't tell me you stayed out carrying on," I say, though by now I am not surprised.

"All right, I won't tell you."

There is a long pause. I wonder if Esther has fallen back asleep. "Hello?"

"Eva, I love you. Now go away."

I realize I had better work quickly.

"You know those blue suede pumps you got last winter?"

"Yes, I know them; they belong to me. And yes, you may borrow them but not until after twelve noon. Do we have a deal?"

"We have a deal."

"Then scram."

"Gone," I promise, and tiptoe off.

I will need Esther's pumps to go with my blue dress for my unofficial coming out. Tonight is the final night of the annual Phillipian Festival, our academic counterpart to homecoming. All week there have been events, but tonight is the talent show. I have decided to contribute a dramatic reading. Maybe someone in the audience will understand why I am doing this; maybe some kindred soul will resonate with my own.

I have always been my own lifeline. I know I cannot expect that to change. But I am full of aspiration.

I primp and fix my hair, so that the ends fall gently on my shoulders. I slip on Esther's shoes and place a fresh handkerchief in my purse, walking across campus and waiting in the audience to hear my name called.

There is a full house for the talent show. A young man from the football squad does magic tricks, then some girls sing a song in three-part harmony. None of them are any good. The audience claps politely.

At last it is my turn. The hall is quiet as I make my way to the center of the stage. I've written some notes on index cards but do not refer to them often, as I recall from memory a story that has stuck with me since I read it in the local newspaper a few months ago. It is the account of a doctor who took a job in a mental institution. He was walking down the hallway on the afternoon of his first day of work and passed one of the patients. The man stood swabbing the floor with a large, heavy, steel-handled mop. As the doctor walked by him, the patient looked up from his work, and their eyes met. Suddenly, a memory was sparked.

A decade earlier, there had been a traffic accident by the side of a rural highway. It was late at night and rain beat down upon the pavement. The doctor slowed and rolled down his window to look at the damage. A woman lay dying, bleeding to death in the lone, crumpled car. Her husband or lover ran from the ditch when the doctor slowed, crying out pitifully and begging him to take the woman to a hospital. The doctor hesitated for a moment, then thought about the appointment he had to get to and sped up, passing the scene, squeezing his eyes shut to block the image from his mind.

Now, as the doctor looked at the patient in the hallway, he realized it was the dying woman's companion from back on the highway. The doctor was silent, full of shame and remorse, reminded of myriad shortcomings that may serve to define a man more honestly and completely than a listing of the certificates and accolades he has accrued.

Just as the bent back of the patient slipped from view, the doctor thought he saw the shadow of the heavy mop head rising up, ready to come crashing down on his skull.

The doctor froze with fear. Time refused to advance. He flinched as he heard the linoleum creak behind him. He could not turn around. He could not step forward. The doctor strained his eyes to one side, trying again to see the patient's shadow on the wall, but there was none. The doctor's heart beat so violently that he was sure it was going to burst out of his chest.

He counted to ten. Slowly, the doctor found the courage to move. He turned around at a snail's pace, still anticipating that at any moment a sharp blow could arrive at the back of his head. When he had rotated enough to where he could steal a glance behind him, there was the patient, the mop planted firmly on the floor, scrubbing back and forth. Oblivious to the doctor's presence, the patient shook his head and wept quietly, mumbling the name Mary to himself in the voice that could belong only to a man bereft.

I draw out the last words of the story for dramatic emphasis, and when it is done, the audience in the little auditorium is still. After an uncomfortable silence, someone starts to clap. It takes a moment to become infectious, but soon they all are standing.

"Yeah! Yeah!" my classmates cheer, pronouncing the word in a way that only Oklahomans can.

Esther is waiting for me as I come off stage.

"Do you hear them? They adore my shoes," she says.

I walk with her across campus.

"Do you think they'll remember me now?" I ask as we get to the girls' dorm.

"My money's on yes, especially that Richie Dunagan."

"Excuse me?"

Richard Dunagan is the last person at Phillips I would expect to pay me any attention.

"He was asking about you right after you finished."

"Well? What did you tell him?"

"I told him you're very busy," Esther says carefully.

"You didn't tell him that I was seeing anybody, did you?"

"No. Well . . . no." Esther shakes her head.

We walk up the stairs toward her room. I pull off the pumps.

"What do you mean? Wh-why do you say it like that?" I stammer.

"I just told him you were very busy," she giggles, "and he probably shouldn't get his hopes up."

"Esther!" I shout and drop onto her bed. We sit cross-legged as we always do when it is time to gossip. Esther rummages through the crumpled paper in an empty chocolate box, but there are no hidden treasures to be found.

Esther's mother sends her a shoebox full of sweets every week, though she knows Esther is on the heavy side and has no business eating any more goodies than the cafeteria matrons dollop on her tray each morning and afternoon. It's her mother's way of showing love, and Esther's way is by eating whatever she is sent. From the looks of it, Esther and her mother love each other a lot.

My own mother sends me a few dollars when she can, but her discretionary funds are more often spent in a doctor's office. It is there she can get a $3.50 hormone shot that leaves her feeling cheerful for days. When my mother has to go without her hormone shots, she does not talk much, preferring to stay in bed with the blinds drawn.

"I know I certainly wouldn't turn down a date with Richard Dunagan," Esther says, savoring his name as if the words were dipped in butter.

Esther's opinion is popular—Richard is a handsome young man, a pretty boy who has the tact to behave as if he doesn't know it's true. He is almost painfully slender and stands straight as a rail. He wears his honey-color hair cut short, but a gentle, lilting Tennessee accent betrays his severity every time he opens his mouth.

It should be noted that I do not know about Richard's charms firsthand; I merely have heard of his reputation. Let it suffice to say that Richard Dunagan is held in high regard by a variety of coeds at Phillips University. While I will admit to having some curiosity about Richard, I have come to the firm decision not to see any boys socially unless they are the marrying type. I am aware that this may leave my social life somewhat restricted, but such a rule is what I need to stay focused on my studies. Perhaps with more people on campus knowing who I am, I will be presented with a greater percentage of qualified candidates. From all I have heard, Richard Dunagan does not fall into the husband category. I figure him to be more of a playboy.

It is two days later when he corners me in the library and bashfully asks me out on a date. As a matter of course, I say no.

"You're crazy," Esther scowls, biting into an oatmeal cookie and launching a rockslide of crumbs down the front of her nightgown.

"Well, honestly," I insist, "I just don't have the time. I'm getting ready to start my mission work. I don't need to get wrapped up in some boy right now, and you know that it's true."

I wonder if she will buy it.

"Suit yourself," Esther says, peeling the wax paper off a piece of fudge and biting into it.

I sigh and picture Richard's face as he asked me out.

"He is handsome, is he not?"

"That's my girl," Esther barks with glee, slapping me heartily on my back, her enthusiasm causing me to gulp a lungful of air.

When I recover, I stand and walk to her frost-laced window, looking out at the old stone buildings of the university.

"I guess one date couldn't hurt," I whisper to myself, my breath fogging the windowpane.

I turn back to Esther.

"Give me a piece of that fudge."

AFTER HE ASKS ME TWICE, Richard and I go to the Haymakers basketball game.

I steam press my Zonta jacket with a wet rag and flat iron, take my date-night sweater out of mothballs, and hook my costume gold chain behind my neck.

The date goes well. Watching the game, Richard and I laugh freely, pointing at the players.

"So what're you fixin' to be when you grow up?" he asks, sipping his malted milk after the game.

"Grow up! I'm all grown," I inform him.

"Is that so?"

A Nelson Eddy tune plays on the Varsity Shop jukebox. Moths flit around the screen door, seeking warmth and light on a chilly evening.

I smile. "I want to be a missionary," I tell him.

"Oh, really?" he asks, raising his eyebrows.

I nod enthusiastically, then parrot the response I have given a hundred times to career counselors and church groups.

"Yes, sir! I want to go to Africa and do mission work."

"Why Africa?"

"Because I like the way Negroes show their feelings."

"Whaddya mean by that?" Richard chuckles as if I have just embarrassed myself. He fiddles with a paper napkin on the red-painted countertop.

"Well, I mean just what it sounds like. To me, I see a lot of value in expressing your feelings. It is important to feel. Negroes really feel; they're not embarrassed. They laugh and cry—"

"And they cook," Richard interjects.

"Well, yes, they do cook," I say cautiously. Is he toying with me?

"What I mean is—like I told you—I'm from Memphis. And I'm not ashamed to say that I grew up poor."

"So did I," I add.

"Well, now," he says, commandeering the conversation, "but you're from Oklahoma City, right?"

"Yes. How did you know?"

"Esther told me."

I wonder what else sweet Esther has leaked.

"So you're city poor, but I'm country poor," he says.

"From what I've heard, Memphis isn't exactly a pasture."

"Well, for my family it was. See, I was born in Germantown, ten miles outside the city limits. As my brother and sister and I came up, we had a cow and chickens in the yard. I'll bet you didn't wake up to a rooster crow in Oklahoma City!"

"True, but what exactly is your point?"

"My point," he says with a smirk, "is that while in the city it's very different for white folks and coloreds, I reckon that when you're country poor there's less difference. My parents didn't have many Negro acquaintances, but I saw enough of 'em to know that our lot in life worked out to about the same. They went to different churches from us, but we all prayed to the same God. Only thing is, their cooking was better. We all ate cornbread and greens, but they knew how to make it taste like they weren't poor. No offense to my mother and my aunts, of course."

I laugh.

"But listen to me running my mouth! Tell me more about you. You want to be a missionary in Africa. A Bible-preaching missionary?"

"Maybe. Either that or the teacher kind. I think I might like to teach."

"Well, if I was in your classroom, I'd certainly pay attention," he says, and I blush. Oily smooth, this fellow is.

"So you grew up in Oklahoma City?"

"Yeah. I went to Talmadge High School, and I wrote for the school newspaper and lettered in forensics and—"

"What about your parents?"

I look at Richard for a moment, feeling cautious. Can I trust him? Oh, what the heck.

"My mother remarried. My real father left us when I was two. I never saw him after that, except once . . . maybe. I'm not sure."

"What do you mean?" Richard asks.

I try to remember the particulars.

"One time, when I was about five, I was playing with my friends, and a man in a long woolen coat came up and started talking to me. I didn't know who he was, but he was so kind, I just wasn't afraid. It's like that with me, I reckon. I get a sense of people quickly. And he gave me a bag of candy and just waved and walked off. All I remember is he spoke kindly and he had black leather gloves. I told my mother about it, and she told me not to be talking to strangers any more."

"Wow," Richard says, finishing his malted milk with a noisy slurp of his paper straw. "So it was just the two of you?"

I nod, wiping my mouth with a paper napkin.

"I had a baby sister, but she got sick, and . . ."

I look down at the countertop.

"I'm sorry," Richard says quietly. "I guess I had it easy compared to you. In certain ways, I mean."

I look up at him.

"I . . . my parents had words sometimes when I was growing up, but I believe they love each another. And my brother and sister and I, we're all healthy, and they're both married. My brother, Peter, is a lawyer," he says.

"Well, that's just as fine as anything," I say.

"Mighty fine," Richard agrees. "He's got that law degree up on the wall and lives with his wife, Peggy, in Bristol. Got him a nice little house. My parents are right proud of him."

In the background, the jukebox plays Bing Crosby singing "Going My Way," and the breeze from the ceiling fan picks up my napkin off the counter. I have to reach out to catch it.

"Are your parents proud of you?" I ask.

"Yes. They will be proud. I mean, they are now already, but they will be even more proud of me. I want to do great things."

"And what does that mean to you?"

"Great things?" he asks.

I nod.

"Well, not the usual sort of things people would mention. I don't want to be Mayor or Governor or anything. I don't reckon I'd be especially good at that."

I realize that, more than listening to his words, I am watching the way Richard talks, noticing how his eyes light up when he gets going. The sensible part of me wants to finish the evening, tell Richard good night, and be done with it. But I cannot; I am taken with him. And he has the most handsome lips I have ever seen. I cannot stop staring at them.

"I want to do something to serve the people around me," he says, "and I don't necessarily mean just people in my own community. I mean people all around me, all people. I know it may sound grand—"

"No," I interrupt. "I want the same thing."

We leave thirty-five cents on the counter, and I take my jacket from the rack by the door. Richard walks me across campus to the girls' dorm. It is still early, so we sit in the lounge and talk some more. As I prattle on nervously, he takes a bar of Ivory soap and a

23

pocketknife from his jacket and whittles away until he has made a crude little elephant.

"Here," he says, advancing the beast across the tabletop on a tiny rampage.

Then he pulls a fresh bar of soap from his pocket.

"Your turn," he says with a smile.

Gamely, I take the soap in one hand and the knife in the other, trying to think of what to create. For reasons I cannot understand, I want to impress Richard. Should I sculpt the Taj Mahal? No, too hard to recognize. How about the white cliffs of Dover? Too simple a design. I settle on a little Hansel and Gretel cottage. Richard attempts to guess what it is I am trying to make, each conjecture getting more and more preposterous. Slivers of soap fall onto the carpet, and we laugh quietly, brushing them under the table when the Basset Hound–jowled dormitory monitor click-clacks down the hallway on her rounds.

When it is ten-thirty, Richard stands and picks up his hat. He takes my little German house and hands me his elephant.

"Thank you," he says quietly.

"No, thank you."

I smile in spite of myself. I must remember not to come off too eager. I must remember not to give away the farm. When I was small, my mother taught me that, when it comes to men, aloofness is a virtue.

"Reckon I should be going," Richard says, gesturing to the door.

"Yes, you should." I wish he did not have to.

At Phillips University, we live by a code of chastity. As in our sponsoring churches, Christian youth are expected to remain chaste until marriage.

"I'd like to see you again," Richard says hesitantly.

"I think . . . I mean, I'd like that as well, yes," I fumble.

I walk him to the foyer of the dormitory, and he hugs me a bit awkwardly. I can smell his aftershave, and it makes me pleasantly lightheaded.

"See me tomorrow night," he demands.

"I can't. I'm, uh . . ."

I clear my throat.

"I'm very busy, actually."

"Okay, sure, I understand." He fiddles with the brim of his hat.

I look into his eyes, and neither of us speaks for a moment. The floor below my feet is not solid.

"Maybe just for an hour," I say, and immediately regret even that much of a commitment.

"Great!" Richard grins. "I'll come by after supper."

He turns and bounds off into the late-autumn darkness with a whoop I am sure will summon the dorm mother. I shut the heavy wooden door behind him and look down at the waxy elephant in my hand, then turn and make a beeline for Esther's room.

Three

October 1956

THIS IS MY FIRST TRIP ON AN AIRPLANE.

The uniformed African steward makes certain we all are tightly strapped to our seats, then perches on a bench up by the cockpit. The DC-3's engines rumble to life, and as I look out my little window over the wing, I see propellers catching sunlight and flinging it defiantly back at the heavens. The hull of the plane vibrates along the dirt runway, the props kicking up clouds of dust. We sit three across, seven rows deep, Africans and Europeans side by side as if it does not matter.

The aircraft gains speed. All of a sudden, there is the incredible feeling of floating on air. We have left the ground. Adrenaline races through me. My toes and fingertips prickle from the thrill that comes with defiance of gravity. The plane pitches backward at a sharp angle, and all I can see out the window is sky, deep blue, everywhere. I feel heavy, as if I am going up in an elevator. It is frightening and wonderful at the same time. The little curtains tacked at the sides of the windows sway and jiggle from the angle of our ascent and the vibration of the engines.

My ears begin to feel strange. It is like the time when I was a little girl and my stepfather drove us up into the Ozark Mountains, looking for his childhood home. We wound our way up through the hills, and I could not hear correctly in my right ear until it popped several days later. Now, I yawn and tap at the top of my jaw to try to work out the same kind of pressure. Richard laughs at me.

"Take your finger out of your ear. It's not ladylike," he whispers.

I laugh along with him. It is anxious laughter. This will be an excursion of firsts—my first airplane ride to receive my virgin assignment from the Missions conference. Richard and I have been summoned from Mondombe to the Missions headquarters in Coquilhatville, a small industrial city near the Congo province's western border.

"Ladies and gentlemen, *Mesdames, Mesdemoiselles, Messieurs*— welcome to Sabena Airlines," the pilot says over a loudspeaker.

He takes us up through the clouds over the tropical rainforest. Below us lies a carpet of green—broccoli and little twigs—broken up by meandering rivers and patches of clearing. Everything seems flat.

"Those are plantations," explains the Belgian gentleman with a waxed moustache seated next to us. He loosens his canvas seatbelt and reaches across my lap, pointing out the window at one of the geometrical patches. Richard sits back so all three of us can share the view.

"Who owns the plantations?" Richard asks.

"Europeans." The man shakes his head bitterly. "They've been raping this land for years."

"None of the Africans own plantations?" Richard wonders aloud.

"There are some. Not many. These Africans can be smart," he says quietly, gesturing with a corpulent finger toward the few native passengers on the plane, as if letting us in on a secret. "They've watched how the Europeans do it. A few of the ambitious ones have cleared their own land and planted cacao or palm-nut trees, and they pick the nuts by hand—"

"They do it themselves?" I ask. I cannot imagine landowners, be they white or Negro, laboring in the midday sun with canvas bags slung over their shoulders.

"Oh, heavens, no," the Belgian says with a genteel little laugh that trails into a cough. "They have slaves."

"What?" This makes no sense to me.

"The Bantus think of Pygmies as their property. It's been that way for a long, long time."

I nod slowly, grappling with this new concept.

"You Americans," the man goes on. "You accuse us of *des actions immorales!* You criticize Belgians for mistreating Congo. But what about the way you took America, eh? Forcing natives to march across the country, shaming and butchering them, stealing their lands. Then when we, in our turn, want natural resources *here*, maybe you forget we, too, need natural resources to survive."

I look at the man and think about the Belgians I have met. They strike me as an honest people, with a good work ethic, but are often short, plump, and have ruddy complexions. They resent non-Belgians for having escaped the indignities that come with being from a country whose very name the French toss off as an insult.

The steward walks down the aisle, interrupting my deliberation with his tray of coffee and fruit juice. I never imagined they could brew coffee right onboard an airplane.

Maybe, someday, it will be possible to live on a plane, choosing the sunset and sunrise that pleases you on any given day, cheating or teasing dusk by flying away from or dead into it. I am not certain I would be able to adjust to a life as grand as that, but right now the notion is entertaining.

In an hour and a half, we land in Coquilhatville. This time the runway is made of concrete. The terminal is crowded and hot, and it reminds me of a bus station back home. As we carry our bags through the room, Richard searches his pockets for the letter that requested our appearance today. We find it, at last, in my handbag.

"So the Missions headquarters is south of here?" I ask, trying to make sense of the mimeographed map that was mailed along with our letter.

"East," Richard says, taking the sheet of paper from my hands and turning it to the side.

"Are you sure?" I ask, gently tugging at the corner of the page so it returns to an orientation that seems proper.

"Haven't you ever read a map before? East. That-a-way," Richard insists, triumphantly snatching the corner of the paper from between my fingers and turning the page sideways. Unfortunately, I do not release my grip as quickly as he had anticipated, and the page rips in two.

I am silent. I turn away and put down my suitcase.

"Oh, what now?" he says, a little too cloyingly to suit me.

Again, I am quiet.

"You know what? Your problem is that you can't take being corrected."

I spin around and face him.

"The problem is the way you correct me," I say, "as though I've wronged you and need scolding, as though we're in some kind of competition. I don't want to compete with you, Richard."

"Oh, Eva, calm down, for Pete's sake. You just don't realize that people talk that way all the time."

"Maybe men do, but women do not," I say, trying to keep my voice from letting on how angry he has made me. "They want to be understood. They try to find something they can agree on."

Richard purses his lips and whistles a quick note that rises and falls with exasperation.

"Let's say you and I try to find the Missions headquarters," he says.

"It says here they're sending a driver," I read aloud, handing over my torn bit of paper.

"Do you see any driver?" he asks sarcastically.

As if on cue, a tall, sunburned man with thinning blond hair approaches us.

"Mr. and Mrs. Dunagan?" he asks in a Midwestern accent.

"Yes," Richard says, setting down his suitcase for a handshake.

"I'm Neil Roberts," the man says, shaking Richard's hand. "I've got the Missions van outside."

The traffic in Coquilhatville is sparse but unruly. It moves like a pack of wildcats going after a kill—lean, swift, and shifting. Mr. Roberts negotiates it with a little too much courtesy to suit the drivers around him. As they pass on the left and right, they salute him with gestures and expressions that seem less than cordial. All the while, Neil sings hymns, sweetly off-key. I look out the dirty window of the wood-paneled station wagon and am struck by how unattractive Coquilhatville is. There is dust everywhere, and the sun enamels it to each available surface. Palm trees and Canna flowers have been planted in a well-intentioned effort to bring civility to block after block of drab industrial and office buildings without proper doors, but the effort is in vain.

"What do you do at Bolenge?" Richard asks Mr. Roberts.

"I train ministers," the driver informs us, seeming pleased to answer, though it interrupts his hymns. "I have three native pastors under me, and we have a sizable congregation. It's good to have new hands coming to share the work, as they say."

In short order, we arrive at the Missions house, an austere red-brick building near the center of town. Richard and I bathe in the ancient washrooms, then eat our lunch as we wait nervously for our afternoon appointment. I yawn and discover I cannot hear well in my right ear. I raise my finger to the side of my head to work out the pressure and realize again mid-gesture that there is no discreet way to put one's finger in one's ear, especially at the dinner table. I lay my hand back in my lap.

"This is it, you know," Richard says, looking up from his soup. His hair is slicked back, wet from washing.

"I know." I smile, adjusting the napkin in my lap uncomfortably.

The dining room is well scrubbed, and the cool plaster walls hold the day's heat at bay. The soup we eat is thin, seasoned with some sort of sliced root vegetable. I realize have no appetite. A battered grandfather clock chimes one-thirty. I look up and notice it for the first time. The clock is as out of place in Africa as the Belgian lace doilies that adorn the armchairs in the Missions house's front room, as out of place as everyone present in the middle of Africa.

At the end of the lunch table sits the director of the Missions house. To my left and right are half a dozen other missionaries: some young, others old, some arriving in Africa for the first time, others leaving after a lifetime's wrinkle-deepening labors. As I look from face to face, I become aware that we all wear the same expression, a lean combination of hope and resolve.

When we have finished our meal, the director stands and invites Richard and me into his office down the hall. We follow him silently. He picks up an envelope from his desk theatrically, as though it contains the deed to Manhattan Island.

"Congratulations, Mr. and Mrs. Dunagan," he says, grinning as he hands it over. Although it is addressed to us, the envelope has already been opened. As Richard removes the letter inside, I see the return address—Missions Building, Cleveland 7, Ohio. I smile. I want to kiss the ink on the paper. Richard lets out a whoop as he reads the letter, hugging me.

"You already know you're headed for Bolenge," the director says.

"Yes, but . . ." I scan the tidily typed stationery. There are grease stains on the paper. The letter confirms that Richard and I will be living and working at Bolenge, an hour's trip downriver from where we stand right now. The letter goes on to say that Richard will be principal of the business high school there, and I will teach classes. So now my husband is going to be my boss, eh? It's not what I had imagined, but it promises to be an interesting experiment. I wonder how I will do at a business school. My grades in first-year typing were what kept me from getting all As in high school.

31

The letter is signed:

With much admiration,
Wallace Hinton

All right, Mother, I am ready. It is time to answer my calling. All those years of cooking and laundering for me, sending me half your tithe to help pay for my board at Phillips weren't for naught. Your little girl will now be able to repay your sacrifice.

I sigh, glad we will soon be at Bolenge, where we will at last be able to settle in and begin to make our home here in Congo. I have been living as a guest for too many months and feel conspicuous. I want to earn my keep.

"I've arranged a transport," the director says.

An emotional "yes" is all I can offer in response.

WE RIDE IN THE MISSION'S YELLOW PANEL VAN for the ten-kilometer trip from Coquilhatville. I try to recall the name of the woman we are supposed to contact once we arrive at the mission. I reach into my purse and pull out the typewritten letter, reading it for the tenth time today. Gloria Snead is her name. Gloria Snead. She is the elderly, exiting principal of the Bolenge high school, having lived in Congo for twenty-seven years now. Gloria is developing Parkinson's disease and, her life's work completed, is going home to Ohio to tremble and fade, surrounded by her family.

I close my eyes and picture what our new house will be like. The letter says it is made of brick, like the one in which I grew up. My mother moved us away from the brick house on 112th Street when I was still small, but as can happen with memories of early childhood, I see parts of it vividly. I walk into the kitchen with its high ceiling, past the spiders that hide under the stairs, and out into the yard and the smell of freshly cut crabgrass. When it stormed, my mother would hurry me into the cellar in case a tornado came. This was just before the bottom fell out, just before the Depression.

I wonder whether living in a kiln-fired brick house in Africa will present Richard and me as people of privilege. The idea worries me. In truth, there are many aspects of privilege that make me uncomfortable. At Mondombe, all the missionaries kept black African wash boys and cooks. Are we not here to teach these people that, equipped with the tools of knowledge and the strength of God, they can grow to do anything—positively anything—they choose? If so, why should we, in our own homes, assign them to perform the most base and menial tasks?

And the missionaries at Mondombe paid them pittance! Some of the house workers were full-grown men whose children and grandchildren were studying in school or decaying in jails or leprosaria. It seems unconscionable for us to come onto these people's turf and subjugate them as such. Also, it reminds me uncomfortably of American slavery and the still-underprivileged status Negroes hold in our own first-world society. Richard and I have discussed the dilemma, and we have decided that the only answer is to not take on any household help, even if the other missionaries at Bolenge are accustomed to such extravagance. We will do things ourselves. Certainly, neither of us ever had any help around the house when we were growing up. Why should we suddenly treat ourselves to such a luxury as someone doing our wash? No! Mission work is supposed to be about sacrifice. We shall do it ourselves. That is how it must be.

Four

September 1956

WE ARE AT BOLENGE. It is mid-afternoon when we arrive.

Several of the African boys from the high school where we will work run alongside the van, shouting and squealing as we near the mission. The African log drums play in the distance to announce our arrival. When we pull up, a hundred Congolese are gathering.

"Hello, white man. Hello, white woman," one calls out in Lingala, having no idea who we are but assuming, I suppose, that we are important.

Gloria Snead, white haired and willowy, waits for us with shoulders stooped from some unseen burden. I stare at her and wonder if Congo has made her look so beaten or if she would have gotten that way on her own, were she teaching school in Ohio all these years. The more I think about it, the less I want to know the answer.

Richard steps down from the payload, knocking the dust from his trouser leg with the back of his hand. I get my purse and hop out of the truck's cab, squinting at the scene in front of us.

"Welcome to your new home," Gloria says, warbling like a wren. She reaches to unburden me of my bag, but the gesture is sadly weak. It looks as though lifting my little bag might do Gloria in.

"Why are all these people here?" I ask her.

"They are here to welcome you, for the *ionza*," Gloria says, waving a fly out of her face.

"The *ionza?*" I ask, being careful to keep smiling. I imagine that it is some peculiar ritual, one that I am far too tired to endure right now, even if it is the sociable thing to do. This has been a long day. I want to get to our new house, lie down, and not rise until tomorrow.

"The *ionza*," Gloria nods earnestly, "is the ceremony where the Congolese welcome you. It's the giving of gifts to the arriving traveler."

I look at the blue-black natives standing in their best clothes, the women adorned with jewelry and brass anklets. In their hands are little parcels wrapped in palm fronds or held in cotton handkerchiefs. One woman pulls a live chicken out from under her wrap and holds it out to me with a smile. I take the bird uncomfortably, flinching when it flaps its wings. One by one, the others come forward and set their gifts on the ground in front of us—canned goods, pineapples, papaya, vegetables, duck eggs, a little pile of coins from an offering they have taken.

All of a sudden, all I can think about is that some of the poorest people in the world are showering us with gifts as precious to them as life itself. Tears well in my eyes at the notion of this generosity.

In the back of the crowd stands Joseph Boale, the white-clad Nkundu I met at the bank of the river in Mondombe. While the other Africans smile and clap their hands, Joseph's face remains stern.

"Thank you very much," Richard says in broken Lonkundo, stepping forward and bowing. The assembled clap their hands in response and break into song. The words sound peculiar—"*Yesu ende boning'okiso*"—but the melody is familiar, and I sing along quietly:

What a friend we have in Jesus,
All our sins and griefs to bear.
What a privilege to carry
Everything to God in prayer.

When the song is done, the oldest Nkundu man present steps forward from the crowd. He is more done up than the rest, wearing a mangy monkey-skin cap and a tattered trench coat.

"Do you have names in Africa?" he asks us in French.

"Beg pardon?" Richard says.

"He wants to know if you have African names, in Lonkundo," Gloria explains.

"Non, monsieur," Richard says to the man.

The crowd laughs.

"You don't address him as *Monsieur*," Gloria says. "He's here in the place of a village chief who would have welcomed you in the old times. Call him *Nkoko*. It means "grandfather." Lets him know you respect him."

Richard nods. *"Non, Nkoko,"* he says.

"Then I shall give you names," the old man replies, acknowledging Richard's courtesy with a smile.

The crowd voices its approval.

"You may be called *Nkoko Bongongolo,"* he tells Richard with much fanfare. He holds up his walking stick and waves it about.

"I, uh . . . thank you," Richard says, then adds, *"Nkoko."*

The crowd likes this.

"And for you," the man says, turning to me, "it will be *Mama Boenga."*

"Mama Boenga," I repeat.

The old man smiles and nods.

We sing another hymn, and the ceremony is over.

An old woman walks toward me with no small degree of difficulty, her ankles feeble, her bare breasts withered.

"Mama Boenga," she says, "You remember when you first came out here. I worked for you."

I nod at the woman and smile carefully. She must be senile. Another native woman, younger and suppler, walks up and stands beside the first.

"Mam'Oenga, it is so good that you return," she says with a look of wonder in her eyes. "You took care of me when I was just a little baby."

I turn to Richard. I am puzzled. Is this some bit of native theater for which I ought to have a response?

"Remember it," the young woman commands me, nodding. "You carried me around in your arms just like that—"

"Yes, yes," Gloria Snead insists, taking me by the elbow and walking away from the women. *"Mam'Oenga* has returned."

"What in heaven's name . . ." I am baffled.

"You and Richard have been paid a high honor," Gloria tells me quietly. "You have been given the names of one of the great chiefs and his wife, very honored in the old times. After that, Mr. and Mrs. Hensley, who came to Bolenge back in aught-six, wore the names. They were two of the first white people here, and they are very well remembered by both the missionaries and the Africans."

"So, because I have this name—"

"The Nkundu will look upon you as an extension of Mrs. Hensley's spirit," Gloria says. "It is a fine thing, really. She was a dear friend to me when I was young and first came to Africa. The

37

Nkundu girl you were just speaking with, Elizabeth, helped deliver her. The girl assumes that since an elder has given you her name, you have the woman's essence in you."

Richard catches up with us.

"That was mighty strange," he says.

"I will explain it later," I tell him.

The crowd is beginning to disperse. I smile and nod gently at the villagers as they depart.

Joseph Boale approaches.

"Bonjour, *Nkoko Bongongolo!*"

"Bonjour," Richard says. "I'm Richard Dunagan, and this is Eva."

"We've met," M. Boale says glibly.

Richard looks at me questioningly.

"At Mondombe," I explain. "Monsieur Boale is a teacher at the high school here."

Richard's expression brightens.

"Ah, yes. Well, then, it's a real pleasure to meet you."

"So they have made you *le Directeur.*" There is a bit of a sneer in M. Boale's voice. "It is a strange thing to give a position of *mpifo* to such a *bonoju.*"

"I'm sorry." Richard shakes his head in confusion. "But I don't under . . . you see, my Lonkundo isn't . . . we're brand new here, and—"

"Yes, you are. Very brand new and very full of big ideas, I am sure. The white man's church sends you here to teach our people how it shall be. But we have our own 'how it shall be.' I am a man of *mpifo,* important like my father before me. The white man's government may make you Directeur, but no one is the owner of Joseph Boale. You would do well to know this."

"Yes, well, shall we be off, then?" Gloria interjects apprehensively.

"Let's go," Richard says, shooting me a look. "Monsieur Boale, it's been a pleasure meeting you."

"Has it?"

"Yes, well . . . we'll see you at school, I'm sure."

"Madame," M. Boale says with a deliberate nod in my direction as he turns to leave.

In a moment, a truck pulls up loaded with the trunks and crates full of household belongings Richard and I shipped by steamer from New York City. Several Nkundu men jump onto the back of the truck to unload it. There is a careless indifference to their actions. As I stand and watch, I want them to treat our things more gently. Richard reaches into his pocket for a few francs to hire one of the boys from the village watch the crates while we go on a walking tour of the mission, but Gloria stops him.

"That's not the custom," she says. "Besides, it's not necessary. No one will bother your luggage in broad daylight."

As we leave, I turn and look at the truck, the pile of gifts from the *ionza* ceremony, the village elder and the scruffy boys playing marbles on the ground nearby. My mind wants to take a picture of the scene to save the memory for always. It will be dearer than any snapshot Richard has captured with his Argus.

"EVA? COME ALONG, DEAR. Now, over here we have the medical station," Gloria says, gesturing in the direction of a sturdy-looking shack to our left. "Nurse Jean Matthews is on full time. She delivers babies and such, gives inoculations, and sets broken bones."

Gloria continues our tour. There are about two dozen buildings of various sizes and degrees of sophistication, all lining a central road patterned after a traditional native village. The largest buildings are Neil Roberts's church and the high school, or l'École Moyenne. The school building has a dozen rooms off a central hall. The more elegant of the houses on the mission have ceilings of corrugated iron, while the simpler houses, with mud walls and graying thatched roofs, are of a design closer to that of the native villages.

"When I got here twenty-seven years ago, it was all mud huts," Gloria says with a laugh. "Every rainy season, we'd have to rebuild half this place. Then again, certain things were easier then."

"Like what?" I ask.

She shakes her head, dismissing my question.

"And when rainy season comes?"

"You've got about a month from now to batten down the hatches. I'm glad I'll be out of here," she says.

We round a corner at the back of the mission, where there are fewer buildings and wider spaces in between.

"And there's your house," Gloria says, pointing. "Welcome."

I look. Surely she is joking.

"Where?" I ask, my confusion genuine.

"That building. Right in front of you at the end of your sidewalk. Go on, now, you've had a long trip. Make yourself comfortable; get a little rest before dinner," Gloria says, gesturing to the derelict shack before us.

I turn to Richard, who looks back at me with a steely expression.

It is three in the afternoon, and I am starting to sweat just standing still.

Dear Lord, I am here to do the work that you have called me to do. I surrender my material wants to Your purpose. I am in your service. Amen.

I keep my eyes squeezed shut a little longer than the prayer requires.

THERE ARE NO PANES IN ANY OF THE WINDOWS, just torn, dusty screens. The house reminds me of some of the abandoned cabins we saw during the Dust Bowl, driving along a two-lane Oklahoma highway.

There is a concrete-slab porch out in front of the house, but it sags at one end. Vine tendrils reach over the floor of the porch, fingers ready to pull the house back down into the soil from which it was wrenched against its will and better judgment.

"Yes, it's going to be okay. Really," Richard says, as though my dismay had come as a question posed aloud.

We walk onto the veranda and the boards groan under our weight. There is termite dust everywhere. The screen door stands ajar. Richard tugs at it gently and nothing happens. He pulls harder. The door gives way, rusted hinges squeaking their displeasure as the wobbly frame swings open. The first thing I notice as I step inside is how the floorboards are so roughly hewn and poorly planed that there are actually narrow gaps between some of the planks. It gives the room the feeling of an oceanfront boardwalk.

"At least sweeping up is going to be easy," I try to joke.

Although the exterior of the house is fired brick, the inside walls are made of mud, some of them laced with termite trails. I walk cautiously toward the kitchen which, although decently sized, is more of an enclosed side porch than a proper room. There is a cast-iron stove and big wooden table in the center. Then I turn and look at the sink, which is flanked on either side by counters covered with sheet zinc.

Once upon a time, the basin must have been white enamel, but almost all the shiny coating has been worn or chipped or weathered off. All that remains is rusty black steel. It reminds me of pictures of Appalachian coal miners' homes, with five people sleeping in each room and no running water.

I bite my lower lip. Admittedly, during the Great Depression, doing without was not uncommon. I think now of a time when I was very young. I see my mother waking at the crack of dawn to go off to work cleaning other peoples' houses or stuffing sausage in a meatpacking plant. Her darkest days were spent trying to find us a room to rent. I had the sense that she knocked on a lot of doors before meeting landladies who would take us in.

Mother was always quiet so as not to wake me, but some mornings I would stir, pretending to sleep as I watched her dress, slowly and sadly, ashamed to put on her silk stockings full of runs. Sometimes we had to take charity. I now know how much mother hated this, but she had no choice. She was divorced, which was not only a shame, but greatly reduced her options in life. In addition, my kindergarten teacher was beginning to ask questions about what I was eating, as I was getting rather thin.

Then my stepfather came courting and things got better, for a while anyhow—at least there was food on the table. I did not fully realize how poor we were until I was old enough to read through the pages of the *Saturday Evening Post*. My step-grandmother kept a stack of old magazines on a shelf over her cracked porcelain toilet tank. I locked myself in the bathroom for hours and stared at the smooth-paper advertisements. There, on the glossy pages, were full-fidelity console radios with polished hardwood veneer, two-tone shoes, electric fans, and big, shiny, aerodynamic Studebakers. All these luxuries were foreign to me. There must be people with money to buy such extravagances, I reasoned, or the Buick and radio people would not put their advertisements in the magazine. I told myself that someday I would rise from poverty. I never wanted to be wealthy—the preacher in church said that earthly riches can serve only to enslave a man's soul.

And now here I sit in a hovel of a house that I am supposed to make my home, and I am to pretend that I do not want more. Richard sees that I am distressed and comes up behind me, laying his hands on my shoulders.

"Eva . . ." he whispers.

"The sink," I say, pointing across the room.

"I'll scrub it out," he volunteers.

"You can not just . . . that's not the point. It's . . . it's—what is *that?*" I shriek, pointing to a strange ripple on the surface of the wall. Richard gets up to inspect it more closely. The ripple turns out to be a thick trail of termites making its way from the floor to the ceiling. So this is what they look like in action.

"And I'll brush them away," Richard says, searching for something to use as a broom.

"You hate bugs!" I remind him unhappily.

"Well, now, that's true," he says, knocking disoriented insects into the sink with our letter of assignment. "But I reckon you've got this basin to come to terms with, and now I've got bugaboos of my own."

He turns on the tap, but no water comes out.

"Be right back," he mutters.

Richard dashes out the already-open back door. The termites reorganize themselves and begin their march with renewed enthusiasm. I pick up my handbag and do my best to compose myself, continuing my tour of the house.

The living room is decent sized, although rooms always look bigger when they are empty. There is a bedroom at the front of the house and another smaller room in the back. From one window, I see a grassy little grove. A tall mango tree is within reach, branches heavy with fruit. From another window, there is a view of the Congo River.

Off the bedroom is a tiny bathroom with a separate toilet closet. I suppose that I should count myself lucky to have indoor plumbing here in the middle of nowhere. I am not sure, however, that I entirely trust the toilet. It looks as though something has been living in it.

There is an electric light in each room, with a switch by each door and cloth-wrapped wire stapled to the mud-plastered wall. From the center of each ceiling hangs a bare bulb. There are two electrical outlets, one in the living room and one in the kitchen. Richard can power a hi-fi and I will be able to run an electric iron when we save up enough to buy them. Gloria told us that the mission's generator is switched on from dinnertime until nine o'clock each evening.

"Be careful about having lights on if you have something plugged in. You might blow a fuse and put the whole mission dark. Also, you'll know when you can run your power," she said, "because you'll hear it. The generator shed is your nearest neighbor, alongside Nurse Matthews, that is."

Richard comes back in the house, forehead slick with sweat, sleeves turned up.

"I don't think we'll be able to use water from the tank until the rain comes."

"Why?" I ask.

"Well, by my figuring, the last rain would have been about four months ago. The water in the tank, it isn't real fresh," he says, catching his breath and leaning against the wall.

"We can't even use it for cleaning?"

He takes out his handkerchief and wipes his face.

"Actually, it's green, Eva. There's a film over the top, and a million dead mosquitoes, and something floating in it that looks like a rat, only bigger. I think that 'til the rain comes, we're going to have to have some of the boys from the village bring water up from the river."

"No, we'll do it ourselves," I say stubbornly. I will not let my principles slip.

"Eva," Richard begins a reproach, but he is interrupted.

"In here!" a small voice shouts in Lonkundo.

We walk to the front door where a half-dozen teenage African boys drag our belongings indelicately up the sidewalk.

"Here! Here!" the littlest one shouts, pointing into the house. He is the child Richard paid to watch our things when we arrived.

"Did you ask them to—" I begin.

"No."

The boys drag our crates and parcels across the threshold and pile them in the center of the living room, four little Africans cooperating to pall-bear the biggest boxes. When they have finished, Richard reaches into his pocket and takes out several dimes' worth of francs, handing them to the child.

"What's your name?" he asks the little one in Lonkundo.

"Liyanza," the boy says with a troubled look. His eyes dart to the bigger boy behind him, then down at the coins in his still-open palm. After a moment, Liyanza looks back into Richard's eyes. He stands motionless.

"Didn't I give him enough?" Richard asks, turning to me.

"I don't know." I shrug. "Give him a whole dollar. He has to share it with the others."

Richard nods, digging in his pocket and pulling out a few more francs. He adds these coins to those already in Liyanza's hand. The boy's face looks even more troubled. He snaps his palm shut and turns quickly, muttering something I do not understand. The boys scurry out of the living room, yelping and laughing as they disappear.

"Why did it seem like . . . ?" Richard wonders aloud, watching them leave. He sits down on a box. "I get so tired just trying to figure out what is and isn't appropriate every hour of the day. They never warned us about it during training. I mean, maybe I should have figured, but . . ." He sighs. "We were just instructed to go forward and do our work."

He rests his arm on a rustic little table that has been left in the room, presumably by its previous residents. The weight causes one of the table's termite-riddled legs to snap, and the table crashes to the floor. We look at the mishap then back at each other.

"Oh, yes," Richard says, assuming the posture of one of our elderly instructors at the School of Mission Ethics. "You will encounter adversity, but you must not let it deter you from accomplishing the goals we are sending you to complete. No, use that adversity to your advantage. Focus it, in your prayers, to help you accomplish your goals. You will have a far keener sense of satisfaction once it's all said and done; of this I assure you."

I applaud his performance, smiling. He takes his seat.

"Have you got a broom packed in one of those crates?" he asks.

"Well, yes, I do," I say but don't feel like standing up. "Would you like me to get it?"

"Perhaps it would be best," he says, pointing to the kitchen wall. "The termites are back."

IT IS LATE IN THE AFTERNOON WHEN, true to Gloria's assurances, the mission's diesel generator begins chugging away from behind a thicket of brush. I discover that only one light bulb in the house works. Richard and I leave it switched on as we go out for the evening. This way, we will be able to find the house when we return home in the darkness.

The other missionaries have organized a welcoming dinner for us at Gloria Snead's house tonight. We arrive to find paper decorations are hung from the rafters of her living room. I look around the improvised tables that crowd the space and realize that Richard and I are the youngest missionaries here by at least a decade. I feel protective of some of the thinner and more wrinkled people before me, who look as though they would be better suited for a rest home Stateside than for a demanding job in the African interior. The menu is peculiar, but I can tell that someone has gone to a great deal of effort to make us feel welcomed. There is wild boar with some sort of green sauce, bread, and steamed plantain. We drink pineapple juice from antique crystal goblets, which one of the missionaries must have, in a moment of grandeur, deemed essential when packing for an extended trip to Africa.

"Hello, there," a middle-age woman says as she makes her way over to Richard and me. The dinner is winding down. The missionaries have served a dessert of Jell-O and papaya.

"I'm Jean Matthews," she says, "and we're just pleased as punch the Missions board has sent you here to Bolenge. We've needed some new blood for a while."

"And what is it that you do?" I ask her.

"I'm the station nurse," she answers proudly. "We're neighbors."

"Oh, yes. I remember. Well, thank you very much."

I look down and notice, suddenly, that an unassuming little monkey accompanies Jean and keeps to her heels like a well-behaved puppy. Jean nods and turns to the buffet to serve herself some more Jell-O without acknowledging her companion, as if it were perfectly normal to have a monkey clinging to your ankles at a dinner party. Gloria Snead stands, clapping her hands and clearing her throat to get everyone's attention. The room settles. Gloria is pale and her blue veins lurk beneath skin so thin that she looks not unlike the Visible Woman diorama in the Museum of Natural Sciences. I am slightly in awe of her fortitude.

"As you all know by now," Gloria says in a voice that remains sweet, though it wavers, "I will soon be going back to the States. I leave my position as secondary principal in the hands of Richard Dunagan, who, from everything I've read about him, is quite suited for the job."

She looks around.

"You probably won't even miss me."

Several of the others at nearby tables offer a reproachful "Now, now, Gloria . . ." and "Of course we'll miss you."

"In any case," she says, quieting her allies and turning to us, "we have a tradition here at the Bolenge mission, a little thing we do every time someone new joins us. It started as a bit of fun, but in truth, it's probably the most valuable welcoming gift we can offer you."

She gazes out at the room, and after a moment I wonder whether she has finished. Then I realize, looking into her misty eyes, that the old woman is lost in her memories.

"We've all had good and difficult times in Congo," she says at last. "It's the nature of this place. We've all learned lessons, and in many cases, we've learned them the hard way." She pauses and smiles.

"What we're going to do now is to go around the room, and each person just stand right up and introduce yourself, and give Richard and Eva the best piece of advice you have to offer about how to get by in our little corner of the world. Now, I'll start. My advice is to always boil the water. Always."

A carefully groomed white-haired man to Gloria's left stands up and speaks in a British accent.

"Hello. Welcome to you both. I'm Henry Adams. My advice to you is to check your shoes thoroughly for chiggers every morning before you put your feet into them. You never know what's crawled in and hid there."

His advice, and most of that which follows, is greeted with laughter and a continuing chorus of "Oh, yes" and "That's so true!"

We have worked our way halfway around the room when a freckled, redheaded lady with a New England accent stands up and says, "I'm Margaret Harrison, and my advice is that no matter how much you trust your houseboy, always keep a lock on your kitchen store room."

Something in me twitches.

"Thank you," I say out of turn, "but we're not planning on having a houseboy."

Everyone is silent for a moment, then they all laugh. I feel my cheeks flush. Their laughter insults me.

"I mean it," I insist, blinking hard several times. The room suddenly feels less safe and the faces around me less kind.

"No offense, Mrs. Dunagan," the lady says a little too casually for my tastes, "but you'll be needing a houseboy. Don't fret about it now—we'll talk later."

I open my mouth to give her a piece of my mind. Why must the world always presume things about me? It makes me burn. I do not think of myself as having a sharp temper—not at all! But when sorority sisters or haughty missionaries assume ahead of time what I am thinking, or what I am capable of, I have to work hard not to give them what for. Richard knows this about me. At present, he kicks me under the table to shut me up.

After the ring of advice has circled the room and met its starting point, an African man serves us all coffee in little stained cups. The missionaries mill around the room, nodding at small talk and complaining about the humidity.

"There's one thing I wanted to mention to you in private," Gloria says, helping herself to a seat beside us.

"Yes?" I ask. I do not like the sound of this.

"It . . . it's about the boys who helped you with your things earlier."

"What about them?" Richard asks.

"The tip you gave them, the payment," Gloria says gently, laying her forearms on the table and touching her fingertips together.

"Well, actually, yes, they acted a little strange," Richard says cautiously.

"It was too much, far too much. I know you didn't know any better, but we can't have that sort of thing."

"Okay," I offer automatically. Then I think about it for a moment and shake my head. She is right that we do not know how much is appropriate, but since when is it a crime to be generous?

"What was so wrong about it?" I ask.

Gloria leans in closer.

"If you give them more, then they'll expect more. And if someone on the mission consistently gives them more money or more free rope, then they'll expect it. It's not that they're not good people," she says, looking around cautiously, "it's just that they think differently from us, and there's no getting around it."

"You're saying you reckon they think differently because they're Negroes?" Richard asks skeptically.

"You'll do well to bear in mind," Gloria advises sharply, "that the best relationship to have with natives is one where you play the role of the parent and let them take the role of the child. If you expect them to act like adults, you'll be disappointed again and again."

"I—" I begin.

"Mark my words, Mrs. Dunagan," Gloria interrupts, raising her wiry white eyebrows. She stands and walks away without waiting for a response.

Richard and I look at each other.

As the party finishes, we bid the missionaries good night and make our way through the blackness toward our new house. True to plan, the lone light greets us from the path as we approach. Once inside, I brush my teeth, using the quart of boiled river water they have sent home with us, and pull back the sheets on our makeshift bed. Richard has emptied six of our sturdy, waterproof crates and laid them two across and three long. Together, we hoisted atop this base the mattress we bought. After we say our prayers, Richard rotates the ancient switch to cut off the light, and we are left in moonless inkiness.

It never gets this dark in Oklahoma City. Even if you draw heavy window shades, there is a border of light from the street lamp, or the neighbor's house, or the collective glow of neon incandescence that blankets big cities. In Africa, if the moon is hidden, you cannot see your hand in front of your face.

I lie listening as Richard walks across the creaking floorboards and eases himself into bed next to me. The generator turbine grinds to a halt next door. My wind-up bedside clock ticks softly. The only sensory experiences left are the redolent dampness of the jungle and the Congo backwash gurgling from across the mission. It has probably smelled and sounded like this here for ten thousand years.

Then, all of a sudden, there is something new, and it is coming from nearby. It's a raspy scratching sound, like sandpaper tickling the head of a snare drum.

"What is that?" I ask Richard with a start.

"Huh?" He has already fallen asleep.

"That! Listen . . ."

We are quiet for a moment. Richard sits up slowly.

"I think it's coming from the living room," he whispers. "Stay here."

I pull the sheets around me. Richard inches his way across the floor, running into the doorframe before he finds the light switch. When he flips it, nothing happens.

"The generator . . ." I lament.

"Where have you got those matches?" he asks.

"They're in my waterproof pouch."

I slip my feet down to the floorboards and stumble toward the bathroom, where I left my bag.

"Here," I say, reaching out my hands to find him and handing him the slender box.

He fiddles with the cardboard and strikes a match. A tiny golden glow spreads through the open doorway and across the living room floor. There, between the gaping cracks of the floorboards, dozens of large cockroaches pass up and down. It is a ghastly sight. Richard recoils.

"Get the lantern," I whisper.

The roaches scurry about, disoriented by the light and noise. Some disappear below the floorboards. Others seek refuge in the corners and crevices of the packed-mud wall. Several flip onto their backs, legs wriggling, and cannot right themselves. I sit on our crate bed and draw my knees up under my chin while Richard goes after the roaches with our broom. He does an admirable job of running off the invasion, killing the upturned crawlers and sending the rest scrambling for safety between the floorboards.

"Done," Richard announces once the room is cleared. "They probably just smelled some of the leftovers we brought home. I should have put the plates in the icebox."

"What icebox?"

"You know what I mean, Eva, that wooden box by the sink."

"I don't think there's any ice on the mission."

"So it's a breadbox then," he says, coming to bed. "Whatever."

"Nobody warned us about this," I whisper angrily, looking down at the ragged floorboards at the edge of the bed. Their gaps leave us as vulnerable as those in the living room. Richard puts out the lantern, and we lie in darkness once again. I awaken several times during the night, startled by the stillness. Now, if I am to trust the glowing phosphorescent hands of my clock, it is four in the morning.

The giant roaches have not come back. In an hour, the lokolé drums will sound to wake everyone. Heaven help us.

Five

March 1953

IT IS SPRINGTIME IN OKLAHOMA, not quite Easter yet, but the buds on the plants are deep green and can barely wait to burst into leaf-being. All over campus, tulips have poked their heads through the mulch that blanketed them during the chilly months, and they passionately promise flowers to any passerby who will stop and listen. I have been listening a lot of late. Early every morning, Richard comes to my dormitory. He stands beneath my window at the break of dawn and whistles the Johnny Appleseed song:

Oh, the Lord is good to me.

On this particular morning, I wake at my desk. My cheek is flat against my comparative religion textbook. There is a midterm in a few hours, and I had planned to study all night. Somewhere along the way, I seem to have fallen asleep.

I whistle back to Richard:

And so I thank the Lord.

We finish the tune together:

For giving me the things I need—
the sun, and the rain, and the apple seed.
The Lord is good to me.

I WAVE TO HIM FROM MY WINDOW, then slip down the back stairs, taking care that my footfalls come at the outside edges of the boards, where the wood is less likely to announce my presence.

Richard is waiting when I get there, his herringbone coat buttoned

51

securely against the damp chill. By the time I reach him, the sun has risen enough that the dewdrops on the lawn glisten and our breath forms clouds as it leaves our lips.

Like most days lately, he has made a stop by the cafeteria on his way across campus. He pays one of the janitors a dime to set aside two glazed doughnuts as soon as they have been iced each day. Richard waits at the side door of the kitchen while the janitor snatches them, putting them into an empty bread wrapper and handing them off. Today, the doughnuts have chocolate icing. Richard and I sit side by side on the back step of the girls' dormitory and eat them enthusiastically.

"So, there's something that's been bugging me," Richard says with icing on his lips. "What makes you want to run off and be a missionary?"

"Didn't your mother tell you not to talk with your mouth full?"

"Never did. Imagine that."

We continue eating in silence. After a moment, Richard tries again.

"I reckon you didn't answer my question."

I realize that he is right. "I, uh . . . it's complicated. What makes you not want to be one?"

Richard pauses a moment, then smiles at me. "Whoever said I don't want to be a missionary?"

"But I thought you were going to be a minister and find a congregation to lead."

"I don't know, actually."

Richard glances across campus, squinting in the sunrise. "I've been thinking that mission work might be worth considering," he says.

I stare at his face. He will not look at me. "And where do you imagine yourself doing this mission work?"

Richard shakes his head. "I haven't got that far yet. All I know is that I've begun to have serious doubts about how beneficial I'd be as a clergyman at some church in the middle of Illinois or Arkansas."

"Oh, really," I say quietly. I have the funny sense that this conversation is going to end either very well or very poorly.

"Because I don't think I'd be satisfied. I don't think my heart would be in it. I'm too young not to be a little larger than that. Am I making any sense?"

"Yes, but—"

"Since I met you, I've been fixin' on it. I reckon I might like to go out somewhere they've got names besides Smith and Jones. I want to go somewhere that I feel like the work that I'm doing, the ministering or teaching, that it's going to affect lives. I don't just want it to be a choice, something to fill up an hour of Sunday morning on Easter and Christmas. There are people who need people like me. I can be . . . they teach us that we are the embodiment of the living Christ, right?"

I nod.

"Well, all right, then. Christ didn't stand in a pulpit on Sunday morning talking about shoulda and woulda. He got his hands dirty. He put his whole self on the line. I have that to give. Do you understand?"

"Yes," I whisper emphatically and feel like shouting for sheer happiness. "Yes! That's exactly the reason why I want to do it. I spent the summer, year before last, working with these migrants across Illinois asparagus fields. Their children don't go to school; they don't know what kind of chance they might have if they would just reach out and take it. They are hungry to learn, hungry to feel liked, to feel accepted. How can I say my prayers and go to bed at night in a tidy little life back in Oklahoma City, next door to my mother and stepfather, when I know there is that kind of gaping, hemorrhaging need in the world? I have a conscience, and my conscience says 'go!'"

"To Africa?"

"To Africa!"

"Well, all right, then," he says and stands up, brushing the crumbs from the front of his coat.

"Where are you going?" I ask.

Richard is silent for a moment, then he sits back down. The air is still. Squirrels play on the lawn. "Eva?" he asks.

"Yes," I say cautiously.

"I . . . I love you. And if you want to go to Africa, or Kansas, or wherever you go . . . whatever it is that you want to do, I want to be beside you. I've fallen hopelessly in love with you."

I am stunned.

"I want to be your partner," he says, as if perhaps I did not understand.

"You're asking me to marry you?" I ask, incredulous.

"Yes, I think I am," he says with a smile.

My mind races, full of pictures of weddings, people throwing rice, children, my mother's face. "We've only been dating for four months, Richard—"

"Four months, is it? Well, what do you know about that? You see, I need you around to help me keep track of things. Will you? I mean, marry me? Wait, I suppose I should do this properly," he says, bending down onto his knee.

"Oh, get up." I feel a smile working the corners of my mouth, and in a moment I am laughing. We stare at each other. I sigh.

My mind races. I have just received a marriage proposal from the man of my dreams. It does not seem real. Marriage. Permanence. Adult life. Oh boy!

"You . . . now, you haven't answered me," Richard says, looking down.

"Oh! Sorry, I thought I did." Now, I cannot stop laughing. The mind is a peculiar thing. I giggle as I speak. "Yes, Richard Dunagan, I will marry you. I will be your partner."

He kisses me on the lips, then picks me up and swings me around. I stand and watch him walk across campus until he disappears around the corner of the men's dorm.

BACK IN MY ROOM, I lie on my bed, staring up at the ceiling. Birds are chirping, the marching band begins its morning rehearsal on the field, and I cannot stop smiling. The sun inches higher in the sky, up over my windowsill, and a few rays spill across my lips right where Richard kissed them. I laugh and close my eyes.

When I wake, I have missed my midterm. Alas.

Six

October 1956

THE RAINS WILL BE HERE ANY DAY NOW. Everyone can feel it. The missionaries and Africans look at one another warily, saying less than they otherwise might, relying on intuition.

I sit on the veranda of our little brick house and close my eyes, breathing in deeply whatever earthy new fragrance the jungle has chosen for me today. Morning chores are finished, and I deserve to rest. I wish there were a breath of a breeze to make my blouse flutter and tickle the ends of my hair across my shoulders. There is only stillness.

I have learned over these days of trial that keeping house on the banks of the Congo is not so like keeping house on the banks of the Mississippi as I had imagined it would be. To the contrary, every chore takes more time, and the effort produces diminished results. In America, even the poorest of the poor can go to the market and buy a dozen eggs as long as they have a few coins weighing their pockets. In Bolenge, we must wait until a frail, several-toothed unpredictable old man comes by our back door with two or three eggs for sale. When he does appear, he may have only one or two for purchase, and they are as likely to be duck eggs as chicken. It would be nice, too, if the eggs were consistently fresh, but that is not the case. I learned the hard way that it is necessary to thoroughly test each egg before purchase by putting it in a glass of water. If the egg drops to the bottom of the glass, it is fresh. If it floats or even so much as begins to tip up on one end, it is too old to risk eating. Then comes the haggling over price. In all, it can take twenty minutes to buy enough eggs to cook up an omelet.

Fresh water, for such frivolous pleasures as drinking and cooking, is another precious commodity. Each morning and evening, Richard and I haul galvanized pails up the slippery river rocks, carrying them sloshing across the mission while the African boys point and giggle, mimicking our capricious steps. Before we can use the water, it must be poured through a fine paper filter, boiled, then chilled to a usable temperature.

Twice now I have burned myself trying to navigate a huge copper pot of scalding river water from the stove to the table. It was in those moments, as I hopped around, yipping and blowing on the reddened flesh of my arms and belly, that I began in earnest to question our decision against hiring a houseboy.

It is not like back home. In Oklahoma, black ants would sometimes show up in the sugar bowl. In Congo, all activity must stop several times a day so that we may divert our attention to brushing thick trails of termites from the living room walls. Again and again, we have to chase hundreds of insects out of the house with a broom.

I hear Richard approaching and open my eyes. He has been to visit the mission's maintenance man about getting new floorboards put down so we may sleep through the night without fear of cockroaches and lizards.

"Who goes there?" I ask, standing and smoothing the creases in my skirt.

Richard walks up the front steps.

"He said they'd have some workers come by and fix the floor in a few days."

"Wonderful!"

Right now, nothing sounds quite as appealing as walking barefoot across fresh planks of timber, smelling the sweet wood when I wake, and telling it good night before bed. I will enjoy sweeping it.

Richard sits down next to me on the borrowed rattan settee.

"The maintenance man gave me a warning about the garden, though." He gestures toward the mess in front of us. In the days since our arrival, the razor grass and brambles have grown quickly.

"A warning?"

"He says there are snakes in it, and if we don't cut it back, we'll have ourselves a mess of trouble come rainy season."

I am not fond of snakes. Richard is susceptible to insects, but in the animal kingdom it is the reptiles that most readily raise my hackles. I look out at the tall grass and imagine a twisting tangle of slimy snake bodies, spiky-toothed cottonmouths and venomous rattlers slithering toward me in the rain.

"Eva?"

"Huh?" I mumble, distracted. "I suppose we ought to cut it down then."

"I reckon that's a fine idea, yes. I asked the fella if there were a lawn mower or some kind of thresher that we could borrow to cut through it. He says someone or other from the medical institute up the road had a big ol' Sears mower about fifteen years ago, but it rusted to bits in the humidity, and they couldn't get replacement parts sent over from the States."

"Swell," I say. "Did he offer any other ideas?"

"He suggested we have some of the local boys cut down the yard for us. He says they've got these machetes—"

I turn away from Richard, feeling betrayed. I thought we had an understanding.

"Eva, I know that we talked about—"

I do not want to hear it. I take a few steps away from him. I shake my head.

"Fine," he says, going into the house.

The floorboards creak under his weight.

I want to cuss, though I could not pretend to know what words to utter. "Darn!" is the best I can produce, but I say it fiercely.

The hot, still, velvety air has been all but unendurable during these first weeks at Bolenge, dampening clothes and arresting enthusiasm. The missionaries and Africans alike assure us that when the rains begin, we will have a whole new set of challenges with which to contend. Apparently, we will have a snake pit out front.

Richard comes back outside carrying a drinking glass. He holds it up to the sunlight.

"Eva? Uh, there's things in here."

"Things?"

"Little bits of—"

"I didn't filter that batch yet. Don't drink it," I say, snatching the water from his hand.

"But I'm thirsty," he complains.

"Well, you'll have to wait," I say as patiently as I can.

He sulks for a moment, then announces that he is going to filter the water himself. I look in at the termites colonizing the living room wall.

"No, you do termites, I'll do water, then I'll start on laundry, and you go find someone who'll sell us a chicken for dinner."

We stand and stare at each other for a moment.

"All right," Richard says in resignation, heading to the closet to get the broom.

As he walks past me, I remain still. What will it be like in a few days when he starts work? How about when I myself start teaching? What will we do when the rains come?

Richard knocks termites off the wall and chases them through the cracks in the floor. As he finishes, he looks up at me.

"Uh, the water, honey?"

He gestures toward the kitchen as if I might need reminding.

"I know," I say irritably, turning and walking toward the kitchen.

"Eva . . ."

"What?" I snap, hearing my mother's voice in my own.

"It's going to be okay," he says.

"I know it's going to be okay! It's just . . . everyone else on the mission has hired help. I'm not saying it's easy for them or their life is all milk and honey, but just running this house, just keeping food in our stomachs and clean clothes on our backs is taking eight or ten hours a day! I don't know how we're going to manage once we have classes to teach, and projects to organize, and papers! We're going to have papers to grade—"

"Whoa, whoa! One thing at a time." Richard puts up his hands and approaches me.

"First of all, we made a decision about not bringing on hired help based on principle, right?"

I nod cautiously. I do not trust him.

"Now, we're here to fulfill certain needs, in teaching and as leaders, aren't we?"

"Yes."

"Then we should see to it that . . . oh, I don't know what I'm goin' on about," Richard says, looking away.

"We should see to it that what?"

"Well," he says deliberately. "Part of me figures that we should do whatever is necessary to make ourselves completely available for the tasks we're here to complete."

"You mean hire someone to come in and—"

"I mean, whatever it takes. But now, that's just one part of me. The other part says what we've been going over all along, not wanting to have any sort of a class distinction between us and them—the Africans, I mean. That it's right, that it's the only way, that our intentions were steering us well."

"I don't . . ." I begin, then realize I truly do not know what to say.

"Take the yard, for instance," Richard says. "If the maintenance man's right, the rains will come in a few days, and we'll have something out of the book of Revelation in the front yard. What are we supposed to do?"

Suddenly my mind is made up. I look up at him.

"We hire the boys," I say calmly.

"What?"

Richard looks as though he cannot decide whether I am, perhaps, putting him on.

"We hire the boys," I repeat. "We find that little Liyanza and have him round up his gang, and I'll use what is left of the lemonade mix and do up a whole jug, and we'll make a day of it. We'll offer to help. We'll all be a team together."

"Eva . . ."

"What? Have you got a better idea?"

Richard is silent, looking around the room. There is a distance between us for the rest of the afternoon. We go about our work, speaking only as often as necessary.

Tonight, as we lie in bed, the full moon glows brilliantly down on the grass in our front yard. The long, tall blades are ghostly gray in the moonlight and shiver with life as insects and snakes make their ways up, along, and through the bases of the stalks. The rolling of the river riles a gentle breeze, and, as it shifts, brings air from the village. There is the faint smell of smoke, and I hear log drums playing, the pattern getting faster and faster, then shifting and starting anew.

The Nkundu are conducting a full-moon ritual.

AS I WAKE, I become aware of the sound of young voices babbling with great animation. I roll over and look out the open window of our bedroom. Liyanza and three other boys from the village are milling around the yard with big, swordlike knives, giggling and chasing one another. Richard must have found Liyanza and talked to him yesterday afternoon.

I smile, watching how Liyanza points his finger and purses his lips, clearly in charge of boys three years older and a foot taller

59

than himself. He **stomps** his dusty bare foot and raises an eyebrow to command their **attention**. Someday, I think, this boy will be a powerful man.

I look over at **Richard**, who remains asleep.

"Hey," I say, poking him.

He opens his eyes groggily.

"Wha . . . ?"

"Your crew seems to have arrived," I say with a yawn, sitting up in bed. I brush the hair from my face with the back of my hand.

Richard looks at me and smiles sheepishly. "Yesterday I, uh . . ."

"Yes, you did, didn't you?"

"I did," he acknowledges.

"Guess you didn't let any grass grow—"

"Under my feet?" he interrupts. "Ha, ha, Eva—No, I did not."

I stand and gather my robe around me, walking to the window.

"Liyanza!" I call out.

"Oui, *Mam'Oenga*" comes the alto reply.

"Go ahead, start your work!" I shout in French.

"Right away," he answers gleefully. The boys gather while Liyanza points around the field, assigning each his duties.

I go to the kitchen and put the final quart of last night's treated water on the stove to boil up for Richard's coffee. In a minute, he comes in from the bathroom, patting a handkerchief against his jaw where he has cut himself shaving.

"I hope you think I did the right thing," he says, examining the bit of blood on his fingertips.

"I think you chose the only reasonable solution, so if I have to label it right or wrong, it could only be looked upon as right."

I set the jar of sugar on the table, struggling to loosen the lid.

"Here, let me," Richard says, taking the jar from my hands. We are discovering that the ants here have a remarkable ability to get into all kinds of containers, thwarting conventional methods of keeping them out. Well-tightened Mason-jar lids have proven effective as a temporary solution, but the other missionaries have warned us that their rubber rings rot quickly in the African climate, disintegrating into orange gum in a matter of weeks.

The ants seem to be especially fond of sugar and dry powdered milk. These are two of our staples here in Congo, as fresh cow's milk is seldom found, and sugar makes everything else just a little more bearable.

I stir a little of each into Richard's coffee, setting the chipped cup down in front of him.

"Thank you, darlin'," he says, his ease salving my irritated conscience.

I go to the bathroom and slip on a light cotton dress, bending over to buckle my sandals. From outside the back door I gather our two tin water buckets.

As I walk down the steps on my way out toward the river, Liyanza looks up from his post as foreman of the boys.

"We do good work for you, *Mam'Oenga*," he says in broken French. I look out at the boys toiling amidst a sea of weeds.

"Oui, oui," I agree. "Do you like lemonade?"

He looks puzzled.

"Lemonade . . . to drink," I explain with a gesture. "Sweet and lemon in cold water."

"Oh! Yes, very much, I think," he says.

"Well, good, then. I am going to go get water for tomorrow. I'll fix lemonade when I get back."

"Liyanza get water for you," he insists, moving toward me to take my pails.

"No. I can do it." I move the pails behind my back and out of his reach. "Thank you all the same."

He shrugs, looking a little cross at my rebuff, and returns his attention to the supervision of the boys laboring in the yard. I walk slowly down the concrete sidewalk, pails dangling from my palms, heavy soles scratching against the pavement. I do not turn to look at the boys as I pass. I just cannot. I am ashamed. The sun beats unkindly upon my shoulders as I walk across the mission to the river, returning with pails full of distressingly murky water. We are told that it is at its most foul just before the rains come. I wonder what kind of misfortune would befall us if we were to drink water straight from the river. Would we contract some kind of fever or stomach cramps? Part of me wants to find out.

Sweat is dripping in my eyes. I stop to wipe my brow. With each step, the straps of my sandals dig into the backs of my ankles. For a moment, I imagine myself slipping Richard a glass of unclean water and watching the reaction. It would not be a kind thing to do. Perhaps a good case of the runs might be just repayment for all the little collected frustrations he has caused me since the day we met—the times he's snored, or left the cap off the toothpaste tube, or deposited his socks on the bedroom floor at day's end.

This whole process will become easier once the rains come. Then water will collect in our backyard cistern and we will need only to pump it from just outside our kitchen door.

As I near the front of our wild garden, I see a familiar face coming toward me. It is Margaret Harrison, the missionary from New Hampshire who gave us patronizing pointers about locking household help out of the kitchen supply closet. I have not encountered her since that first night, nor do I have any desire to speak to her now. I have not had my breakfast and am feeling rueful about the boys toiling in our yard.

Margaret is getting closer. I am almost home. I turn quickly, pretending that I have not seen her, and hurry toward the house. Water splashes out onto the path, soaking my feet.

She calls out from behind me.

"Yoo-hoo! Eva!"

I realize that she has caught me. I turn slowly, putting on a brave face.

"Hello, Margaret, how are you?" I ask cheerfully.

"A little wilty from the humidity, if you'll pardon my saying so."

She looks around the yard and smiles unpleasantly.

"I see you finally took my advice. I knew you'd come around eventually."

I feel my face flush.

"Forget about it, Margaret. If we could find a mower, trust me, I'd be doing it myself. I'm not afraid of hard work," I say, turning and striding through the open doorway into the living room.

I am furious, not so much at her as at myself for being prideful and hard headed. What should I have said? I set my pails down on the kitchen floor and slump into one of the rickety chairs. Richard looks up from the skillet where he is scrambling our precious eggs.

"What was that all about?"

"It was all about me letting my temper fly off the handle," I say.

"Whom were you talking to?"

"That Margaret Harrison who runs the print shop," I answer.

"Oh," he says gravely. "So I suppose she saw the—"

"Yes," I snap.

"What did she say?" He sets his spatula down on the counter.

"What you would expect."

"Was she insulting about it?"

"She didn't have to be. Just her standing talking to me like that was embarrassing enough. I'll bet she was watching and just waiting until I got home."

Richard stands and looks at me, shaking his head as he sets a plate full of eggs and plantain on the table. I am struck by the way he looks so comfortable with an apron strung around his midsection. I cannot recall a single occasion when my stepfather entered the kitchen to do more than freshen his glass of iced tea. Times change. I am fortunate.

"Eat," Richard says sternly and, as he has so bluntly ordered it, I feel compelled to comply.

After we finish, I clear the table and Richard walks out into the heat of the garden to check on the boys' progress. After a minute, he comes back in, smiling.

"Liyanza says that the boys are thirsty, Madame, and you are instructed to hurry with the lemonade."

I nod, setting a huge copper kettle on the burners. The water will need to boil for twenty minutes.

The stove in our house is a pregnant-bellied black iron monster with flat eyes and pigtailed corkscrew handles. It is slow to heat and slow to cool, taking the temperature of the room along for the ride. Visiting our kitchen during the late morning can be less than pleasurable, especially now, just before the rainy season. Air that would otherwise circulate through the unshuttered windows and cool the room now stands still, at times funereally so. I sweep the floor as the water in the kettle rises to a boil. Richard has spread the workings of a bicycle gear shift across the table, soiling one of my dishtowels as he tries to repair the mounting.

"I was watching those knives, the machetes they use to cut down the brush," he says. "Liyanza tells me they've made them from bands of packing steel from around pallets on the big freighters. The boys make off with the metal and take it to a machine shop where someone cuts the pieces into swords and sharpens one edge 'til they're like razors."

"Who taught them to do that?" I ask, trying to imagine one of our missionaries arming a cavalry of little Negro boys for battle.

"Funny, Liyanza didn't want to say." Richard gets up and walks toward the front door.

"You *are* helping them out there, aren't you?" I ask.

"As much as I can," he says over his shoulder. "This is their world, not mine."

"Richard," I call as he walks out onto the porch.

He stops and turns around.

"Yes?"

"We're doing the right thing here, aren't we?" I ask quietly, drying my hands on the front of my dress.

"In Africa?" he asks facetiously.

"You know what I mean."

Richard is quiet for a moment too long.

"Of course," he says without looking at me.

When I finish with the lemonade, I serve it to the boys. It is not cold, but it is remarkably well received. I get the feeling this is the first time some of them have tasted a sweetened drink. One of the older boys gulps so much that he gets a stomachache and has to lie on the veranda for a while. I sit and talk with him. Liyanza watches us suspiciously. When he mutters "lazy" under his breath, I do not know if he is referring to his disabled worker or me.

IT IS WHILE I AM FIXING DINNER that Richard comes in carrying a letter he has received via special dispatch from Coquilhatville.

"Lookie here," he says, holding out the single sheet of paper.

I dry my hands and take it from him.

The letter is from the Ministry of Education district office. Apparently, it is time for the quarterly inspection of the various little elementary schools that have been organized in the rustic backcountry surrounding Bolenge. Under ordinary circumstances, this inspection would be handled by the principal of the Bolenge mission's elementary school, but he is home in the States on furlough. Thus, the responsibility falls on Richard.

I look up from the page.

"Well, how about that?" Richard says.

We sit at the dinner table and discuss the matter. The trip will require Richard to be away for several days, and several days away are something we cannot spare just now. The school term begins soon, and we have yet to put our house right for the rainy season.

"I'm thinkin' maybe I should send one of the Nkundu high school teachers."

"But you haven't met any of them yet," I say, tending a pan of canned green beans on the stove. "I mean, once the new term is underway, sure, but—"

"Now, hold up a minute. We met the one teacher. What was his name, the tall one with the dark glasses at the *ionza?*"

"Boale. Joseph Boale."

"Maybe I oughta send him."

I turn and look at Richard.

"Honey, I have to tell you something," I say. "I don't think I like him very much."

"C'mon now, Eva," Richard says reproachfully, "I know he came off a little . . . well, I reckon you could call it rigid . . . when we first met him, but not everyone we meet out here is going to be someone we might choose to have as a close personal friend. It's a different world. You know that. The point is to be able to get along and work with them—"

"Richard, I don't trust him," I say sharply.

"Because?"

"It's in his eyes. I just know, okay? As a woman. He isn't trustworthy."

"I don't know how you could say that. He had sunglasses on the whole time."

"Don't be funny." I frown.

"Well, what? You think I should go do the inspection myself?"

"It's just . . ." I shake my head. "You seem awfully eager not to go."

"Well," Richard says, sitting down at the table and stretching, "I was thinking, being a manager and all, there's a lot to be said for knowing when to delegate. This is a perfect instance. White missionaries have been in charge of the back-country schools for over fifty years now, right?"

"Right . . ."

"So let's give them back some autonomy. The natives, I mean. It may seem like a trifle, but I reckon it's a step. Don't you think?"

I sigh my concession, for he does have a point.

Richard folds the letter and slips it back into its envelope.

"And you want to send Joseph Boale?" I ask.

"Why not?" Richard says with a shrug. "It's not a very complicated assignment."

MARGARET HARRISON IS COMING TO VISIT. I had Richard ask her to stop by this afternoon so we might discuss an unseemly matter.

"Hello, there," Margaret says with artificial cheer, taking off her broad-brim hat as she comes through our front door. The hat is more of a necessity than the affectation it would seem Stateside, as the equatorial sun is not favorable to Margaret's freckled complexion.

"Please, sit down," I say, finding my manners. "Would you like a cool glass of tea?"

"No, thank you," Margaret says with a smile, obviously pleased to be received so courteously. She looks around the house uninvited, inspecting our new sofa. The furniture squeaks slightly as she presses on the arm, the still-green wicker slowly drying into shape. We bought the sofa in the village and I stitched the cushions myself, stuffing them with the innards of old pillows. It is homely but serviceable.

"How are things going for you two? I understand Richard has been meeting with the teachers at l'École Moyenne, and he's already very popular."

"I think he's a little overwhelmed just yet, trying to find his way around the office, learning how things are done out here—"

"It's no easy task," Margaret says. She drags her index finger along our newly azure living room wall. "How did you manage this?"

"Richie did it," I tell her proudly. "We didn't know how to cover dirt walls, really, so he took two boxes of whitewash and stirred the powder into a pail of water. But I wanted it to be some color other than white, so before he brushed it on the walls, he mixed in some bluing I had brought out for the laundry and mineral salts he ordered from Coquilhatville. It's kind of like the calcimine paint they used in Tennessee when he was little. We're thinking of doing the bedroom yellow, if we get to it before the rains come."

"Well, I do declare," Margaret exclaims, "that Richard certainly is a talented man, isn't he?"

"Yes," I say uncomfortably, wondering whether Margaret has a husband. I do not recall seeing him at the welcoming dinner.

"So you start teaching when?"

"Tomorrow," I say, "which is why I had Richard ask you to come by."

I suppose we must get to the business at hand.

"Yes," she said, adjusting the pleats of her floral dress as she takes a seat.

I gather my wits before speaking.

"You know how I feel about having people around me working as servants. . . . I mean, hired help . . . at least I think you do."

Margaret sits up a little straighter.

"It's hard for me to justify our being here . . ." I say, "white people with store-bought clothes and sturdy houses in the middle of the black people's poverty and hunger, and we're here to help them . . . at least, that's what we all signed up to do. Then when Richard and I get here, we see all of you, everyone, with native houseboys and laundry boys, and it just reminds me of the way things were back home, all the way since slavery. I didn't like it back in America, and I don't like it here."

There is a long pause.

"But?" Margaret asks expectantly.

"But," I say with a sigh, "keeping house here is just so . . . I don't know how we're going to manage once I start teaching tomorrow. It's a full-time job running this place. We have to do everything for ourselves, and it is more than we can manage—"

"I could say I told you so—"

"Margaret, don't. Please, just don't." I interrupt, shaking my head. "This is hard enough for me as it is."

"Eva, I understand. Maybe you don't think that I do, but I came here with a lot of the same sweet, pure notions you're talking about. Trouble is they just aren't practical. I know that sounds cold, but it's true."

I turn away.

"Now, then," Margaret says very deliberately, "there's someone I'd like you to meet."

I sigh, but do not answer.

"His name in Lonkundo is Ta Pierre. I call him 'Papa Peter.' He lives in the village. Why don't I bring him by after supper so you and Richard can meet him?"

"Meet him for . . . ?"

"He's very good, very efficient. He used to help out around the print shop when things were busy. I don't think he's working now. Maybe . . . I mean, perhaps you and Richard could help him out."

I am quiet. This is, after all, why I have asked her to come.

"All right," I say, turning around slowly. "Why don't you bring him by after dinner, about six-thirty? Ta Pierre, you said?"

"Yes. You'll like him a lot."

Margaret picks up her hat and rises to go. As she reaches the veranda, she turns back around. "Eva?"

"Yes?"

"Oh, never mind," she says with an odd smile. "I'll see you tonight."

Margaret carries herself from my porch with perfect posture.

I manage to buy a chicken for dinner, and by a stroke of good fortune it is already plucked. The barefoot old woman who came by peddling it forgot to mention, however, that the chicken probably died of natural causes. I find a large tumor in its gullet while attempting to clean the bird.

"Another night for canned horsemeat," I muse to myself.

Richard walks in and kisses me on the back of the neck, setting down his leather bag on a kitchen chair.

"So? How was school?" I ask, wiping my forehead with the back of my turned-up sleeve. I've been wearing one of Richard's broadcloth cotton shirts all day. I like smelling him when he is not around.

"There's so much to figure out. The deeper I get, the less capable I feel," he says.

"Are you going to be a bully once you're my boss? Margaret Harrison says all the African teachers like you."

Richard snorts a laugh in response.

"I don't see how Margaret Harrison would know about that," he says.

"She works in the print shop. We may not have a newspaper, but the gossip seems to filter through her office all the same." I set a knife and fork in front of him. "Thank you, by the way, for having her come over here. I just couldn't go in there, onto her turf, I mean. She's coming by again this evening, bringing a man with her. She says we'll like him."

"I feel like an unwilling participant in some kind of arranged marriage," Richard says.

I answer by setting a plate of horsemeat and bread in front of him. Richard takes my hands and sings a simple prayer:

Mealtime has come. The board is spread.
Thanks be to God, who gives us bread.

"So how was your day," he asks, "other than Margaret?"

"Well, I had half a dozen old women come by begging for food."

"And?"

"And I gave them what I could. It's hard to know where to draw the line."

I look at the boxes and tins of staples that sit on our counter.

"I could give them everything we've got, and it still wouldn't be enough. It wouldn't be a fraction of enough. When those women leave, there are a dozen right behind them. I get the sense that we could work every day of our lives and not make a dent in the poverty of this place."

I look down at my plate of horsemeat, and I am not hungry anymore.

MARGARET ARRIVES AT A QUARTER TO SEVEN, knocking on the front door frame.

"Come in," I call from the bedroom, where I sit working on a letter to one of our sponsoring congregations in Memphis, writing white lies about how our every hour is consumed doing God's work.

Richard walks in through the kitchen, wiping his hands on a work rag. He has been in the backyard, negotiating with our cistern pump in the rapidly fading evening light.

"Hello," Margaret says to him. She wears her hair up, and as I walk closer I notice that she smells like perfume.

Behind her, in the deepening shadow of evening, stands a tall African man. He is wearing a pair of much-mended trousers and a shirt that looks as though it used to be black but is now the color of the sky just before a thunderstorm. His clothing may have fit him when he was twenty years younger and twenty pounds heavier, but the way it hangs on him now gives me the impression that I am being introduced to a Negro scarecrow that has lost its straw. On his feet are battered brown oxfords with no laces.

"Meet Ta Pierre," Margaret says, and the old man steps humbly forward.

"Bonsoir, Madame et Monsieur," he says, bowing in subservience.

Ta Pierre is a gentle man. He wears Coke-bottle glasses that make his eyes look cartoonishly large, and as he walks toward us I wonder if he can see much at all.

"Come in, sit down," Richard says, gesturing toward the sofa and switching on the light bulb. We have fashioned a paper shade for it that looks surprisingly good.

"Would you like a cup of coffee?" I ask them. Both refuse, so I take my seat next to Richard. I want this to be over with quickly, whatever the outcome.

"Ta Pierre is a wonderful cook, *n'est-ce pas?*"

"Oui," he says, then continues in clumsy French. "I have cook since a boy. I once work for a Portuguese man, and he teach me the recipes to cook all food. I can cook all food."

He smiles proudly, showing off each of his ten teeth.

"Papa Peter does so many things, really. You'll find him to be very versatile. Down at the print shop, he kept the machinery oiled and cleaner than it was ever before or has been since."

Richard looks over at me, and I catch his glance. Having someone good with machines would be very helpful for us. We have ordered a gasoline-powered washing machine from Sears & Roebuck with gift money my mother sent us. The delivery boat should have it here by the end of the month, but acquisition is only the first step of ownership. Richard and I both fear that the belts and gears of the washer will be difficult to keep in working order so far removed from civilization.

We have heard horror stories about missionaries who mail off letters Stateside, asking for small replacement parts for broken machines. It may take six months for the requested part to arrive, and then, as likely as not, the wrong screw or gear or bolt has been sent.

I look at Margaret.

"How much does he charge?"

Margaret purses her lips, smiling tightly.

"It is proper to pay a houseboy five francs a day."

"We'll pay him ten and Sundays off."

"But—"

"He is not a boy; he's an elderly man. He says he's been cooking all his life. Surely that counts for something."

"Ten francs a day?" Margaret asks Ta Pierre, extending my offer without any further argument.

"Oui! That is good," the old man's eyes brighten.

"How soon is he available?" I turn to Ta Pierre and re-pose my question in French. "When can you start?"

He thinks about it for a moment, placing a dark, lumpy-knuckled index finger against his lip so that it touches the tip of his white mustache.

"Tomorrow morning," he says after a moment.

Tomorrow morning is good. I look at Richard, who looks at Margaret.

"Tell him he's hired," Richard says.

Margaret translates, and Ta Pierre smiles broadly. A chill goes through me, radiating from my center and extending out to the hair on my scalp and the tips of my toes. I have just become one significant step closer to the vague and various "them" I have long regarded with haughty disdain. We wish Ta Pierre and Margaret good night and see them out into the stilled, chirping darkness.

I look at the nearly empty water dispenser in the kitchen. It is almost bedtime, and tomorrow is a big day.

Richard and I are alone in our living room. We lie on the couch, nestled like spoons in a silverware drawer, the back of my head resting on his chest. I can feel his heartbeat.

"Oh, by the way," he says, stretching with a yawn. "Margaret isn't married, is she?"

"Do you recall meeting a husband?" I ask with a twinge of displeasure.

"No, no, can't say as I do," he says.

"Well, then."

There is a pause.

"Why do you ask?" I challenge.

Richard shakes his head. "No reason," he says, getting up and walking toward the bedroom with a sailors swagger.

"That Margaret, she's an odd bird," he adds as he exits.

I smile, realizing that it may be in my best interest to keep an eye on her.

IT IS IN THE EVENING several days later that Joseph Boale returns from his inspection of the backcountry elementary schools and comes by our house to make his report to Richard. He climbs the stairs onto the veranda as Richard and I work together upholstering an improvised armchair for the living room.

The visitor steps up to the screen door. He is dressed in white, as always, and wears dark sunglasses, although it is dusk. M. Boale clears his throat to announce his arrival.

"*Entrez, je vous en pris*," Richard says, setting down a tack hammer.

M. Boale comes in and takes off his glasses.

"I have your report," he says.

"How did everything go?"

"You gave me too little money."

"What? I figured up all the salaries and material allotments carefully and checked them again before I—"

"You didn't give me enough to pay all the salaries. I told the teachers in the north region that they will have to wait for next time to be paid."

"There must be some mistake. I . . . I'm sure I took enough out of the cashbox for all the salaries. I don't know how this could happen."

"Here," M. Boale says, handing him the report. "All the expenses are there. I've put each thing on its own line, just as a white man likes to see it."

Richard takes the page from him, squinting at his handwriting. "What's this?"

"I needed a new suit of clothes for traveling," M. Boale says, pointing to the first item on the list.

"Yes. Yes, I see. So what is this charge you put down for umbrellas? You bought twenty-five umbrellas for your trip?"

"For gifts. A man of *mpifo* who goes into the backcountry must behave in a certain fashion or he will get no respect."

Richard continues to check the list.

"Twelve cases of Pepsi-Cola?" he asks, incredulous.

"More gifts."

"Maybe I wasn't clear with my instructions," Richard says. "But the money you've spent on presents here . . . I mean, a hundred and twenty francs plus another forty-five francs, and the suit you bought—that's enough to pay those teachers' salaries."

M. Boale shakes his head condescendingly. "You do not know how things are done here."

Richard sets the report down on the table and clears his throat before answering.

"Lookie here. I know that I gave you money from the government to pay people to work. Simple as that. And you spent the money on soda pop. *That's* what I know," Richard says, almost shouting.

M. Boale's expression changes. "You cannot speak to me this way in front of a woman," he protests, acknowledging my presence for the first time since he walked in the door.

"That woman is my wife," Richard growls, gesturing in my direction, "and in a few weeks, she'll be your colleague. She deserves to know why she won't be getting supplies for her classroom next term, because now I'm going to have to take money out of the high school budget to pay elementary teachers whose salaries you squandered on . . . on . . . ."

Richard looks down at the list again and smacks his hand against the page. "On ladies' perfume! What on God's earth were you doing buying perfume?"

M. Boale smirks.

"School teachers are not the only people a man of *mpifo* visits when he goes out of town. There are certain pretty, young women along the way who must be made to feel—"

"Get out," Richard says in a voice so calm it frightens me.

M. Boale is silent for a moment.

He looks at me, then back at Richard.

"I warn you. Do not speak to me in that way."

"Get out," Richard repeats very slowly, this time pointing to the door.

M. Boale sniffs, then turns casually and leaves, carrying himself as though the departure were his idea.

From far away, I hear the rumble of thunder.

Seven

October 1953

THE RAIN BEGINS.

I stand on a busy street corner in Chicago. I wait at a bus stop in front of Northwestern University for the ride that will take me back to the hotel room where Richard is waiting for me. I look at my watch. It is a quarter past five in the afternoon. I have been waiting here for almost half an hour. The leaves on the trees glisten and hang on for dear life in the chilly wind blowing off Lake Michigan. I step back beneath the awning and button the top of my raincoat. I hope the bus comes soon, as it is beginning to get dark.

Only a week has passed since Richard and I were married in a clapboard church in Oklahoma City, smiling for photographs and feeding each other cake, trying to look comfortable in stiff, ill-fitting clothes. During the last twelve months, we graduated from Phillips and sweated through a northern-Illinois summer with a group of Mexican migrants as they stooped to harvest peas and asparagus and lettuce at starvation wages.

Richard has finished all the appropriate course work to get a Tennessee teacher's certificate. It should arrive in the mail at his parents' house any day now. I, on the other hand, have spent so much time absorbed in my religious studies that I will have to settle for a Mississippi certificate, unless I want to spend another year in school. Right now, all I want to do is to get to Africa.

In the end, the particulars of my teaching certificate will be an issue only where my pride is concerned. The Belgian Ministry of Education does not care from which state my credentials come, just that I have them.

On the other hand, the Missionary Society *does* seem to care a great deal that its candidates be able, motivated, and mentally well balanced. Richard and I have spent the last three days undergoing a battery of psychological and physical examinations at Northwestern University—blood tests, Rorschachs, aptitude and IQ exams.

I have been asked "Are you sure you want to be a missionary?" and "Why?" so many times in the last seventy-two hours that I have begun to feel as though a desire for field work is a disreputable thing to own up to. And still, after three days, as it has been after the past three years of waiting, my answer remains an unequivocal and resounding "Yes!"

I cannot be merely a housewife. I steadfastly refuse to do such a thing. I cannot sit and gossip about small things as I cut quilt pieces out of patterns that I pass around a table ringed with women whose lives are as grocery-sack drab as my own. I cannot be a church lady, primly sipping coffee and sniping behind her neighbors' backs on Sunday afternoons.

I will not end up like my mother, sad from too many deaths in her childhood, out of options, poor as a church mouse, immobilized but for her hormone shots and Pepsi-Cola, which she likes because of the way it tickles the inside of her nose. Today, my mother's only outlet is giving piano lessons to marginally willing teens in the front room of her apartment and playing the church organ on Sunday mornings. The lessons are her main means of socializing, as well as how she supplements the dollar-a-week grocery allowance my stepfather gives her. It is how Mother can afford to buy herself the hosiery, pimento cheese, and Pepsi-Cola she "owes herself."

No, that will not be me. The Lord has blessed me with talents I must use. The Lord also has supplied me with a conscience that burns to direct those talents toward His service. I know no choice but to go out into the world and roughen my hands in the name of Christ.

I have to get away. That is the only way I have any hope of being happy. I remember, clear as a bell, the afternoon when I picked up that slender pamphlet at church school. It was during my freshman year of college. Across the front fold was the title *A Hard Job: The Requirements, the Romance*. It talked about the kind of fortitude that was needed to become a Christian missionary.

Since that day, my course has been set. I feel as though my life will truly begin when I step off the boat in Africa.

The doctors' questions buzz in my head:

"Have you ever committed a felony crime or been rejected for U.S. military service?

"Would you feel uncomfortable eating a meal at the same table as someone who is not white?

"Do you feel a desire to dominate people?

"Do you feel like a failure in your current life?"

I have tried to dismiss my concerns as unfounded. The questions they asked simply needed to be broached in order to sort out the bad seeds, the delusional people who are attracted to mission work for the wrong reasons.

I sat next to Richard as one of the doctors grilled him.

"I was always eager to be good," Richard said earnestly. "I wanted to do the things my parents and the Church said were good for me to do. I walked down the aisle and was baptized into the Church when I was eight years old."

"Isn't that a bit younger than usual?" the doctor asked, looking up from his notes.

"Yes. But I felt sure about certain things." His voice was charismatic. "Then when I was a teenager, I began to realize that I wanted to make my living working for the Church. I mean, isn't that the highest ideal? I looked at Jesus, at His life, at His call.

"Christ Jesus told us to continue His work of teaching and preaching and healing. That's the part of Jesus that always has impressed me, not the doctrinal part about His being the Son of God and salvation from sin."

The doctor nodded.

"I got an undergraduate scholarship to Phillips University, and as I went through all the hours of religious studies there, I became certain that I want to work in direct service."

As he spoke, I looked around the room, taking in the wall of books, the heavy drapes, the diplomas hanging behind our shiny-headed examiner.

"One of my favorite things to do on Friday nights—before I met Eva, that is—"

I smiled then, and Richard winked at me.

"I'd walk across the field a couple of miles to the County Farm with the King's Messengers volunteers. The County Farm was a nursing home, really, for old indigents who couldn't pay for a better place to live out their . . . to stay before the Lord took 'em. It wasn't such a pleasant place, and there was this smell sometimes that made you turn your head away. A lot of the old people were sick or senile. We'd go and sing familiar songs with them, hymns and such. We'd pray and have a little devotional talk.

"I reckon some of the old people sat in their rooms thinking, 'There goes all that racket of the religious fanatics,' but those who came down to the parlor in their wheelchairs or hobbling on canes—they'd talk to us as well as they could. Not all of 'em were coherent, but it gave me a feeling like I've never had before. It's a most extraordinary thing, I have to tell you."

"And that is why you want to be a missionary?" the doctor asked.

"That's part of it—the feeling, the gratitude. I thought for a time that I'd become a doctor, but I never even got as far as signing up for a pre-med anatomy course. See, I don't know if doctors get a feeling of reward from their work like I got just from walking over that field to the County Farm on Friday nights, but if they do, they must be few and far between. Now, I know Eva said this, too, but I can't think of doing anything else."

The bus is late. The other people waiting grumble to one another. I stand apart from them. I hear the doctors' questions in my head again. Silently, I answer.

Yes, I am sure I want to be a missionary. I want to be a missionary because as of today, as of right here and now, on a bus stop in Chicago, in the October rain, I cannot imagine myself being anything else. I want to be a missionary because I need to get away from where I have been. There is no oxygen left for me to breathe in Oklahoma. I need the Serengeti, not Seventy-Third Street. I need a field hospital, not the blood drive at the First Christian Church.

"I want to be a missionary because I want to help people." Every time I say those words before a congregation or guidance counselor, I imagine they sound trite, but they are as sincere as any that have been spoken. I want to be a missionary because I believe it to be the will of God.

Truly, it is God's resolve and my own fused as one. I must make a mark in this life, must count for something. There is this wanton largeness in me. I must go and be large with it, or I will be as disconsolate as an animal caged at a zoo.

In the world, there is much pain. I have seen but a fraction of it, yet I know it exists, looming. There is also much hunger—for nourishment, for knowledge, for hope. Since I was very young, I have been blessed and cursed with a chronic perception of that need. It haunts me by night and pales all other purpose by day. I must attend its call. And that, dear Doctor, dear Professor, dear Minister, is why I wish to be a missionary.

Let me.

Eight

January 1957

I WAKE TO THE SOUND OF THE LOKOLÉ DRUM. High and low, high and low, it speaks, bottle-shaped mallets falling against a large hollowed log. The percussion carries well across lush forest, waking workers and farmers and advising them, in singsong code, of the village's latest goings-on. I wonder what it is saying.

Today is the first day of the new term at l'École Moyenne. I was restless last night, anxious about what the day might hold for me. Now I do not want to rise. I try and ignore the lokolé, hoping the drummer will be done soon. I put my pillow over my head, but the pounding will not be muffled.

At last I sit up and throw my pillow in exasperation. It lands at Richard's feet. He wakes and turns to me with a look of confusion. Sunlight streams in the window. The drumming ends.

"Good morning," I say tartly.

A cock crows. Richard grunts his reply. I loosen the mosquito netting, tugging at a corner of the gauzy fabric I tucked behind the frame of the bed last night.

Shuffling into the bathroom, I find a small cockroach on my toothbrush. I shake the brush over the toilet and watch with improper delight as the bug falls to its watery grave. Richard comes up behind me and kisses me on the back of my neck. I am startled, though his stubble is still soft like that of a boy and causes my skin little trouble. I smile and breathe him in. His hair smells sweet from last night's Lux shampooing. He kisses my neck again. I finish brushing my teeth.

"Here," I say, handing Richard our bottle of Niquavine tablets.

We take a dose of the medicine every day to combat the symptoms of malaria. Richard swallows and hands me the bottle. I place a bitter tablet on my tongue. It is jungle communion. In a certain respect, we disciples do this in remembrance of Christ, for any action taken here is a component of our presence in Congo, and that presence is as much a remembrance of Him as anything I can imagine.

Richard turns and leaves the bathroom. I look in the mirror and address my class, shoulders back, in the posture of authority.

"Bonjour, garçons," I say, but as the words form on my lips they sound demeaning, so I try again.

"Bonjour, classe." This is better. I try it both with and without a smile.

"What?" Richard calls from the bedroom after my third or fourth attempt.

"Nothing," I answer.

I turn my attention back to the mirror.

When we came to Africa, I packed four tubes of Max Factor lipstick in my toiletry case. Those four tubes must last me three years. As I smudge a little red across my lips, I do so with the intention of economy.

Richard, now dressed, combs his hair into place. He wraps a piece of bread in newspaper and puts it into his trouser pocket. He is the principal of the school and must get there to see to matters before anyone else arrives. He kisses me goodbye and heads out. I stand near the front window and watch him disappear around the bend before once again considering my own preparations for the day. I pressed and laid out my best skirt last night, and it waits for me, leaning back against the sofa cushions.

I dress and return to the bathroom mirror.

"Bienvenue à l'École Moyenne," I welcome my students.

They all smile at me. I pull my hair back off my face and fix it in place with two barrettes.

There are footsteps on the porch, followed by a cough that indicates a visitor. I walk to the door and draw it open. Across the threshold stands a blouse-less old woman, skin so slack and weathered that she appears mummified. She wears a piece of brown-and-orange cloth around her bony shoulders as a hedge against the early morning cool, but it affords her scant protection. The old woman asks me in Lonkundo whether I am awake. I look down at myself, fully dressed, coifed, and shod.

"Yes," I tell her, "I am awake."

She offers to sell me some breakfast.

I tell her that I will try to get my breakfast later at school.

"Bokele, Mama," she says and holds out a big duck egg. She looks me in the eye and nods shrewdly, as though this surely must be an offer I cannot refuse. I think for a moment of buying her egg purely as a gesture of good will. Just last week, this same woman brought us a gift of banganju stew, which she promised was made from palm-nut gravy and the peppers in her garden. It might be rude not to take her up on her present offer. We stand quietly for a moment, she and I.

I take the egg into my hands. It is fat and heavy. I cannot tell if it is warm from being freshly laid or from a long journey in the palms of the old woman's hands. I look at her drawn expression. Under the skin of each hollow cheek she carries the tattooed image of a single leaf. Down the center of her forehead is a straight black line that terminates between her eyes, where it resembles a furrow of worry. I hand the egg back to her.

"Wait a moment," I tell her and go to the kitchen pantry, unlocking it and taking out a can of tuna fish.

"Keep your egg and have this," I say, walking back to the door. I hold out the tin can.

"Eoto-e," she thanks me matter of factly, taking it from my hands without a moment's hesitation. I wonder if this charity was her goal all along. The old woman turns to leave, muttering a polite entreaty that I might stay in good health.

The lokolé sounds again. The sun has risen. It is time for school. I gather my things and leave. As I walk hurriedly toward l'École Moyenne, I hear the boys singing the Belgian national anthem:

Marche joyeux, peuple énergique, Vers des destins dignes de toi!
Dieu protège la libre Belgique et son roi!

In the final lines of the song, the boys beg God to protect the freedom of Belgians and their king. Though the song is many generations old, the appeal was a pressing concern fifteen years ago, when Nazi troops drove through the central square in Brussels. I think about this as I hike across the field.

The students finish singing just as I take my place among the other teachers on the porch of the principal's office. I catch my breath while Richard gives the morning announcements and offers

83

a prayer. I realize that in my haste I have stood next to Joseph Boale. Neither of us acknowledges the other.

As Richard speaks, I look down at the rows of bowed heads in front of me, a dozen slender teenage boys, skin ink-black against their white cotton drill shirts and shorts. Their clothes are clean and mended. My skirt is ironed. I am nervous. Richard finishes the prayer and dismisses the boys, turning and walking past me with no greeting beyond a cursory glance of disapproval. He is mad at me for being late, if only five minutes. I turn and watch as he rings the old-fashion school bell.

I want to be mad back but cannot. Richard has every right to be on edge this morning. The weight of the world rests on his shoulders. He is a new arrival, not yet thirty years old, charged with teaching, disciplining, and seeing to the care of a generation of young Nkundu men, the hand-picked future leaders of the villages that surround Bolenge.

There is a new solemnity to Richard's step as he walks down the packed-dirt hallway toward his office door, greeting the other teachers with handshakes. I pick up my things and follow him.

My classroom is across the hall from the office and one door down. Once I enter, I will be a different person. The torch will be passed. I will be an educator.

In the final footsteps before I go into the classroom, my mind is flooded with pictures of my favorite teachers. Each one of them must have had a day like this, though it is hard to imagine. Sentiment wells in me, but then as I pass through the doorway, I do so not with mawkishness or fear but with a sudden, keen sense of understanding, of place, of order.

The boys rise and stand at attention. I stop in my tracks. I did not expect this. Three dozen of them stand beside their desks, in tidy rows, crisp clothed and bright eyed. After a moment, the young men silently take their seats. The room is larger than I expected. I walk to the long, hand-hewn teachers table and set down my bag of books and supplies. Richard has typed up a class list. I take it out of my folder.

"Bokunge," I say, beginning to take attendance.

"Present, Madame," a tall, bright-eyed boy says from the back of the room.

"Lokolutu," I continue, and another speaks his acknowledgment.

When I reach the last name, I walk around from behind the table and sit, as casually as my self-conscious arms and legs will allow me, against the front of the massive piece of furniture. For several days I have debated how to begin my first class, but now it seems simple.

I take a deep breath. "Today is a very special day for me," I tell the class in slow, deliberate French. "You all have been in school for seven or eight years. And I have sat as you are sitting now in many, many classrooms. But today is my first real day as a teacher. I hope it will be all right with all of you if we learn together."

The boys smile and nod. Several chuckle, displaying their filed teeth.

I ask the boys where they are from. Surprisingly few name Bolenge as their home. Some hail from as far as eight hundred kilometers up- or downriver, having made the journey with the blessing of village elders wise enough to see the benefits of having a man in the tribe with a high school education.

I introduce our first French essay exercise. I pass out paper and pencils and ask each student to recount his first day at school.

While the boys work, I look around. The classroom is bare but not unpleasant to the eye. The whitewashed walls reflect plenty of light. The row of windows to my right is large and open, so the room is airy, though I do not know how much of a benefit this will prove during the rainy season. I question the advisability of taping maps or students' work to the walls. Any bit of wind surely will tug fragile pages away from the whitewash and land them on the floor. Perhaps I can hang things up above the windows.

I turn around to inspect the wall behind me. There is a black slate chalkboard, cracked and weathered from much use. It seems I will have to forage for chalk should I wish to use the board, as none seems to have been provided. Looking up, I am struck by the idea of enlisting the boys' artistic skills to stencil a border around the top of the walls. It will let them see the room as their own and not a manifestation of the austerity of Belgian rule. I must ask Richard for some clear varnish, in addition to the chalk, so the drawing may be preserved.

My stomach rumbles. I wonder if the boys can hear it. I should have taken the egg the old woman offered me. I drum my fingertips on the tabletop. A student in the front row looks up at me quizzically, then returns his gaze to the task at hand. The teacher in the next classroom has her students singing.

I wonder, twenty minutes into my first class, whether I am a good teacher. In front of me, thirty-six pencils dull against thirty-six sheets of assignment paper. Thirty-six foreheads wrinkle with concentration. These boys look distressingly alike to me, all dark-skinned and bony, all eager, all filled with the conceit that comes from knowing they are smarter than their village peers. I fear it will be some time before I am able to properly associate their names with their faces.

Sooner than it seems it ought, the class bell rings, and the students file to the front of the room, making a neat pile of essays on my desk as they leave. Once the last boy walks out of the classroom, I sigh. I realize I have been clenching my jaw for an entire hour.

Second period is my break for teacher's preparations. I am hungry. I look at the stack of essays in front of me and pick up one of the pieces of paper. It is difficult for me to read the handwriting. I realize I have three dozen of these to correct by tomorrow morning, three dozen stories in three dozen French dialects. Already this morning, the class confronted me with a variety of expressions I have never before heard. Now, looking over essay after essay, I grasp at the limits of my own knowledge of the language. I do not know if the queer things the students write are perfectly serviceable French sayings or perhaps pidgin betrayals of the tongue, which I ought to root out lest they reduce some future prospective employer's estimation of the boys.

I close up the papers in my folder and drop it into my bag. I am too hungry for this right now. I must go home and find something to eat.

On my way home, I pass Margaret on the footpath. She looks somewhere between official and officious—dress tightly fitted, a clipboard tucked under her arm and a pencil over her ear.

"How's the new school marm faring?" she asks.

"All right, I guess." I do not really feel like stopping to chat, but Margaret plants herself squarely in my path, so I suppose it would be rude of me not to stop.

"Say, I understand you filled out a road paper for one of my workers last week," Margaret says, fiddling with the clasp of her clipboard.

"Yes, that's right," I tell her. "He needed to go to Coquilhatville for supplies and he couldn't find you, so he came and knocked on our door. I wrote him a note saying that—"

"Do me a favor: next time, use the proper form, okay? There's a whole stack of travel forms right by my desk. They're two-part carbons. If I'm not around just leave me a note saying what you've done."

I nod, trying to think of an appropriate response.

A tentative "Okay . . ." is all I can muster.

Margaret shifts. Behind her, a steady stream of natives files past, heading to the river to bathe, to drink, to launder their clothes.

"Another thing—"

"I'm sorry, I need to get back to class." I back away from her.

"Well, all right, but I need to talk to you about your duties. I'm the station chairman this year. Everybody takes on at least one job beyond his or her regular assignment. We need to find assignments for you and Richard soon, or the only thing left will be tending the native cemetery near the village."

I consider this and stop my retreat.

"I thought they did that themselves, looking after the dead, I mean."

"Back in the old days," she says with a laugh. "Now there's all kinds of government regulations about sanitation. The natives don't like it much. They've got some notion that we're messing with their ancestral spirits. I hear tell that a while back, one of the elders had a ceremony to send the spirit of the missionary tending the graves into what they call the evil forest. Didn't work, though. He was healthy as a horse all the way through till he went home on furlough."

I shift my bag from one shoulder to the other. The sun is rising higher in the sky and, in response, the heat of the day has begun to come up.

"Maybe I'll be charitable and make you the social chair. You any good at throwing parties?"

I squint at her.

"I'm all right, I reckon."

"Good. Then it's done. I'll catch Richard later," Margaret says, turning and continuing on her way.

I stand and watch her disappear. When I reach the house, Richard is sitting at the kitchen table going over some papers.

"You were late," he says without looking up.

I pass behind his chair and go to the pantry.

"I was late," I acknowledge matter of factly. "I can explain—"

87

"And I've come to the conclusion," he continues, "that math is one big mystery to most of these boys."

He marks a D-plus on the assignment he is correcting.

I hold my tongue.

"You making breakfast?" Richard asks, looking up for the first time.

"That I am," I say, taking a tall tin of margarine from the cupboard. Today is not a day for a balanced meal. There is not time to cook up Spam before I return to class. I will toast us some bread in the skillet.

Thankfully, Richard and I have been able to borrow a countertop kerosene burner. That way, we can heat a pan quickly, rather than waiting the half hour a potbelly stove takes to heat. Richard eats greedily and dashes back to school, leaving me with a greasy peck on the cheek. I look at our dirtied plates sitting on the table. I must clean them and bury the trash in the backyard, or the kitchen will be swarming with ants when Ta Pierre gets here at lunchtime.

For some reason, I am overwhelmed by the notion of washing dishes. I look around. Of course, no one is watching me. I open the old icebox and put the plates quickly inside.

"There," I say quietly, shutting the door and turning to leave. But before I can get out of the room, my conscience nags me to deal with the situation in a more adult manner.

There is a noise outside. I startle, as several native women step up onto the back porch.

"Ol'eko, Mama," they call, grinning for having spied me through the screen door.

It would only be courteous for me to say "Loy'endo" and welcome them to my home, but I am too anxious about what waits for me back at school to bow to propriety.

"I'm sorry, I have to go teach now," I say.

Their faces fall. Their shoulders sag.

One 'tsk 'tsk's her disapproval. Another shuffles her feet. None of them, however, move from where they're standing. A sudden draft brings their smell across the threshold and into the kitchen. It is musky with smoke and fermented manioc.

"What do you want?" I ask, and I hear an edginess in my voice that I do not like.

"Dresses, Mama. We want dresses."

I look out beyond them to where two of my dresses hang on the clothesline beside Richard's trousers and underwear.

"I really have only a couple saved back," I tell the women, "and they have to last me through the end of next year."

The women's expressions do not change. While they have made sense of my words, they do not understand the concept of saving back dresses. It must be because nothing lasts out here. It molds, it rots, it becomes riddled by insects, it is stolen. It would be foolish to hoard anything for a month or a year. It would be stingy and presumptuous.

We are here in Congo, promoting the notion that a man who is pious will give a beggar the shirt off his back. I suppose now, in these women's eyes, I am not behaving in a Christian manner. I am a hypocrite, my action a contrast to that which I teach. There is nothing I can say, at present, to ameliorate the situation. I pick up my books.

"Go well," I mumble as I walk out the door and push past them.

AFTER MY LAST CLASS, I return home.

Ta Pierre makes no mention of the dirty plates I left in the icebox.

I pour myself a glass of tea and take a seat in the corner of the kitchen, away from the open windows and doors. There are times when I relish this quieter light found in afternoon shadows. It suits my eyes. I write out my lesson plans for tomorrow, heavy on review, in accordance with the principles I learned in a correspondence course from the Peabody College for Teachers. I hope the district school inspector will be impressed by my preparations when he visits later in the term. I must come up with a Bible lesson for the boys in my afternoon class but can think of nothing.

Today, we read together one of Jesus' parables about being prepared. When I asked one student to stand and retell it in his own words, he enthusiastically reinterpreted things so that the bridegroom in the story was taking his ten wives to a wedding feast for his newest wife. After the boy was done and the class had politely applauded, I wasn't sure how to respond.

For the moment, I do not feel very close to God.

I close my eyes and listen to the sounds of the mission. Natives tell themselves stories as they pass the house on their way to the river. Washtubs clank against one another at Nurse Matthews's house across the way. A wooden bell clacks at the neck of one of the natives' shy-throated Basenji hunting dogs. A local carpenter goes by, his steps weighed down by the load he is carrying home to finish.

As the carpenter passes below my window, he breaks into song. I think it's the Hallelujah Chorus. I smile.

Thank You, Lord.

Nine

April 1957

THE RAINS HAVE COME AGAIN TO CENTRAL AFRICA, turning the mission into a soggy mess, filling our backyard cistern until it coughs out rainwater onto the scrubby grass nearby. Wind blows the rain sideways with amazing force. The screens in our big open windows do nothing to prevent the arrival of the elements. In fact, they seem to invite the weather in with utmost hospitality, and sometimes it seems as if a fireman's hose were opened on the proceedings of our home life.

We are more prepared than we were in late October, when the first squalls of the season came. For several days, every room in the house was drenched each time the wind blew. Then Richard got a hammer and rusted saw from the mission's shop and tore apart the remaining packing crates from our move, fashioning the sides and tops into wooden shutters that more or less cover the windows.

This time, the windows are secured, but Richard and I begin to notice the roof is leaking terribly. We move furniture around, trying to find dry patches of floor. Below the leaks we place coffee cans, soup bowls, and our one wash pail, emptying them over and over during the heaviest downpours.

The Congo River is swollen, the fast-moving murky water inching up the banks until it snatches away sapling trees, dragging them downstream. The Africans have warned us that the river is dangerous now. It can steal people, they say, steal them for sure. Crocodiles take their bodies away to underground tunnels, where they keep them for three days before returning them to the surface somewhere downriver.

We hear the roar of the rushing water every night as we drift to sleep and every morning as we rise. Sometimes, in the wee hours, I lie awake, counting drops of water that fall from two leaks in the roof of our bedroom. The leak by the door is worse. It allows ten drops to tap on the floor in the time the leak nearer the bathroom allows but three. There is music to the pattern of their interaction. I sigh and put my pillow over my head.

The whole world smells wet. Clothes get musty all on their own. Towels do not dry properly between baths. Doors, swelled with humidity, scrape on the floor and refuse to shut. Last week, the mission's generator got waterlogged, and we endured two evenings without electric power.

Perhaps the worst thing is that the mail boat has not come for more days than I can count. This must be what is like to live deep in the interior, like the early missionaries, entirely detached from civilization. For a moment, it was exciting, bracing. Now it has begun to weigh upon me. Despite my best efforts, I end up wet several times a day. It is the worst when I slip in the mud while traveling to or from school, ruddy mire streaking my shins until I reach my destination and can clean up.

I try to remember that the rainy season is a waiting game. Richard and I endure the squalls with as much patience as possible, prayer and our half-dry towels helping us through.

I have been teaching at l'École Moyenne for seven weeks now, and Richard and I are becoming used to our roles. By day, he is Monsieur le Directeur and, therefore, my supervisor. But in the evenings, he and I work side by side as equals, reviewing the school's antiquated curriculum. I am beginning to understand why, upon our arrival, the other missionaries seemed so pleased that we are young. While Gloria Snead may have done an admirable job of running the school, her course work and methodology were left over from an earlier part of the century. It seems to me that the lessons being taught in l'École Moyenne are designed to prepare young men for a life of no greater achievement than entry-level office work. In truth, such a station is usually all that Africans can hope, as yet, to achieve.

And what of dreaming? There is no provision made in our lesson plans to fuel the students' imaginations or feed their spiritual selves, save for the compulsory Bible lessons, dispensed like spoonfuls of medicine first thing every morning. As I look at the faces of the boys in my class, it saddens me to know their favorite part of the day is typing class. I lie restless at night, nursing the notion that there must be something Richard and I can do to change this.

Schooling ought to be something about which our students are passionate. They are the chosen ones. They are brighter than their peers who will not go beyond the sixth grade. They are the hope for the future of Congo. I think of the parable about teaching a man to fish and thereby giving him the tools to provide for himself. As educators, we must teach our students to fish for ideas, for poetry and music, for the liberation of hope.

As most of the students hail from the deep backcountry, their long days in class are followed by long nights in an overcrowded dormitory room with few comforts and even less privacy. They do it all so they may have the privilege of education. I feel sorry for the boys who must be away from home at a tender age, and yet it is hard right now to think about anything but rain. Every day, we ask the Africans when the rains might be over.

"Madame, we do not know," is the singsong answer. "Madame, we do not know," again and again.

Today, however, brings a different response.

"The rains will finish soon," Ta Pierre promises as Richard and I are getting ready to leave for school.

I stop and turn to look at him.

"Excuse me?"

"I say, the rains, he will travel soon."

"What makes you so sure?" Richard asks.

Ta Pierre just smiles and nods as though we have paid him a compliment. There is a smudge of white flour across his forehead. He and I have spent the early part of the morning in the kitchen together. I promised, on his request, to teach him the instructions for some favorite American dishes. I credit him with wanting to expand his repertoire.

My first thought was to make him a little recipe book, penning recipes for biscuits and key lime pie on little index cards. I immediately dismissed the notion, however, when I recalled the daily image of Ta Pierre leaning low over the stove until his glasses fogged from the steam rising out of a saucepan. Aside from being nearly illiterate, Ta Pierre is nearly blind.

I discovered this morning that the way to teach Ta Pierre to cook something like Southern fried chicken is to go through the steps as he watches closely, making exaggerated facial expressions, drawing his nose up close to the measuring spoons to inspect the contents and quantity.

"Then," I explained to Ta Pierre after showing him how to shake the cut-up chicken in a paper bag full of flour and spices. "You fry it in oil until it turns the color of the bag."

"You fry it in oil!" he exclaimed. "You mean from the palm nut?"

"No, no," I said. "Regular oil."

"Regular oil?"

"Yes, does that not make sense?" I asked.

He shrugged, still looking confused.

"Oui, Madame," he said after a moment.

TODAY THE BELGIAN GOVERNMENT SCHOOL INSPECTOR comes through Bolenge. We are told he makes a circuit that takes him past every school in his district once each term. If a school does not, in his appraisal, measure up to standards that officials in Brussels have set, the school's funding is cut. It can be quite a rude consequence. Officially, the budgets of the schools in our region are used for classroom supplies and instructors' wages. In practice, however, many schools find it necessary to borrow from other mission programs to buy meal rations for their students.

Teenage boys who fill their days with studies of Christianity, French, and *dactylographie* do not have the time to go to work on plantations, as they would otherwise by about age fifteen. They are, therefore, often reliant on the Belgian schools for the food on their plates. Richard, the African teachers, and I serve up cupfuls of dried rice, butchered meat scraps, dried fish, and whatever else is available in the village on a given day. If it were not for the rations we dispense, some students would go hungry. The Belgian government may disagree, but I do not believe that a sixteen-year-old boy is in good condition for learning when he is faint with hunger.

There are weeks when we can give the boys rations five days in a row, and there are times when there is only enough in our coffers to provide food every other day. It is painful for me to go home at night to a full meal Ta Pierre has cooked up for us when I know that some of my students are spending the night hungry. I look down at my plate and get a lump in my throat. Then I tell myself that if I do not eat, I will not have the energy to teach. Truly, then, nothing will be accomplished.

THE SCHOOL INSPECTOR ARRIVES AS ANNOUNCED, looking like Teddy Roosevelt in nose-pinching spectacles.

"Bonjour, Mesdames, Messieurs," he addresses the faculty in harsh-voweled French. He stands before us in the thatched-roof common area as rain drips rhythmically from a leak near the corner of the room.

"Today I wish for you to conduct your classes as usual," he says. "I will stroll amongst you and observe. Just pretend I am not here."

We do our best, but the inspector keeps poking his head into the classroom at all the wrong moments—when students are making errors, when the pretty young mathematics instructor gets her menstrual period unexpectedly and has to rush from the room, when my termite-gnawed chalkboard, its grasp of the wall tenuous on a good day, comes crashing to the floor with a deafening thunder crack. Between classes, I find Richard and pull him aside in the muddy concrete-floored hallway.

"So? How do you think it's going?" I ask, trying not to sound troubled.

"It's too soon to tell," Richard says the way a parent might talk to a toddler. "I reckon you just need to keep doing the excellent job I've seen you doing since the day you began, and everything will be fine."

I take a small step back to get a good look at him. Either Richard is bluffing exceptionally well, or the fresh-pressed cool he is sporting is genuine. If the latter is true, he must know some information about the school inspection that I do not. Richard smiles gently and walks past me up the breezeway. I turn in bemusement, watching him go.

At the end of the day, Richard gives the recess bell a vigorous shake, and the boys scramble from the building and out across the waterlogged field to their dormitory. One of the instructors comes to my classroom to tell me that the inspector has summoned Richard to the school office.

One by one, the teachers and I gather under the eaves of the courtyard, anxious to receive the results of our evaluation. Several times we hear mumblings from Richard's office. For a quarter hour, we stand in rapt silence, straining to make out any intelligible bits

95

of conversation. M. Boale is the only one who does not seem concerned about the goings-on inside the office. He stays with the rest of us but says he is doing so only for the pleasure of our company. I do not believe him.

"Are you not at least a little nervous?" I whisper.

He shrugs. "Why should I care what a foolish white man thinks of me?"

And yet he stays.

Then at a quarter past three, the door opens. Richard and the inspector walk out, grinning and shaking hands. Richard shows the man to the end of the hallway, waving goodbye at the front door before returning to where the teachers wait. As he walks up to where we stand, Richard is silent for a moment. Then he starts laughing.

"You should see yourselves," he chuckles in French, mimicking our frozen, anxious expressions.

"Well? What did he say?" the prematurely menstrual teacher calls out from the back of the group.

"You all should be proud of yourselves. He's giving us high marks for the term in almost all areas."

"Hooray!" several of the teachers cheer, but Richard quiets them.

"This rating shows the hard work your students have been doing, and to reward them, if the weather shows any signs of clearing up as we've been promised, I'm of a mind to declare tomorrow a day of athletics. There will be no academic studies, just games of physical fitness in the field. Who'd like to be in charge of organizing soccer teams?"

"I will, Monsieur le Directeur," a teacher says, raising his hand.

"Who will coordinate marching?"

My hand goes up before I think about it.

"Eva? Marching?" Richard looks surprised.

"Why not?" I ask. I directed three different plays in my neighborhood during high school. Getting some African boys to remember a few marches has to be simpler than dragging a gaggle of teenaged Oklahomans through "Blithe Spirit."

"Well, all right. If you're sure," Richard says, writing my name on his pad of paper with a chuckle. "Let's see. Who can organize a foot race?"

Hands go up around the room until, one by one, every teacher is assigned an event. When the meeting is finished, Richard and I walk home from school.

"The inspector said some more things," Richard tells me once we are out of earshot of the school building.

"Like?"

"Like he hopes we have no connection with the CIA, and he doesn't want us teaching pacifism, even if Jesus Christ approved of that sort of thing. He told me that Belgium may sometime need the Congolese to defend this colony, and we need to teach them to be patriots."

"The CIA!" I exclaim, laughing. "Well, I never!"

A silence settles, scored by the squishing of our soles in the mud. The rain continues to fall, but the sky is not as threatening as usual.

"Oh, by the way—marching? What on earth possessed you?" Richard asks.

I remain quiet for a moment. Then a giggle forms and I cannot stop it from surfacing. Richard looks at me and laughs along.

"I was just excited, okay?" I tell him. "I didn't think about it. It's called initiative—"

"Oh brother—" he smirks.

"Just you wait. I will have them marching like little soldiers." I demonstrate, straightening my back and right-angling my knees with each step.

"Well, isn't that a regular hoot? The Army of l'École Moyenne," Richard laughs. "I'll have to see it to believe it. Too bad the school inspector came today and not tomorrow. I'm sure he'd be mighty impressed."

We walk on. We are approaching the missionaries' houses, and I can smell the sooty smoke of wood-burning stoves heated for the cooking of dinner. Sometimes I think the smell of smoke is more appealing in the rain.

"You know," Richard begins, quieter now, "the only area where the inspector gave us a mediocre rating was French classes. I've been wondering if we shouldn't try a different approach. I reckon... remember when we had those intensive language study records?"

"Uh-huh."

"Well, now, I wonder if we could get hold of something like that. Maybe a set of French records. Then we could borrow the record player from the mission and put it in one of the classrooms, and the boys could spend, I don't know, maybe an hour a day with the recordings. I think I'll write that professor—what was his name?"

"Monsieur . . ." I try to remember the name of the rumpled little white-haired man who ruled his Ivy League lecture hall with an enthusiasm bordering on panic. I wonder whether he is still alive.

"Wait a minute. Becktart, that's it," Richard interrupts, snapping his fingers. "Professor Becktart. I think I'll write him and see if he's still got those records."

The rain has decreased to a drizzle. As we walk through our front garden in the twilight, I see that the plants are flourishing from all the moisture. Where there are no roots to hold the soggy ground together, the dirt has washed away to a slick, muddy brown. We step carefully.

"Come! Come!" Ta Pierre calls to us as soon as he hears our footfalls on the veranda. "Time to eat. *Mama y Nkoko* Dunagan late! It's special dinner. Raining will be finished. Time for chicken bird."

"You really think so, about the rain?" I ask, and Ta Pierre nods vigorously.

"I'm sorry," Richard says, trying to find the right words in Lonkundo. "We were slow at school. Here now."

I can smell something cooking in the kitchen.

"You sit down," Ta Pierre invites, affecting a cartoonish maître d's flourish that would disquiet a well-starched Parisian restaurateur. Ta Pierre has done a careful job of laying the table. Once again, I am reminded of the comfort of upholding certain convention.

"Join us," Richard says, dragging another chair to the table.

Ta Pierre stands and shakes his head as though the notion is absurd.

"Why not?" I ask. "If you cooked a whole chicken, then there is surely enough for three."

"No, Madame," he says, still shaking his head and now laughing, "I do it for you. It is celebrating of rain go away."

We set down our books and papers and take our seats at the table. Ta Pierre hurries to the kitchen, returning with plates of steaming vegetables and golden-brown, deep-fried chicken. I am delighted.

"Thank you," I say, and Ta Pierre grins, nodding with satisfaction as he returns to the kitchen.

Richard says a quick prayer, then picks up a chicken breast, biting into it hungrily. The moment he takes the meat back away from his lips, an unpleasant expression comes across his face. He grabs the napkin from his lap and spits the unchewed bite of chicken into it, hastily refolding the fabric.

"What's the matter," I whisper.

"It's—taste it yourself," he says, reaching for his water glass and taking a generous gulp.

I pick up a drumstick cautiously, holding it under my nose. There is definitely something wrong with the smell. I take a tentative bite and immediately repeat Richard's action of spitting it into my napkin, for the chicken tastes like Vaseline.

"Ta Pierre?" I call, and he comes in from the kitchen.

"You like the chicken?" he asks hopefully.

"Ta Pierre, which oil did you use to fry the chicken?"

He looks puzzled.

"Regular oil," he said with a shrug. "Like you say."

"Show me," I gently insist, rising from the table and wiping my tongue on my napkin.

I follow him into the kitchen, where he pulls two empty motor-oil cans from the trash.

"Oil," he says with a decisive nod. "I have to look long time to find enough for the cookings. I got cans from the generator shed."

I smack my forehead with my palm. Richard and I are as diplomatic as possible, thanking Ta Pierre and hurrying him out the door before we dig a hole out back and bury the chicken to hide the evidence. I am determined Ta Pierre not carry the blame. It bothers me how misunderstandings with natives often end in whispers and cutting looks from my peers—as if they themselves had no part in the confusion.

At bedtime, Richard and I laugh about the fiasco until my sides hurt.

"At least it's better than finding out he lubricated a truck with Wesson," Richard guffaws.

After we settle down, Richard goes into to the bathroom to brush his teeth. Left alone, I think about Ta Pierre, about his wisdom and his frailty. We know little about him, despite the weeks he has been with us. There is something peculiar in the way he smiles, in the way his eagerness to please is sometimes replaced by reserve.

"Do you really think the rain'll be done by morning?" Richard asks.

I listen to the gentle rain drumming its fingers on the roof, and I am too sleepy to answer. Richard comes back into the bedroom.

He stands at the foot of the bed, looking like a little boy in his striped cotton pajamas. I stare at him and he stares back. Then he begins to grin.

"What?" I ask, feigning indignation.

"I'm thinking about the day of athletics tomorrow, trying to imagine you leading marches. What're you going to do?"

"Are you asking as my husband or as my principal?"

He thinks about it for a moment.

"I'm asking as your principal," he decides.

"Then you will have to wait until tomorrow. I never discuss work outside of the office."

"Whaddya mean, never? You've been teaching for, what, a whole seven weeks now?"

"Doesn't matter," I say defiantly.

Right on schedule, the gentle rumble of the generator next door stills as the contraption grinds to a halt. Our lights dim rapidly and go out.

"I suppose that's the end of the scene," Richard offers in the darkness.

"Not quite," I say, reaching under the pillow for my flashlight. I switch it on and find myself a blank notebook amid the pile of books and papers on our dining room table. Richard snores gently in the bedroom, while I sit up writing words for a tomorrow's marching exercise. Will he be surprised? Perhaps so, although he should know by now not to underestimate the power of my conviction.

I WAKE TO A SOUND that is not immediately familiar. The river is roaring with the kind of raw ferocity only nature can muster. But beyond that, there is a delightful stillness. I rise and walk to the packing-crate shutters on our bedroom window. As I open the latch and swing them open wide, I see patches of sunlight on the grass.

All at once, I feel like singing. Yes! Hooray for the blue sky overhead! Hooray! Nothing here in Africa is as simple as I wish, but, as is always true in life, adversities pass. I am learning this important lesson as I age. Living in Congo gives it deepened resonance.

I wake Richard by dancing a little dance across the bedroom floor. We eat our breakfast on the veranda, delighted by the change of weather but anxious to get to school.

"Smell that air," Richard says, drawing in a noisy breath. "It makes all the trouble of the rainy season worthwhile."

"Yeah," I agree, "but let's not get carried away."

I thought I, as a woman, was supposed to be the one prone to hyperbole while Richard, the man, would be grounded and sensible. But, I learn, to every rule there are exceptions. We are exceptions.

"What were you doing up so late, anyway?" Richard asks.

"My homework," I answer. I am intentionally vague, but Richard does not take my bait, instead scowling at a seed from his fruit salad that has ended up between his teeth.

I look at our garden growing out of control. In a few days, once the soil is firmer, it will be time to have Liyanza and his workers return. Now I know that in exchange for their labors, it is kinder to offer them a solid lunch than a pocket full of francs.

Richard frees the seed from his molars and holds it up for inspection with a simpleton's grin. I go into the house to get my things so we can leave for school.

The rain is done and my boys will march. I have a feeling this will be different from the way they have marched before. I imagine Gloria Snead sending students out, stomping to the drear of centuries-old hymns. In truth, not long ago I myself probably would have insisted on "Onward Christian Soldiers"—this is a Missions school after all.

But I'm changing.

I line up my regiment as the day begins, teaching them the whimsical rhyming song I wrote last night:

À l'École Moyenne, je promène mon chien, il veut tellement entrer dedans . . .

I lead my barefoot group from my classroom out to the schoolyard, where other instructors have their students warming up for foot races and long jumps. Richard turns from where he has been watching a soccer team decide their positions. He stares at my motley infantry in disbelief. I pay him no mind, marching the boys out onto the main street of the mission. I think up some simple choreography as we go, then stop the boys in the middle of the square, handing off the lead to the first student who comes forward. The rest of us stand behind, mirroring his gestures.

Once we have exhausted my little rhyme, we break into French folk songs they have learned from the river trade. The boys stomp, laughing loudly. I laugh with them. I feel giddy, as if I can do anything. Look at me! I've reached these people and helped them feel a bit of joy. I want it to go on and on.

Several small boys come running up from the river. Liyanza is among them. He sets down the load of sticks he's been gathering and waves both arms in the air.

"Madame! Madame!" he cries for my attention, hopping with excitement when I wave back.

My boys and I wind our way to the far side of the mission. As we pass, Margaret steps out from the metal shed that serves as the mission's print shop. She's looking cross, wiping her hands on her apron.

"Good morning," I call to her.

Margaret shields her eyes from the sun with her hand, watching us pass, saying nothing. Mbenze Antoine, one of the older boys in the back of my group, dallies a bit. He waves at Margaret.

"Bonjour, Madame Marguerite." The boy's voice is husky with the awkwardness that accompanies puberty. Margaret sees him and turns away, stepping quickly back into the shadow of her doorway.

Mbenze's face falls. He stares at Margaret's darkened door.

"HERE'S TO DRY WEATHER," Nurse Jean Matthews says, raising an empty coffee cup in a toast. She sets the cup down forcefully, and her hairdo shifts slightly on her head. Jean reaches up quickly to secure it with bobby pins.

It is morning. Jean and her pet monkey are joining us for breakfast. They have just returned from a trip downriver, and Jean has brought fresh bacon back from the city market. Because of the rains, the steamboat's passage was treacherous and slow, and the bacon has begun to spoil. We must eat it all before it is too old. I set two cast-iron skillets on the stove, laying slice after slice against the blackened metal until both skillets are full. I brush disoriented ants from the counter onto the floor and laugh as Jean tells us about her trip.

Her wire-rim glasses and white hair give her the appearance of a frail, storybook grandmother. But when she speaks, her jaw juts out and her eyes flash, letting everyone know she means business. Jean likes to boast that she has delivered over a thousand African babies during her tenure in Congo.

"So there we were, rain coming down in great big torrents." She waves her hands in the air. "The boat's trying to navigate the current, and this hippopotamus wouldn't move! The captain, he was drinking and cursing and taking the Lord's name in vain, and I thought, 'My goodness, I hope he's sober enough to navigate this thing.' He pulls the steam whistle, and it's this big, deep 'Whoo,' so the hippo turns and looks at all of us standing there soaking wet and leaning against the railing of the boat, and what does he do? He opens his big old mouth and brays back at the boat. Bless him— he thought he was singing a duet!"

We laugh. I set the plate of bacon on the table, and Richard and Jean exclaim how good it smells.

"Sometimes you don't realize how much you'll miss something as simple as bacon until you just don't have it anymore," Richard muses, laying his napkin across his lap.

Jean looks at him, quiet for a moment.

"What you've got to learn is how not to hold on to things so tightly," she advises, each word separate from the one it follows.

I pour the coffee and take my seat. Richard says grace and we begin eating.

Jean's monkey sits on the floor, watching patiently as we have our breakfast. At one point, his hunger seems to get the better of his manners and he reaches up a long, hairy arm to steal a slice of bacon.

"No, Edgar!" Jean says, slapping his hand.

The monkey lets out a little shriek and cowers. I realize that it is the first time Jean has called him by name in our presence. I have come to accept her pet as her perennial shadow, almost an extension of who she is. It seems that the heat and duress of the jungle accentuate everyone's eccentricities, much in the way age is wont to do. At first it is disturbing, but after a while it is normalcy that would seem unusual. I look at Jean, really study her, and think about all the rainy seasons she has seen come and go in Congo. I begin to speak, and my words are hesitant.

"There is so much here no one at the Missions board told us about—good things and bad," I say. "I wish there were an easy way to talk to people back home about what's working and what isn't—be real honest, just tell them the truth."

"Eva," Jean says, setting down her fork. "If they'd told you everything, you might not've come. Besides, even if you were to speak out, nobody would listen. Honestly, I don't reckon they really care. Don't you get it? We're here to send home success stories—starving babies fed, leprosy treated, young men educated, word of God spread. Nobody at the Missions Society's going to publish a pamphlet about how the Belgians are impossible to deal with and how we sometimes don't even have enough money to feed the boys at school or buy sulfa for the clinic. No way. See, it's not good press. It won't make folks back home want to send in their pennies and nickels to help further the cause. What they want to hear are success stories, Eva. They want to feel good about what's goin' on over here. Keep it for your journal, and discuss it amongst yourselves. In the end, it's better that way."

I am about to offer a retort, but Jean shakes her head.

"Nothing's going to change, Eva. I've been here long enough to know that."

IT IS LATE AT NIGHT.

Richard and I lie in bed talking about the other missionaries until the generator cuts off and the glow of the bare bulb overhead fades. Why is it that among such decent, duty-driven people I feel more isolated than ever before? There is a weariness and cynicism here that I did not anticipate. Perhaps it is because everything in Congo is a struggle and those around me are simply tired. But ought not their faith in God sustain their optimism?

Richard asks me about school, and I am glad for the change of subject.

"Problem is," I say to him, "French is hard for the boys. It's a shame that our grasp of Lonkundo is so small. Where's the common ground? I keep on thinking that if we could talk to the boys more clearly—I don't just mean give 'em instructions, but really talk and listen and not be so removed, not operate at such a distance—we could get more done. Sometimes I just sit all quiet in my classroom when I'm grading papers during prep hour, listening to the voices from the next room—the teacher's and the students', too—and I feel like all we're doing is keeping up the separation that got 'em to this state in the first place."

We lie silent for a bit. The river rolls, gurgling past the knotted palm roots that upset the flow near the bank. I think about language, about understanding, about the Belgians and their king, who has promised a visit next month. His armies may conquer territories that have a millennium of cultural history and languages of their own, but then he insists the conquered-peoples' government be administered in his native tongue. Therein lies an arrogance that I am just beginning to appreciate.

I turn toward the sound of night birds quarreling down by the river. I suppose the dilemma that began their row is of just as great a consequence to them as my present concerns are to me.

"Maybe we should find someone to teach us, a tutor in Lonkundo," I suggest. We still need better French as a tool, but Lonkundo is key to really knowing the Nkundo.

Richard does not answer for a moment.

"Well?" I prompt him.

"I'm afraid to ask any of the teachers in the school to tutor us," Richard says at last, "because frankly, they're all so overworked as it is. I mean, surely you know—"

"Yes," I interrupt uncomfortably. This is the first time the subject of salary has arisen between Richard and me. "I know. I hear it in the staff room. All of them want to be paid more. It's as if you have money that you are . . . I don't know . . . withholding or something. I tell them if you got more from the government, then you would pay them more. But they just look at me. I am white, and they are Negro. What I think clearly doesn't carry a lot of weight."

"I'm sorry," he says, taking it personally. "I reckon I'm doing what I can—"

"You think I don't know that? You think I don't see you working twelve hours a day? Really, Richard."

"Okay, now, you don't have to take that tone—"

"What tone?"

"It's just . . . I don't know how I became the bad guy here."

I think about it for a moment.

"You accepted the job as the principal. That made you the bad guy."

Richard sighs. I listen to the river again.

"I have an idea," I tell him. "I think I know where I can find us a tutor."

In the darkness, I see Margaret's face the way she looked yesterday, warily watching my parade of marching boys. I have a feeling she knows the Nkundo better than she is letting on.

"Okay, fine." There is resignation in Richard's voice.

"I'll take care of it tomorrow," I say, as though it is a done deal.

Margaret steps back into the shadow of her door.

THE OLDEST AFRICAN TEACHER shakes the noon bell, the din of the iron clapper echoing through the hallway.

"That will be all for now," I say, closing my textbook.

The boys in my class put away their *cahiers* and leave the room noisily, scrambling out into brilliant sun. I follow them, tying the ribbons of a broad-brim hat beneath my chin and walking to the boys who sit on the matted grass near their dormitory, talking and laughing while they eat manioc. The more fortunate among them have pieces of fruit for dessert. As I pass, they nod their acknowledgment.

"Madame," a few mutter.

I follow the path past our house to the far side of the mission. As I open the door to the print shop, Margaret looks up from her mechanical press, squinting in the bright light. She wears a denim work shirt with the sleeves turned up. There is a scowl on her face and black ink all over her hands. It appears as though a piece of paper has jammed her contraption.

"Eva!" Margaret says, her expression becoming more favorable as her eyes adjust to the light. "What brings you here?"

"Is it a bad time?"

Margaret walks toward me slowly, wiping the sweat from her forehead with the back of her arm.

"Of course not," she says. Wisps of hair have crept out from under her barrettes and stick to the sweat that lines her forehead.

"Come in," she says, picking up a rag to wipe off her hands. "How is Ta Pierre?"

"Very good, thank you. You did well for us."

"Yes," she says matter of factly.

I am silent.

"So what is it, then?" she asks.

"I—well, Richard and I were wondering . . . we have been thinking about trying to learn more Lonkundo. Our orientation at Mondombe was so short. . . . I mean, the Missions board sent us here after we had only been in Mondombe for three months. I feel as though there are still a lot of pieces missing."

"That's pretty typical for orientation these days," Margaret says. She leans against the counter.

"I was wondering if you knew someone, a native, I mean, who would be willing . . . we are looking for a tutor, someone to help us learn more Lonkundo."

"I see," she says, running her rag across a piece of machinery.

I look around the shop. It is a mess of broken-down equipment and metal drums of printing ink. Stacks of paper sit on the counter, jobs in progress, I assume. There is only one window, high on the rear wall. I wonder how Margaret can stand the heat during the daytime.

When she speaks again, her voice startles me slightly.

"Can you pay for this tutor?"

"Huh? Oh, yes—very little, but we will pay what we can."

"Anything more than very little would be too much," she says, picking up her rag and walking back to the press. "You need to learn that, Eva."

I watch her move, noticing how the freckled skin of her arms shakes slightly as she struggles with the paper stuck in the machinery. Margaret is well kept, but she is no longer a young woman.

After a moment, she pauses. "Come by my place on Saturday morning," she says. Her head is buried in the big, greasy-geared machine. "I'll take you and Richard to meet someone in the village."

"What time shall we go?" I ask.

Margaret looks up.

"We'll go when you get here," she says, smiling faintly, then returns her attention to the machine.

"Thank you," I say hesitantly, not sure whether I have been dismissed.

"Say hello to Richie for me, would you?"

I let the shop door shut behind me, pretending I have not heard Margaret's last question.

RICHARD IS WASHING THE DINNER DISHES, whistling to himself. Ta Pierre has gone home for the day. I sit and write on fragile pages of airmail paper:

Dear Mother,

We have survived the rainy season here in Congo.

The King of Belgium is supposed to come to this part of the country for a visit sometime next month, and everyone is terribly excited. The Belgians have done a good job of spreading the notion that the king is an unusually powerful and wise man. We shall see whether it is so.

We are both working now. Richard is heading up the mission high school, and I am teaching a variety of subjects.

It can be frustrating. We talk to the boys in French, but many of them have a hard time learning the language. Last week, I gave a compulsory essay assignment, where the boys were to tell about their lives back home in the village.

One wrote: "I live in Congo with my parents! They are married! Every night we eat dinner together, but some nights we do not, as we do not have any food!"

Another wrote: "I have seven brothers and four sisters. Someday I will have slaves and be white."

A fourteen-year-old student came to Richard last week with a great dilemma. A missionary is paying him to do yard work, and the student's salary is two francs a week. He told Richard that he wanted to follow the teaching of the Church and tithe, but the smallest coinage we have in Congo is a single franc. If he were to give any of his money each week, it would be half his earnings.

"Keep the money," Richard told him. "Give Jesus your commitment to service and that will be enough."

We try to communicate with the Africans, but the differences between our cultures seem to stand in the way. The poverty here is overwhelming. Sometimes we have a dozen villagers who come to our door in the course of a day, begging for something or other. I do what I can, but I invariably turn away some of the appeals, and it keeps me up nights.

Because we are teachers, we are afforded the same respect that is given to elders of their tribe. Sometimes, when children come begging, they want not only food but help with their studies or answers to difficult questions that are plaguing them. We stop and listen to their dilemmas as often as we are able, trying not to be impatient, though the questions always seem to come at the most inopportune times.

There are a hundred students in our high school, three hundred and fifty more in the elementary school, and perhaps a thousand in the village of Bolenge. They all need something.

Please forgive the delayed arrival of the slides Richard has been taking so you can see what Bolenge looks like. I know I promised the package in the last letter I sent, but we are both so terribly, terribly busy.

I love you,

Eva

I sign the letter and look up at Richard. It is almost ten o'clock. He is sitting at the table, looking over papers he brought home from school. From the corner of his eye, he catches me watching him.

"I'll beat you at a game of canasta," he offers.

"You probably will," I concede, though I intend to prove him wrong.

We play until they shut the power off, at which time I am easily ahead.

Ten

Missions—A Hard Job
The Requirements, the Romance
by Wallace P. Hinton

The Qualifications

Modern Missions work is not a snap course. The standards for Christian service abroad are high. The training required today is stiff. This is truly a hard job.

But the challenge of foreign missions never has been greater, and the romance of the task can't be equaled in any other calling.

No Simpletons Wanted

This means you should be above "medium" or "average" intelligence, as others look upon it. Grades do not tell the whole story, but we shall study transcripts closely. We require each candidate to submit a copy of both secondary and college records. Poor grades in the early years, if followed by good or superior work, tell a story of improvement and give promise of higher attainment in graduate days. But a poor record throughout eight years will need some explaining.

These scholastic requirements apply to all, even to exceptionally average candidates who may become engaged to men or women with a higher record of academic achievement. We value the combined resources of missionaries who apply as couples, but there are no free rides. That fact should stimulate activity among gray cells all over the country.

No Kilkenny Cats

The ability to get along with a variety of other people comes near the top of the list. Personal relationships count most in making Christ live and breathe in the field. If the missionary cannot adjust his life and ways to those about him, he gives the wrong conception of how Jesus lived His life and what He expects.

Get Help and Self-Help

The candidate can begin early to find out what help he needs, if any, to make the personal adjustments that a successful missionary career demands. Does he turn up his nose at spicy foreign foods and spicy foreign ideas? Does he think all Japanese are devils? Would he be ill at ease or perhaps insulted if a nonwhite person sat at a table next to him? What social niceties does he know how to practice? Does he know which fork to use at a formal dinner table? Is he just as able to eat with his hands, if protocol demands? Does he sing in his bath at midnight or at four o'clock in the morning? Can he play or does he consider all forms of recreation a waste of time? Can he relax? Does he know how?

Some corrective measures may have to be prescribed by a psychiatrist, others by horse sense. In either case, correction does not spell out failure in the field. To the contrary, it foretells success.

Firsthand Christian Experience

A deep, sane experience of God is paramount. A coldly intellectual concept of the power and function of Christ in personal and community life and in the remaking of the world order is not adequate. A sloppy, emotional, uncritical response to human need and to divine ability to meet it is even worse. Weepy Williams and Winifreds ought to seek their outlet serving a Thanksgiving meal to the local destitute in their home church's basement. In the field, the meaning of Christianity must be grasped by the mind, and the power of it must be felt by the "spirit," for religion without emotional drive is like a fully equipped, completely fueled automobile stripped of its spark plugs.

High School

More than 80 percent of the Protestant Church membership in all mission lands is rural. The people live on farms and in villages of 2,500 or fewer. They need all kinds of practical help. If the missionary can make a chair or a horseshoe, he can contribute something worthwhile to their daily lives and win their respect while he is doing it.

Therefore, each candidate should attend a high school where academic studies are supplemented by industrial or technical education. It is no disgrace in this day and age for a girl to know how to bake a loaf of bread or make a dress, even if she intends to go to cosmopolitan Manila or Buenos Aries instead of to a rural demonstration center in China or Africa.

THE PAMPHLET GOES ON, but my eyes are tired, and I have read it many times. I refold the paper and put it back in the display stand where I found it.

Richard and I are in the marble lobby of the United Missions Building in Cleveland, waiting to meet with Mr. Wallace Hinton, the pamphlet's author. We are at the point in our training when our progress must be reviewed. We sit patiently. It feels all right to wait, as I believe an appointment with Wallace Hinton is worth the delay. I am excited to meet him. I have heard his name spoken so many times at church lectures and classes that I feel I know him already, like the way I feel I know the stars of radio shows. Mr. Hinton is Director of Candidate Education. He is a guidance counselor of sorts, advising missionary candidates about the joys and perils found in the field and steering their education in the years that lead up to their formal commission.

I make an effort to sit up straight. Stern-faced men and women travel through a revolving door, puddling the marble floor with the remnants of a summer downpour that has slicked their overshoes and soaked their umbrellas. I check my wristwatch.

"Mr. and Mrs. Dunagan?"

We both look up. A plump, middle-aged woman approaches us.

"Yes?" Richard sounds as though he has just been woken.

"Mr. Hinton apologizes that he's running behind schedule, but he's ready to see you now." The woman smiles again, and her cheeks pucker like apple dumplings poked with a finger.

"Thank you," Richard says, and we gather our things.

The elevator is crowded with theologians and their solemn secretaries. We stand in the cramped compartment, and as I watch the dial over the door move floor by floor, Richard whistles a John Philip Souza march. I smile, but wish he would be quiet. When Richard is nervous, I feel it and grow nervous as well.

By the time we reach our floor, Richard and I are the only ones left in the elevator. The hallway is dark, its floor tiled with worn black-and-white linoleum squares.

"Are you sure this is the right floor?" I ask.

"I think so," Richard answers hesitantly, then discovers a sign with Mr. Hinton's name on it, accompanied by an arrow pointing to the end of the hall.

Wallace Hinton's door is heavy, and I have to give it a sturdy shove before it swings open. He stands before us, shorter than I had imagined, in an over-starched shirt. The knot in his necktie is exceedingly tidy. He has an unruly shock of graying hair and wears wire-temple eyeglasses that make him look older than he probably is.

"Come in, please, come in," Mr. Hinton invites. He walks around to the back of his big console desk, knocking into one of its corners on the way. A pewter pencil holder tips over from the impact of his leg against the desk, spilling paper clips and pencil shavings across a stack of mimeographed papers.

"Darn it," he mutters, then looks up at us. "It's been a long afternoon."

Mr. Hinton takes a seat in a squeaky armchair and, clearing his throat, pulls a thick manila file folder out of the rectangular wire in-basket on his desk corner.

"Now, then," he says, fiddling with the spilled shavings and taking a sip from the stained china cup that sits in front of him.

"Oh, you want some tea?" he asks.

Richard and I decline in unison.

"All right, well, then, I'm pleased to meet you both. I was impressed when I looked over your files. All the doctors and test-givers back in Chicago, they were happy with you as well. Everyone thought you ought to make good missionaries."

"Thank you," I say.

"We're very sincere in our desire to be the best we can be," Richard adds, then nods as if this will drive his point home.

"Yes," Mr. Hinton says slowly, looking up at Richard through his spectacles, which have slipped down dangerously close to the tip of his nose.

"The only problem I have is . . ." He opens a desk drawer and pulls out a pipe, reaching for a polished wooden canister at the far corner of his desk. "Oh! Do you mind?" Mr. Hinton holds up the pipe.

"Well!" Richard looks at me with what looks like surprise, then back at Mr. Hinton.

"Oh . . . no, of course not," I say.

Honestly, I am shocked. How can a man of such a position smoke? Worse, he has displayed his ugly habit within minutes after we met him! This is not a bar or a speakeasy, and this is not how I was raised, cursing and smoking and whatnot. I cannot remember anyone smoking around me when I was growing up, with the possible exception of men in the movie theaters, but they were strangers. The beam of light from the projector would turn into a luminous, expanding rectangle when obscured by their sinful exhalations. The people on the screen smoked, too, but that was different. That was make-believe, where such things as smoking and drinking were more easily excusable. This, on the other hand, is real life, where there are real consequences to lapses of morality.

Mr. Hinton fiddles with his brass lighter, shaking it absentmindedly. He rubs his thumb over the flint, but it will not light.

It was rumored that one of the philosophy professors at Phillips smoked a pipe, but if he did, he must have puffed on it at home where no one could see him. Such a habit is not the kind of thing upon which the regents of a Christian institution would likely cast favorable regard.

"The problem I have . . ." Mr. Hinton continues slowly, giving the better part of his attention to his pipe. At last he sets it down on the desk and looks up at us. "The problem I have is with your education. Now, I don't mean that you appear to have had any problems in school—to the contrary, all the teachers you listed as references had kind and generous things to say about you both. Even when we checked secondary references, everyone was complimentary."

Mr. Hinton takes a pinch of tobacco from the wooden canister and pokes it into his pipe. He tries to make his lighter work one more time, then pulls a box of matches from his desk drawer. I watch closely as he strikes a slender stick of wood against the strip of red sandpaper, holding its tip to the round, upturned barrel of the pipe and sucking the flame down inside.

I shift uncomfortably in my chair, smelling the sulfur from the match mix with the mustiness of the rain that beats against the office window.

"My concern lies not in what your references said, but rather who they were."

"What do you mean?" Richard asks a little anxiously. He rubs his palms on his trousers.

"Well, take the college you went to—Phillips University. Good school. In fact, great school, highly rated, very religious, but it has a reputation for turning out graduates who have trouble adjusting to what we like to call the real world."

Mr. Hinton raises his eyebrows and peers at Richard over the rim of his glasses.

"In your transcripts, there seems to have been heavy emphasis on Bible study. Now, that's not a bad thing in and unto itself. After all, we're an outreach of the Christian church and religious scholarship is valuable. The problem is that in your case, these years of classes in the Old Testament and religion seem to have come at the expense of course work that, uh, that gets your hands dirty."

The smoke from Mr. Hinton's pipe smells sweet, like cherry wood in a bonfire. I sit up straight in my chair, listening intently to what he is saying, not liking what I hear. Mr. Hinton has a little twitch in his lower lip, and he places his pipe there, sucking on it between thoughts.

"What I think will be best for both of you at this point—and don't get me wrong, I believe you're well on your way to being fine missionaries—but what I think you both need is some more work in the social sciences. I'm going to send you back to school, if that's all right with you, but as soon as your next term is done, I want you to leave Phillips."

I look over at Richard, who is nodding with great sincerity.

"Where do you think we ought to go?" I ask.

"Well, I'd like you to think about making a move to a bit of a colder climate."

Mr. Hinton is a riddler, and I am not in a mood for riddles.

Richard takes a breath as though he is about to say something but then lets it go without speaking. He turns to me tentatively. I give him a nervous smile.

"Connecticut can be lovely in the fall," Mr. Hinton continues. "I want you to spend some time at the Kennedy School of Missions up in Hartford. You'll learn how to do all kinds of things they don't teach at Phillips, like dealing with malaria and throwing social functions where you don't know the language of the people you're inviting. Also, I'm completely in love with the language department at Yale."

He clasps his hands together. "The way they're teaching there is extraordinary, using phonograph records and bringing in native speakers. They're only set up to give classes like that in Japanese and Chinese, but I've had a number of conversations with the principal there, and I've convinced him to offer a specialized track in French and Spanish for us, starting next year. You two can be in the first group of students."

I look again at Richard. Imagine us at Yale! Would I look out of place at an Ivy League school? Would they laugh at the way I talk, at my lower-class Oklahoma manners? I think of trying to fit in with my Zonta sisters.

Mr. Hinton continues. I hope Richard is listening closely, for I am not.

I recall the conversation with my mother. Honestly, she seems happy for us. So does my stepfather, in his peculiar step-fatherly way. He looked at us, stunned for a moment, when we told him we were going. Then he chuckled, showing off his big teeth, and began doing jungle monkey impressions.

"I saw a man with an elephant gun once. Are you going to get to have elephant guns?"

"Stop that now!" my mother insisted, clucking as she cleared the dinner table. Richard and I were home, visiting them from college, midway through the months that separated our engagement and wedding.

I wish I could have told them then, "Yes, we are sure about going to Africa, and to prepare ourselves, we're going to go up to Yale University to study."

Although it might not have put to rest her fears about my safety, ten thousand miles out of her motherly reach, it would have given her an appreciation for the fact that Richard and I were not just going out with pith helmets into the primordial stew to commune with crocodiles and chimpanzees. No, it is going to be serious study. It will be work to be proud of. She will be able to brag to her Sunday-night church friends with their brooches and pinned hats.

"Mrs. Dunagan?"

Mr. Hinton looks at me with an odd smile.

"I . . . I'm sorry. I was just thinking," I stammer, my thoughts returning to the present.

"Thinking about what?" he asks gently.

Richard reaches over and takes my hands in his.

"Just about going to Yale."

"Do you have reservations about making a move like that?" Mr. Hinton asks.

I shake my head. "Not if it's where we need to be," I say, turning to look into Richard's eyes. "I have no hesitation whatsoever."

"Fine, then let's consider it done and point in that direction, shall we?" Mr. Hinton smiles.

Richard and I both nod.

"Now, I'm sure you've been asked this before, but I'm curious to hear for myself," Mr. Hinton says. "Why Africa? According to your paperwork, you have been resolute about that from the start."

I take a deep breath and begin telling the story one more time.

"When I was growing up, Oklahoma City didn't have a lot of Negroes. I only saw them occasionally, and they'd be downtown mopping floors or running elevators, doormen standing outside of hotels—you know, that sort of thing. I remember walking down the sidewalk holding my mother's hand and asking her why it was that those people only had that kind of job. She looked down and told me it was the best they could do.

"I knew about slavery. I'd seen it in the movies. It's funny . . . the movies," I say, thinking about sitting in the air-conditioned theater for the Saturday matinee. "I've always liked the Negro actors. I look at them performing—they're so much more real than the white actors. It's as if they have a bigger capacity for expressing their feelings. What's the man's name? Robinson?"

"Paul Robeson," Richard corrects me.

"Robeson, yes. Robeson's really the cream of the crop. When I see him in the movies, I just can't take my eyes off him. It's a pity that they won't make a film, like a big MGM musical, and let him star in it. These people, I reckon I like the way they look at life."

"Negro people," Mr. Hinton says, nodding.

"Yes."

"Well, why not work in a home mission to better the lot of the Negroes here in the States?"

"No, that wouldn't do," I insist. "You see, we spent the last summer working with the Mexican migrants at the home mission south of Mount Vernon. It was fine, and I reckon we did good work there, teaching the Mexicans and helping the missionaries with their service, but I feel a calling to work abroad. It's too comfortable working somewhere we can just pick up a telephone and call home any old time we feel like it. I want to go somewhere our assistance is vital."

"And you don't think your assistance would be vital here?"

I consider the question for a moment.

"It's not that. It's just . . ." How can I explain it? The right words don't make themselves available. I feel frustrated. The simple truth is that I have to get away, lest I become trapped like my mother.

"I think, perhaps, I understand," Mr. Hinton says after a moment.

I exhale, realizing this is the first time I have done so properly for several minutes.

Mr. Hinton has finished smoking his pipe. He taps it against a glass ashtray on his desk, dislodging the charred tobacco inside. After a moment he looks up.

"Do you two love each other very much?"

Richard and I look at each other in surprise.

"Yes, very much," Richard says.

"Good. Before you go, then, there's a quote from Reinhold Niebuhr I want you to think about. He's the dean at Union Theological; you've probably heard of him. Anyway, I want you to take this to heart: I was sitting in a service one Sunday night when Niebuhr was in the pulpit, and he said that nothing worth doing can be achieved in our lifetime, so we must be saved by hope. Nothing in this world that is true or beautiful or good makes sense in any immediate context of history. Therefore, we must be saved by faith. Nothing we do, however virtuous, can be accomplished all by ourselves. Therefore, we must be saved by love."

Mr. Hinton smiles gently, marking the end of his thought with a little nod. He looks each of us in the eyes, first Richard, then me.

"Out there, who knows what kind of trouble you're going to find? Just remember, every day and every night, you're each other's lifeline."

"We know," Richard insists.

Mr. Hinton smiles.

"Well, then, make us proud," he says, laying his palms on his desk as if to seal the deal.

Eleven

June 16, 1957

To Our Sponsoring Churches:

Thank you for the money you have collected to buy berets for the boys in our Bolenge high school. We have sent for sturdy green felt ones from Coquilhatville and are sure the truck will bring them any day.

It is Sunday evening on the Bolenge mission. This morning, we had a glorious service with much pageantry. We find that the Nkundo are good actors, for they are natural mimics. It is most satisfying to preach to them, for they sit rapt and never take their eyes off you.

It seems as though they are hanging on each word of Scripture. But this is not exactly so. In truth, what they are watching are our movements. They are taking in the musical score played out by our shifting posture and the rise and fall in the tone of our voices. This can be verified later, when we catch one of them imitating us to a tee.

In fact, it seems that the Congolese are such good actors that they can have trouble sorting out what is real from what is make-believe:

"I can't figure out what you mean by this 'truth,' Madame," one of the boys in my class told me recently. "Our people don't think in that way."

I find that their custom is to exploit the temporal nature of expression, saying (and perhaps believing) what is most pragmatic at the moment—like making up the lines for a play as they go along. Artistically, this is delightful. Yet from a moral standpoint, it raises troubling questions. What we call lies, they dismiss with a shrug.

The distance between our worlds, in miles and centuries, also adds difficulty to the process of teaching:

Suppose that you can draw pictures and conjure up simple stories that prove, incontrovertibly, that two and two make four. No matter, for your class may only be watching the manner in which you scratch your nose as you explain it.

Last week, I gave my class a mathematics exam. One of the boys turned in a paper on which he had not managed to solve even one of my word puzzles correctly. Yet it was with a convincing display of shock that he approached me after class:

"Madame, you gave me a failing grade on this test!"

(Yes, I did. It was what he had earned.)

"But couldn't you pardon me this time?"

"Pardon you?" I asked in disbelief.

"Yes, like on Sunday you teach us the Bible says. Are you not like Jesus in your ways?"

Our differences and eccentricities daunt us, but they also can, on occasion, bring me delight. This morning's worship service was glorious! Though it is half a year away from the correct date, the youths of the village have been begging us to let them have a Christmas pageant like the ones we tell them about back home in America. At last, we gave in. The Nkundo attacked their roles with great passion. Never has a king looked wiser, nor a shepherd more awestruck, nor a baby Jesus more angelic in disposition.

"Have you seen this man Jesus?" they ask us. "Does he live in America?"

How many members of the cast or assembled audience realized that the child in the story is the Son of God? Only a few. Yet it is those few who justify our being here. For cannot a little yeast, in time, leaven the whole loaf?

In Christ's service,

Mrs. Richard Dunagan
Bolenge CCM, via Coquilhatville
Congo Belge, Afrique

AFTER BREAKFAST ON SATURDAY MORNING, Richard and I walk our bicycles to Margaret's print shop. It takes several knocks before Margaret answers the door. When she does, a flowing skirt has replaced the denim work getup in which I expect to find her. Margaret has her hair pinned up, and I think I smell Chanel No. 5.

"Such a pleasure to see you both," she says, smiling broadly enough that I can see a gold crown on one of her molars. Margaret may be perfectly sincere, but if her voice were any more brittle it might break. Richard and I are trusting that Margaret will do as suitable a job of finding us a Lonkundo tutor in Bolenge as she did delivering us a houseboy. We ride astride three balloon-tire bicycles, from the mission to the heart of the village.

"I'm going to introduce you to a man named Ekebe Jacques," Margaret says as we wobble along, our spoked wheels navigating truck-tire tracks. "You'll like him. Old as the hills. He lives next door to his niece. It's gotten to where she has to look after him pretty closely, bless his heart. He's still sharp, though." Margaret points her index finger to her temple and nods. I look at her hand as it returns to the bicycle handlebar. Her fingers are raw from the daily stains of printer's ink and subsequent scrubbings with lye soap.

"How old is he?" I ask Margaret.

"Ekebe Jacques?"

"Yes."

She takes a moment to answer.

"You never can tell with Africans," Margaret says as deliberately as if this were an aphorism.

We pass villagers walking along the road, women with baskets of laundry balanced on their heads, men with tall, skinny walking sticks.

"Hello, white people," they call out in singsong Lonkundo, waving enthusiastically. Sometimes the little ones chase after us, scampering barefoot on the gravel until rocks poke at the soles their feet and they have to stop.

We arrive at the center of Bolenge.

"Well, then, here we are," Margaret says, catching her breath as we stop our bicycles.

I look around. Though we have been at the Bolenge mission for several months, this is my first time visiting the actual village.

Bolenge is laid out in a traditional arrangement, with several parallel rows of packed-mud houses. Smoke finds its way through the palm-frond thatch of many of the roofs. Everywhere I turn, ducks chase chickens, goats bleat, pigs snort. A fisherwoman passes in front of us, naked but for her grass skirt and the canoe paddle she carries tucked under one arm. The village blacksmith hammers away under a small, leaf-roofed shelter. Old women and babies sit in front of dingy houses, eyes glassy, jaws slack.

When I was a little, I used to believe that the porch-sitting crones in my neighborhood could actually see time passing. I am reminded of that as I watch the African women sit as still as stone, looking out at something I cannot see. Flies crawl around the corners of their mouths; chickens peck in the dirt at their feet; sugar cane and banana plants grow slowly in their dusty yards.

Margaret clears her throat. In the shade of the house directly in front of where we have stopped, a blue-black old man sits at a dilapidated card table, naked but for a threadbare piece of fabric wrapped around his midsection. I realize it's the same man who spoke to us at our welcoming *ionza* ceremony. His feet are cracked and gnarled, leathery as his elephant-tail fan. The man's hair is white, and it circles the back of his bald head like a lucky horseshoe. He looks up at us and grins, his few remaining teeth making him resemble a wrinkled infant.

"This is Ekebe Jacques," Margaret says in Lonkundo, then turns to us and continues in English. "He is a respected elder, but you're teachers, so he'll treat you as equals."

Richard and I step forward and nod our acknowledgment. The elder returns the recognition, raising himself slightly from his chair and bowing in our direction, gripping a wooden cane for support.

"I have brought them to learn from you," Margaret explains to the old man in Lonkundo loudly enough for the neighbors to hear and slowly enough for me to understand. "Once again, you have to teach teachers."

Ekebe Jacques laughs and gestures for us to join him at his table.

I look at Margaret.

"Well, go on," she says after a moment.

"Thank you," I tell her, taking a seat on a large stone near the card table.

"I'm sure you'll find some way to pay me back." Margaret shrugs casually and turns to go.

"Goodbye, Richard," she says.

Richard looks up and nods distractedly. I watch her watching him and for a moment, part of me wants to pick up a rock and throw it at her. Margaret gets on her bicycle and rides off. I turn my attention back to the card table.

"So what is it that you want to know?" Ekebe Jacques asks Richard.

"Everything," I say.

We spend over an hour speaking simple Lonkundo with Ekebe Jacques. He explains, in the long-winded nature of an old man who has all day to get to his point, about some of the queerer African customs and the distinctions among the tribes of the region. At one point, he pauses to go inside the house and get a drink to cool his throat. When he returns on shaky feet, he sets cups of water in front of Richard and me. He takes his seat with a pensive look.

"What is your proverb?" he asks me after a moment.

I'm confused. "I'm sorry, my . . . my proverb?"

Ekebe Jacques looks at me sadly. "I see you do not have one. Every man who is wise must have a proverb," he explains. "Everyone, even a white man and woman like you. If you are to find respect, you must tell your proverb when someone calls out asking for it."

"Who would ask you for a proverb?" Richard wants to know.

"Anyone" is Ekebe's quick reply. "Before they see you, they must know your nature."

"So what is your proverb?" I ask him.

"*Aobola wato*," Ekebe Jacques says matter of factly, then breaks it down into simple word-pictures we will understand: "He broke his boat."

"Once more?" I ask, shaking my head.

"The unwise fisherman broke his boat."

"Yes?" Richard asks.

"Yes," Ekebe Jacques' tone is resolute.

"Is there a story to that?" I ask.

"Of course," Ekebe Jacques snorts. "There is a story to everything. It is unfortunate that people as wise as you know so little."

"That's why we're here. Today, I mean," Richard explains, then blushes, and he and I exchange a look.

"I will tell you the story," Ekebe Jacques says, pursing his lips and looking off at the lush horizon for a moment before he begins.

"There was once a fisherman who went out across the big river. It was just before the rains, and the river had dropped to the point where the water that remained was thick with fish. The fisherman cast his line and fished all day, filling his boat until the fish were flopping over the sides and his boat rode very low in the water, almost up to the rim. That night, he went back to his little house on the shore and cooked the fish, eating until he was stuffed. There was still a giant pile of fish left."

Ekebe Jacques gestures to indicate just how big the pile of fish was.

"The next morning," he continues, "the fisherman wanted to cook more, but he was all out of wood. He looked at his boat. 'Surely I will not need my boat any longer, for look at all the fish I have caught,' he said to himself. So he broke apart his boat for firewood and cooked up more of his fish, eating until he was full once again. That day, the rains came and washed away his house. He had nowhere dry to sleep, and soon he had nothing to eat, for he ate much of his fish and the rest spoiled. He realized then that he also had no boat from which to cast a line or return across the swollen river to his home village. On the last day of the rains, the unwise fisherman died from hunger."

I look at Richard, who is nodding slowly.

The afternoon passes quickly. Ekebe Jacques laughs and tells more stories. Richard and I repeat Ekebe Jacques's words and phrases like school children. We talk through lunchtime. We talk as the heat of the afternoon rises and recedes. We talk as the sun dips toward the horizon. At last, Richard and I tell the old man goodbye, giving him several francs for his time and trouble. He makes an effort to stand up straight and smiles with a gentle dignity, waving one knobby hand from side to side as we prepare to go.

I wish we could talk through the evening, but my stomach is rumbling, and Richard and I must ride our bicycles back home to the mission, where Ta Pierre, a far more tight-lipped African, is cooking for us.

AS WE PEDAL AROUND THE CORNER and head up to our house, I see our new kerosene-powered washing machine on the back porch. It arrived this week in a big crate from Sears & Roebuck. What a joy it is! Once we find where to buy laundry soap, we actually will be able to use it. We have acquiesced to the notion of hiring Liyanza and some of his boys to tend the yard on a regular basis and to haul drums of gasoline that power the washer and kerosene for our new icebox. It gives the boys something productive to do with their time and allows us to give them money to buy food without it being a handout.

Richard and I walk our bicycles up the front path and lean them against the porch. Liyanza has just finished scything the thick grass in our yard and is resting on the steps.

"*Bonjour, Madame,*" he says.

126

I lay my hand affectionately across his back as I walk past him. "Stop!" he protests.

"Are you ticklish?" I ask, and Liyanza responds by wrinkling his nose at me.

Richard goes on into the house, but I linger in the doorway, turning around and watching Liyanza from the back. His hand-me-down clothes don't fit him as well as they did when we first arrived. Soon Liyanza will be old enough to attend l'École Moyenne. I must remember to discuss his future with Richard. It would be a waste if such a bright mind doesn't go beyond the sixth grade.

"*Aobola wato,*" I whisper to myself. "A wise man plans for the future."

MIDWEEK, THE MAIL BOAT ARRIVES IN COQUILHATVILLE. The mission postal officer drives his truck to Bolenge, loaded with parcels, and brings several wooden boxes to our house late in the afternoon. There is a crate from my mother. I set it on the kitchen table, using a hammer to loosen the nails that hold the top fast.

When we are sent store-bought food from the States, the Belgian post office charges us a 25 percent tariff on the items. Most times they figure the value up higher than I think Mother actually paid, but there is not much to be done about it. In the case of food from home, the bride is worth the dowry.

I take the officer's *douane*, checking it against the cans and jars in Mother's box:

Chocolate-cake mix, 12¢
Two cans beef in barbecue sauce, 19¢
Two cans collard greens, 4¢ apiece
Two pounds coffee, 65¢
Baking soda, 3¢
Cream of tartar, 6¢
Pumpkin-pie spice, 14¢
Replacement rubber-shoe soles, 29¢
Shoe nails, 4¢

Everything looks to be in order. I put the food away, admiring the way the brightly labeled cans look on the shelf. For a moment, it's like being back home. Richard comes into the kitchen and starts sorting through the rest of the letters and packages on the kitchen table. He seems to be hoarding one particularly large package, wrapped in butcher paper and tied with twine. I try to get a look at the return label, but Richard covers it with his hand. I hear him ripping paper in the other room, then he laughs excitedly.

"I knew it! Eva, look!" Richard says, coming back in from the living room. He holds a stack of battered record sleeves, each one boasting "French without Toil."

"From New Haven," he says giddily.

"Oh, Richard, I love this!" I am stunned, applauding, then hugging him.

"I wanted it to be a surprise," Richard says. "C'mon."

We go into the living room, where the phonograph sits. Richard borrowed it over the weekend so that he could listen to his Roger Wagner Chorale album in higher fidelity than on a hand-crank phonograph. Everyone has something that makes him or her feel like home. For Richard, it's choral music.

We wait. In a few minutes, the generator comes on. Richard plugs in the record player and watches the tubes as they begin to glow orange. I pick up one of the record jackets, reading the endorsements of senior educators on its label.

"The boys are going to love this," Richard says, rubbing his hands together and giggling tremulously, as he does at moments of excitement.

"Bonjour," the record's basso host greets us, and we answer an impromptu "Bonjour" in unison, then look at each other and start laughing.

The records are scratched from many semesters of classroom use, but the voices are still as unintentionally amusing as when Richard and I first heard them back in New Haven.

"Excusez-moi," one actor over-enunciates. "Can you direct me to the Hôtel de France? My poodle Geraldine is waiting in the taxi and she is very tired."

Richard and I fall to the floor laughing.

"No, wait. Wait. Play that again," I beg, and Richard moves the needle back to the beginning of the passage. Only, this time he sets the record player to forty-five RPM so the actors sound as if they've been sucking helium from a balloon.

"My poodle Geraldine is waiting in the taxi and she is very tired."

We laugh until we absolutely must stop listening to the records and eat dinner because we are both so hungry. If any of our neighbors have been walking by, they must fear we have lost our firmness to some tropical fever.

"Whooo-eee! I'm plum exhausted," Richard says, dropping into a kitchen chair.

For some reason this strikes me as funny, and it sets me off all over again.

We finally settle down. I set a pan on the stove for rice. Richard takes a thick file folder from his portfolio, starting in on the evening's homework.

"Thanks," I say.

THE NEXT MORNING, Richard carries the record player to school. I set it on a table in front of my class, placing the needle carefully at the beginning of the first record. I send one of the boys running across the mission to give Jean Matthews the prearranged signal to switch on the generator early.

For the next hour, the students are transfixed, staring at the record player or out into space as reactions to the stories and exercises play across their faces. I look at them, at the art projects we have hung on the wall, at the tribal stencils with which we have bordered the ceiling, and I feel like a success.

"*Bonjour, Madame,*" the man on the record says.

"*Bonjour, Madame,*" forty teenage African boys repeat.

"*Comment allez-vous aujourd'hui?*"

"*Comment allez-vous aujourd'hui?*" comes the single response. In between phrases, a complete stillness fills the classroom. I can't believe these are the same boys who, day after day, are so reticent to learn, distracted by anything and everything.

"*Bienvenue a l'Hôtel de France,*" a haughty-sounding woman says.

"*Bienvenue a l'Hôtel de France,*" they repeat.

The technology is wonderful and amazing. Word of the new curriculum spreads quickly through the school. At lunch, several students who are not in my class approach me, asking if they can come and "talk with the machine" after school. I assure them that they may.

Richard walks up as I am getting ready to go back to my classroom.

"So?" he asks. "How did it go?"

"Come to my room after school and see for yourself."

"It went well?"

I smile and nod. Richard hugs me, then turns to address a tug on his sleeve from one of the younger students.

"Monsieur, I have a question for you . . ."

I walk back toward my classroom, a gentle breeze blowing cool air against my skirt, tickling the stubble on my legs. I hold a rumpled paper bag at my side. In it are two sweet, syrupy mangoes for my afternoon snack. I close my eyes, feeling the breeze, seeing the faces of my morning class before me, rapt, soaking up the lessons on the phonograph record like a collective sponge, looking at me in wonder.

The afternoon session with the records proves a repeat of the morning's spectacle, only now fifty boys are cramped into the typing room in a semicircle around the record player. Richard and I stand in the back of the room, holding hands and watching. This is how it was in my imagination. This is what makes all the rest worthwhile.

SATURDAY COMES AGAIN, and Richard and I go into the village to study with Ekebe Jacques. As we ride up on our bicycles, the frail old man sits at his table. He is dressed as we found him before, only this time he wears a headband decorated with straggly bird feathers and his table is laid with a bright red cloth.

As we rest our bicycles against the side of the house, Ekebe Jacques looks up from his meditation.

"Such a pretty color," I say, pointing to the tablecloth.

"For my distinguished visitors," Ekebe explains, leaning forward in a geriatric bow.

Richard and I return the gesture and take our seats on the makeshift stools beside him.

There is a peculiar odor to Ekebe Jacques's house, a mix of oil smoke and old age. This should not come as a surprise. The villagers in Bolenge keep small cooking fires burning day and night in front of their houses, and the greasy smoke from their cooking clings to the thatch roofs until the smell becomes permanent.

I look at the round, rusted cooking stand under which Ekebe's fire is laid. He must have owned it for decades. I wonder how the fire is lit each morning, for surely he cannot afford matches.

"When the fire goes out, how do you restart it?" I ask him.

"I take an ember from the neighbor's fire," he says.

"How do you ask them? What words do you use?"

Ekebe Jacques shrugs.

"You don't ask them," he says. "You just take it."

"Even if they're sitting right there?"

"You don't have to speak. Everybody needs fire sometimes."

Ekebe Jacques smiles. I look around at his tidy yard.

"What have you done so far today?" I ask him.

Ekebe corrects my syntax.

"In Lonkundo say, 'Done today already.' I have swept the dirt around the house and had my lunch. The King of Belgium is coming, you know, and the village chief told us we have to have all the houses looking their best in case the king decides to visit here."

"Would you like the King to come here?" Richard asks.

"Of course," Ekebe Jacques says.

"Why?" I ask.

Ekebe shrugs.

"Because it would be a great honor. The King of Belgium is an important man."

I look again at his little iron stove. There is no cooking pot in sight.

"What did you eat for lunch?" I ask.

"I had only one piece of manioc bread," Ekebe Jacques says, "But it made a good lunch."

"And what did you have for breakfast?" Richard asks.

"I did not have time for breakfast. I was too busy sweeping the yard and laying the table in preparation for your arrival and the arrival of the king."

"Then what will you eat for dinner?" Richard persists.

Ekebe Jacques looks out at the village, squinting in the bright sunlight. He nods as he considers my question.

"I don't know," he says at last. "But the Lord has always provided for me in the past, and I know that He shall provide for me now."

I am quieted by this, and cannot look at him for a moment. Ekebe Jacques clears his throat.

"Tell me where you come from," he instructs Richard.

"Me? I come from the city of Memphis," Richard says. "It's named after another famous city way up in the north of Africa. My Memphis is a big town, bigger than Coquilhatville."

"How many people are there?" Ekebe Jacques asks.

Richard thinks about it a moment.

"A thousand thousand," he says, which may be an exaggeration but puts the scope of things in terms that Ekebe Jacques can understand. "Imagine if for every grown man in Bolenge, there was a village the size of Bolenge, and it was all put together in one town."

Ekebe Jacques's eyes grow wide.

"Are there many automobiles?"

"Many, many," Richard says. "Most white families have cars; a lot of them have two. Some of the Negro families have cars as well."

"But the Negroes have fewer cars than the white people?"

"Yes," Richard says. "Just like here."

"Do you have Negro friends in Memphis? Did you have Negro boys in your high school?"

"Well, no," Richard says.

"Just like here," Ekebe Jacques says quietly, nodding.

"But we have African friends now," Richard says defensively.

"Now you have to. Now it's your job."

"Yes, I reckon you're right," Richard says. "And it's a job that we've chosen, despite the fact that we could've made more money for less work in America."

Ekebe considers this.

"You have made a good choice," he says with a finality that seems to indicate we have exhausted the subject at hand.

I'm increasingly distracted by a plump, young Bantu woman who has been loitering in front of the house next door for the past several minutes. There is an anxiousness about her. She shifts her weight back and forth from one foot to the other and seems to be staring at me.

"*Nkoko* Ekebe," she calls out shrilly.

Ekebe Jacques turns and notices her. He greets her and they carry on for several minutes, talking too quickly for me to understand. During the conversation, the young woman seems upset, standing with one hand on her generous hip and wagging a pointer finger in the air.

"Excuse us for that," Ekebe Jacques says when they have finished and the young woman has gone back into her house.

"What did she want?" I ask.

"She's my youngest niece," he tells me. "She said that she wants to talk to you."

"Me?" I ask, surprised.

"Yes, Mama." Ekebe Jacques raises his eyebrows.

"Now?" I wonder what her interest in me might be.

"No, no. She wants you to come back another day."

"What day?" I ask.

"On the day that you choose," he says in the way one might explain something to a small child. "Ask me another question."

I try to think of something good. "Are there still cannibals in Africa?" I ask. It's the best I can come up with.

"Oh, yes!" Ekebe Jacques says. But then he pauses and his expression changes.

"Actually, not many," he amends his answer. "No, not many at all. Ask me a different question."

Richard wants to know how justice is carried out in the interior, which leads to a lengthy explanation of the more ghoulish forms of punishment exacted by various tribes. After a while, I look at my wristwatch. Several hours have passed. I must get home so that I can lead a Bible study class after dinner.

"We've got to go," I tell Ekebe Jacques.

He nods and wishes us well.

"Good. Bye," he attempts in English, standing on unsteady feet. His ragged shawl shakes as he waves his farewell.

I look at the threadbare cloth. It needs to be laundered, although I fear that it might not withstand a good washing. I have a few yards of fabric at the house that might do him much better. I will have to get out my sewing kit before our next visit.

When we get home, Ta Pierre has dinner ready. I look at the chicken and canned green beans and bread, at the pitcher of milk that waits in the icebox, at the chocolate cake I baked this morning. Then I think of Ekebe Jacques sitting hungry as the night falls.

"Go get Liyanza to run an errand, please," I tell Ta Pierre.

"D'accord, Madame," he says and leaves.

"What's the matter?" Richard asks with his mouth full. He has snitched a bite of chicken. I can only shake my head in response. I take a paper box from under the kitchen sink and fill it with a can of horsemeat, a chunk of bread, a fat slice of chocolate cake, and a Mason jar of cold milk.

Ta Pierre returns with Liyanza. I put a one-franc coin in the boy's palm, giving him directions to Ekebe Jacques's house and handing him the box.

"Hurry now," I say, dispatching him with a gentle swat on the backside.

"Oui, Mama," the boy calls over his shoulder as he scampers out the front door and down the steps. I walk to the front door and watch him go. Richard and Ta Pierre come up behind me. The sun has set. There is a dreamy purple-orange glow to the western sky, and as I look out, it frames the mission exquisitely. Jean Matthews's pet monkey chatters from across the way. Missionaries and Africans stroll by the path in front of our house, carrying their buckets to the river in the never-ending procession to get fresh water.

"How many villagers came by today looking for food," Richard asks Ta Pierre.

"Four," Ta Pierre says.

"How much did you give out?"

"I gave nothing. There is nothing to spare this week, 'less you and *Mama Boenga* going to go hungry."

Richard nods. We are all quiet for a moment.

"I leave now. You have a blessed Sunday," Ta Pierre says, breaking the silence. "I see Monday morning."

Richard takes his billfold out of his pocket to pay Ta Pierre his weekly wages.

We're silent during dinner. Midway through the meal, a little gecko hops from the counter onto the table, landing near my plate. Rather than brush him away, I take a bit of my bread and hold it up to him. He turns his little wrinkled face aside in scorn, unmoved by my charity. I laugh halfheartedly, then look at Richard, who gives no reaction. I set my napkin on the table and shove my plate gently away.

IN THE FOLLOWING WEEK'S MAIL comes the written version of the school inspector's report on l'École Moyenne. It begins with a reiteration of what he told Richard in the school office, then the letter's tone changes markedly:

Upon reflection, it is my recommendation that Directeur Dunagan make provisions for new student dormitory accommodations directly. It is with regret that the district informs Directeur Dunagan that we will not be able to provide him financial assistance in this endeavor. It is recommended that he employ the keen skills of improvisation that have apparently served him well thus far in his young tenure.

"What?" I ask, incredulous.

Richard and I stand in the living room, home from school for lunch.

"Keep going," he says. "It gets better."

I continue reading. The inspector's handwriting retains its bureaucratic conceit, even after passing through three sheets of carbon paper.

A district inspection of the new facility shall be attempted forty-five days from the issuance of this report, weather permitting.

It is essential that in accordance with government regulations, l'École Moyenne de Bolenge provide its students with proper housing facilities. Any variance from regulations in this regard may be looked upon as grounds for rescission of the school's certificate and funding by the Ministry of Education.

Sincerely,

Jean-Baptiste Dupont

I drop onto the sofa, letting the letter slip out of my hand and drift to the floor.

Richard steps forward, picks up the letter, folds it, and tucks it back into its envelope.

"We've been set up," he says quietly.

"What?"

Richard sighs. "I have this feeling," he says, pacing. "I get the sense that my approach . . . our approach—it flies in the face of how M. Dupont thinks these kids should be taught, all the art projects you've started with the boys, the way we try to get them to do creative-writing projects, you know?

"It would make him look bad to say in his report that he finds fault with our having the students stay after school and paint pictures or listen to French records from America. Heaven forbid if he knew we were doing that! He has to find fault with something, you see? Make some recommendation that'll either take all my time and energy away from the stuff he doesn't like or, better yet, he makes the recommendation something I can't possibly achieve so that I'll either resign or be removed."

"Why would he be against trying out some new teaching methods?" I ask, growing angrier by the moment. "The boys like it better now. They pay more attention. The teachers like it better, too. Is the inspector afraid we'll fail?"

Richard sits down next to me.

"Maybe he's afraid we'll succeed."

"And what?" Now I am infuriated. "The Africans will come out of school with the expectation that they might go on to be something more than office assistants? Oh, now, there's a threatening concept!" I'm shouting now.

"Eva—"

"No, this is wrong! This just isn't fair."

"So what do we do?" Richard asks, walking to the front window where he stands, looking out at the river.

I think. I rise. Slowly, I cross the room. "We give him what he's asking for," I say quietly from just behind Richard's back.

"Wha—" he says, spinning around, startled by my proximity. "What do you mean?"

I smile slowly. "We give him the dormitory he's asking for," I say.

"Great. How do we build a dormitory with no money?"

"We use those skills of improvisation he wrote about—such a snide little man. Maybe we don't build. Maybe we convert."

"Hmm," Richard nods, considering this. "Okay, convert what? And with what labor force?"

"Well," I say coyly. "I can think of a captive work force of about a hundred able-bodied boys who could be very helpful, if properly supervised."

"Okay, but that still leaves a larger problem."

"Close your eyes."

"Eva, I'm not in a mood for games."

"Come on."

He obliges.

"Good. Now take an imaginary walk with me down to the river. Can you see it?"

"Yes . . ."

"Now turn to your right. What do you see up ahead, beyond the thicket of trees?"

"The old steamboat repair shop!" he says excitedly, opening his eyes.

"Precisely! I was over there last week poking around, looking for spare junk for art projects. Since the mission doesn't have a steamboat any more, it all but closed the repair shop. The first floor is full of rusting machines and big old engine parts, but the whole second floor is empty. I mean, there are some old desks and office junk up there, but I'll bet we can get the mission to let us use it if we're willing to fix it up."

"I don't know, Eva. I reckon that's pretty ambitious."

"Ah, those skills of improvisation that have served you so well during your young tenure," I say, mocking the inspector's letter.

Richard doesn't laugh. Instead, he turns and looks back out the window, still for a moment.

"Richard?" I say hesitantly.

"What if this plan . . . what if it backfires?" he asks quietly. "The school, the funding, all the boys' lives, their hopes, their dreams—where do they go?"

"I—"

"The inspector knows more about Congo than we do. He's been here longer. What if what we're talking about just isn't possible?"

I stand and look at Richard's profile. I don't have good answers for his questions.

RICHARD CALLS A SPECIAL STAFF MEETING.

"What are you talking about?" one of the teachers calls out angrily from the back of the room. "You pay us too little already. Now you want to make us take a cut so you can impress the government inspector?"

"I'm not doing it to impress anyone," Richard says with exasperation. "You know as well as I do that we need more dormitory space. The boys are overcrowded in the old building, which is falling apart anyway. If we take on any more students, it's only going to get worse. You've seen the pamphlets from l'Institut de Santé. There is disease all around, and if we crowd the boys any more, they're going to start getting sick. As it is, it's hard for them to get through their homework with all the elbow bumping. Remember, all we're talking about is twenty-five francs from each of you, and it's only for a few weeks."

The teachers grumble.

I am silent, but my heart beats quickly. Can't they see what he's trying to do? The teachers are ungrateful; that's the problem. They are ungrateful and short sighted.

Richard writes on the blackboard, adding up columns of numbers.

"Twenty-five times ten, times four weeks, let's say. With that money we can cook extra meals for the boys while they're working, buy twenty beds, and get the paint and nails and flooring we need to make the place habitable."

Richard finishes his tally and sets down the chalk, dusting off his palms.

M. Boale stands. "Why don't you pay for it out of your salary?" he wants to know.

"Oh, I'll take the pay cut just like everyone else," Richard assures him.

"You should take more of a cut! You're white. You're rich. You can afford it. We can't." He sits back down to applause from several of the other teachers.

"Look," Richard says, his voice cracking slightly. "I came to this job with the belief that we had a common goal. If that's not the case, then Eva and I have no business being here. If it *is* the case, then let's quit bickering and get on with the business of teaching. Now, these boys need a roof over their heads. If we don't put it there, we have no more school. Simple. You think I should pay for it? I wish I could, Monsieur Boale. Even if you put my whole salary and Eva's together, it wouldn't be enough. This is a group effort. We need to think not of ourselves but of the students. You all can get jobs somewhere else in the province, but what about the boys? If this school is shut down, I reckon that hundreds of lives are going to be affected. I want you to think about the faces of the kids in your classes. Can you stand up in front of them and tell them that their school is closing because you aren't willing to spend a few francs to see that they have somewhere decent to live?"

Richard's brow is beaded with sweat. He looks around the room. No one speaks.

"I'm putting it to a vote. All those in favor of sharing the cost of the new dormitory, raise your hands."

I hold my breath. One arm goes up tentatively in the back of the room, then another, and another. The staff approves the salary levy by a margin of one vote—mine.

AFTER DINNER, Richard stands before the station meeting, where the assembled missionaries discuss issues of concern. Someday, I hope station meetings will be extended to include our native teachers, pastor, and nurse, but for now, the voting privilege is limited to white people.

I raised this concern several days ago while talking with Margaret. She shook her head.

"Oh, Eva, be smart. You know as well as I do that all they'd want to talk about is more money for themselves."

I held my tongue, choosing to let the matter rest until later.

While Richard is gone to the meeting, Liyanza and one of his friends from the village come by the house asking for food. I look around the kitchen.

"I'll give you both some bread if you help me with some chores," I offer.

They agree, and I come up with a small task for each of them to complete. I know I'll need to put almost as much energy into supervising them as if I were doing the work myself, but it doesn't matter. What does matter is that they're doing legitimate labor in exchange for legitimate wages. I can't help but believe this is necessary for them—to give them a sense of pride and to help them appreciate the value of labor and initiative.

I have Liyanza fetch water from the river while the other boy, a buck-toothed eleven-year-old, helps with the dishes. With my sewing kit, I slowly hem a piece of fabric into a new shawl for Ekebe Jacques. I look up occasionally, making sure that the boy's doing a good job of scrubbing the pans.

"Make sure you get the dishes all the way clean," I advise.

"Yes, Mama," he says, plunging his dark little arms into the soapy white bubbles of the dishwater. He stands on a wooden milk crate, so he can reach the dish drying rack.

As he nears the bottom of the stack of dirty dishes, he holds up an eggbeater for examination.

"What is this?" the boy asks me.

"It's a tool I use for mixing things. Powdered milk, for instance."

The boy rotates the beaters a few times, then goes back to his work.

After several minutes Liyanza comes back with a water bucket in each hand, laughing to himself as he tromps up his way up the front stairs making rhymes. I get up to help him with one of the buckets, and as I cross into the living room, there is a crash of breaking glass from behind me.

"Ooh!" comes a startled voice from the kitchen.

"What happened?" I ask, immediately turning around to look.

"The pitcher," the boy says, pointing to shards of glass lying on the floor.

"Did you drop it?"

"No, Mama," he answers with a shrug. "It broke itself."

"What do you mean it broke itself?" I ask, becoming angry as I look down at the remnants of my favorite water pitcher. It was a wedding present, one of the few pretty things I brought here to Congo. I can still see the satin-lined department store box in which it arrived.

The boy steps down off the crate, drying his hands.

"It just broke. It broke itself," he says casually.

"How did this happen?"

"It was on the drying rack, and it just went onto the floor, there, where you see it."

He's far too nonchalant about the whole thing to suit me.

"But . . ." I begin, then realize it's useless.

"Here," I growl, breaking his promised piece of bread off the big, yeasty loaf and thrusting it toward him.

"Go on."

He takes the bread and dashes for the front door. Impulsively, I give him a sharp smack on the backside as he scrambles away. The boy starts to cry. Liyanza stands in the doorway as the boy passes.

"You hit him. Why did you do that?" Liyanza asks.

He turns and stares at me defiantly, his slight frame silhouetted in the gray dusk.

"He needs to learn to take responsibility for his actions," I say, kneeling to clean up the glass. "He just broke my favorite pitcher but wouldn't admit it. He's old enough—you're both old enough— you ought to know better."

"But he told you—the vase broke itself!" Liyanza shakes his head.

"Liyanza, vases don't have the ability to break themselves. Somebody has to help them."

He stands still, shaking his head and tsk-tsking.

"She got angry," he says in Lonkundo under his breath.

"What?" I almost shout at him.

He stares at me for a long moment, then walks forward.

"May I have my bread, Madame?" he asks sullenly.

"Here," I say, hastily slicing off a chunk and handing it to him.

He takes it and leaves without another word.

AFTER SCHOOL ON WEDNESDAY, I go to the village on my own for the first time. As I ride my bicycle down the winding path, the tires pick up dust and fling it against me, soiling the white socks that wilt around my suntanned ankles. I must be quite a sight. I wear an old book bag slung across my back like a mail carrier, and I pedal with my head down, squinting from the brightness of the sun.

A small African boy, maybe five or six years old, runs beside me for part of my trip, joyfully shouting, "White woman! White woman!" I wave to him.

When I reach the village, I walk my bicycle toward Ekebe Jacques's house, leaning it at last against a tall tree that separates his little patch of property from his niece's. She's waiting for me. I walk up to where she sits bolt upright, thick lipped, thick armed, ample bottomed, wearing a piece of bright red flowery fabric. When I get closer, I realize she is about my age, perhaps a little older.

She stares at me without speaking. I wait for her to greet me, but she won't. I don't understand. Was it not she who requested I come and pay a visit? She noticed me in the first place. Her inhospitality confuses me.

She hums a long low note that trails off at the end. She pushes herself back from the table and stands, coming toward me with an unmistakably haughty expression. She passes without looking me in the eye and circles behind me, inspecting me up and down. At last she returns to her chair, adjusting the peculiar bustle she wears under her garish outfit.

She snorts. "You can sit down. I see you're no competition." She sneers.

I laugh, despite myself. "Pardon me?" I ask, choking on my words.

She answers me with another snort. "I say you're no competition."

It's at this moment that I remember Gloria Snead's telling me how Bantu men prize plumpness in a mate. A voluptuous woman, with full, heavy breasts and a generous backside, makes a good bride. This ideal would be considered nearly obese by familiar American standards.

I think about my own modest frame, lanky armed and slender hipped. If the African standard is that by which Ekebe Jacques's niece is judging me, then I suppose it's true—I'm no competition for her. The one attribute that she might covet, however, is my white skin. African women seem to have a fascination with European complexions, emulating them by patting talcum or even white baking flour on their faces before coming to our Sunday church services. I want to tell them there's nothing wrong with blackness, that they can be beautiful without copying someone impossibly different. Moreover, I am tempted to tell them that the smelly white powder they pat on their faces does more to make them look like cadavers than it does to make them look white.

But I can't tell them these things. It wouldn't be appropriate for me to speak to them so frankly, and even if I breached propriety and did so, there would be no reason to believe they would listen to me. After all, what's my voice compared to the bitter reality they see before themselves every day? Those who *have* are white; those who *have not* are black. It's as simple as that.

Richard and I live a frugal life, but to the Africans in Bolenge, we are rich. The other Europeans they see—the doctors and plantation owners who sometimes pass through the mission—are rich by anyone's standards. They fly in airplanes. They have gold watches and wear shiny leather shoes. They eat meat three times a day if they like. They own land. They keep slaves. This last bit of information particularly shocked me as I became aware of it. While it no longer is legal in Congo to own another man's life in the truest sense, the plantation owners maintain broad power over their servants, withholding wages or restricting workers' right to travel by denying them road papers.

European plantation owners sometimes stop by the Bolenge mission during their travels to and from the port cities, staying overnight in unused missionaries quarters. They revel in the company of others who speak their native tongue, though the accommodations we can offer them are spartan. Nowhere in our missions training was there a chapter or a lecture on how to extend social politeness to ungodly men who make a living by owning the lives of others. As I was raised in the South, it's possible there were slave owners among my ancestors, yet I'm not aware of any. I try to be cordial to the plantation owners, knowing it's the Christian thing to do, but I find it one of the more difficult tasks I'm asked to undertake.

I look up into the face of the young woman who sits opposite me. She has some kind of red cosmetic smeared across her lips in imitation of European lipstick. Her eyes hold a peculiar expression. As I study her, I realize what lies there is not truly conceit but fear. She's afraid of me. But why?

A moment passes. I want to reach out and put my palm against her cheek. I want to talk to her like a sister, but I cannot. I don't move.

She stands and stiffly tells me goodbye.

I nod, unsure how to proceed. I choose the simplest option—I get my bicycle without attempting any further conversation.

As I pedal home I realize that although Richard and I have been babbling in Lonkundo in the middle of Congo for almost six months now, we're no more able to truly talk with the Africans than on the day we arrived.

THE BOYS FROM THE HIGH SCHOOL work hard on their dormitory. We get a good price on cots from a wholesaler in Coquilhatville, and the boys spend several days sweeping and mopping, hauling out junk, and painting. Richard lets them out of school to do the work, and their appreciation for the release from classroom tedium is evidenced by the enthusiasm with which they attack the process of cleaning and painting the dusty, cobwebbed building.

I sit in the shade of a banana tree, glancing over my lesson plans and supervising the boys' progress.

"Look here, Madame," one of my students calls to me, demonstrating a rope-and-pulley contraption he's made to help lower pieces of rusting machinery out the window and down to a junk heap by the river.

I applaud, then cover my mouth to hide a gasp when he loses his grip of the rope, and the oversize gear he is lowering drops the last few feet of its trip, landing on a pile of refuse with a loud clatter.

Richard walks up. "What was all that ruckus about?" he asks.

"Oh!" the boy calls down sheepishly from the window, and Richard's question no longer seems to need an answer.

"How's it coming?" Richard asks, reaching into my book bag to steal a banana.

"They say necessity is the mother of invention," I tell him, shooing him away. "I think these boys must be cousins of invention. Or nephews of necessity maybe."

"We're all related to necessity, some way or other," Richard says with a chuckle.

I look up at the building, admiring how a fresh coat of paint improves its appearance. There is, however, a problem with the building that all the youthful inventiveness in the world can't solve. It's something neither Richard nor I thought of as we laid our plans. There is no place to put a latrine.

OUR STUDENTS FINISH THE WORK on their new dormitory in just a few days. On the morning the last coat of paint is drying on the corrugated metal walls, the truck from Coquilhatville comes onto the mission carrying the beds we have ordered. The boys cheer, running alongside the truck, grabbing hold of its side rails as the driver makes his way through the mission and on toward the steamboat shop.

I stand in front of l'École Moyenne. M. Boale walks leisurely from his classroom, summoned by the sound of the spectacle.

"There you go," I say, smiling at the boys' enthusiasm. "Now tell me that's not worth a few francs a week out of your pocket."

M. Boale looks at me for a moment, then turns his attention back to the students' whoops and hollers as they disappear around a bend in the road.

"There are many things worth a few francs. Too bad I don't have more francs to spare. I might be able to fix the world." He turns and goes back into the school.

A few hours later, at lunchtime, Richard and I are at home when one of the boys comes to get us.

"We are ready for your inspection, *Monsieur le Directeur,*" he says.

Richard and I put our plates in the icebox and walk with our escort down to the river. When we arrive, we discover that the boys have spent the last few hours making a sign to hang over the front door of their new home. They've hoisted it up with my student's makeshift winch and nailed it to the rusting metal wall over the front door. Richard and I laugh with delight at the sign, whose bold black-and-green hand-painted lettering advertises L'HÔTEL DE FRANCE.

I wonder if the school inspector will find the reference equally amusing.

Twelve

September 1957

I HAVE BEEN AT THE BOLENGE MISSION FOR A YEAR. The anniversary of Richard and my arrival passes without fanfare.

Once again, we wait for the rainy season. If the air contained any more humidity, it would weep from the effort. Everyone is irritable with anticipation. There are days when clouds are visible on the horizon, but they're billowy and light, unwilling to pay off their promise. They present themselves only to mock us.

The tension on the mission builds until not a soul dares speak to another for fear that violence will erupt. Students in my class will not raise their hands to answer questions. Instead, many lay their heads on their desks. I allow them to make paper fans to cool themselves. The river is low. The air is deathly stagnant. In the middle of the day, I can stand in the mission square and hear nothing but my own breathing. We wait.

Then, at a time about which no one is willing to conjecture, there shall come a gust of wind and a rippling of lightning on the horizon. The skies will open up, and all heaven and hell will cascade.

When the rains come, a wall of water drops on Congo like a pitcher pouring its contents onto a saucer. Whole villages wash away. The tempest snatches corrugated roofs off buildings. Boats refuse to travel. The natives tell me elephants drown in the river and wash up in gruesome pieces on the banks.

But now, everything is still. It's an ugly kind of stillness.

Saturday, Richard and I ride our bicycles, greasy gears grinding, from the mission station down the rutted road to Bolenge to see Ekebe Jacques.

We're making headway in our quest to learn Lonkundo. If we are truly going to teach these people what they need to know to grow beyond the poverty that cripples them, we must learn to treat them as equals and have them afford us the same consideration.

The language lessons aren't easy for us. Lonkundo is especially challenging for Westerners to learn because of its tonal nature. The rise and fall of the speaker's voice gives the words meaning, just as much as the difference between consonants and vowels.

When we raise our pitch at the end of a sentence, it shows we are asking a question. That is true in English, just as it is in French, Portuguese, and Russian.

In Lonkundo, however, a rise in tone may give the word an entirely new meaning. Elevate the end of a sentence into a question and you just may have accidentally challenged someone to a fight or asked whether they were *eating* rather than *reading* the Bible.

The best example of this phenomenon that I have encountered is the word *nkolo*. It's pronounced exactly as it's spelled. Say the word like a statement, and it means "God." Raise your voice, however, on the second syllable—as in *nkolo?*—and you have just said "oil." The distinction between oil and the Lord is one I would like to know.

Also, intonation helps separate present tense from past tense. Ekebe Jacques tells us that, in the previous generation, the bungled preaching of leaden-tongued zealots led the residents of Bolenge to believe that Jesus Christ was not only risen but was rising on an ongoing basis. The Congolese understood Jesus to be alive and well and living in his father's house somewhere in America, perhaps down the street from the minister who was preaching.

There are moments, however, when I realize that all the trouble of learning is worthwhile. When I speak Lonkundo correctly and the words come out smoothly, it's the most liberating thing I can imagine. It feels like singing. It must feel like this for a gymnast when she dances with the bars, defying gravity.

Ekebe Jacques smiles.

Richard and I work hard to learn the nuances of the tongue, not just the simple words and phrases that the Missions board feels we need to know in order to bully our way through day-to-day negotiations with the Congolese. I must be able to laugh and grieve with the Africans on their own terms. That is the least respect I can pay them.

Today we spend the afternoon with Ekebe Jacques, as has become our Saturday tradition. The old man tells us fantastic yarns, explaining why water is blue and why the sky does not fall down and crush us all. I watch the spark in his eyes as he speaks, delighting in whatever it is he's saying.

When at last it's time to leave, I walk across Ekebe Jacques's yard to get my bicycle. As I reach for the handlebars, I'm hit by a sudden wave of nausea. I let the bicycle go, and it clatters to the ground. The bell jangles as it falls against packed dirt, sounding like the cry of an offended animal.

Richard rushes over to me. "You okay?" he asks, leaning over to steady me.

"I . . . I don't feel so well all of a sudden." A second wave of dizziness hits me. "It's . . . in my stomach . . ." I put my hand on my midsection.

"Here?" Richard asks, laying his hand over mine.

I wince and nod. "I think I ate something bad," I say.

Richard looks troubled.

The nausea comes again. It feels as though a giant purple-black lacquered African beetle has lodged in my intestines, pinchers flailing.

"I'll be fine," I tell Richard. "Just give me a second."

"Okay," he says hesitantly, taking a step back.

I lean against the wall of Ekebe Jacques's house and feel myself starting to sweat.

I'm wearing my good blue dress today. I fear my perspiration will dampen the fabric and, in turn, allow it to become soiled by dampening the packed mud against which I am leaning. But the mud feels cool against my cheek, so I stay there.

I lean my head back and count silently to ten.

"Let's go," I say, and my voice sounds peculiar to me, as if it's far away, as if someone else is talking.

"Are you sure?" Richard asks, looking concerned.

Then he looks blurry. I see prickly stars and my head hums.

"Yeah, let's just . . . I need to get home."

All I can think about is lying down. Twice I try to mount the bicycle, each time nearly collapsing from the effort it requires. What on earth is going on? If I can just lie down, I will be fine.

"Easy now," Richard says, his expression tight.

"*Mam'Oenga* has a bad spirit in her body," Ekebe advises from his seat across the yard, but neither Richard nor I acknowledge his warning.

Gingerly, Richard helps me on the bicycle and I grip the handle-bars. He steadies me with one arm, steering his own bicycle with the other. It's a clumsy operation, and we move slowly.

At the edge of the village, a woman crouches, shrilly scolding a goat for eating the laundry she has hung out to dry. As we pass, she stops to stare at us.

"Are you well?" she calls to me in Lonkundo.

I smile at the woman and nod slowly, not because I'm well but because I'm pleased I can understand her words.

The nausea comes again, stronger this time, and steals my smile. It takes forever for Richard and me to wobble our way back to the mission. Along the way we pass a group of boys trying to start a fire by the side of the road. They point and talk in hushed voices as we roll by. I want to be courteous and acknowledge them, but it's all I can do to stay upright on the bicycle, head hanging. Could it be food poisoning? Ta Pierre's cooking sometimes renders other-wise serviceable dishes bland and greasy, but it would be harsh to presume his methods pathogenic.

What else could it be? Am I feverish? I don't think so, although I'm shivering.

This feeling in my gut is not how malaria is supposed to start, though it's true that Richard and I have been lax with the mosquito netting of late.

We make our way into the mission. Jean Matthews, in full uni-form, sits outside her house typing on an old upright typewriter in the afternoon sun, her monkey on her shoulder. She sees us ap-proach. A worried look spreads across her face.

"Are ya hurt?" Jean asks, shooing Edgar aside and rushing to our aid.

"I don't know," Richard says. "We were just in the village, and it was time to come home, and all of a sudden Eva got real sick."

"Are you in pain?" Jean asks.

Weakly, I shake my head. Moving my neck is suddenly taxing.

"C'mon, let's get her lying down."

They put my arms around their shoulders, and our bicycles fall to the ground. I wince, as much from concern for the bicycles as from pain. They walk me across the compound like a drunk, the toes of my shoes dragging wobbly parallel lines in the dirt. In every doorway, missionaries and Africans appear, voicing their curiosity in concerned whispers.

Once we're back in our house, Richard helps me to bed. Sitting hurts. Lifting my legs up onto the mattress hurts. Raising my head, so that Richard may adjust the pillow, hurts.

"I need my medical bag," Jean says, hurrying out of the room.

Richard takes a seat in the chair by my bedside. Neither of us speaks for a moment.

"Richard?" I whisper.

"Yeah?"

"I'm scared," I say, and once the admission passes my lips, my throat constricts with emotion. But I will not cry. My mother cries too much—enough for the both of us. I'm not her.

Richard picks up my hand and fiddles with my fingers for a moment.

"Don't be," he says, but he sounds scared himself.

There is the sound of feet shuffling on the porch. Richard sets my hand against the sheet, patting it awkwardly. Jean comes in with a black leather bag, sitting down on the mattress beside me. She balances a pair of wire-rim glasses on her nose and untangles the rubber tubing of her stethoscope.

"Breathe," she urges me, laying the cold metal stethoscope face against my breast.

I draw a shallow breath, looking up at her face. She looks back sternly, putting the back of her hand to my forehead.

"You're cold," she says to me, then looks over at Richard. "Eva's cold," she repeats, as though Richard might not have understood the first time.

"Have you drunk any untreated water?" Jean asks me.

I shake my head. She puts away her stethoscope and stands.

"Only thing I can say is, hopefully, it'll be gone by morning, whatever it is. If she gets a fever, why, you call me back. Meantime, this will help the pain," Jean says, taking a small, cotton-choked bottle from her bag.

"Take two."

"What is it?" I ask in a whisper, which is all I can manage.

"Aspirin," she says curtly and turns to go. "One must work with the tools God affords us."

EVENING COMES. The sky slowly darkens. I can't move very well. I lie on my back, staring at the rippling corrugation of the underside of the roof. The generator chugs away next door. I catch occasional whiffs of its diesel exhaust. The river rolls, quieter now than it will be once the rains begin.

Richard sits beside me, looking over the teachers' most recent reports, breathing noisily in the way he always does when he's preoccupied.

"How are you feeling?" he asks entirely too often.

"Fine," I lie, fearing I'm less convincing each time I say it.

He looks worried. There is something very wrong with my insides. This isn't food poisoning. I got sick off some bad mayonnaise at a church picnic when I was eleven, and it didn't make me distressed like this. I feel bloated, but it's not time for my period. I wonder if I have appendicitis. I move my fingertips around my stomach, trying to remember from school where my appendix would be. I give up.

Richard gets to the bottom of his stack of papers, setting them aside with an exaggerated sigh. He turns his attention to me, easing my hair out of the ponytail in which it's been bound all day. Richard runs his hands through my hair and lays it to the sides of my face before leaning in and kissing me on the forehead.

"You just need to rest. You've got Bible school in the morning. If you get some sleep now, you'll be all better by sunrise service; I just know it."

I can only shake my head.

"I don't think I can sleep," I say.

"Eat some dinner, then."

"I'm not hungry."

Richard sits silently beside me. I stare at the ceiling some more, but my eyes grow tired. I close them.

When I wake, it's the middle of the night. The lights are out, and Richard lies next to me, curled on his side. I have to go to the bathroom, but I feel too weak to stand. I don't want to wake Richard, so I slide myself to the edge of the bed, sucking in air when my midsection hurts. I manage to get myself down onto the floor and hunch there on all fours, like a baby about to make its first attempt at crawling.

The only way I'm able to make it to the bathroom and stay conscious is by hanging my head so that I look directly at the rough-hewn floor. Any attempts to raise my neck bring stars to my eyes and ringing to my ears. I struggle up onto the toilet and urinate with my head leaning against the wall. I wince silently, defying tears. I sit there for what feels like half an hour before I feel strong enough to make my way back to bed.

Dawn comes. Cocks crow. The lokolé drums clamor.

Richard stirs, turning to look at me.

I have been awake for an hour, drawing shallow breaths.

"How are you?" Richard whispers.

I shake my head. My lips are cold, and I feel as though they would not move if I tried to say something.

"Okay," he says, sitting up in bed. "I'll go get Jean again."

He pulls on a pair of rumpled khakis and searches through a pile of laundry for a clean T-shirt.

"Right, okay," he mutters anxiously to himself. "Go get . . . uh . . . everything'll be fine."

In a few minutes he returns with Jean, who wears a bathrobe and looks freshly wakened. She squints at me, raises my wrist to take my pulse, then sets my arm back down and turns to Richard.

"I'd better fetch a doctor," Jean says with a creepy calm. "Shame that Dr. Baker is away on furlough."

Her remove stills my breath.

"You go on and get ready for church," Jean tells Richard. "I'll make a call then stay with Eva."

"I don't think . . ." Richard hesitates.

"It's best." Jean's pizzicato response discourages any further discussion.

Richard sinks into the chair beside me, his face growing pale. "Fine," he says to himself.

The smell of bacon and coffee drifts in from the kitchen, but I'm not hungry. I picture the kitchen table set for breakfast. I planned to bake a cake this afternoon, do some mending, and enjoy time to myself. Now I doubt I'll have the luxury of such privacy. At the rate things are going, I wonder if I'll have the luxury of consciousness.

"I hear tell there's a British doctor visiting down at medical dispensary. I think I'd better go see if he can come up here and . . ." Jean gets up and walks toward the front door. Her words trail off, marking her exit.

Richard helps me sit up and get out of my clothes. I insist on wearing my favorite pale-yellow cotton nightgown. It has lace trim at the neck and sleeves, and it reminds me of my mother, who gave it to me. I wish she were here with me now.

Minutes pass. Richard makes a halfhearted attempt at getting dressed for church. Jean bustles back in, her bathrobe replaced by the nurse's uniform to which I am more accustomed.

"Go on, get yourself off to church. Eva and I will just have a little chat, isn't that right?"

She pats the back of my hand as one might pat the head of a little dog.

"I have to go to class," I croak, and Richard and Jean turn to me, each wearing a look of surprise.

As I hear my own words, I realize that the notion is absurd.

"Eva," Jean says with a reproachful edge.

"Please, give us a minute," Richard says, moving toward me and gesturing her out of the room.

Jean shuts the door behind her as she leaves.

"Darling," Richard says, laying his head next to mine on the pillow, so he can whisper softly in my ear.

"You need not to go to church today." He takes my hand gently in his.

I try to protest, but he cuts me off.

"Shh. You can't. You're sick. You're too weak."

"I have to," I interrupt. "I promised the children we would start a new art project this afternoon, and if we don't, they'll be—"

"Eva," he interrupts again. "That doctor, he'll be here soon. I'll come home after the first service and check on you. If you like, I'll go to your class and tell the kids you're not feeling right, and they can start the art project next Sunday."

"Could you?" The thought makes me feel better for a moment. Richard kisses my cheek.

"When will the doctor be here?" I ask weakly.

"Let me just go find out," Richard says, standing.

Jean opens the door on cue. "Hello?" Jean makes her way toward me, toting her nurse's bag. She stops. Both of them stand and stare at me as though they're waiting for something to happen.

"What?" I whisper, confused by their manner. Is there something they're not telling me? Jean takes a seat on the bed. She looks up at Richard, then at the open doorway.

"Well?"

"Well . . ." Richard echoes.

"Go on, then. We've got things under control."

Richard is still for a moment, then awkwardly gets his things from beside the bed.

Jean holds a mercury thermometer up to the light, shakes it, then inspects it again.

Richard stands at the foot of the bed looking helpless. "I, uh . . . . I'll be back soon," he says awkwardly.

"Everything's under control," Jean replies without looking up.

"Right. Okay, then," Richard says. As he is about to walk out the door, he turns around. "I love you, Eva," he says quietly.

Then he is gone. I look up when I hear a disturbance in the outer room of the house, and I realize I had drifted off to sleep. Jean is showing a middle-age European man into my bedroom. The visitor smiles broadly when our eyes met.

"Good morning, Ma'am," he says in a tidy English accent. "I'm Dr. Horton. Nigel Horton. Miss Matthews asked that I come by. Now, I understand you're feeling a bit peckish."

I try to smile back, but simply don't have the energy.

The doctor pinches a pair of glasses onto his nose. "Now, then," he says, approaching the bed. He takes my wrist and presses his fingers against it, looking down at his wristwatch.

The doctor's brow furrows. I look to Jean for a reaction, but her expression is impassive. Dr. Horton sits down beside me on the bed, leaning in close and placing his fingers under my eyes. He pulls down the lower lids and looks at them, his fingers smelling like tobacco and Lipton tea.

"Hmm!" the doctor snorts. He picks up my hand again and looks at it closely. "Do you mind?" he asks, drawing back the bed sheet.

"No," I whisper.

He lifts my nightgown, touching my stomach gently with his fingers.

Jean stands and watches.

I cry out in pain when he presses on the flesh of my abdomen.

He pulls his hand away as though he has been scolded.

"Where is this young lady's husband?" the doctor asks, turning to Jean.

"I sent him on to church. I thought it would be better than having him hang around and get in the way of—"

"Go and get him straight away," Dr. Horton interrupts. "We'll need to get a transport. Send someone to the dispensary and ask if we may borrow their station wagon. Then get word to the European hospital in Coquilhatville and arrange an operating room."

"Yes, Doctor," she says. "I'm sorry I didn't call you right away when she—I just thought that—what's wrong with her?"

Dr. Horton ignores Jean's question and turns his attention back to me.

"Are you pregnant?"

"No," I say, shaking my head. "Not that I know of."

It's true that my period is late, and the last one was uncharacteristically light.

"Forgive the indelicacy of the next question, but are you and your husband practicing birth control?"

"Well, no, I mean we . . ." I fluster, trying to figure up the days of the month.

"Are you using contraception?"

"No," I say.

"You've lost a lot of blood, Mrs. Dunagan, a great deal. The insides of your eyelids and fingernails should be pink, but they're a grayish hue. I can barely get a pulse. My best guess is that you're bleeding internally. I believe it to be the result of a ruptured ectopic pregnancy."

"Ectopic?" The word is new. "What is . . . ?"

"If what I'm thinking is correct, an egg was fertilized on its way down the fallopian tube from your ovary, and it's attached itself there."

"I'm pregnant?" I ask, puzzling over the notion.

"Sort of. If a baby starts to grow in the fallopian tubes, pressure builds up until the tube bursts. Once that happens, the woman starts bleeding into her abdominal cavity, which is a very serious matter. Now, let's get you off to hospital so we can deal with this situation."

I nod weakly. *Dear God* . . . Richard and I aren't ready for children, not yet. Maybe next year but not now, not here. I envision blood leaking out of my fallopian tube and filling up my insides.

Jean is pacing.

"I'm sorry. I didn't think that . . . I just tried to do the best—"

"Never mind that now, just go and get the van, will you?" There is an edge of urgent irritation in the doctor's voice.

Jean's face flushes.

"Yes, I . . . right," she stammers and hurries out of the room.

Moments later, Richard reappears.

"I had to come back," he says apologetically. "I was walking to church, and I realized that I have no business being anywhere but right here while you're sick." He looks at the doctor. "I'm her husband," he explains.

They shake hands and mutter pleasantries. I am starting to feel faint again. The heat of the day is coming up, and when Jean hurries back in, there's sweat across her forehead.

"Neil Roberts is out in the van, delivering some Bibles downriver, but he should be back soon."

"Good!" the doctor says. "Then let's have a spot of tea." He raises his eyebrows expectantly.

I feel as though I might fall unconscious at any moment. Concentrating on the pain is all that keeps me coherent. They drink tea, or at least, the doctor drinks tea, sitting next to my bed. Ridiculous—hot tea on a hot day in the middle of the African jungle!

I laugh out loud, or maybe I just imagine it. I'm not sure of anything.

At last, Neil returns from his errands. Richard and Dr. Horton carry me out and lay me across the back seat of the van. Richard drives.

"I'll follow you up after lunchtime," the doctor shouts after us as Richard pulls away.

Every bump, every twist in the road is agonizing. I squeeze my eyes shut. It feels as though my body is being ripped in two. I do my best not to cry out.

"Thataway," Jean keeps saying, looking down at me. I take this to be some kind of encouragement, although it effects little good.

As the crow flies, it's not a great distance from the Bolenge mission to Coquilhatville. But the road is so rutted and its surface so cracked from scorching sun that a driver must travel only a few kilometers an hour or risk destroying his car's shock absorbers. I can now say that I know every bump and depression of that road intimately. I feel as though I am being dragged to Coquilhatville. It's a cruel sensation. What have I done to deserve this pain? I feel like a man being beaten for a crime he didn't commit. I try several times to say a prayer, but with each attempt the pain seizes my attention before I have spoken more than a few words. So I lie staring at the underside of the roof of the van, which is stifling hot, as the back windows are sealed shut.

All of I sudden, I get the sense that this is my coffin. This is where I die. My life ends now, here, on a derelict road, late for a date with a Belgian surgeon. This is not how I wanted to go. I wanted to grow old, to become noble through long service to Lord God. I wanted to see Richard age and grow wise and wrinkled from the sun, and grow patient, as I'm sure he will, with or without me. I wanted to have grandchildren, to have a shelf in a house somewhere in America where I kept photo albums full of happy little faces that look like me. I wanted to gather them around me on the front porch, grandchildren with sweets in the summertime. I wanted to tell them stories of Africa. I wanted this life of mine to have some meaning. Now, no one even will remember who I was.

Gradually, the road improves: first a finer gravel under the wheels, and a bit further we hit pavement. We're near the city.

Dear God, Bring me safely through this trial. I know there are reasons for all Your actions, but I don't want to die yet. I'm not ready. There's still so much more I can do to serve You. Please, Lord, please bring me through this, and I'll recommit my life to You with redoubled fervor. In Christ's name, I offer this prayer. Amen.

Richard pulls up to the European hospital–emergency entrance. Big-hatted, gray-complected nuns crowd the back of the car, prattling to one another in harsh-sounding French. Their headgear looks like seagulls flapping in vain.

I laugh again. The nuns pull open the back door to the car and slide a board up under my back. It feels like the blade of a knife. They ease me onto a gurney and begin rolling me through shiny metal doors into the building. A stout, jowly nun takes a pair of scissors from her apron and hacks open my yellow nightgown.

"No!" I protest, but Richard appears at my side to quiet me.

As we move into the bright white operating room, the nun finishes slicing the gown and slips it off me. Another gull-winged nun wheels up an intravenous rack with a cylinder of clear liquid and a tube leading down from it. She fiddles with my arm as they move me onto the operating table. I don't hurt as much now.

I begin slipping in and out of consciousness. I feel a prick in my arm, then another and another.

"The veins—they're collapsed!" one of the nuns exclaims in French.

After that, everything is black and cold.

WHEN I BECOME AWARE OF MY SURROUNDINGS, I'm alone. I'm taken by the notion that I may be dead.

I hear sound, or the lack of sound—the dull rush of nothingness that meets our ears, the thing we call the "ocean" but which is merely matter striking against matter, millionfold, on such a small scale that we discount its significance. I open my eyes. Everything is bright. I must squint. I adjust. I look around the sparsely furnished room. I am in a hospital. This must be the European hospital. I am lying in a bed. Next to me there's a rolling table, typical of hospitals. On the table sits an oversized bowl of oatmeal, typical of Belgians, and laid next to the bowl is a set of silver cutlery, sized on a similarly exaggerated scale. The oatmeal is steaming, so it must have been just set there.

Am I indeed dead? Perhaps Belgian saints run heaven. What a fine comeuppance this would be for untold generations of dead, disparaging Frenchmen. For a moment, I try to recall whether there actually are any Belgian saints, then discard the notion as too exhausting to explore.

"Hello?" I say, looking around.

No one answers. I become aware that I cannot turn my head, nor can I lift it, for it's simply too heavy. I look down at the oatmeal, and for reasons I cannot understand, I start crying—really weeping.

"Hello!" I sob.

A wing-hatted nun comes through the door. "Are you in pain?" she asks me in French.

"I . . . the oatmeal. Everything is so heavy, and I can't move. See? I can't even lift my arm."

"Wait," the nurse says, putting up her hand. She disappears back out the door.

I can't stop crying. *Dear God, Drat the Belgians! Why have they brought me this heavy oatmeal when I'm lying here either dead or dying?*

Dr. Horton comes into the room in a hurry, looking rumpled and the worse for wear. He picks up a clipboard hanging at the foot of my bed. The doctor's arrival gives me a strong suspicion that I'm, indeed, still alive.

"Shh. It's going to be all right," Dr. Horton says, flipping through pages tacked to the board.

"Where's the transfusion?" he asks.

The nurse shrugs. Dr. Horton looks up at her.

"Where is the dratted transfusion? We brought this woman in almost dead from blood loss. You sewed her up, and all you gave her was a glucose drip? Where in God's name is your supervising surgeon?" He storms out of the room.

I close my eyes. *Dear Lord, Please bring this ordeal to an end.*

Dr. Horton and the nun come back into the room in a flurry.

"Never mind," the doctor says. "Start a transfusion right away or we'll lose her. What's the blood type?"

He picks up the clipboard, flipping furiously through the pages.

"A-positive," he reads, forcefully tapping his index finger on the page as if to punish the information for being other than what he hoped to find. "Have you got A-positive blood in storage?"

The nun looks at him for a moment, then, almost imperceptibly, shakes her head.

I feebly turn my gaze toward the doctor. "Richard's A-positive," I whisper.

"Good! And so, by the Grace of God, am I. We'll take as much from each man as either one of us can stand. Let's go! We haven't got time to waste."

The nun whispers something to Dr. Horton and he explodes again.

"What do you mean? Equipped or not, we're doing it! Where the hell is Dr. Dupré? Go round up every syringe in the hospital, and sterilize the lot."

"Mais non, nous ne pouvons pas—" the nurse begins to protest.

"Do it!" Dr. Horton interrupts with such force that the nurse is left to mutter *"sacré Dieu"* and leave the room shaking her head.

Dr. Horton turns to me, and his expression changes.

"Bear with us, Mrs. Dunagan. I think you're aware of some of the complications we're facing, but we'll get through this just fine, all right?"

He smiles. I appreciate the fact that he is trying to comfort me. That's what doctors ought to do. But this time it's not working. I nod slowly. It's all I can manage.

The doctor leaves. I am alone. The room is very quiet. It's a small space, exceedingly sunny. The walls are bare. There is a large section of windows to my left, but I can't turn to look through them because the light is too bright and hurts my eyes.

A different nun comes in and walks to the edge of my bed. She looks down at me with a peculiar expression. She is silent for a moment.

"Oui?" I eventually prompt her.

"What is something you would very much like to eat?" she asks me quietly in French.

I'm confused. Why on earth would she be asking me this question now? There's an untouched bowl of oatmeal before me. I stare back at the nun and realize the look on her face is sadness. Suddenly, I understand why she's asking.

Oh, dear God. I'm dying. I really am. They don't think I'm going to make it. This is my last request. So this is how it happens. I look at the nurse for a long time without moving. I scarcely breathe. When I speak, I do so softly.

"I would like to have a sandwich of fresh tomato slices on white bread with butter."

The nurse nods gravely, turning to exit the room without looking back. Dr. Horton returns with Richard and one of the Belgian physicians in tow. The nun and an orderly trail them with a tray of syringes. The room is suddenly crowded. I feel as though I should leave.

"Now, here's what we do," Dr. Horton begins, rolling up his sleeve. "The equipment here is . . . I find it's not the very best."

Richard walks past the doctor to my bedside. He places his palms on my cheeks and looks down. I have never seen such sadness in the eyes of another. He's already begun to grieve. He kneels and lays his arm across my chest, burying his face in my neck.

"What have they done with my nightgown?" I whisper to him.

"What?" he asks through tears.

"My yellow nightgown. It's my favorite. They cut it off me. I want it back."

"It's all right, darling—"

"No," I insist, "I can mend it. Have them bring it back to me." Suddenly, I can think of nothing else.

"Okay, yes," he weeps. "Anything you want."

The doctor lays his hand on Richard's shoulder.

Richard doesn't move.

RICHARD AND DR. HORTON sit side by side on little wooden chairs.

The nun kneels in front of them, drawing their blood one syringe at a time, emptying the red stickiness into a small bowl that shakes slightly as she holds it.

Together, we are a meticulous, horrifying assembly line.

No one speaks.

After a sufficient quantity of blood has accumulated in the dish, the nurse draws it into a larger syringe and presses the tip of the needle to the bluish flesh of the inside of my arm.

"The veins . . . I can't get one," she exclaims, scowling as she turns to Dr. Horton. "They collapse."

"Keep trying," is all Dr. Horton has to offer in reply.

I close my eyes. The process goes on all afternoon. The nurse pokes so many holes in me that if I were a window screen, the bright African sunlight would shine right on through. It takes the nurse seven or eight punctures each time before she finds a vein, then all the blood she can deliver to me is contained in a slender syringe. I fade in and out, the sounds in the room echoing around my head.

The Belgian doctor stops at one point, declaring, "C'est impossible!"

"Keep at it, man!" Dr. Horton chastises him again and again.

The nun mutters a prayer aloud.

"Notre Dieu, protégez cette jeune femme . . ."

When it's done, they bandage my arm, lest the blood they have just put in me leaks back out the plentiful perforations.

"Mrs. Dunagan?" Dr. Horton whispers.

I open my bleary eyes. He smiles. Behind him and all around, there is blood on the sheets, blood on the floor, little spatters of A-positive blood on the wall. Whose blood? I wonder.

"We've given you about a half a tank. Now it's up to you. You've got to make the rest on your own. How's about it?"

I try to work up a smile to lay across my dry, cracked lips. I try to do anything, but all I can manage is to close my eyes and nod gently.

"Let's let her rest," Dr. Horton says, then I hear them shuffle out of the room.

The last sensation I recall is the touch of a hand, unmistakably Richard's, stroking my cheek.

I WAKE WITH A START, as if from a nightmare, but I've had no dreams that I can recall. I'm not sure how long I've slept, as there is no clock in the room. Night has fallen. The curtains are open. The glow from the street lamps on the *rues* and *boulevards* of Co-quilhatville is just strong enough to demark the white walls' corners and seams. The glow gives me a comforting sense of being grounded, of being in place. I feel a little stronger. I can lift my head again. I turn and look around, wincing when I try to shift my bruised, puncture-riddled arm.

The blood has been cleaned off the wall, and a freshly ironed sheet covers me. Someone has laid my mutilated nightgown on the chair next to my bed. I draw a deep breath of evening air. It loiters inside my chest for a moment, leaving me in the form of a silent sigh. I wonder if the fact that I'm alive means I will not get my sliced-tomato sandwich.

Thirteen

I BELIEVE THIS IS MY THIRD DAY IN THE HOSPITAL, although I'm not certain of it, having lost count of the sunrises and sunsets.

I am still too weak to leave the room. At mealtimes, I need help to eat. I spend most of the day napping.

At present, the sound of someone entering the room startles me.

When I open my eyes, Liyanza stands before me, holding a ragged little parcel.

"*Bonjour,* Madame," he says, shifting his weight from one foot to the other. The boy has more energy than his body knows how to disburse in a gainful manner.

"*Bonjour,*" I whisper back. I smile as Liyanza, scrubbed, gawk-ishly preteen, and dapper, walks cautiously to my bedside.

He sets a ripe avocado on the table beside me. Beside the avo-cado he places a small parcel as gingerly as if it were made of frag-ile crystal. I look at the little bundle of palm fronds, sweaty and soiled from its journey in a boy's hands. One of the fibrous leaves is curled back, allowing a glimpse of the package's contents.

Liyanza rotates the treasure so I may have a better look.

"It's peanuts," he says, holding the gift up and shaking it.

Several nuts fall onto my bed sheet.

"*Nkoko* Ekebe sends these. He says he wishes you fast health and to be free of evil spirits."

I nod and smile at Liyanza. "Sit down," I whisper.

I'm given pause. Liyanza has walked all morning to bring me these peanuts. He has come ten kilometers from Bolenge, the same ten kilometers I traveled a few days ago, along the same treacherous road. Ekebe Jacques, too frail and bow-legged to venture out this far, has paid Liyanza to come on his behalf.

Liyanza sits, as I have bid him, but soon begins to fidget.

I do not speak.

Liyanza gets up, walking around my bed for a look out the window. "Busy, busy," he says.

"You like coming to Coquilhatville?" I ask.

"Coq is good, yeah, Mama," he says with a smile.

I watch as his eyes explore the room.

"Is this your first time in a hospital?" I ask, imagining he may have seen a crowded native hospital but this private room for Europeans is comparatively spacious, with a bathroom and an enclosed veranda.

"No," he scoffs, shaking his head at the absurdity of my question.

I have to smile. The adamancy of his denial tells me that I'm right.

"Have you ever been sick?" I ask.

Liyanza wears a pensive look for a moment, then shakes his head firmly.

"The Nurse Matthews gave me a shot in my shoulder when I was this small," he holds a down-turned pink palm at waist level, "so I wouldn't be sick. Now I will not be sick, no way."

"She gave you an inoculation, yes."

"Yes," Liyanza echoes proudly.

At the side of my bed is a bouquet of paper flowers made by my first-year French class at school. They created the display from recycled homework assignments, which I find poetically just and even more amusing than perhaps they intended. Liyanza continues to walk around the room, curiously inspecting anything remotely medical, the sweat-soaked soles of his sandals slapping dully against the tiled floor.

He picks up a blood-pressure cuff lying on a low table at my bedside, fiddling with the chrome fittings of its black rubber hose. A nurse comes in, her ceiling fan of a hat nearly grazing the doorframe on either side. Hurriedly, Liyanza sets down the apparatus and stands erect with his hands behind his back.

"It's all right," I tell him. The nurse looks at the clipboard hanging from the foot of my bed and takes a pencil from the folds of her robe, touching the lead of the pencil to her tongue and making a notation on the chart. She mutters something to herself in French and leaves.

I lay my head back against the pillow.

My bed linens are white. Everything's white. The sunlight streams in my window, making crisscross patterns that crawl across the bed as the day passes. I have been observing the advance for almost a week now. At the moment, it's taking too much energy to watch Liyanza explore, so I close my eyes again.

"Do your parents ever bring you to Coquilhatville?" I ask quietly.

"I don't have parents, only father. My mama almost have another baby after me, but she get sick and we have no money for the hospital so . . ."

We're both silent.

"I'm sorry," I say finally.

I hear the sound of several men on the street arguing in Lingala. I can't make out their words.

"What does your father do?" I ask Liyanza.

"What does he do?"

"For work."

"He is in the diamond mines. Many kilometers."

The diamond mines are indeed far from Bolenge. I think about Liyanza's father toiling beneath the earth, under what I have heard are almost inhuman conditions.

"How often do you see him?" I ask.

"Sometimes three or four months."

"So who takes care of you?"

"My auntie. My mother's sister. Or I take my own care."

Liyanza crosses his arms proudly across his chest.

It's a queer thing, but for a moment I covet his blind self-assurance.

WHEN I WAKE FROM A NAP, Margaret is standing at the foot of my bed. In her hands, she holds a single hibiscus flower. She smiles gently as I open my eyes. The first thing I notice about her is a smudge of printers ink on the waist of her dress fabric. I'm surprised she has allowed herself to go out of the house so besmirched.

"Hi," she whispers.

I look at the flower she has brought me. The base of its stem disappears into a crumple of newspaper whose ink matches the stains on Margaret's dress and the perennial darkening of her fingertips. She wears her wavy red hair up today, and carved-African-ivory earrings in the shape of little war masks hang beside each of her cheekbones.

"Hi," I say back.

"I brought you a flower."

"It's lovely."

"Where should I put it?"

"Maybe one of the nuns can find a vase," I say.

Margaret goes out into the hall. I hear her speaking with someone, then she reappears. "I closed the print shop early and got a ride here from the paper-delivery truck. The driver had to make a stop in Coq, so I just rode along."

A nun brings in a cylindrical metal vase and sets it brusquely on the bedside table.

"I figured you could do with some brightness in your room," Margaret says to the grizzled nun's back as she leaves us.

"Wherever did you get such a pretty flower? I hope it's not improper to ask," I say.

"Goodness, no," Margaret replies with a laugh. "I got them from the side yard of one of the wives over at the dispensary. She let me cut a few when I was down there yesterday dropping off a batch of printing. She orders seeds from a catalog. Tried raising some of the more exotic varieties, but not much from back home will bloom in this climate."

I shift the pillow in my bed so that I'm sitting up at more of a sociable angle.

Margaret continues unabated. I don't know whether her garrulousness springs from a newfound comfort in my presence or the nervousness that hospitals can bring about in ladies, but in either case, it's entertaining.

"One time her laundry boy asked if her flowers were for eating, and she said no, they were there just there for decoration. He smiled at her quite peculiarly, and she later found out he went around telling all his friends that the American lady had gone crazy and she was raising strange plants just to look at 'em."

Margaret laughs, and I smile.

She drags the chair from my room's writing desk and parks it alongside the bed, fluffing the back of her inked dress before she sits down.

After a moment of silence, she sighs. "Oh, Eva." She lays her hand on mine, looking at my bandaged forearms.

She tells me about the goings-on at the mission, how the schoolboys were distressed to hear of my misfortune, how everyone misses me and is concerned about me.

"It's disgusting," she says with a laugh. "All the attention you're getting. It's like you're some kind of saint or something!"

Margaret smells like Chanel No. 5.

She shifts. "Is Richard fixing to come by?" she asks.

"You mean coming here? Yes, pretty soon."

Margaret looks uneasy. "What time?" she asks.

"About five," I say, "as soon as he's done with school."

Margaret glances at her watch. "Well, then, I'd better head up out of here. I can't have him see me looking like this," she says.

"No, it's all right," I tell her. "You're welcome to stay."

I'm surprised, as I realize I'm not just extending social courtesy; I would genuinely like her to stay a bit longer.

"I think I can get a ride if I hurry," Margaret says, rising to go.

"All right," I concede limply.

"'Bye, Eva. Hope you're better soon." She's already at the door.

I'VE MENDED MY YELLOW GOWN, but it looks as though it had a Cesarean section. I won't be able to wear it when anyone other than Richard is around to see me in it. I'd be too embarrassed. I suppose I should throw the nightgown away or give it to one of the African women in the village. It would be more useful for them than me. But I cling to the mended fabric. It means something to me, though I'm not sure what—security, I guess. Or perhaps it simply means that I'm alive.

For the next few weeks, I'll need to wear more presentable-looking sleeping clothes. I fear I shall not lie in my own bed for some time.

I'm paid a visit by Dr. Burton. He has pulled bureaucratic strings to get me a government-paid stay of convalescence. It's necessary so that I may rebuild my blood. I'm starting as nearly from scratch as a woman can and still be breathing.

Dr. Burton has arranged for Richard and me to stay in the town of Thysville, eight hundred kilometers down the Congo River. He insists that the air in Thysville will be beneficial—cooler, clearer, and better suited for the kind of recovery I have ahead of me.

Thysville does not benefit from as pristine a climate as that which I understand can be found high in the eastern mountains around Kivu, with its temperate game reserves and European sanitarium. That level of luxury is reserved for plantation owners and European aristocracy far better heeled than Richard and I probably will ever be. The Belgian government, at the urging of Dr. Burton, is footing the bill for my convalescence, and Thysville fits much more tidily into the budgets the Belgians afford government employees and missionary school teachers.

Richard helps me onto the airplane to Léopoldville, walking me across the dirt runway to the shiny DC-4. I still am not steady on my feet, and the African flight attendant anxiously hovers near us during the whole flight.

From Léopoldville, we ride a train to Thysville, where we find the pallor of our skin and hair to be even more of an anomaly and magnet of attention than back in Coquilhatville or Léopoldville.

Thysville is a small railroad town, located midway between Léopoldville and the seaport at Matadi, gateway to all shipping from New York and Antwerp. The town is important enough to the diamond and coffee trade to warrant the stringing of telephone wires from tree to tree. Thysville boasts a hotel, where we're headed, and according to our stooped porter, an infamous tavern.

As we pass through the town's dusty central square, it's as though a circus barker has walked ahead of us to announce our arrival. The underfed, half-clad populace parts as we progress. I smile and nod at their earnest faces, but what I really want is to lie down.

The crowd, seated and squatting, calls out to us in tongues both new and familiar. The manner in which we are received brings to mind the way movie stars are treated in newsreels detailing Hollywood premieres and USO shows during the war. Who are we to deserve such notice? I know that the entire hubbub is because we are white. Yet, aberrant from their daily routine as we may be, do we really warrant such histrionics?

SEVERAL MONTHS AGO I was walking home from school in the afternoon, taking a shortcut by the back of one of the mission's common buildings. From an open window, I overheard a bit of a private conversation between two young men from Bolenge who had been hired to clean the kitchen inside. From what I could make out, they were having a rather philosophical discussion, debating the order of the universe.

"The white man is *bonto mongo*," one of them said dogmatically. The other responded by snorting disdainfully. I stood beneath the window and listened further, swatting mosquitoes and hoping

I'd be able to figure out the meaning of this term, *bonto mongo,* from the context of the conversation.

The next day I rode my bicycle to Ekebe Jacques's house and asked him to explain the expression. He closed his eyes and nodded as I reenacted the conversation.

"Yes, yes. *Bonto mongo,*" he said. "That's the thing which is essence of all mankind. It's the thing that goodness and life come from. All else is not true *bonto mongo.*"

I looked at Ekebe Jacques, nonplussed, thinking about the men and their discussion the day before. What in God's name are we teaching these people?

IT'S A COOL DAY IN THYSVILLE. Our porter walks us into the lobby of the modest hotel where Dr. Burton has arranged for me to spend my convalescence. We cross the worn tile floor—past rotted, potted palms—and up to the battered desk, where an African clerk sits napping, slouched in his rumpled uniform. Richard rings the desk bell and the clerk chokes himself awake.

"Yes?"

"Sorry to disturb you. We have reservations here, under the name Dunagan," Richard tells him.

"Ah, yes, I see," the balding, crooked-tooth clerk responds, running his finger down the page of his oversize register. "I see here, Monsieur, that the gentleman making the reservation requested a room on the ground floor so that no unnecessary climbing of stairs would be encountered?"

"Yes, that's right," Richard says. He sets down his suitcase and pulls off his hat. I take a seat nearby. Several African women sit on the floor in native dress, chattering and clucking amongst themselves like cooped chickens. Now and again, they pause and steal curious glances in my direction.

"White woman going to die," one of them says in Lingala, shaking her head. "Too skinny. Too skinny for living."

I turn away, wishing I couldn't understand.

The clerk has Richard sign the register and then, large brass ring of keys in hand, takes us to our room. As we walk, he makes small talk with Richard.

"We have newspapers here for you from Léopoldville and Paris, if you should like to see them."

"Swell," Richard says absentmindedly.

"I'll bring one to your room in the morning."

The clerk has a degree of poise and facility with French language that I would not expect from a man working behind the desk of a small hotel. Perhaps the clerk previously held some more important station and through unfortunate circumstances has fallen to the conditions of his current employment. I hope, for his sake, it's not the reverse. The clerk isn't a young man. It would be a cruel thing if, on his ambitious ascent, this was as far as fortune had yet allowed him to rise.

The floorboards of the hallway, worn smooth by decades of shuffling feet, sink slightly and creak as we walk from one to the next. We move past a long series of faded photographs, framed portraits of notable guests from generations gone. European dignitaries and bounty hunters display, respectively, their obscene jewelry and the kill of the day. Each photograph looks to have been taken in the hotel lobby. In each, the celebrity stands rigid and serious, as is common to photographs of a certain age. Also in each picture, at the feet of the subject, a dozen or so cross-legged Africans sit looking just as sternly into the camera, a hollow-cheeked, loin-clothed welcoming committee. In most of the photographs, the Africans' faces are blurred and indistinct. Apparently, the natives weren't of sufficient significance in the mind of the photographer to deem bringing into focus.

I sniff. There was a peculiar, unpleasant smell in the lobby, and it's becoming more intense as we pass through the narrow, low-ceiling hallway.

"What is that?" I ask Richard quietly, wrinkling my nose.

He shakes his head. "I don't know. Bug spray, maybe."

When the clerk opens the door to our room, I am greeted with an intense wave of the sour, peppery smell. It makes me sick to my stomach.

"What is that smell?" I ask the clerk.

He looks surprised. It's the first I have spoken to him. "It's the powder to keep the insects away," he says, "so that you may have a pleasant stay with no sickness."

I shake my head.

"Never mind the insects; that smell alone is enough to make me sick." I slump against the wall, resting my head on the mildewed plaster. I look down the uneven row of picture frames. Another wave of the prickly smelling insecticide sweeps past me. My stomach is unsettled.

"I can't stay here," I tell Richard, who looks at me warily.

"I don't . . . think this is going to work out," Richard tells the clerk in French.

The clerk nods and begins spouting insincere-sounding apologies, shrugging and gesturing with limp wrists as only a French-speaking, Belgian-educated African can. I have quit being curious about the clerk's station in life. I just want to be rid of him.

"Is there another room we can see?" Richard asks.

"I can show you a room, but I do not think Madame will like it any more than this one," the clerk says. He insists upon speaking to Richard as though I'm not here, as though I am a hundred miles away and must be appeased in absentia. It saddens me when I see Africans adopt the chauvinism so typical of the French. Then again, I have begun to find traditional African society to be just as sexist as any in the world. I bristle, and Richard sees it.

"Let's see what we can work out," Richard says, putting his hand on the clerk's back and leading him down the hall and away from the wrath of my irritability, riled as it is by illness.

They disappear around a corner, and I turn so that my back rests against the wall, sliding down the whitewash until I'm sitting on the floor in a rather unflattering, but comfortable, position.

Without the distraction of conversation, my ears are met by the sound of children playing in the courtyard that opens at the end of the hall.

I smile. It strikes me as reassuring that when echo and distance blur the individual syllables of their speech, children from central Africa and central Oklahoma sound alike at play. I draw a deep breath. It's lush in Thysville. There are birds and plants and flowers I haven't seen for many, many months.

I swallow. There is a peculiar taste in my mouth. Our luggage sits on the floor beside me, and I dig through the outer pocket of my carrying bag until I find a packet of Beeman's pepsin chewing gum. I sit and chew, savoring how it tastes cool even on a warm afternoon, listening to the children shriek and laugh, enjoying the minutes until Richard returns with the clerk I have decided to dislike.

Too soon the floorboards announce their arrival.

"Are you all right?" Richard asks as he comes around the corner and sees me on the floor.

"Yes, I'm just . . . tired."

"Well, let's get you out of here."

I nod.

"I don't reckon this hotel is gonna work out," he says. "How about you?"

I shake my head and try hard not to look at the clerk.

"Right, so I got him to let me use his telephone, and I called down to Kimpese, where Jane Davis is stationed. Remember?"

I close my eyes and nod.

"So she said to come and visit there. She has an extra room that you can stay in."

"Okay," I say.

It will be good to see Jane. She was a kind friend back at Yale, when Richard and I spent our sweaty summer there studying French. Jane sat beside me in class and kept me constantly entertained by muttering a running commentary on the day's lesson. On our own, Richard and I might otherwise have asphyxiated under a stack of textbooks and lessons. We have a tendency, he and I, to take a very deliberate tack in everything we do, and sometimes an infusion of jocularity is beneficial. Esther always helped me with that back at Phillips. Jane assumed the role once Richard and I graduated to the Ivy League.

Now Jane is a medical technician stationed at Kimpese, about sixty kilometers south of our current strait in Thysville. She works at the Union Mission Medical School, running blood tests in their little laboratory. Jane and I have written a few letters back and forth, but it's been over three years since I have seen her.

"So we'll go to Jane's?" I ask listlessly, opening my eyes.

Richard hesitates. "Yes, well, I can stay a day or two, but then I'll need to go back on home to Bolenge. Remember the new term at l'École Moyenne starts next Monday."

"I don't know, Richard, I—"

"We'll still get the government allotment for your convalescence, so you can give Jane part of the money. I'm sure she could use it."

There's nothing to debate.

"Is there a train?" I ask Richard.

"Huh?"

"From here to Kimpese, to Jane's?"

"Oh. Yes," he says, nodding. "All the major lines go through here. The clerk says there's one out Jane's way every morning and afternoon, so we may be able to get the late train if we head back to the station now. How you feelin', darling?"

To be honest, I'm very tired and my insides are unsettled. Also, the unpleasant sulfuric taste in my mouth has triumphed over the pepsin of my chewing gum. I wonder if Richard can smell the unwellness on my breath.

"I'll be fine, once we get on the train and I can rest a bit," I say, and I hear the weakness in my own voice.

Our porter escorts us back to the station.

Richard and I sit on the bench in the shade of a palm tree whose fronds arch so high and broad that I feel, in the quiet moments that come and go, as though I am in a cathedral.

Richard stands and squints.

I wait, as patiently as I am able, for the afternoon to pass and the train to scrape and clack its way down one of the sets of rails that connects Thysville with civilization—or the Dark Continent's version thereof.

What is civilization? I find myself wondering. What, for that matter, is civilized behavior? Are we to believe it is the manners of people who live close to others in some sort of a civic assemblage, where each individual is reliant on the group for his standard of living? If so, then it seems to me that the concept of what is civilized should be much more loosely defined. Certainly, there are just as many varieties of civic assemblage and interreliance as there are cities on the planet. Whose place is it to say that the manners of the city of Bolenge, Belgian Congo, with its thatched-palm roofs and outdoor stoves and particular code of moral behavior, are any less civilized than those of Enid, Oklahoma? It's not mine. Of this, I am sure.

I swallow and feel the clay dust of the streets of Thysville in my throat. Also, I can't get rid of the peculiar taste in my mouth.

"Can you get me a drink of water?" I ask Richard.

He gets up with a muttered acknowledgment, dusts off the seat of his trousers, and ambles away, presumably in search of a fountain.

I shade my eyes and look out at the figures of a company of laborers a dozen yards up the track. They scythe at the brush that threatens to swallow up the railroad tracks if it's not kept in check. I wonder if the men are slaves. They are sweat-shining figures—sinewy, bare backed, blue-black. They wear tattered, patched trousers, snorting furious and crimson eyed with each stroke of the scythe, like so many Clydesdales straining to do their master's bidding.

My great-uncle was a hard drinker with a livery stable in Arkansas around the turn of the century. He died before I was born. My mother told me bedtime stories of how, late at night, he would go after the horses in his lantern-lit stable with a hickory switch in one hand and a brown-glass bottle of bourbon in the other. He would laugh madly in the moonlight, tormenting the beasts until they feared him and their spirits were broken.

I wonder at what point the spirits of the men I see in front of me broke. At the age of fifteen? Seven? Two? I wonder if we are each born with a belief in the ultimate possibility of our lives and are raped of it, over time, by the reality of circumstance. Or maybe we're born with no expectations at all. Life's options, which we later will claim as birthright and compensation for our mortality, were learned along the way.

Certainly the latter is true when it comes to luxury: A man who has lived all his life in a poor culture and never has known such comforts as indoor plumbing, air conditioning, and crisp bed sheets doesn't miss them. The people he sees around him are in the same lot as he, so there's nothing to covet. He has no cause for resentment.

But a man who's indentured or of a subordinate class is all too aware of his condition. There's someone above him, someone richer, fatter, more powerful, someone whose elevated stature is made possible by his own diminished life. The indentured man's awareness of his position isn't innate. It's learned. It's observed. This awareness grows with time. As the man's experiences of subjugation accumulate, his recognition of the disparity between his and his master's privilege can grow into resentment. Ultimately, it may become a virulent, blinding indignation.

I think again of my great-uncle and his livery stable. My mother told me he died from injuries suffered when one of his noble beasts finally had enough of the old man's torment and railed on him late one night, trampling him in an avalanche of wild-eyed whinnies and snorts. Justice is not always gentle.

RICHARD BRINGS ME A PAPER CONE OF WATER, holding it out like a new lover offering his sweetheart a bouquet of flowers.

"Thanks." I take the water and sip it.

"How you feelin'?"

"Not so hot," I tell him.

"Your eyes," he says, squinting. "You look a little sick."

"What do you mean?"

"Like I say, it's in your eyes. They're not clear."

I frown, opening my handbag and taking out my compact. I rub the powder off the mirror with my thumb and stare into my eyes. Richard is right—they're jaundiced.

I hear the sound of a train whistle in the distance.

Richard gathers our things and pays our porter, who has waited patiently nearby as the afternoon passed.

The train grinds to a halt in front of the station, a blast of steam escaping between the large, iron wheels. This style of train I remember from when I was a child, tie arms linking each set of wheels to make the cars look like a long convoy of iron animals galloping across the plain, adding to my sense that the train's indeed as much a living thing as the passengers it carries.

Richard and I take seats on the last car before the caboose. The train sighs a grand plume of steam and starts up, moving past the bent and burdened laborers, swaying through the warm, dry, mountainous midafternoon. The air coming in the window feels cool against my cheek and I close my eyes, taking in the breeze with as many of my senses as are available to it.

We travel through forest and glen, winding through passes as we progress from one ridge of rock to another. The shadows cast by the afternoon sun look grand and golden against the craggy mountainside, but I'm not in so pleasant a humor as to be moved by the sight of them.

A little before suppertime, the train pulls into the station at Kimpese, lurching as we roll across the yard. This station isn't as busy or built up as the one from which we departed, but several buildings and switch houses foretell the medical facility nearby.

We rise, Richard quickly and I less surely, taking our hand luggage and climbing down the solid stairs onto rocky soil. Around us, uniformed African railroad workers bustle to check the train cars and unload parcels. Richard looks around for a porter, but after several gesture-filled exchanges with railroad men, returns to inform me that none are for hire.

"How far is to the Union Mission?" I ask him, sighing at the burden of carrying my one small handbag while he juggles two suitcases and a knapsack.

"It can't be far," he says optimistically.

Sometimes Richard's faith in providence dismays me.

We walk along what turns out to be a quarter-mile uphill path toward town. I have to stop several times to rest, and Richard puts his hand on my shoulder, stroking my hair softly and encouraging me. He tries to take the bag out of my hand, but I won't let him.

"C'mon," I say each time, and we are back on our way. The longer I delay us, the longer it will be before I can lie down somewhere cool and close my eyes.

When we reach the center of Kimpese, walking past row after row of small packed-dirt houses, we see the Union Missions medical building, with its row of various national flags hanging limply. There are European doctors and nurses walking across the square. I hear Parisian French and German spoken around me, and I feel comforted.

The Missions building before us is two stories high and a hundred feet long, made of rough hand-fired brick. Out front, three-foot-wide boulders lay next to one another on either side of a walkway leading up to the heavy wooden front doors. As we approach, an upstairs window opens and Jane appears, calling down to us.

"*Bienvenues,*" she greets us. "Welcome!"

She wears a practical, short haircut and has put on a few pounds since last I saw her. She meets us downstairs and throws her arm around me, taking one of Richard's suitcases in her free hand.

We walk slowly to her house.

The little four-room building's of a similar construction as our house at Bolenge but forty years newer and better kept, with cotton-lace draperies and brass door handles and shuttered windows that close against the elements. Also, because Jane lives so close to the medical school, she has underground plumbing to bring her hot and cold running water. I'm envious the moment I see the shiny handles on her tap.

Jane sets our bags in her study next to the kitchen. We sit at the table while she puts a kettle on for afternoon tea. When she has finished, she dries her hands on a towel and sits down across from me.

"Could I . . . would it be all right if I lie down?" I ask.

Richard gets out of his chair abruptly, coming over to my side. Jane walks us into the room next to the kitchen.

I lie on a narrow camp mattress, and Jane sits beside me, talking quietly while Richard unpacks the books and journals I had him bring, setting them on the shelves that line one wall of the little room in which I will be staying.

"I've been doing really well since the last time I saw you two back in Connecticut," Jane says, looking out into the kitchen. "I couldn't have asked for a better appointment than I have here."

"What exactly do they have you doing? Some kind of medical . . . what was it you said?" Richard asks without turning around. He snaps closed the clasps of my battered, leather-trimmed suitcase and slips it under the bed.

"Well, as you know, this is a Union school, so there are doctors from all over the world here to study."

"Aren't they already doctors when they come here?"

"They're already doctors, but that doesn't mean they know anything about how to treat what you find in Congo."

"Such as?"

"Malaria, leprosy, yellow fever, sleeping sickness," Jane says like a short-order waitress listing the day's specials.

"I see."

Jane walks into the kitchen and turns off the burner under the whistling tea kettle.

I rest my eyes.

Jane raises her voice so Richard can hear her over the clatter of cups and saucers she's getting out of the cupboards.

"So anyhow, I work in the lab, running blood samples and keeping the practical nurses out of trouble." She lets out a horsy laugh and tucks her bangs behind her ear with her index finger.

Richard pours the tea and brings it in on a wooden tray, setting it by my bed. Jane fixes me a cup, and I sit up to sip it. The murky water is hot and I blow across its surface. We never have hot tea in the middle of the day in Bolenge, but the magnetic pull of propriety is stronger here, and we, like dime-store compasses spinning to point at the pole, pay it due without question.

I raise the cup to my lips and sip the tea delicately. It's sweet and lemony. I take another tentative swallow. Richard and Jane chat about our trip to Kimpese and her lab, and they are oblivious to me for the moment.

I feel the tea in my stomach. I shudder. I don't feel at all well. I set down my cup.

"Eva!" Jane says, noticing me.

I lean over the edge of the bed and vomit tea on the floor, gasping afterwards.

"That's okay," Jane reassures no one in particular, hurrying to the kitchen and returning with a towel to wipe up the mess.

My mouth is full of the horrible taste from earlier in the day.

Richard helps me lie back against the pillow.

Everything grows hazy.

I draw the back of my sleeve across my lips.

Time slips.

I am on my feet and Richard's trying to get my arm through the sleeve of a coat, although I don't understand why. There are florescent lights and some women in white coats and a hallway, and I want to sit down, but they make me keep walking all the way to the end of the hall and through a set of double doors. Richard keeps talking to me in a low voice, but I don't remember anything he says. I try to nod, but I can't tell whether or not my head actually is moving, because everything is moving.

I am young again. I sit in our apartment by myself. I want to know where my mother is. She's supposed to be back from giving a piano lesson, but she never came home. It's getting dark, and the walls are frightening me. The room is getting smaller.

I start to cry, but then I am at Phillips, feverishly studying for a final exam, and I'm so tired I can't keep my eyes focused on the textbook I am supposed to read, and the words on the page jumble and blur, and there are voices talking and overlapping, and it smells like ether, and finally I fall asleep with my face in the crease where the pages meet, only my eyes are open and I can see with utmost clarity the words that lie just beyond the tip of my nose, as large as if they were a newspaper headline.

I notice that my body has gotten heavy. I must weigh a thousand pounds. There is something foreign weighing on me, and I believe it's something to do with the taste in my mouth and the swoon in my step and the unsightly yellow hue in the whites of my eyes. I sense now that my eyelids are definitely closed. Yes, I am sure of it. I could not open my eyes now if I wanted to. I'm asleep, or mostly so, against my will. I hear a clock ticking. It is Jane's mantle clock.

I let sleep take me.

Fourteen

September 1957

Eva?"

I open my eyes. I'm back in Jane's house, in the room next to the kitchen. I feel a mountain breeze on my face. The air is sweet and gentle.

The curtains sway. The clock ticks. Jane stands beside me, holding a tray with a glass of water on it.

"Eva?" she says again.

I sit up slowly in bed.

"Yeah . . ."

My lips are dry. My tongue feels as though it's made of burlap.

The breeze subsides. The curtains fall slack. I sense a peculiar smell in the room. It's similar to the taste I had in my mouth in Thysville, something like spoiled eggs or a vitamin pill without the sugar coating.

There is an unsettling closeness about the odor. I hold the palm of my hand to my nose and breathe in. The strange smell is coming from my own skin.

"Are you ready to give it another try?"

"Another try?"

"The water," Jane says. "You couldn't keep any down during the night, but the doctor says you need to drink liquids."

"The doctor . . ."

"At the medical school. You have serum hepatitis."

"What?" I ask.

"It's from all of the transfusions you had back in Coquilhatville. Some of the blood must have gotten contaminated. I'm surprised they didn't see it coming on before they sent you down here."

"There's this taste in my mouth, a smell—"

"It's bile. It's all backed up in your system. Your bilirubin count is ten times what it should be."

"Bilir . . . where's Richard?" I ask, and as I do, I feel my lower lip crack.

Jane notices. "Here," she says, setting down the tray and taking a handkerchief from her pocket. She touches it to my lip where I have begun to bleed. "We need to get some water in you before you parch up."

"Where's Richard?" I ask again. My tongue is now fascinated with the split in my lip and insists on exploring it.

"Sleeping. He was up all night with you. Don't you remember?" I shake my head.

"Well, all I can say is that you're lucky to have a husband like that. Now, see if you can get this down," Jane says. "I have to get back to the lab."

She holds the rim of the glass against my bleeding lip. I let the water into my mouth. As it mixes with blood, it picks up a rusty taste. I swallow the cool water, and I feel the liquid as it travels toward my stomach. It swims there for a moment, then I vomit water back up on the front of my nightgown.

I gasp and put my palm to my lips. "Oh my God," I say, but a second gag cuts short the Lord's name before the blasphemy can fully leave my lips. Jane sets a ragged towel across my bosom. I begin to apologize, but she interrupts.

"Shh, Eva. Everything's going to be all right. I promise you. You just need to get your system going again."

I look down at the towel laid across me like a baby's bib. I try to regain my composure.

Jane sits down beside me. I sigh. It would seem appropriate to say something now, some bit of apology perhaps, but I find myself with nothing to contribute to this wretched little scene, as speaking would require more energy than I can spare.

Jane takes my hand in hers. I lie still and listen to my own labored breathing. It's like a squeezebox being opened and closed at a tempo just a little slower than that which would produce a musical note. What comes out, instead, is a raspy wheeze. Jane raises the glass to my lips again. I hold my mouth firmly closed. I don't want to drink her water.

"Eva . . ." Jane reproaches.

I take the smallest sip of water imaginable, and I feel it crawl down my throat to my stomach where it lurks, restless, chasing its tail. I rest my head against the pillow.

"There," Jane said, stroking my hair with the heel of her hand. "Later on we'll try some apple juice."

Time moves slowly, as it always does when I'm not busy—it was Mother who always called me "Miss Run Ahead." I nap feverishly and cough up virtually everything Jane tries, patiently, to get me to drink.

SEVERAL DAYS PASS IN A HAZE. Richard and Jane take turns sitting with me, reading books and singing little rhyming songs that make me smile. I get to where I can stomach plain, tepid water and a little lukewarm apple juice, but the chicken broth they bring me isn't so easy to keep down.

On what I believe is my sixth day at Kimpese, I ask Richard for a look at the calendar he carries in his little folding lap desk.

"It's Thursday, August the fifth," he tells me.

"And the school term starts Monday," I say, turning to look at him.

"Yes," he says, after a pause.

The next morning, I drink spoonfuls of rice broth that Jane has strained through cheesecloth. Then I kiss my husband goodbye. I think about him arriving at the Bolenge mission alone. I wonder how Margaret will greet him. Will she be wearing one of her flowered dresses? I try to bar her provocative glances from my mind, but the more I try, the more persistent the images become.

I swear I can smell Margaret's Chanel No. 5. My skin begins to itch.

CLOUDS ROLL BY. Some bring to mind elephants, others school buses or lobsters.

I lie in bed all day, bored silly but for the bit of goings-on I can see from my window. Doctors come and go; African villagers pass with loads on their backs and heads; a stray dog mills about, showing off gaunt ribs. I'm as yet too weak to get up and explore the compound here at Kimpese.

Attempts at napping are futile, as the contagion in my blood makes my legs and arms itch incessantly.

I feel caged. The closest I get to being out of doors is just after dawn, when the heat of the sun urges sweet morning air up the side of the mountain, and it sighs its balsamic breath across me through the open windows.

It's only after knowing how the jungle near Coquilhatville quivers and caws in moldering irritation that one can appreciate the lovers' whispers that weave through the air at Kimpese. They come disguised as breezes in late morning, when sunshine has made it full of last night's cedar-brewed dew.

I find, in time, that the purity of the air here soothes my spirit as surely as it does my body. Jane has an old leather-bound collection of classic literature, and I turn musty pages of a volume of Rudyard Kipling as long as my interest holds up. I try to write letters home, but even the simple task of moving pen across paper tires me. Time drags by. The clock counts to twelve, unburdens itself, and begins its tally anew.

I watch afternoon shadows slowly prowl their way across the kitchen walls, consuming all that lies in their path. It occurs to me that shadows move at precisely the same rate here as they did in my hospital room in Coquilhatville. Time passes, and the inevitable approaches at an identical rate in Africa as in Oklahoma, the same in New York City as in the palace at Versailles. This universality, though of little practical benefit, provides me with bit of comfort. My ears are met by the sound of children talking outside. I believe, from what I can make out, that they are conspiring to torture a stray dog. Darkness is near. One by one, mothers call the children home to their evening meal. The dog is left alone.

The arrival of dusk makes it difficult to see the words on the page I'm reading. I light the lamp beside my bed. The smell of sulfur from the match reminds me of the pungent taste I've been enduring, a taste that diminishes each day, as I become less bilious.

I rearrange my bed pillows. In a tin bin, just at the edge of my adjusted view of the kitchen, lies Jane's stock of potatoes. Kimpese's mountainous clime is forgiving enough to allow their cultivation, something that's not possible back in the equatorial stew that surrounds Coquilhatville. It's been over a year since I've eaten potatoes of any sort. Now, I eye Jane's as if they might become animate and run away, should I not duly stand sentinel. I stare into the fat potatoes' dark eyes, and they stare sullenly back at me.

This standoff strikes me as amusing, and I laugh out loud. It's a high, sharp, startling thunder-crack "ha!"

I've begun to crave boiled potatoes.

The afternoon draws to a close. The evening star appears along with a fat, ripe moon. Jane returns. She warms some broth on the stove and tries to entertain me with the details of her day in the laboratory. I appreciate the company, but as I gulp down the soup, I only half listen. My mind is fixed on the potatoes in the tin bin.

As evening passes, I find myself craving the potatoes like a street-corner preacher yearns to find sinners: I want to consume them and convert them into something of value.

I don't tell Jane about the audacious hunger I've developed. I don't want to announce it prematurely, lest the notion prove fickle.

I sleep restlessly. I dream of Richard back in school. I wonder how my French class is faring without me.

They're in the classroom, sitting at their desks, as Richard rings the school bell in the hallway. Then there's silence in the room. I sit at my table. I don't know how I got here. I try to speak, but it's as if someone has stuffed my mouth full of cotton. I scream, but it's of no use.

"Where is the teacher?" one of the boys asks the class in Lonkundo.

"Where is *Mama Boenga?*" another echoes.

They all shrug and look around, and I want to shout at them that I'm right here! I'm right here! None of them can hear me, and I can't move. I wake from the dream in a sick-smelling sweat.

The next afternoon, I'm ready when Jane gets back from the clinic. I call to her when I hear her coming across the front porch.

"Hello, there, Eva. How are you feeling?" she asks, drawing up beside me.

"All right, I guess," I say. "I was just wondering one thing, actually."

"Uh-huh?" Jane sits.

"How many potatoes do you have in there?" I ask.

"What?"

"There," I say, pointing to the bin.

She gets up and walks over to the kitchen, swinging open the tin lid.

"I don't know—six? Maybe eight? How come?"

"Can you cook me one or two of them?" I ask.

Jane stands and stares at me for a moment, hands on her hips. "Potatoes?" she asks, wrinkling her nose at my unlikely request.

"If it's not too much trouble."

Jane cocks her head to the side. I raise my eyebrows and nod to indicate that I've spoken in earnest.

"Well, all right," Jane says at last, shrugging.

While I watch, she sets a pan to heat on the stove, peels and quarters two potatoes, and drops them into the boiling water. In a few minutes, she brings them in to me on a tin plate. They are steaming and velvet-white.

"I would have done up some onions and bacon grease with them, but I wouldn't figure on your keeping all that down," Jane says, as she lays a napkin across my lap.

"I've got it," I say, propping myself up by the elbows. I take the plate raptly from Jane. I pick up my fork and plunge it into a chunk of potato, slipping the warm morsel into my mouth. I've never tasted anything so good.

"Thank you," I say again, but this time my mouth is full.

Bite by bite, I eat the quartered potatoes. Jane watches me closely. When at last she clears away my plate, she does so clucking her tongue and shaking her head.

"I thought you were going to leave some for me," she jokes.

I laugh for the second time today.

Jane turns around in surprise. "Eva, now isn't that a queer sound?"

IN THE MORNING, I FEEL MUCH BETTER. I'm able to eat several slices of dry toast without excessive concern that they will revisit me. By day's end, I nibble at the bits of chicken that Jane brings in on my dinner plate, rounding up the scraps with a formidable crust of bread.

"That's right," Jane says, "get all the starch in you that you can. It's the starch that rebuilds blood. Look at you, so thin." She lays her hand on my arm. "Keep on eating bread and potatoes and we'll have you healthy in no time."

I nod, brushing crumbs from my lips.

"Oh!" she says, taking a piece of paper out of her front apron pocket. "The mail came. I think you might be interested in this."

I take the envelope from her. It's a letter from Richard. My heart skips a beat. I thank Jane and slide my finger under the flap of the envelope, pulling out the notebook paper inside. With anxious palms, I spread smooth the folds in the page so I may read the familiar handwriting more readily:

August 14, 1957

My love,

I miss you awfully, but I know that it's best that you are where you are and that I'm here in Bolenge, running the school. I miss you every morning and every night and pray that God may speed your recovery.

I got back just in time for Sunday-night Bible study, and everyone asked about you—the missionaries and the students—and I told them that you're doing fine and will be home very soon. Please prove me right!

The district inspector will be here next week, so we're organizing the students to give the school a whitewashing before he arrives.

Unfortunately, we have had to close the Hôtel de France in your absence. It seems that while you and I were gone, workers moved into the shop downstairs and complained that the boys weren't going outside to relieve themselves by the river at night. They were urinating on the floors of the dormitory, and it made a horrible smell and dripped through onto the machinery. It isn't feasible to dig them a pit toilet, for the ground is too low. A shovel wouldn't produce so much a toilet as a water well. The workers in the shop tell me they talked to the boys, but it fell on deaf ears.

I guess the next time we get the enthusiastic impulse to convert an old building into living quarters, we had better make provisions for indoor bathroom facilities.

As with everything, we live and learn.

I'm assuming you'll be home before I get a chance to send you another letter, so I'll mention this, just so you can get to thinking about it—Ngkala, the math teacher, was reading in an old copy of a magazine about our American Halloween traditions, and they want to have a costume party for all the missionaries and teachers next month. Isn't that a swell idea? We'll need to help them round up materials for costumes. I think that's more your department than mine.

Margaret came by yesterday with a couple homemade pies. She said that she'd made them in case I got hungry while you were away. She offered to serve me a slice, but I wasn't especially hungry. I tried a sliver of one of the pies today. I think it was supposed to be mincemeat, but I'm not sure. Margaret is not much of a cook.

With adoration,

Richard

I touch his signature with the tips of my yellowed fingers, as if by feeling the same spot in which his pen caressed the paper, I could be inside the words, inside Richard, where I belong. My attention has been so occupied by my recovery that I haven't, until just now, realized how much I ache for him. I must remember to let him know I appreciate the way he didn't tell me my idea for the dorm was nuts.

I AM GETTING STRONGER. Today, I tie a rayon scarf over my head, slip on my sandals, and go with Jane for a walk around Kimpese. I have to stop and rest several times, but the breaks give me occasion to visit with some of the locals and use my Lonkundo with nurses who hail from the equatorial region. I have missed speaking the rhythmic, singing tongue.

Jane and I walk past the Kimpese Union Medical Building where she works. Twenty or so African women stand around, talking and gesturing. Some wear heavy packs tethered to their bent backs, but they all have the unmistakable look of entrepreneurs.

"What are they doing over there?" I ask Jane, pointing.

"That's the hospital market. The head of operations at the school buys what they bring in to feed the patients. A lot of the time it's just manioc or yams, but sometimes hunters bring in fresh meat. Mostly it's antelope they hunt themselves, but Dr. Sandoval, he pays the same no matter what they bring. That's the deal. He'll give seven francs a kilo whether it's antelope or an old anteater."

I squint at the women.

I sweat, despite the constant cool breeze that moves across the square.

"C'mon," Jane says, taking my hand. "Let's get something to drink."

We walk back to her house, and I lie down in my room by the kitchen, content for the moment, staring at nothing in particular, listening to the mantle clock's stately ticking.

"I got a letter from my mother today," Jane says, coming into the room.

"Yes?"

"The letter was just . . . she worries about me over here. In her church—our church—they talk about me all the time, almost every Sunday, she says, and after the service all the old ladies come up and ask her questions about me, and it makes her so proud. But some of the things they ask start her worrying about whether I'm safe and whether . . . I mean, the situation here isn't exactly stable, you know?"

"I can't say, as I really don't pay much attention to politics," I admit. "You see, upriver, where we live, it's so far away from Léopoldville, and—"

"I don't know if it's 'cause we're closer to Léo or on account of this being a Union station—so there are people from all over coming in and out—but there are a lot of Africans who keep yapping about how they aren't happy with the Belgian government poking around in their affairs all these years. Back . . . you know . . . before, they were used to taking care of things in their own tribes—how many wives they took, arguments over land, punishing murderers and thieves, such business as that. My mother reads about it in *Look* magazine and cuts out the articles, then she wants me to talk about it in my letters home to the church, but there's nothing I can really say. I mean, the Missions board tells us over and over again that our letters should be uplifting and give a positive sense of what we're getting done, spreading the word of God and curing everything. But Eva, you know as well as I do that it isn't always pleasant around here."

"This is true," I say.

"Well, of course it is. And you're not going to be able to write any letters home to the Missions society about how you almost died because the doctors in the hospital where they sent you had no idea how to give a transfusion. That's not good press. And if it's not good press, they don't want to hear about it."

She smacks her palm against the top of the bedside table.

"Baptisms and conversions—*that's* what they want to hear about. Baptisms and conversions. So is a revolution coming, Mother, like your little articles say? I don't know." Jane guffaws. "I'm just a missionary minding my own missionary business. I wasn't sent here to deal with revolutions, Eva, and neither were you."

I am silent. Jane stands, crossing her arms and looking out the window with a grave expression on her face.

After a moment, her stiff posture softens. She sighs. "Sorry I get so worked up. It's just that I . . ." Jane falters. "Never mind. What do you want for dinner? Potatoes, again?"

"If it's not too much—"

"Trouble?" Jane interrupts. "Now, you just put that out of your mind this instant."

I close my eyes and doze uneasily before dinner. What if the things Jane's mother says about the coming unrest are correct? No. There would be signs. We would feel it.

I think of Bolenge, less primitive and pastoral than Mondombe, but still I try to imagine the village's occasional squabbles and grumblings turning into some kind of organized revolt, and it seems ludicrous. There's no revolution coming to Bolenge.

Tsetse flies and Sears Roebuck deliveries and thunderstorms and Christmas are all on the way, but no revolution.

Fifteen

October 1957

I TRAVEL THROUGH THE FLATLANDS.

The train conductor is racing the diesel engine. We go fast, speeding around curves in the track. It is a rollercoaster ride, and at every turn I feel as if the locomotive will jump the rails and plow down into the muddy ravine. I wonder what lives down there, what razor-tooth creatures lurk in the algae-slick backwash below. The sultry perfume of the water rises, pulled along and swirled up into my window by the momentum of the speeding train.

I'm going home to Bolenge. I am thrilled. I want to smell Richard. I want to lie in my own bed between sheets whose mended places I know by touch because I myself have done the mending. I want to see the faces of the boys in my classroom, smiling at me, posing the absurd, exasperating questions that chase around in their heads. I will have patience for them. For, now I am new. I'm repaired. Nothing can harm me.

I have seen the face of death. I know its dizzying leer and the stench of its breath. The Creator has seen fit to send me back to do more of His work, and, strength redoubled, I will roll up my sleeves and tackle the task.

The train slows as we near Léopoldville.

I checked my bags with the porter so that now I carry only my purse, which sits on my knee. I wear white gloves and a ladies straw hat. Mr. Hinton advised us that as we are emissaries of the church, we always must look presentable when in public.

The train rounds a bend, and we're in shadow. I inspect my hat in the reflection provided by my window, wondering whether it's still in style back in the States. There are certain choices we make in this life. I've made mine.

The train has stopped. We are at the station.

RICHARD CRIES WHEN I GET HOME TO COQUILHATVILLE, running up to the rolling stairway of the plane that has brought me upriver from Léopoldville. He takes me in his arms and kisses my eyelids. On the airstrip's packed soil, I hold Richard as tightly as I can and don't let go.

Once behind closed doors, I light into him like a love-struck teenager. Afterward, I lie in bed, watching Richard walk around the room naked. I take in his lean body, smiling at the farmer's tan that stops midway up his arms.

I have a beautiful husband. I want to have babies with Richard. I have watched the way he talks with the boys at l'École Moyenne, gently and strongly. I want to see him do that with our own child. It was a troublesome thing, my brief, fruitless pregnancy. When it began, I had no sense of what it might be like to have a life inside me. Now that it's come once and gone, I'm left with a yearning to be in such a state once again.

Richard puts on his pajama bottoms and sits down on a wicker armchair in the corner of the bedroom. It's his turn to watch me dress. I step into my nightgown and brush my hair.

"You're back," he says quietly.

I look at him and laugh at the plainness with which he has spoken.

"Yes, sweetheart, I'm back."

He shakes his head. "No, I mean, you're back from the dead." He pauses and looks down. "I . . . I was frightened," he admits. "I figured you needed all the . . . you needed my support. I was afraid you'd never have that peach color in your cheeks again, Eva. You got so gray . . ."

I go to him and sit on his lap, putting my arms around his neck.

We're silent for a comfortable spell, then Richard begins humming a familiar tune. After a verse, I sing along quietly:

Let me call you sweetheart, I'm in love with you
Let me hear you whisper that you love me too
Keep the home fires burning in your eyes so blue
And let me call you sweetheart, I'm in love with you.

When we've finished, neither of us speaks. I lay my head against his chest and listen to his heart beating, slowly and steadily. At last I rise and climb into bed. Richard follows, snuggling up close behind me and kissing my shoulders. I look up.

"Honey, the light," I say, pointing to the bulb still glowing over our heads.

He looks at me. I look at him. He looks at the bulb and back at me. I shake my head.

"All right, fine, then," Richard mutters, making a silly face. He slides out from underneath the covers, crossing the room in stocking feet to the light switch by the door.

"There," he says, and with a dramatic click of the switch we're in the thick of the Congo darkness.

Dear Mother,

I have returned to Bolenge.

My health is much better. Halloween has come and gone. We're in the middle of the school term, and the boys at our École Moyenne are doing well.

I'm the new social chairman of the mission, and since I've recovered from my illness so ably, I decided to organize a Halloween party for the teachers and missionaries this past Friday evening.

We did Richard up as Scheherezade. I figured out how to make those Turkish pantaloons from old bed sheets. One of the African women lent us a carved anklet. (The married women here wear a lot of them.) I put it on Richard, along with a long black wig and gold earrings. I myself dressed up as Bluebeard, with a turban, whiskers, and all. When we got to the party, everyone thought we were the doings.

Some of the other missionaries put together costumes as well—Jean Matthews, our medical nurse on the Bolenge mission, came as Joan of Arc, although in this incarnation, the French martyr was accompanied by a chattering monkey (Jean's pet doesn't like to leave her side after dark.) Margaret Harrison, in charge of our print shop, dressed as Marilyn Monroe. She gave herself a beauty mark on the cheek and used a white string mop in place of platinum blond hair.

A few African teachers from the school came, but they didn't wear costumes. Actually, I think they're a little confused by the whole notion of Halloween. From what I understand, when they dress up in costumes it's a serious affair, usually for a shaman's religious ceremony or to call up the spirits of their ancestors.

Dr. Baker, one of our newer arrivals here, won the prize for best costume at Bolenge. He came to treat infectious diseases in Congo, bringing along his wife, Betty, and ten-year-old son from Augusta, Georgia. At the party Dr. Baker scared everyone to death by showing up in full official regalia and announced convincingly that the governor was arriving. He had on a hospital jacket trimmed with all the gold braids, medals, pins, and costume jewelry he could find. When I opened the door, my heart jumped into my throat!

Can you imagine? Just as we were all gathering in all these outlandish getups? I should mention that the governor of this district is a devout Catholic, and although he's always respectful of the charitable intentions of our mission, the missionaries think he's suspicious of our Protestant mores. Oh, did we laugh when we realized that the emissary was only Dr. Baker.

We look forward to Thanksgiving. I've just opened your package. Thank you for the pumpkin-pie spice and dried eggs, and the cans of yams and condensed milk, as well. We will have pie after all! The milk is especially a blessing, as the tsetse flies keep us from being able to keep cows in this region. What bit of canned milk we manage to order from Coquilhatville goes to the crying babies, who seem to be arriving left and right. (Nurse Jean Matthews is keeping busy!)

Love,

Eva

RICHARD AND I GO TO SEE EKEBE JACQUES. We find him sitting in his familiar posture in front of his house, proudly wearing the cotton-denim waist wrap I made for him.

He tells us that his rheumatism is better and asks if I have found a similar recovery.

"I have," I assure him.

"Did the boy bring you peanuts in the hospital?"

"Yes, he did, and thank you very much. They were delicious," I say, though in fact I was far too ill to eat any of them.

Ekebe Jacques smiles and nods.

I look around his raked-dirt yard.

"What have you been doing lately?" I ask in Lonkundo.

He squints and shakes his head. "I got all ready for the King to come, but he never came. It is a shame. The rains will be here any day now, and then it's for certain that the King won't come. The roads will be washed out. No, he is not coming. I don't think that Bolenge matters very much to the King."

"I, uh . . ." Suddenly, and strangely, I feel as though it is my duty as a white woman to justify the actions of the King of Belgium.

"King Boudoin is very busy," I say. "I'm sure that he had every intention of coming, but just like we can't always go and visit our relatives as we'd like to, it doesn't mean we don't care about them a great deal. I'll bet it's the same way with the King."

Ekebe Jacques nods and considers this, stroking his wiry white beard.

"What is your proverb?" Ekebe Jacques asks us, suddenly very serious.

Richard and I look at each other.

"We still don't have proverbs," Richard said apologetically. "We've been busy fretting over Eva's health, and what with the new school term—"

"It is all well," Ekebe Jacques assures us, shaking his head and clucking. "I have proverbs for you." He smiles gently.

"For you, *Mama Boenga,* when they ask you, you may say '*Batsala buke nko nzala.*' It means 'Lots of gardens, no hunger.' I watch you and listen to what you say. You have come from far, far away to teach Nkundo to tend after their own gardens. You are a great gardener who uses her imagination when droughts and insects come in her way. It suits you to have this proverb."

"Thank you," I say, feeling awkward in the face of praise. "How about Richard?"

Ekebe Jacques purses his lips and looks skyward.

"For le Directeur, it is '*Tomboofomana*'—this I say."

Richard repeats the phrase slowly, Ekebe Jacques correcting his pronunciation. *"Tombo-Ofomana."*

"And what does mine mean?" Richard asks.

"It is the proverb of a chief. It says, 'We will meet again. Do not cross me.'"

"Well, now," Richard says, hesitating. "I don't know whether that is really exactly how I would describe my—"

"Oh, yes!" Ekebe Jacques interrupts, putting up his hand and shaking his head. "You are the chief of the young African men at the white man's Christian school. You must have a proverb that shows your position."

"All right," Richard says, accepting his new mantle uneasily.

When we've finished our visit and are getting ready to go, I walk my bicycle along the space between Ekebe Jacques's house and that of his niece. As I pass her front window, I see her inside, sitting on a low chair. She stares at me as I pass. Our gazes fix upon each other. She turns her head to continue looking at me as I get on my bicycle to leave.

I watch her. She watches me. Neither of us say a word.

WE HAVE ENDURED ANOTHER RAINY SEASON, and the only compliment it warrants is that it was less severe than the furies that beset us in the spring. Still, it rained for days and days on end. The sky blackened, the river rose, and we wore long pants every day and slept with all the musty blankets in the house tucked beneath our toes every night.

For sixteen mornings we rose to the drumming of rain on the roof. For sixteen days we acquiesced to half attention from the boys at school and in church, knowing that things much more dramatic than our typing lessons were stealing their concentration. For sixteen nights we shivered through damp dinners and early bedtimes.

Then, yesterday, the seventeenth day, rays of sun poked through the murky clouds, columns of light against the misty dark green of the open glade near the mission. It was the day before Thanksgiving. Now we have reason indeed to celebrate.

I go to bed happy, but wake with a start in the middle of the night. Someone is banging on the front door.

"Mr. and Mrs. Dunagan?" demands an anxious, boyish voice.

There is more rapping at the door.

I recognize the voice as Tommy's, the ten-year-old son of Dr. Baker, who has become our nearest neighbor, save the generator.

"Just a minute," I call to him, fumbling for the matches, so I may dispel the darkness. I hear the sound of chickens cackling frantically from Dr. Baker's house fifty yards away.

"Richard, wake up." I nudge and prod him until he rolls over and sits up in the darkness.

"Come quick!" Tommy pleads. "The ants are in the chicken cages!"

"We'll be right there," I call back.

Hurriedly, we pull on our clothes, grab flashlights, and rush over to Dr. Baker's house. I trip on a low vine as we pass through our garden. A snake hisses noisily.

I get to Dr. Baker's coop moments before Richard does, making my way around back, where the fowl are sounding their alarm.

Dr. Baker keeps his chickens in locked cages to prevent the villagers from helping themselves to the hens. The natives have peculiar views on the transitivity of property. Dr. Baker can insist until he is blue in the face that his chickens should be left alone, but it will do nothing to prevent them from disappearing when he is out on rounds. If he were to complain to an Nkundo elder about the theft, the elder likely would shrug and say that whoever stole the chickens was probably hungrier than Dr. Baker. This doesn't sit well with our Western notions.

Richard catches up with me as the beam of my flashlight makes its way across the cages.

I have heard tell about the ravages of driver ants, but as always, secondhand stories never prepare one for battle. As my beam reflects off the locks on the cage doors, I take in a truly horrible sight: a foot-wide stream of driver ants marching resolutely to their prey, rippling shiny-backed black, pouring through the wire and rattan cages and swarming over the chickens. The birds flap their wings and stamp madly. The yard is full of their frantic screeching.

"Get the keys!" I holler at the house, but Dr. Baker is already coming out the door with a blowtorch in one hand and a brass key ring in the other.

"Eva!" Richard shouts, pointing to my feet.

In the moments I've been standing here, a thousand ants have swarmed across my shoes and are about to make a supper of my ankles. I drop my flashlight on the ground and begin hopping frantically, brushing ants off onto the ground with one hand and clearing them off my wrist with the other.

"Just remember to keep moving," Richard warns.

Once I have gotten most of the ants off my own body, I pick up my flashlight and go after the chickens.

Driver ants work en masse, hundreds of thousands of them, covering any living thing that stands in their way, burrowing their heads and pinchers under the surface of the flesh and eating until they can hold no more. Before the missionaries came, Nkundo tortured wrongdoers by tying them down in the path of the ants. Ta Pierre told us that driver ants can clean the flesh off the bones of a goat or a dog in a matter of minutes. He also told us that driver ants are afraid of nothing but fire.

Dr. Baker lights his blowtorch and points the flame down at the ground where the ants are advancing, its blue flame instantly scorching their armored bodies by the hundreds.

Richard and I pull open the cages and drag the chickens out one by one, brushing off as many ants as we can, tossing the flailing birds in a galvanized washbasin that terrified, blubbering little Tommy has dragged out his back door.

Soon the basin is full.

I think fast. "Put 'em in the bathtub!" I call to Richard.

He carries two hens up the back steps and into the Bakers' kitchen.

The larger chickens in the cages nearest us seem to be all right, but the smaller, more tender birds are chirping frantically from their cages in the back.

I'm so anxious to get to them that I can hardly breathe. I knock aside empty cages to reach the chicks, dancing from one foot to the other to keep the ants from crawling up my legs. Feed mash and rancid feathers fly. Chicken droppings splash across my ankles.

At last we get to the babies.

Some of them are well on their way to being eaten alive, already rippling black gargoyles, every inch from eyes to open beaks covered with ants. Richard picks up the locked cage in both arms and shakes it violently. This knocks some of the ants free, but most have their pinchers embedded in the chicks' flesh.

Dr. Baker lays his blowtorch on the ground and, with trembling hands, tries to remember which is the right key for the lock. He attempts one after another.

"Move," Richard says, pushing Dr. Baker aside. He leans in and rips the door off the cage.

The beam of my flashlight shakes. I'm repulsed by the idea of touching the flailing birds, but there is no other option. I take a handkerchief in my hand and reach in to grab the little chick that is the most covered with ants, pulling it out and batting the insects off its back and head. I shake the bird, but there are a score of little black devils under its wings and in its tail. The bird coughs a last breath, and several ants scramble from its mouth.

I lay its limp body in my basket and reach back into the cage to try and save the chick's siblings. How many doctors have been confronted with a patient so injured that he would rather let the man die quickly than work on him while he continues to suffer?

We run out of places to put the chickens, so I begin relaying them back to our house, handing them one by one to Tommy and instructing him to put them in the bathtub.

The ordeal goes on and on. I feel as though the chickens' screeching will drive me mad. Soon, Tommy tells me that our bathtub is full. I have him start filling up the kitchen sink. Dr. Baker, dripping with sweat, keeps working his blowtorch until he has killed tens of thousands vicious little ants. Those that survive scatter, confused and disoriented, into the grass. Soon, though, they regroup and head off to a more inviting environment. Perhaps a warren of rabbits, trapped below the earth, will lose their lives tonight.

In a few more minutes, it's over.

We sit outside the Bakers' house, sweating, spent, shaking. The doctor's wife has at last brought out a kerosene lamp. The light is pale, but I can clearly see the disarrayed cages in front of us, broken, wire frames dented. Feathers and dead ants litter the ground. I glance down into the basket at my side. In it, the first chick I tried to save lies limp and contorted.

Then I look closer. It's with great surprise that I realize he's still alive, his ravaged little body trembling slightly with each fast, shallow breath.

"Richard!" I call.

He walks over to the steps where I sit. I reach into the pail and lift the bird out, recoiling at what I see. The ants have eaten clear through his feathers and skin in spots, and patches of bald flesh are exposed on his breast and head. The little thing opens his eyes and then closes them again. I lift his wings, picking with my fingers at the ants that remain, pulling some of them away from his body with their heads and pinchers still buried under the surface of his skin.

Dr. Baker draws some tweezers and a tin of sulfa powder out of his bag.

"Here," he says.

I take the tweezers and pick the last dozen ants from the poor little creature's flesh.

"Dust him with the powder," Dr. Baker advises half-heartedly. "It might keep his wounds from getting infected."

I comply with a numbed heart, for I can tell from the doctor's tone that he does not expect the chick to live any more than I do. When I'm finished, I steal a look at Richard's wristwatch: The hands glow radium-green in the night. It is three o'clock.

The jungle roils and shivers, restless in the dark.

"C'mon, let's get some sleep," Richard says, taking my hand. We walk home, and I carry my chick with me in Dr. Baker's galvanized pail.

The chick lies huddled up and still. He doesn't make a sound.

When we arrive home, I let the beam of the flashlight lead me into the bathroom. The bathtub is full of fowl. It is an absurd, troublesome sight.

I go to the kitchen, where there are more. Right here and now, I say a prayer of thanks to God for the fact that the birds in the sink are silent and not pleading for their lives, as they were an hour ago. That sound of panicked desperation touched my heart in a way I won't forget.

Richard and I don't bother changing back into our bedclothes to lie down. I set the pail containing the tragic little chick at my bedside and close my eyes, waking at the too-soon Thanksgiving dawn to the crowing of a rooster and the beating of the lokolé drum from the village.

When we rise, aching and bleary eyed, I look into the pail to see if my baby chick has passed.

Instead, I find him almost chipper. I'm thrilled. Can it really be so? I clap my hands with joy and gingerly pick up the bird.

He looks up at me, opening and closing his beak, mutely demanding his breakfast. I realize that during their torment of his throat, the ants made their way to his voice box. My chick will never have a voice again. But nonetheless, he's alive!

Richard and I look around the house. Mud and chicken blood are tracked across the floor, lending the living room the eerie ambience of a butchering house, but from the bathroom and the kitchen come the contented clucks of a henhouse's worth of fowl. I go from room to room, inspecting our patients. We haven't lost a single bird during the night, and in defiance of farmyard logic, one of the hens has even laid an egg.

I slip across the yard to tell Dr. Baker the good news, singing a song as I walk.

When I get to Dr. Baker's yard, I stop short. There, the cages we emptied last night lay strewn about. The grass is blackened from Dr. Baker's torch and littered with charred feathers. A million ant carcasses pepper the packed dirt of the yard.

It takes me a moment before I'm able to proceed up the stairs to the Bakers' house.

When I knock on the door, Betty opens it, greeting me with a tired smile.

I must look exhausted, as well.

"Morning, Eva."

"Morning," I answer. "You up already?"

"Yeah, got to get my yams going for the dinner later. You want some coffee?"

"I . . . that's okay," I decline, not feeling proper about having her husband and son see me so bedraggled. "I just came by to let ya know that they all made it through okay—the chickens, I mean."

"Well, praise be," Betty says. "I don't know how to begin thanking you for what you did."

I nod and turn to go.

"C'mon, have a cup of coffee. It came out real good," Betty insists.

I hesitate, then smile and follow her inside. Betty's right. The coffee is hot and strong. I sit and watch her chop onions.

Today, we celebrate Thanksgiving. The date is nothing but a number on a calendar to me now. The seasons of Congo—the rain and drought, the celebrations of harvest and the hunger in between—these are becoming the milestones I count. We Americans cling to what's familiar. The holidays we bring with us from back home are purely ceremonial, remembrances of things gone by. In Africa, intervals of time are measured by more immediate concerns. It's all about rain and soil and life and death in the present tense, not the past.

Betty takes her chopping knife and eases the onions she has been cutting off the board and into a waiting skillet. They sizzle when they hit the grease, and the sweet smell fills the room. I feel at peace.

Because it's Thanksgiving, we, as a mission, have decided to give our household help the day off after cleaning up the grim remains of the ant invasion. We'll do the cooking ourselves. I finish my coffee and go. It's time to start my own preparations for the mission's holiday meal.

Margaret volunteered to make pumpkin pies and I signed her up, but Richard said that if the mince pies she made while I was sick could serve as any indication, Margaret should be kept as far away from food preparation as possible. I had a boy take a note over to her in the print shop last week, inviting her to help me with decorations instead.

Richard and I spend the better part of the morning cleaning up after the traumatized poultry, taking them back home to the Bakers' place, while the doctor rights the cages, shaking his head at the mess.

"I'm sorry for all the trouble," Dr. Baker says.

"No trouble at all," Richard congenially lies, putting a squawking hen back in her cage.

"If it weren't for you two, I don't know how many of these I might have lost. I'm really rather indebted," the doctor says.

"Just being neighborly," I insist, looking down at the cages. "Shame you have to lock them up like that."

AS RICHARD AND I ARE MIDWAY THROUGH cleaning our own house, Liyanza comes by, walking into the kitchen without waiting for an invitation.

"Hello, there," I say, looking up. "I'm very busy right now."

Liyanza stands and watches for a moment. "You have sick chickens from the ants," he says.

"Yes," I tell him, picking up one of the few remaining birds. "Here, you can carry one back to Dr. Baker's house."

I point toward the open door. Liyanza looks closely at the bird I have handed him, peering into its blinking eyes and forcing its beak open with his index finger and thumb. This amuses me. I try not to laugh as Liyanza turns the chicken upside down to get a better look at its underside, startling the fowl. It complains and tries to free itself of his grasp. Liyanza holds down the wings and clears his throat.

"Yeah, Mama, this bird will be good," he says with a nod.

"Thank you, Dr. Liyanza."

He takes the bird and scampers off toward the Bakers' house.

I must go see Margaret. She's printed Thanksgiving place mats for the table with brown and green ink and made little cursive place-marker cards that fold, like at a wedding or a fancy restaurant. She described them to me in a long-winded manner yesterday. I'm eager to see if they're really as divine as she claims.

This is the first time I've been inside Margaret's little house. I wait in the living room while she takes the rollers out of her hair. There are old photos sitting on the hutch. I pick up some of them, blowing off dust to get a better look at the faces.

"That's my mother and daddy on their wedding day," Margaret says from the hallway as I set down a picture of a beaming bride and her rigid groom, in a World War I officers uniform.

"Who'd have guessed that he'd end up leaving her for his stenographer?" Margaret says with a callous laugh as she comes in from the bedroom.

"I'm sorry," I say.

"Oh, really, don't be. 'Cause I'm not. He's not sorry, and my mother's dead. End of story."

Margaret looks at herself in a hall mirror as she hooks a modest string of pearls around her neck.

"Maybe his leaving is what did her in. Actually, I think the whole family fell apart after I became a missionary. They couldn't stand the shock."

While I watch Margaret put herself together, I think about my own mother and her solitude. My real father wore his officers uniform on his wedding day, like Margaret's daddy. He wandered off, just like Margaret's, although in his case it wasn't with a woman. In truth, I think something bad must have happened to my father over in Europe. As my grandmother put it, when he got back, he "wasn't right."

It wasn't long before he left us and shacked up in a boarding house on the seamy side of town, with few possessions beyond a ham-radio receiver and a bottle of whiskey. My last clear image of him is that of a frail man sitting in a dark, roach-infested room one afternoon late in the fall of 1944. He was hunched over a Morse code button, quickly tapping as if he had some sort of nervous tic.

Then there was that time he came by and offered me candy. I was standing in the street. At least I think it was him. I'll never really know.

I look again at Margaret's pictures and, this time I think about Richard. I imagine him standing in the kitchen in my apron, baking pies and whistling tunelessly. I have done well. Richard is a man who holds me when I'm frightened, who rarely raises his voice or loses his temper.

Although my health has suffered this year, there's much for which I ought to be thankful this Thanksgiving morning.

"All right," Margaret says, checking her lipstick in the mirror before leaning down to pick up a pile of printing on her kitchen table.

"Shall we?"

She and I walk to Jean's house. We'll be eating Thanksgiving dinner surrounded by tongue depressors and smelling salts, but we'll make the best of it, for she has the most available room for such functions. I borrowed an American flag from the dispensary, and Margaret and I hang it from the corners of the glass medical cabinets that line one wall of Jean's living room.

As Margaret sets the place markers in front of dishes I have borrowed from several households, she hums quietly to herself.

"What's that song?" I ask, trying to remember the melody.

"It's Nelson Eddy," she says.

"Oh, yes," I remember. "They used to play it on the jukebox at the Varsity Club when Richard and I were first dating."

I hum a few bars, but Margaret stops me.

"Tell me something, Eva," she says, straightening the last place marker and looking up at me. "How'd you find a man like Richard? I've been thinking on it, and I sincerely want to know."

"What do you mean?" I ask, taken aback. "First of all, he found me."

"Well, okay, then, what did you do to nab him?"

"*Nab* him?" I ask, surprised.

"Yeah. You can tell me. I mean you didn't let yourself get pregnant; that's plain to see. What was it, then? Are you some kind of amazing cook?"

I steady myself. "Look here, Margaret," I begin, and then I think the better of where my tongue might lead me. "I didn't do anything to 'nab' him. Our relationship isn't like that."

Margaret turns her back to me and crosses her arms.

I continue. "From the very beginning, when I met him, we did things for each other. It's a two-way street. I think that's the only way to survive out here—or anywhere for that matter.

"Not that I need a husband to survive—that was my mother's way. She couldn't make it on her own. After my daddy left, she needed to marry my stepfather to give her life meaning again." I've walked around Margaret so that I'm now facing her.

There's a pause. Margaret's very still. "Well, honestly, Eva," she says demurely.

"I'm sorry," I stammer, and feel my face flush. "Forgive me. It's just . . . it's been a difficult day. Night. I shouldn't have said, uh . . ."

Margaret stands looking down at the table then, after a moment, walks slowly toward the door.

"I'm sor—" I start to say.

"No offense taken," she says without looking at me.

She rises so that we may leave. But as she does so, she pauses for a moment and lays her hands atop mine, squeezing gently before she lets go.

I PUT ON MY SUNDAY DRESS, the blue one.

We have a marvelous dinner, sixteen of us, gobbling a roasted hen from the Coquilhatville meat market and spooning canned cranberry relish by candlelight. We use linen napkins to wipe our lips. We drink grenadine punch and coffee with the pumpkin pie that Richard baked from supplies my mother sent us.

We tell stories and sing hymns. Dr. Baker takes out his guitar, and he and Richard offer crude renditions of "Oh, Susannah" and "My Darling Clementine."

Betty and I tell everyone of the chickens-and-ants ordeal, receiving much sympathy. Several of the others say they thought they heard some of the ruckus last night.

"Why didn't you come to help?" I ask too quickly.

"Things aren't like they used to be," Jean answers. "Back when I got here, it was a lot more civilized, believe it or not. Nowadays, what with the natives getting their heads full of crazy talk from down in Léopoldville, you hear something in the night, there's no telling what it might be. You do best just to make sure your front door's locked up tight."

Others mumble their agreement.

By the time Richard and I walk home to our end of the mission, singing the chorus of "Careless Love" in the moonlight, the generator has chugged to a halt and the shadows on the ground are pale.

As we reach the front of our garden, I hear footsteps behind us. Richard walks toward the front steps, but I lag, hiding myself behind the trunk of our mango tree, curious about who or what has been accompanying us on the path. I shiver, recalling Jean's cautionary comments from dinner.

As the footsteps on the path become more distinct, I see it's Margaret who has followed us—only, she really hasn't been following. She's merely walking home by herself. Her face looks ghostly

in the moonlight. She sings quietly and slowly as she passes, echoing the words Richard and I have just finished:

> *Love, oh love, oh careless love . . .*
> *You see what careless love has done.*
>
> *I cried last night and the night before . . .*
> *Gonna cry tonight and cry no more.*

Sixteen

August 1958

Y SECOND ANNIVERSARY IN CONGO APPROACHES.

I'm beginning to feel that the Dark Continent is my home. I have come to appreciate that there's a rhythm to the process of living, the waking and falling asleep, the laboring and resting, the adjustment to heat and chill that varies from one season to the next. It's taken me some time to find my step in the local dance, for it is tricky and I've had no teacher but my own intuition. In recent months, I've ventured more time among the natives in Bolenge. Saturdays are devoted to Richard and Ekebe Jacques. Our Lonkundo lessons are progressing nicely.

On Sundays, I've been returning on my own to sit and talk with some of the Nkundo women. What I learn saddens me. With good reason, women in Africa view themselves as little more than chattel. They're their husbands' possessions and as such can be bought and sold for a handful of cowries or an animal skin. They cannot vote, own property, or bring legal action against a wrongdoer. The constant awareness of their subordination weighs just as heavily upon them as the brass anklets with which their husbands like to see them adorned. How can it be that for an entire generation, our Christian missionaries have not been able to turn that injustice around? Am I to simply stand by and watch?

The women of Bolenge don't know how to read, so I've taken it upon myself to teach them. The trouble is, they have never been inside a classroom, and therefore they don't have the associated academic discipline.

Today, I'll conduct a grand teaching experiment. I asked Margaret to come along and watch, for I was sure she'd be impressed with my ingenuity. I wasn't greatly surprised, however, when she declined, saying she lets boys from l'École Moyenne come by the print shop on the weekend and practice their typing lessons, and this afternoon she'll be busy supervising them.

So I ride my bicycle to the village alone. We're midway between rains: the time when living things flourish. I pedal quickly, enjoying the way the breeze whistles in my ears and tugs at the ribbon that binds my ponytail.

When I arrive, the women are waiting for me. Eight of them are gathered around the front of a house. The youngest is about my age and the eldest looks as though she could be my grandmother. One woman is breastfeeding her new baby as I approach.

"*Lol'eko,*" I call out to them.

"*Oy'endo,*" they respond in chorus, welcoming me.

I sit down and open my bag, taking out the stack of flash cards I've prepared. It seems to me that to teach a grown-up who's never been to school, it might be smart to use the same tools as with a child who is, likewise, at the beginning of his or her journey.

I stayed up late last night with a stack of three-by-five index cards and a box of crayons, making little line drawings for each letter of the alphabet. Every American child knows that A is for apple and B is for boy. But in Lonkundo, B is for *bokele*, which means "egg." I have drawn a fried egg and colored in the yolk.

The women sit cross-legged on the ground, studying my pictures closely and nodding their heads seriously. They say the words over and over. After a while, I quiz them. They get most of the letters wrong. I'm patient, they are patient, and we repeat the exercise. On the second go-round, they do better. One of the older women surprises everyone by remembering nearly all the sounds.

"Very good! You're a good student," I congratulate her.

She looks as though she has won the Nobel Prize.

"*Mam'Oenga,* I have something to tell to you," one of the other women says, raising her hand politely.

"Yes?" I turn to her.

"I have a husband who is a teacher at the same school you come from."

"The high school?" I ask, surprised.

"Yes," she says, nodding.

"What is his name?"

"Boale." She pronounces the word succinctly, as though its sound is inherently prestigious.

"Joseph Boale?" I ask, surprised at the notion of his having a wife. He's never discussed the matter with me, and he certainly carries on like a bachelor.

"Yes," she says. "He's an important man."

Before I go, I show each of the women how to write her own name. I pass around pencils and a stack of index cards, holding up the series of little pictures that have become familiar. Woman by woman, letter by letter, they make tentative lines and circles—shapes familiar to me but foreign and exciting to them. They speak to one another in hushed whispers, asking questions and critiquing one another's penmanship.

When I've given each woman the spelling of her name, I tell the group to take home their name cards and study the letters until they have been committed to memory. I then give them each a pencil with which to practice writing. For these simple gifts they thank me so profusely I must finally insist they're welcome, really, but it's time for me to go.

"Please, soon come back," they beg of me as I hoist my satchel onto my shoulder.

The old woman who was first to commit the alphabet to memory decides to perform for the group, standing up and reciting each letter she's learned. Her singsong voice trails in the distance behind me as I ride away.

WHEN I GET HOME TO THE MISSION, Ta Pierre is fixing dinner, and Richard is going over student progress reports, whistling "Rock-a My Soul in the Bosom of Abraham," operating under the assumption that there's no one nearby to listen. He pauses here and there, pronouncing a word or two of the lyric before going back to whistling. I snicker as I walk into the room.

"What?" Richard says, looking up.

"Nothing," I tell him and head to the bedroom to rest a few minutes before dinner.

"How was your afternoon?"

"Right nice."

As I pass our packing-crate desk, I look down at the calendar that lies there. I realize that my period is eleven days late. Eleven days is a long time.

I slip off my shoes and climb onto the bed, lying on my back. Dusk has not yet arrived, but afternoon's rapidly surrendering its hold on the day. I breathe deeply, tracing my index finger along the serpentine scar from my great illness. The doctors claimed that the torment I endured would not affect my chances of becoming properly pregnant.

Perhaps we shall find out.

WE HAVE VISITORS. For several days, Bolenge pays host to a family of church leaders traveling from India to America and visiting missions along the way. The father, an associate pastor from Kansas City, asks all sorts of questions about life in Africa. On the third morning of the visit, we have a communal breakfast at Jean's house.

"I was thinking," the pastor says, "if it isn't too much trouble and won't take but one day, I'd like to get a lion."

Nurse Bateman coughs at this, telling the man that she has seen only one lion in all the years she has been stationed here. Lions are grass-country animals. Only a hopelessly lost beast would make an appearance in these parts. Besides, game safaris make a two-week business out of such a pursuit.

The missionary also expresses regret that it took fifteen days for the letter announcing his arrival to travel from India. We decide not to tell him that it often takes that long for mail to make its way the short distance from Mondombe to Coquilhatville.

IN MY CLASS AT L'ÉCOLE MOYENNE, I give a social studies essay assignment. I ask the students to write about the differences between the races. As usual, their responses surprise me.

One boy writes:

The white missionaries are smart people. But they don't give us enough things. We need more food and clothing, but the white man keeps it all for himself. Independence should come to Congo like all the peoples are saying. Then black mans would not have to pay to ride the train and we could go into a store and take what we want and not have to pay the white man money for it. That is Independence and that is what is best.

Another suggests:

Things were better in the world when everybody was in charge of their own people. Before the white man came to Congo, Nkundo of power gave out the women and slaves and meat. It was better then.

Finally, at the bottom of the pile, I find evidence that one of my young students is walking around with disturbing notions in his head:

There are many things different between the races. The blacks have less evil spirits that the whites. The whites evil spirits have very powerful! Whites get injection in their arm of vitamins and against the illnesses but also for being smart. So they kill black man and put him in tin cans. I see a can of Niggerhead Oysters they call them with a black man face on the paper label in Coquilhatville.

I am sitting alone at my desk when I read this last essay, and I don't know whether to be amused or appalled. As I consider what I might say to its young author, M. Boale passes my window and I call him into my room.

"What do you want? I am very busy," he warns as he enters.

"We're all very busy," I remind him and hold up the paper. "Here, have a look at this."

He takes it from me and reads the essay.

"And so?" he asks when he has finished.

"So? Where on earth do you suppose he got notions like that?"

"Like what?"

I stare at M. Boale for a moment, wondering if he's playing dumb.

"Like white people eating Africans, or that we have evil spirits that we use against you," I say.

"There is more that exists beyond the horizon here in Africa, things that a young white woman like you cannot see, Madame Dunagan. Perhaps when you have grown a little older and a little wiser . . ."

He begins to go but pauses before he reaches the door. "Oh, by the way," he says, turning around, "I understand you have been down in the village teaching my wife to read."

"Yes, and she's a good student. You should be proud."

"You have no business there and may stop."

"Why?" I ask, surprised and a little hurt.

"A woman has no business with reading and writing. It makes her insubordinate."

"Yes, just look at me," I mutter.

"They don't need to know about all that," M. Boale says with great assurance. "My wife, if she knew how to spell, she would only write notes to her lovers."

"Really, Monsieur Boale—"

"I would thank you to stop teaching her right away," he says in a manner that lets me know our conversation is finished. He leaves the room, shutting the door behind him. I sit and stare at the doorway. I feel like throwing something heavy at him.

I return to my papers. I can't believe that he would promote such hogwash about whites eating blacks. I think about the education Joseph has received. Didn't he learn a bit of social studies along with mathematics and penmanship?

When there's a knock on the door, I hope it might be M. Boale, returning to make amends, but it's Richard. From the minute he walks into the room, I know there is trouble.

"I was . . . can you come down to the office for a minute?" he asks. Perspiration covers his brow.

"Sure. I mean, what's the matter?"

"The police commissioner from Coquilhatville—he's here. There's a letter. He thinks one of the boys has done something terrible."

I follow Richard into the hallway, trying to make sense of what he's saying.

We reach the office. The corpulent commissioner is waiting inside with a grave look on his face.

"Madame," he says, rising with the aid of an ivory walking cane and shaking my hand. I mutter an anxious acknowledgment. The commissioner takes a typed letter out of the folder he carries and holds it out to me. I take it.

"I was telling your husband, *le Directeur,* there has been a series of letters distributed around Bolenge and Coquilhatville that aren't entirely flattering to the government. I'm curious to know if they may have come from your school. The way they're typed, you see . . ." He taps his index finger against the letter that I'm now holding.

"There are no accent marks. We believe the letters have been typed on an American machine, with its peculiar Q-W-E-R-T-Y arrangement of the keys and no provision for accents and circumflexes. The typewriters in your classroom are the only such machines we're aware of in this region."

I pause to read the letter:

To All it May Concern—

White man has wealth. The time will come and we will have it. We do all the work. They steal from you. They have guns. Why aren't we free to carry guns with more than four shotgun shells a month? Be ready to decide if you are your own man or white man's slave.

The letter isn't signed.

"I told him I didn't think anyone here would be writing things like that," Richard says.

"Nonetheless, I must conduct a systematic investigation," the commissioner says. "If you'd be so kind as to lead the way . . ."

Richard opens his mouth to speak but then closes it.

"It's okay," I whisper to him as we leave the office, but my nerves are knotted tight. For as surely as there exists mistrust between the Catholic Belgian government and our Protestant mission, so surely would such an inflammatory letter generated in our school bring difficulties for us. At minimum, it would be a great embarrassment, the likes of which our peaceful mission has not known in its half century of existence. My deeper fear is that the school would be shut down, branded a hotbed of revolutionary discontent, in a decision ripe with the kind of paranoid generalization to which the despotic colonial government seems prone.

I look at Richard's wan expression and guess he may fear the same. It's well past the end of classes for the day, so all the boys have gone back to the dormitory or out into the field for their afternoon soccer drills. As Richard and I walk the commissioner down the breezeway toward the room where the school's typewriters are locked up at night, the only sound I notice is the rattle of Richard's keys as his hand trembles.

"I'm sure it wasn't anyone from the school," Richard tells the commissioner as we reach the door to the typing classroom.

"We shall see," the man says.

I think back to the indignant tone of the essays I've just been correcting, and I'm not so sure Richard's right. One by one, Richard and I take the typewriters from the cabinet and set them on the dozen desks that fill the small room. It's a peculiar police line-up. The typewriters all look alike, enameled black-and-chrome Royals, but one of them is now a potential enemy. I hope we don't find the commissioner's culprit among them.

Richard gets typing paper from the cabinet and rolls a sheet into the carriage of each contraption.

The commissioner approaches the first suspect. He extends accusatory fingers and pecks out a sample sentence, then pulls the sheet of paper from the carriage and compares the characters to those of the letter he has brought as evidence.

After a moment, he shakes his head.

I breathe a sigh of relief. The commissioner moves on to the next machine.

Please, dear Lord, may he finish his investigation and not find any of our typewriters culpable.

As the commissioner finishes testing each typewriter, Richard and I return them to the cabinet. All of this takes place wordlessly. At last the commissioner looks up at us.

"Are there any I have not seen?"

No, we tell him, there are not.

"Very well," he says, looking at us warily. "I'll leave you with one of the letters, just in case you think of anything. If any suggestions about its origin should come to mind, give me a call right away."

We show him out to the Mercedes-Benz that he has left parked next to the school. Half a dozen École Moyenne students are gathered around the sedan, sitting on its hood or cupping their hands to peer inside its tinted windows.

"Get away!" the commissioner shouts at the boys when he sees them pressed up against his car. He waves his cane, and the students scatter like discontented dogs being sent off from their dinner.

Once the commissioner starts up his engine and pulls away, I turn to Richard. What do you think?" I ask.

"I think Congo is a very complicated place," he says quietly, watching the cloud of dust that the commissioner's car has raised in the road. As the dust settles, M. Boale's figure appears in the roadway about a hundred yards away.

FOR SEVERAL DAYS, I spend my free time studying the reactionary letter.

I've noticed something odd about the characters on the page. The lack of accent marks isn't the only distinctive feature of the typewriting. The letter Q appears several times, and in each instance, the type is faint and only a partial impression has been made through the ribbon. Perhaps this is what the commissioner was looking for when he tested our machines.

I wonder, secretly, if it was M. Boale who typed the letters. Surely he is farsighted enough to imagine its dissemination could mean an end to the school, thereby his teaching position, thereby his position as a man of *mpifo* in Bolenge. It's hard for me to think of any revolutionary ideal, however noble, being more important to M. Boale than his own social rank.

Richard and I have decided it's best not to discuss the letters with anyone for the time being. After all, it was Richard, not a church official, whom the commissioner approached with his concerns. Therefore, it's technically Belgian school business and not of direct concern to the mission or the Disciples of Christ. Undue paranoia or gossip need not be fueled.

At last the weekend comes, and my attention is diverted. I'm tempted to tell Richard that my period is now fourteen days late, but I decide to keep it secret. It's becoming a little game: Will the bleeding come today? Tomorrow?

I say a prayer that my period might not come at all.

On Saturday morning I wake feeling tired. I lay my palms flat against my stomach and wonder what's going on beneath my skin. Since our arrival in Congo, my insides have been subject to more than their fair share of distress.

From my window I hear the mission stirring, making its morning sounds. Chickens cluck, houseboys walk to the river sharing village gossip, Jean's new kerosene-powered icebox chugs away like a Ford Model T.

I get up slowly and prepare to go to the village for another language lesson with my Nkundo women. I won't let the mystery letter or M. Boale deter me from this task. If his wife doesn't want to learn to read and write Lonkundo, then she ought not come by when I'm teaching. It's that simple.

Another reason to go to the village today is that I miss Ekebe Jacques and want to visit him. I miss our language lessons and afternoons spent laughing and musing about the world. Having lived so many years, Ekebe Jacques has a peculiar perspective on this. He's also the only of my Nkundo acquaintances who was alive before the missionaries pitched their tents in Congo and began seeking converts. Surely, if he took as much exception to our being here as the incendiary letter writer, he would have told us by now.

On my way to the village, I stop by the print shop to see if Margaret wants to join me. When she comes to the door, she seems displeased that it's I who has come to call.

"Eva, you know I have the high-school boys over to practice typing on Saturday," she says, pinning up her hair. She's wearing lipstick. "I'm expecting the boys any minute now, and—"

"I won't stay long. Is your typewriter American or French?" I ask her.

"What?"

"Is it an American model or—"

"It's a Royal upright they sent over years ago from the Missions board in Cleveland. How come?"

"Might I see it?"

She squints at me for a moment.

"Well, all right," she says, leading me hurriedly to the back of the building where her cluttered desk is located.

"There," she says, pointing at the machine.

"May I type on it?" I ask, determined.

"I suppose—look, Eva, what's this all about?"

"Nothing, I just . . ."

I put a sheet of paper in the machine and type the letters Q-W-E-R-T-Y. I look carefully at the characters on the page, and the Q is as clear and dark as any of the other characters.

"All right," I say, tugging the sheet of paper out of the roller and crumpling it.

"Would you like to tell me what's going on?" Margaret asks.

"It's nothing really," I tell her. "Thanks for letting me, you know . . ."

I walk toward the front of the building feeling a little embarrassed.

"By the way," Margaret says.

I turn around. "Why was there a policeman at the high school a couple of days ago?"

"How did you know about that?" I ask nervously.

"Oh, Eva, I know about everything that goes on around here. So what did he want?"

A knock on the door saves me from having to answer. Margaret and I both turn to look. It is Mboto Antoine, a boy from my class.

"Come in," Margaret tells him.

"Mesdames," Mboto says, nodding politely as he approaches.

"Where are the others?" I ask him.

"Pardon, Madame Dunagan?"

His eyes are unusually shy and won't look at me.

"The other boys, for typing practice," I say. I would have expected them to arrive together.

Mboto looks at Margaret then back at me for a moment without answering.

"I came alone," he says quietly.

I turn to Margaret for a response, but she's diverted her attention elsewhere.

"I should be going. Have a nice day," I say, walking to the door.

Mboto and Margaret stand awkwardly still and don't tell me goodbye. Just before I leave the building, I turn around again to look at them, and I notice that Mboto has come bearing a spindly wildflower, which he holds behind his back.

I close the door quietly behind me.

WHEN I ARRIVE TO TEACH THE VILLAGE WOMEN, there is one fewer that I had hoped to see. M. Boale's wife has not come out for the lesson.

Today I help them write one another simple one-sentence letters. It's a slow process, for I must tell them how to spell each word.

After we finish, they swap letters and read them aloud. This part of the exercise requires even more patience of all parties.

As the sun moves to a place in the African sky where it casts no shadows, I give each woman the assignment of memorizing the spellings of several words—manioc, franc, woman, child, Congo, and Jesus. I've made more note cards, and I hold them up, one by one, while the women transcribe the words.

Richard approaches on his bicycle to accompany me for the visit with Ekebe Jacques.

"Try to have the words in your memory for next week," I say to the women. "There are many words to be learned."

They laugh at my humor. I love making someone laugh in another language.

Richard and I walk our bicycles up the row of houses, arriving at last in front of Ekebe Jacques's yard. The old man sits at his outside table with a piece of wood in one hand and a native carving knife in the other. He is fashioning some sort of fetish. I can't tell exactly what it is, for Ekebe Jacques's hands are no longer steady, so the cuts his knife makes are not precise.

When he hears the sound of our bicycle tires against the dirt path, he looks up and smiles broadly.

"Loy'endo," Ekebe bids us. "I did not know whether to expect you."

"I have been busy," I say. "After you took the time to teach us Lonkundo for so many weeks, I went to the women of Bolenge to show them how to read and write it."

"Women reading and writing Lonkundo?" Ekebe Jacques asks, his eyebrows raised as if he isn't sure whether I'm serious.

"Yes," I tell him.

"Why this?" he wants to know.

"For the same reason anyone would want to be able to read and write. To make a letter to a relative, to look something up in a book."

Ekebe Jacques nods his head seriously and considers this.

"But they have no books, and I believe their relatives cannot read," he reasons.

I sigh as I sit down at the table. "Maybe the women will get some books once they learn how to read them."

"Maybe," Ekebe Jacques says, then chuckles to indicate he has dismissed the deliberation.

Richard takes his seat. Ekebe closes his eyes and draws a deep breath.

"It's a good day," he says. "Good for hunting. The sun's warm enough to put the animals at rest. When they're napping, or have just woken, they're good prey. And today the air's still. You see? It wouldn't carry a hunter's smell to the animal to warn it danger is nearby. I remember many days like this when I was a boy. I would carry my bow on the hunt. I couldn't wait until I was old enough to have a spear like my father."

"Were things better back then?" I ask.

"Better?"

"Before the missionaries came," Richard explains. "Better for the Nkundo."

Ekebe Jacques thinks about this. "It's a long time past. Why do you want to know this today?"

"We've just been wondering," Richard says. "I mean, living here in the village, you must have heard some of the talk that's going around."

"I hear talk about many things."

"I mean talk about how it would be better if the Europeans went away from Congo, about how it would be better if they'd never come," Richard says.

Ekebe Jacques nods slowly. His eyes are far away. "If it were not for white man's medicine, I would be dead now," he says very seriously. "Ten rains and twenty ago, I had bad fever, very bad. A powerful evil spirit wanted to take my body. The shaman gave me no more breath to draw. But the white man's medicine shots made the fever leave me, and it doesn't come back, and now I'm here to talk to you."

Ekebe Jacques looks down at the piece of wood he's been carving, then sets it aside.

"These young men who carry on," he says. "They talk of what they don't know. If you cut down a tree, there's no more fruit."

I shake my head, trying to grasp Ekebe's meaning. "What exactly does that—?"

"It is a proverb," he says. "The young men see that the white man has more wealth than Nkundo. They think that if the white man were to leave, all wealth would be theirs. But they don't know that the white man brings them many gifts they can't see. I remember when I was a boy, many babies died in the village. No one thought anything of it, for that was how it had always been. A wise woman knew not to grow too close to her child until it had passed its first year. For as often as not, the baby would die before the year was done. If she loved her babies too much, she would surely be in sadness all the days of her life. My mother—after me, there came fourteen more babies, and only four of them lived past two rains."

Ekebe Jacques's voice is slow and measured. I know better than to interrupt.

"Now things are different. White man's medicine saves all the babies except those born already sick or cursed with the missing of parts of their body. If the white man took his medicine away, surely many Nkundo babies would die. The young men who speak so hot, they don't think of this. They don't care to, I think. All they want is what is before their eyes."

"But were there *some* things that were better before the missionaries?" Richard persists.

Ekebe Jacques clucks and nods. "When the white man came, I was this tall," he says, stretching out a frail arm so that his downturned palm is about the height of my bicycle handlebars. "Bolenge was smaller, but there was much singing and the ceremonies were very . . ."

He gestures in the air with great animation.

"Like so, you see? After the harvest, there was the drinking of palm wine by all the men of *mpifo,* and everyone stayed awake through the night with much laughing. That's gone now. The minister tells us that Jesus doesn't want us to have worship of many gods with dancing and masks, so we must do it quietly or not at all. The minister says a man who disciplines his wives harshly or dances to the gods at harvest time will burn in a hot fire for all the rains that come. The minister makes the Nkundo so afraid that he feels as though his ankles are weighted by shoes of heavy clay. He could not dance, even if he wanted to. This is something not good about the white man's coming. A man who doesn't dance is a man who doesn't live."

We're all quiet for a moment.

"Thank you for explaining," Richard says at last.

A FAMILY OF NIGERIANS has come to stay with distant cousins in Bolenge in order to escape some predicament about which none of them wishes to be very specific. I had not paid them much mind until yesterday, when one of the old Nigerian men came by the school.

Though his arrival took me by surprise, I decided to set aside an hour's worth of instructions so that he might tell my students proverbs and stories from his part of the continent. None of my boys have ever traveled as far away as Nigeria, so to them, it seems virtually as foreign and exotic as the Americas. Today, I've written down several of the old man's stories and set my class to the task of making accompanying illustrations. When they've finished, I shall bind the results into a sort of picture book.

It is with no small amount of forethought that Richard has scheduled art class as my last subject at l'École Moyenne each afternoon. By one o'clock, the heat has risen and the sun has warmed the clay walls of the building, idling my students' minds. By one o'clock, they are full of lunch and drowsy. Thus it is beneficial to present them with subject matter that is as unchallenging to the intellect as possible.

I look around the classroom where the boys are intent on their drawings. I can't ever remember my American classmates being as enthusiastic about art class as the Congolese. I have observed that every culture has its predilections. Americans are fond of commerce, while the Congolese take great delight in finding colorful ways of expressing themselves. Though raised in the very heart of America's heartland, I myself am less inclined to the former than the latter.

All of a sudden, my attention is drawn to one of the desks in the back of the room. There, one of the younger boys has slouched in his chair, eyes closed. His head is tipped awkwardly to one side, and green paint has spilled all down the front of his shirt.

There's a commotion around him.

He doesn't move.

I dash to his side, catching his weight before he slides off the chair.

"Bokande," I say his name anxiously.

His eyes flutter, and his gaze slowly meets mine.

"Oui, Madame," he says weakly.

"Get him some water!" I say to the circle of boys who have surrounded us. Several dash out the door at the same time.

"Are you sick?" I ask Bokande.

"No, Madame," he says, straightening in his chair with what seems like a fair amount of embarrassment. "I am very sorry to have caused this trouble."

"What is the matter with you, then?"

"I am very hungry, Madame. I get dizzy."

"Have you not eaten?" I ask him.

"Not since four days, no," he admits.

"Why not?"

One of the boys approaches us with some water.

"Thank you," I say to one, taking the cup and setting it in front of Bokande.

He stares at the glass.

"Drink," I command him, and he takes a sip. Then he notices the paint spilled down the front of his shirt.

"Madame, I'm very sorry for causing a trouble in the class," he says again. "May I go to the dormitory to put on my other shirt?"

"Stay here," I tell him. "You're in no shape to be walking around by yourself in the hot sun. What you need is some food."

I walk to the front of the room and take a banana out of my bag. I had intended to eat it after class as I corrected assignments.

"Here," I say, returning to his side and starting to peel the fruit.

He takes it from me greedily and gulps it down without chewing.

"Why have you not eaten for four days?" I ask him once he has finished.

"My ration from the school, I have to sell it."

"Why?"

"I have need to buy a special thing."

"What sort of thing? I don't want to play a guessing game with you, Bokande. You can tell me now or I can send you to talk to le Directeur, and you can tell him about it. It's your choice."

"I needed to have money to send away in the mails for a fetish to help me have power with my mathematics studies," he says tearfully. "I sold my food rations to the other boys."

His explanation does not make sense.

"How did you order something in the mail?"

"I didn't send for it in my own name. Monsieur Boale has a catalog from Chicago in America with magical pencils and coins. We pay him the money, and he sends away for what we need."

I'm aghast. At the end of the breezeway, Richard rings the class bell. The boys stare at me warily.

"The rest of you, go on," I say. "We'll finish the pictures tomorrow."

The boys scramble noisily out of the room.

"As for you," I say turning back to Bokande, "Tell Nkutu I said for him to go with you. Put on that clean shirt, then march over to Nurse Matthews's place and fetch yourself some bread."

"But—"

"Go on, now. I'm going to get your money back from Monsieur Boale."

"Don't get me in trouble," Bokande begs.

"You're already in trouble," I tell him. "Now, skedaddle!"

Bokande gathers his books, holding them up in front of his paint-stained shirt as he approaches the door.

"But, Madame, I need the fetish," he whimpers.

"No, you don't. Now go get yourself something to eat. We'll talk about your mathematics work later."

Bokande nods his resignation and leaves.

I head immediately for M. Boale's classroom, which is at the far end of the school building. I suppose I ought to talk to Richard about the matter, but right now I'm too angry to defer to Monsieur le Directeur.

I find M. Boale alone in his room, sitting at his desk.

"Opportunist!" I snap from the doorway.

"Won't you come in?" he asks, officious in his cordiality.

"How dare you!" I say and hear in my own voice something akin to metal grinding against metal.

"How dare I invite you in?" M. Boale asks, raising his eyebrows.

"Monsieur Boale, how long have you been taking our boys' money to send off in the mail for little voodoo trinkets? Money they sell their school rations for—"

"Voodoo? What is this 'voodoo' you speak of?"

"Fetishes, whatever you call it," I say, annoyed to be interrupted. "I had a boy in my class pass out from hunger just now because you took his food money. You, always talking how you are a man of *mpifo*, you should be acting as a leader, not—"

"I did not take anything from him as you say," M. Boale says indignantly, rising and walking around his teachers table toward me. "I performed a service for him for a small fee. I should be thanked for this, but no. Instead you scold me like a child. Such a rude white woman you are!"

"I can't believe you," I say, almost shouting. "Do you have no conscience, no sense of what's right and wrong?"

"Not a white man's sense, no, and that's a good thing. You have a fine perception of yourself, all of you white men and women, come here to rape our people and our land of its wealth, then you accuse *me* of taking advantage—"

"You think Richard and I came here to steal the Nkundo's wealth?"

"It's so obvious, white woman," he says, shaking his head condescendingly. "Why else would you be here? There's no cleverness to you."

"And there's no wisdom to you. You're a greedy, ignorant man who doesn't deserve to call himself a teacher in a classroom of God."

"*Chienne!*" he sneers, cursing me.

"Oh, so now we fall to name-calling, do we?"

"Who asked you come here, white woman?" M. Boale seethes. "What Nkundo wrote you a letter saying, 'Please come across the ocean and be in charge of me. Please come take what is rightfully mine and claim it in the name of some King who I have never seen.' Eh? No one. So why don't you just pack up your boxes and go home. You're not wanted."

"Monsieur Boale," I say decisively, though my voice isn't steady. "Again and again, you've made it very clear that you don't like me, and we both know why that is."

"You think so highly of yourself," M. Boale says with a hostile laugh. "If you were my wife, I'd beat some sense into you right now, you insolent—"

I step forward to within striking distance.

"Go ahead," I challenge him. "Hit me."

In a flash, M. Boale raises his arm to take a swing. Then he simply stands and stares, his hand trembling in the air. The veins on his neck bulge. I brace myself. Very slowly, M. Boale lowers his hand to his side.

"Get out," he whispers disdainfully.

"Give me Bokande's money back," I demand quietly.

"Go on," he says.

"Give . . . me . . . the . . . money . . . back," I repeat.

There is a pause. Joseph Boale reaches into his pocket and pulls out several tarnished coins, dropping them onto the floor at his feet.

I stoop slowly and pick them up, looking him in the eye the whole time.

Seventeen

September 1958

FOR EVERY ACTION, there is an equal and opposite reaction. For every harsh word spoken, there shall come a repercussion. Since the hour of my schoolroom argument with M. Boale, he's avoided me, seemingly at all costs. I'm certain I haven't experienced the last of his enmity.

At present, my attention is focused on something else—my womanly cycle, which is now two and a half weeks late. After school, I pay a visit to Jean, so we may discuss the matter. For the last several days, I've been tired in the morning as I rise and prepare for my classes. My appetite has turned finicky but has not decreased. If anything, I'm hungrier than usual.

It doesn't take an especially thorough examination for Jean to come to a conclusion: "You're pregnant," she says, "and it's for real this time."

I stare at her.

The words are queer, like something in a foreign language. I look around Jean's little examining room and am suddenly short of breath.

"Eva? Did you hear me?"

"Yes, sorry," I say, then begin giggling. "I'm just a little stunned. Are you sure about this?"

"Sure as shooting. Congratulations."

I float back to the house, where Ta Pierre is just leaving for the day.

Richard sits at the table, starched white sleeves rolled up to his elbows. He's going over paperwork and requisitions for our upcoming trip to the backcountry.

Richard's had occasion to go out into the field three times already. Next week's expedition will be the first on which I accompany him.

"Hello," he mumbles as I enter the room, but doesn't look up from his notes.

"Hello," I say. I pass behind him, running my hand through his hair.

"Where were you?"

I take a seat opposite him, shuffling through the stack of government forms as if they held some bit of interest for me.

"Over at Jean's," I say demurely. I want to see how long it will take for him to discover the big news.

"That's nice. How is she?" he asks but is clearly concentrating on a column of rural teachers'-salary figures he is attempting to balance.

"She's ecstatic," I say, fiddling with a paper clip.

"That's nice," Richard says again. Then he pauses to look up at me. "Why is she ecstatic?"

"Because of our news."

"Oh, okay," he says, returning to his work.

After a moment, his brow furrows and he sets down his pencil. "What news?"

"The news about us having a baby," I say playfully, getting up and walking toward the kitchen.

"What!"

"You heard me," I tell him over my shoulder.

"You're not serious!" he says, following me over to the sink.

"Oh, I'm serious."

"You're serious."

I nod.

"You and me, we're having a baby," he says very deliberately.

"Congratulations, *Nkoko*." I grin.

Richard hoots and takes me in his arms, dancing me around the kitchen.

We eat our dinner quickly. Afterward, we are too keyed up to sit and do schoolwork, so we take a walk around the compound.

"How do you want to tell people about it?" Richard asks, shooing a mother goat and her kids off the path. She bleats her indignation.

"Let's wait until after we're back from the backcountry," I suggest.

We follow the curve in the path as it approaches the river. The world is blue-gray as the coming dusk casts its calm across the land. The air's still, perfectly still, and lazy trails of smoke climb straight toward the sky from the stoves in each of the missionaries' houses.

"You feeling all right, not too tired?" Richard asks, putting a hand to the small of my back.

"Oh, I'm fine, thank you," I tell him, then laugh. "There'll be plenty of time for all that later, I reckon."

As we make back to our house, darkness has fallen, and we have to mind the ruts and bumps in the path. This bit of business, the concentration on the surface below our feet, effects a silence between us.

I begin to think more about what it means to have a child inside of me. There's a new life of which God has given me guardianship. The life isn't my possession. Rather, it's at once my joy and my responsibility. There is a spark of something remarkable in me, arrived with the same weightless grace as a kiss, a murmur, a bit of cattail fluff alight on the wind. It's something universal that, like most of what is truly valuable, has begun small but is mind boggling in potential.

As I walk through the cawing and rustling of the jungle on what has become a possibly perfect evening, I feel the same effervescent limitlessness as when I first fell in love. I suppose that's what this is, really—falling in love. The only difference is that this time around, the object of my affections isn't just a person but a process, as well, and both object and action lie within me.

IT IS THE AFTERNOON OF MY FIRST TRIP into the equatorial backcountry.

I have just now finished reading *West with the Night*, a collection of journals by a young female aviator named Beryl Markham, who was raised on the plantations and game reserves of British East Africa.

Mrs. Markham begins her volume by noting there are as many different Africas as there are books about Africa. I have found this to be true. There's good reason—if one's willing to travel, there also are as many different Africas as there are days of one's journey. Every author who has put pen to paper to record impressions of this continent surely has seen a different facet of its daunting breadth than any other observer.

As distinct as New York City may be from Appalachia, or London from the pastoral English countryside, these contrasts are nothing compared to that which exists between bustling Léopoldville and a tiny backcountry African village such as the one we are approaching. The exaggeration of this disparity has to do, I suppose, with the historic difficulty European armies and mercenaries have encountered navigating the African interior. Penetrating this hostile land requires stoicism, determination, and a keen native guide, as the locations of river portages and seasonal swamps are unpredictable. The twentieth century, with its mechanization and obsession with immediacy, is far too impatient to consider most of the Dark Continent's interior worth its bother.

The land is left to its various contentious native tribes, who hunt and plant their crops year after year while scuffling with neighbors, taking slaves, celebrating the harvest, waiting out the rains, falling ill, getting well, giving birth, drinking, aging, dying.

Into this age-old cycle I come, lurching along in a noisy, bright-yellow panel van with Richard, Neil Roberts, and Nsimba, our tall, lean Nkundo guide. We travel through moor and boggy marshland, where the road is reduced to thirty-foot logs, split and laid end to end in pairs. For fifteen days we will inspect backcountry schools, pay teachers, and baptize converts.

We must be either very wise or very foolish to make this our vocation. There's no electricity here in the backcountry, no newspapers, no mail delivery, no radio transmissions, no gasoline, no ice, no cows milk, no leavened bread, and apart from a few far-flung rural dispensaries, no one to give out tonics and set broken bones. Almost without exception, the only white people who make it into these parts are the missionaries, like us, who come through for their inspections several times a year.

The farther we travel from Coquilhatville, the more I become aware how entirely dependent we are upon the supplies loaded in our van. While natives can live off the land, a white man would be dead within days were he to try a trip such as this without adequate preparation. I find this vulnerability thrilling, bracing, and full of the brand of young romance that lures sailors to sea and soldiers to battle.

It's late in the afternoon when we find our first destination. The place where we'll stay isn't so much a village as it is a widening in the road that runs beside the Ruki River. We are sweaty and out of sorts, yet we are received as celebrities, something between demigods and a sideshow attraction. It's the same phenomenon I encountered at Thysville during my illness, but there the natives' enthusiasm was subdued by the relative uneventfulness of a white man's appearance.

In the backcountry, our arrival is almost a holiday. When we pull in and Neil Roberts sets the van's hand brake, barely clothed families appear in their doorways, anxious, wary, faces stern. We get out of the van and look around. I take off my sunglasses and scarf.

There are about ten houses, most of them of crude construction and without windows. It's hard to tell where one family's property ends and the next begins. They don't have yards to contain animals, like in Bolenge. One by one, children break from their parents and gather cautiously around us, reaching to touch our skin.

"They want to see if some of our white magic might rub off on them," Neil explains. He walks around to the back of the van to unload our kerosene lanterns and mosquito netting.

"Aha," I say uncomfortably as a naked little boy tugs at my skirt. He looks up at me and babbles a Mongo dialect so different from the Lonkundo spoken around Bolenge that I can only understand two of his words—"I" and "mother."

Neil pauses to run his fingers through his thinning hair. The natives watch him intently, studying his every movement. Once Neil's back is turned, they gesture to one another and mimic his actions without a trace of self-consciousness. They watch me, too, and I watch them. It's a little game. Everyone is fascinated.

"*Bienvenues,*" the village's native teacher calls to us, appearing in the doorway of the school building, which doubles as his home. He waves enthusiastically, summoning us in. The grinning Nkundo is giving up his single bed for the night so that we may have a place to sleep.

"*Merci,*" Neil says with a nod, following the teacher toward the dilapidated building.

It's decided that Richard and I will sleep on the bed. Neil and Nsimba will sleep on the mats normally occupied by young students too far from their own villages to make the journey home each night. I look around. There's no bathroom.

I prepare our evening meal, heating canned horsemeat and making biscuits in the pressure-cooker kettle we have brought along. We invite the native teacher and our guide to join us in front of the little school. By the time the biscuits are cooked over the open fire, it's very dark.

We eat by the light of two kerosene lanterns. This dual illumination is an act of minor self-indulgence, for we have a limited supply of fuel with us and it must be carefully rationed. It's not until I taste the food that I realize how hungry the day has left me.

"I must announce," the native teacher says, putting two biscuits in his mouth at once, "Madame is a fine cook."

At the edge of the pool of golden light that spills from the lanterns, a circle of spectators lurk. It's mostly children who watch us, silent and curious. In the dark, all I can see is their wide eyes.

"Thank you for giving us your room," Richard tells the teacher.

This is met with a nod of acknowledgment as the teacher reaches for more biscuits. Nsimba seems less enthusiastic about my cooking. He's obtained some sour-manioc mash from one of the local households and eats it, silently, beside me. When we have finished our meal, I wash Neil Roberts's tin plates in the river. Richard puts out one of the lanterns, and the African night swallows up more of the little schoolyard. This far from civilization, the darkness has a personality all its own. Back in our home on the Bolenge mission, we are close enough to Coquilhatville that no wild monkeys or lions dare come to call. Here, so many kilometers from any threat other than a cunning hunter's spear, all God's creatures do as they will.

Tonight, their will is to do a great deal. I hear them in the brush behind us and wonder whether I should fear for my safety. It's comforting for me to smell greasy smoke and see the orange glow from the cooking fires in the native houses that ring the clearing in the path. These bits of sensory familiarity afford the night boundary and substance.

All the children have gone now, called back to their houses, to bed. While Neil and Nsimba busy themselves with preparations for tomorrow-morning's baptisms, Richard and I put out chairs and talk with the native teacher about serious matters.

"How much schooling have you had?" Richard asks the teacher.

"Four years à l'école à Mondombe" is the proud reply. "I have learned both how to worship Jesus and how to spell his name."

"And you're good with reading and writing?" I ask.

"Very good," the teacher assures us with a nod, switching from French to Lonkundo, as though we, too, were being examined and this were a language class.

It's understandable that he would wish to size us up. The Nkundo take great care in studying their opponents' strengths and weaknesses before directly engaging them. An observer to our present conversation might conclude that the teacher perceives Richard and me as foes. But I know that isn't so. The teacher understands that we are merely messengers, instruments of a process. The real foe is tomorrow-afternoon's school inspection. He must demonstrate that his students are well on their way to achieving literacy. Only then can Richard justify paying the man his three-hundred franc salary.

As we sit and talk, I think about what three hundred francs would buy. A good pair of patent-leather shoes? Perhaps. One night on the town? A few hardcover books?

I look at the gray-hair teacher.

He is a lonely sentinel of a mission he may barely understand, in a village far from those to whom he must answer.

He must be a man of great faith.

I think about him gobbling biscuits at dinner. I suppose there are times when it's a wise man who takes what he can get when opportunity presents itself.

"Do you like your job?" I ask, then realize I have interrupted what Richard was saying.

There's a silence. Richard and the teacher turn to me.

"My job is a good job," the teacher says thoughtfully. "I don't have the luxury of liking it or not. Days, they have changed since the white man comes."

"Yes?"

"Yes," the teacher says, nodding gravely. "You make it so we're all the same. One African is another African in your eyes, as though none were smarter or had better ancestors. But before, everyone had their rightful place. There was some fighting, but my people, who are much better than the simple fishermen who live on the Busira—"

"What do you mean . . . better?"

The teacher shrugs. "There is no simpler way to say it. We know we're superior to them, and they know they're inferior to us. It's a fact. It's obvious."

I glance over at Richard. "And if the Congolese people—" I ask, "all of you—if there were a revolution or you got independence from the white government—"

"Then things would go back as they should be. My kin would be boss again over the weak tribes, and we would have the riches we deserve."

A child cries out from one of the houses that neighbor the school, and the teacher makes a sour face.

"My daughter has gotten into some kind of trouble, I fear. Excuse me," he says, getting up to go. *"Locikalo-o."*

Then he nods to each of us courteously and exits into darkness.

WE STAND WAIST DEEP IN WARM WATER. There are three dozen of us, Christians bedecked in flowing finery on a fine sunny Sunday morning, soaking wet, performing Christian rites. Richard takes snapshots to send Stateside.

Neil Roberts questions each of the African supplicants about the teachings of Christ. The converts have come from miles in every direction, walking in their best robes since before sunrise. This is a big day in their lives—the new Christians are turning from their old ways, leaving the past buried in the water, so that they may rise and walk in the newness of a life in the Lord's service.

"How many disciples did Jesus have?" Neil asks one of the comers.

"Twelve, Monsieur," the man answers.

"Who was His father?" Neil asks another.

"God in Heaven, Monsieur," the second man replies.

"And His mother?"

"Mary is her name," says the next in line.

I think about Jesus' message. He did not say, "Don't go around naked," nor did he warn, "Don't eat humans, not even enemies." There was nothing in his teaching that could be translated as "Don't commit adultery, even if you can pay the fine," or "Get to work on time, and saw your boards straight every day."

What, then, did he preach?

"Love one another. Be kind to one another. Give to those who ask of you—give them the shirt off your back. Tomorrow will take care of itself."

As Neil finishes his quizzing, I wonder if it's truly he, and not his Nkundo supplicants, who should be asking the questions about the teachings of Christ.

"Bokonji, kel'onkemy'emi. The Lord strengthens me," they sing.

As the verse comes to its end, several Africans break into a sort of harmony. It's endearing, although I suspect it to be no more than a happy accident. There are broad smiles all around. One by one, vows are taken and heads are dunked beneath the surface of the brown water. I feel, in my chest, a swell of affirming correctness to all that is taking place before me. Yes, this is why I am here. I had forgotten. I must not let the distractions sway me.

In the end, it's a very successful morning. Neil deems all but two comers to have accrued enough knowledge of Christ in their humble backcountry in-gatherings to make an informed decision in this most important matter.

Once we've finished with the baptisms, we return to the little village and change into dry clothes, laying the wet ones out in the midday sun.

Though it's Sunday, the children are assembled in the schoolhouse. It's a special session of class, arranged for the purpose of our inspection.

The native teacher wears long trousers and a white shirt. One of the pant legs bears the stamp of the manufacturer. Inside a circle, the word "irregular" is stitched in thread.

Richard and I watch the teacher put his wide-eye youngsters through their paces. I'm pleased to observe that in schools as rural as this, boys and girls are taught in the same classroom, with no preference given to one or the other. The children sit bolt upright on rough-hewn benches. They know they are being tested and presumably have been well coached.

I think of my own appraisals by the Belgian inspector. It is nerve-racking business. So much hangs in the balance.

Some of the young faces in the room are already familiar to me. I saw them around us last night as we ate dinner and again this morning as I stooped to brush my teeth at the river's edge. I suppose they must have wondered what on earth a dramatically pale woman was doing, pulling a stick of wood with bristles back and forth across the front of her mouth. They stood and watched, bare bellied, acting terribly excited to be near me.

Now Richard hands one of the little girls a classroom book he's picked up.

"Read for me," he says gently, kneeling at her side.

The girl looks frightened. She turns to the native teacher, who nods. Then the girl looks at Richard. "Yes, sir," she says softly in Lonkundo, opening the book to begin.

I watch as she stumbles along, giving some words extreme emphasis and faltering on others. She is six or seven years old, no more. Her dress is a drab and worn blue, and the fabric has been washed on rocks so many times that it's thin as cheesecloth.

"Thank you," Richard tells her once she's finished a few pages.

She nods sharply and hands the book back to him. Then comes a nervous little smile that breaks my heart. I know the girl's stumbles and hesitation have not diminished Richard's appraisal. To the contrary, they make it clear that she was truly reading the words on the page, not just reciting language she's learned by rote. Richard told me this distinction becomes an important one when inspecting schools that might own only half a dozen books.

We continue our drills, asking the children questions in mathematics and geography. We don't expect great scholarship, nor do we find it. But the native teacher is clearly doing his job to impart to the next generation what little formal education he himself has received.

Once an hour of observation has come and gone, Richard takes the teacher aside, and I help the children paint their blackboard. We have but one can of black paint for all the classrooms Richard and I will visit, so I must be sure none is wasted. Once the board has its fresh coat, I take the children with me to the van so I may retrieve their quarterly allotment of chalk and the prize they have been eagerly anticipating—a new soccer ball. We purchased twelve in Coquilhatville as we passed through, one for each school on our junket. Neil Roberts suggested we supply the teachers with the balls, as their lure would draw more students to the backcountry classrooms.

I'm glad to lighten our load, even if it's only by a little, for the next leg of our trip won't take place in the van. It's time to transfer all our gear into log canoes and leave our last link to civilization parked at the shore. The river will take us where roads can't. We've hired two boats from the villagers.

I soon find out how wisely designed these craft truly are. Their long, slender hulls slice through the water of the winding channel, making light work of our paddling.

Neil and Nsimba man the lead boat, piled high with supplies that will sustain us for the days of our expedition: bicycles and lanterns, mosquito netting, and canned food. Richard and I follow in the second boat, equally burdened. We must take care to avoid the sandbars and debris that litters the murky wash.

For a time, all goes well. We glide forward, singing rowing songs, and the jungle answers, birds and monkeys cackling their comments as we pass. At one point, we see a snake swimming alongside us. I shiver at the way it weaves through the water.

"*Njwá!*" Nsimba calls out a warning from his position in the bow, and we all raise our paddles until the reptile has passed.

The trip takes the better part of the afternoon, and I'm glad when Nsimba announces we are nearing our destination. Richard and I relax in our rowing and fall a boat's length behind. Though we have been instructed to follow closely, the current distance between our boat and Nsimba's does not seem to present any cause for concern.

I am enjoying the afternoon, feeling the warmth of the sun against my back, watching the passing fauna, thinking of how I shall someday tell the child inside me about its first trip on an African river. This pleasant abstraction is interrupted by a sudden shimmy in the boat's bearing. At the same moment, I hear the sound of splintering wood. I turn around to look at Richard, who has a most peculiar expression.

He lifts his paddle from the water. The bottom half is missing. It looks as though it has been snapped in two.

"What happened?" I ask.

"Something got a hold of it," Richard says anxiously.

We begin drifting sideways, rotating in the current. I turn and look toward Nsimba and Neil's boat. They are now several lengths beyond us and have not noticed our predicament. I call out to them, but in the rush of water they can't hear me.

"What do we do?" I ask Richard.

Nsimba and Neil disappear around a bend in the river.

There is a disturbance in the water to the left of the boat.

"Eva!" Richard whispers sharply, pointing.

Two animal ears have appeared at the surface of the water, large pinkish-brown things. In short order, they're joined by a pair of bulbous nostrils, then eyes, and finally the rest an adult hippopotamus head. I remember as a child, thinking that hippopotami were clumsy, cuddly creatures that could bring about no great harm. Now, confronted with the reality of the behemoth before me, I adjust my assessment.

The hippo opens his mouth. The cavity is immense. Then he lets out a deafening roar. Surely, I think, Nsimba and Neil will have heard this bellowing and return to rescue us. Yet as I crane my neck to see around the river bend, no boat appears.

Our hollowed-out log twists perpendicular to our original course. We're drifting slowly toward the hippopotamus. I am terrified.

"Should I paddle?" I whisper to Richard.

"I don't know," he answers, his posture frozen. "That might make him mad."

The hippo's brown back emerges from the murky water. It resembles a well-waxed Volkswagen in both size and texture.

"Oh, gracious," Richard says to himself.

Then, with another rippling on the opposite side of the boat, a second hippopotamus begins to make its appearance. Meanwhile, the current has drawn us to within ten feet of the first beast.

"I . . . I think I should row now," I say uneasily.

"Go!" Richard agrees, suddenly animated.

I plunge my paddle into the water and pull for all I'm worth.

"Switch sides back and forth!" Richard commands me.

I run the boat with the kind of fury only a woman can summon, propelled by the knowledge that I may not be saving just my own life but my baby's as well.

"Faster!" Richard calls. "He's coming toward us."

I hear the hippo roar again but can't turn around to look. We come upon the bend in the river. My arms and shoulders are aching. I have no breath to spare. I work the paddle hard.

At last I see Nsimba and Neil, who have been warned of our distress by the hippo's latest roar. The horror that registers on their faces is by no means comforting.

"My oar's busted," Richard shouts at them.

"Steady, then," Neil calls back and begins paddling toward us. "Mind the sandbar."

When they have drawn to within two boat lengths of us, Nsimba stands, balancing his weight gingerly, and throws his paddle like a spear. It arcs over the surface of the water and seems to hang there for moment, finally landing with a clatter in the middle of our boat. Richard grabs it. We row ferociously. With both of us pulling, we quickly put distance between the rampaging hippopotami and ourselves.

Neil pulls their boat up alongside ours. We look at one another, but no one speaks.

In another quarter hour, both boats are safely on shore beside the village where we will spend the night. I stumble out of the craft and collapse in the thick grass that lines the bank. I'm drenched in sweat.

"What is wrong with the white woman?" asks the native pastor who has come to meet us.

"She is *bompele,* with child. Also, she has just defeated a large hippopotamus," Nsimba says matter-of-factly.

"Oh-oh-oh" is all the pastor can muster as a reply.

WORD OF OUR ARRIVAL TRAVELS RAPIDLY through the village, and the natives soon come out to meet us, many bedecked in elaborate attire. There are women who wear a string around their midsection with a little bustle in back and several men of mpifo with regal skins and ornaments.

From where I sit, in the late-afternoon shade of the pastor's front yard, I can see an Nkundo man walking the path through the village. He is accompanied by several women and children, all of them carrying spears and heavy bracelets.

"What's that all about?" I ask the pastor, pointing.

"That man, he is taking his family to another village tonight to buy a new wife. He must have gifts to use for the bargaining."

After the entourage passes, I notice the local witch doctor walking across the square with the labored gait of a tortoise. The man is probably fifty years old, but his hollow cheeks and stooped posture make him look a hundred and fifty. He wears a loincloth, a monkey-skin cap, and a necklace of leopard teeth.

"*Nkokonyango-o,*" the pastor calls amiably to the witch doctor. "Will you come to the prayer meeting tonight? The white Jesus-man has traveled many miles to honor us this day."

The old man continues his slow, deliberate amble. As he passes, he raises his hand in a way that leaves me unsure whether he has dismissed us or agreed to attend.

Richard walks up with his Argus in hand.

The witch doctor turns to assess him and notices the camera.

In short order, the old man is animated, shaking his rattle and dancing as Richard snaps pictures. As soon as the roll of film is used up, however, his diffidence returns.

After dinner, we go to church service. Richard, Neil, and I sit on split logs in the front row. Behind and beside us, two dozen natives have come to worship. The pastor has great plans for the spiritual conversion of his village but at present is without much of a church from which to deliver his message. The building's but a rickety frame with palm fronds spread across the top. I fear for the arrival of any good gust of wind.

Just as the sermon's about to begin, the witch doctor enters the sanctuary, bedecked in colorful splendor. He takes a seat across the aisle from us.

I turn and greet him with a smile and a nod, but he's stone-faced.

For some reason, the young pastor feels it necessary to deliver an exhortation on the subject of idolatry. "Take a look at this," he says, stepping down from the pulpit and standing directly in front of the witch doctor. The pastor reaches out and tugs at the long feathers sticking out of the witch doctor's ceremonial cap.

"Do you see this?" the pastor asks the assembled. "They're chicken feathers. Where do they come from? An ordinary chicken, the kind you eat. Now, I ask you, is there anything particularly godly about a chicken?"

"*O nye,*" a few members of the congregation say, shaking their heads.

I look over at the witch doctor. He wears the same expression as when he came into the service.

"A chicken is just a chicken," the pastor says. "But you take a few of their feathers and you make this your god. You shouldn't put your faith in something so ridiculous as feathers!"

He goes on for some time in this vein. I suspect he's showing off for us. I wish he wouldn't. A Christian worship service should be about righteousness, not showmanship and derision.

But then the young pastor makes a valuable observation:

"The gods you worship, you must understand that they're a different sort of god than the God in heaven we talk about in church. The African gods are things you must pay off in order to keep them from harming you or your family. You make offerings to them: meat or fire or dances. Their job is to punish you if your offerings aren't good enough. The Christian God is very different. He doesn't punish people who believe in Him. He loves all those who believe in Him as a father loves his sons and daughters. Sometimes He isn't happy to see what they've done, but He doesn't strike them down with accidents or terrible fevers. If you think of the Christian God like you think of the Nkundo gods, you will never fully come to know Him."

One or two members of the congregation nod gently, but most of them stare straight ahead, blank expressions on their faces.

When the sermon is done, we sing a hymn. Then it is time to go. The witch doctor shuffles off without a word.

The pastor sits down, sighing, beside the pulpit. "They haven't understood," he says sadly, shaking his head.

DAYS PASS. Our load lightens. African boys love soccer balls. Everyone loves Jesus. We leave some of our gear behind and approach the village of Longa on bicycles. This is the farthest we will be from Bolenge and Coquilhatville. I've given up trying to keep my arms and legs protected from the sun, forgoing any attempt at fashion in favor of a sleeveless cotton dress. Quickly, I turn brown. Who would have thought I would so enjoy the sun?

On the eighth afternoon of our journey, we roll along beneath the high canopy of trees, singing folk songs and laughing. Neil tells us a long and bawdy joke about a Christian, a Jew, and a Hindu who were shipwrecked on a deserted island. There are few travelers on this path, so when we see two figures approaching from a hundred yards ahead of us, we stop to talk with them.

As they get closer, we see they're a couple of Batswa natives. They come toward us, waving and carrying the carcass of a large snake.

"*Ay, bosingalétteurs de Yésu,*" they call out, "it's good you meet us. We've killed this snake in the swamp beyond the clearing ahead. Now it won't trouble you."

Richard and Neil thank the travelers enthusiastically, but I'm not able to say anything; I'm busy trying to keep from laughing after being greeted as a "bicyclist of Jesus."

On we go. The afternoon isn't anxious to give way to dusk today. I can't blame the fat egg-yolk sun for resting on the horizon, reticent to drop below. It's been a glorious passage across the savanna, both for the sun and for our little party. We arrive in Longa just as day becomes twilight, greeted by natives who have been told of our coming by the lokolé.

Longa is a large village, nearly as big as Bolenge. Were it not so well hidden in the backcountry, it might have developed a like measure of sophistication. Yet Longa remains utterly provincial. The evidence of this is all around, from the blacksmith forging arrowheads in the middle of the central path to the goat kids that wander unchecked, bleating and pulling at tufts of grass wherever they may.

Richard and I hurry to the school, so we may have a look at it before darkness is total. It's the largest building in the village, with three small classrooms so that different subjects may be taught at the same time. We find only the head teacher. He's fiddling with the end of his necktie, waiting anxiously for us.

"I'm so sorry it's just me here," he says, jumping up and ushering us into the building before we even can greet him. "My colleague's baby has taken ill. He is gone to the medical dispensary on the other side of the big swamp. He hears the announcement of your coming and thinks you might be traveling with a nurse or doctor, so it's very excited that he grows. But the lokolé this afternoon, it says you are only teachers and one minister. So he packs the baby up and goes away. Please don't let it make your judgment of our school harsh!"

"Of course not," Richard says. "What was wrong with the baby?"

"*Lokosu ja jitsoka*, the whooping cough you call it," the teacher says, shifting his weight from one foot to the other.

"How old is the baby?" I ask.

"Only two months now," the teacher says, "and very, very sick."

Richard and I steal a look at each other. It will be a miracle if the child survives the illness at such a tender age.

The teacher walks us through the school. I smile at the children's artwork he has hung from the walls. It reminds me of my own classroom.

"Where do you get the paper for this?" I ask, pointing to one of the pictures.

"The India trader comes in between each rainy season. They bring many things for sale. I have paper and ink and sometimes the Lux toilet soap."

"And you pay for it . . . ?"

"From my own salary, Madame," the teacher assures us, nodding. "I want to have the best school in the region for you to see. I'm so sorry that my other teacher has this sickness in the family."

"It's okay," Richard assures him.

The sky has gotten dark, and it's not easy for us to see our way to the government-built guesthouse on the other end of town. There, we find beds. According to Richard's agenda, there was supposed to have been a native cook to prepare dinner for us. But as no such assistance shows itself, I break out the one pan I have brought along in my knapsack.

238

In the morning, we put on our good clothes and go to the village church for worship service. This sanctuary is much sturdier than the ones we've seen so far on our trip. It has a raised floor and a traditional cross erected at the front. At the door we're met by the head teacher.

"The baby, it dies," he says quietly.

"And the parents?" I ask.

The teacher points hesitantly into the sanctuary. In the middle of the front row sit a young man and woman, still and straight-postured, both dressed in white. I look at them from behind. There is a terrible stillness to them. In a heartbeat, I come to understand how it's possible to know someone is grieving without so much as a glimpse of his face.

The service is simple, the Nkundo pastor making no mention of last night's loss. I'm surprised at this, hurt almost. Does the sadness not merit any acknowledgment? As we leave the church, the head teacher introduces us to the bereaved parents.

"I . . . I'm so sorry," I say. "It's so . . . I'm expecting a baby too, and I . . . I don't know how you can be here this morning—"

"I have told my wife that we're teachers," the young man says, mercifully interrupting. "We must bathe and come to church. I iron my clean shirt, you see? We must be an example."

I look at the young woman. "How old are you?" I ask.

"I am fifteen, Madame," she tells me. Her voice is sweet and sad. I find it impossible to match her gentle composure in the face of tragedy. I hold back tears by swallowing hard.

"Don't worry, Madame," the young mother says, taking my hand. "It isn't a sadness greater than any other. Jesus has taken two babies from me already. I know how to make this peace."

As she lets go of my hand, my fingers move instinctively to my own belly. I watch the young teacher and his wife slowly walk away, and I can't respond to anything Richard's asking me. Suddenly, all I want is to be back in some semblance of civilization with antibiotics and stethoscopes and my baby safe inside me.

Eighteen

October 1958

WE RETURN TO THE HOUSE AT BOLENGE.

It's late on Friday afternoon when Neil drops us off. I can think of nothing but taking off my wrinkled, soiled clothes and falling into bed.

I'm first to reach the porch. My pace slows as I sense that something in the house is amiss. I ease the pack off my shoulder and set it down. The front door stands slightly ajar. This is most peculiar, as Ta Pierre hasn't been here in almost two weeks.

"What is it?" Richard asks, coming up behind me.

"We've had visitors," I say, pointing to the crack between the door and the frame.

We exchange uneasy looks. Richard opens the door cautiously. On the floor a trail of burnt matches proceeds toward the kitchen.

"What in heaven's name . . . ?" Richard says.

I discover the cupboards lie bare, doors open on their hinges. All my spices and canned goods are gone. So, too, are our drinking glasses and most of our silverware. This can't be true.

Richard picks up the matches one by one. Apparently, whoever broke in came at night and didn't have a flashlight. If the burglars had chosen another occasion for their looting, we might have been there, lying in our bed.

"How could they?" I ask no one in particular and sink into an available chair. I slowly look around the room, imagining how the kitchen cabinets will look once they're fitted with padlocks.

DAYS BECOME WEEKS. My blessing grows. Mornings bring a challenge to my constitution, but the soda crackers Richard carried home from Coquilhatville help quell my distress. I'm almost three months along now. My pregnancy has begun to show even in loose clothes. I grow clumsy. Once-simple tasks are becoming difficult. The air's muggy and hot as we wait for the rains, and I don't move about any more than I must. Everyone at the mission is excited for me. Even M. Boale congratulates us.

"Now you can earn your title of *Nkoko*," he tells Richard.

I think that more than anything, the other missionaries are amazed that I can be pregnant after all my body has endured. They have no idea how stubborn I really am.

The one person who's been standoffish since my announcement is Margaret, so I'm surprised when she comes by our house after church on Sunday afternoon. When she arrives, I'm stooped on the back step, washing communion cups. As deaconess of a church whose membership has grown to almost a thousand, my Sunday-afternoon duties are considerable.

"I've got to talk to you," Margaret says as bluntly as if we were already in the middle of a conversation.

I stand and stretch, wiping the sweat from my brow. "Talk," I say.

"Down by the river, if you don't mind."

Margaret fidgets. Something's wrong.

"Okay," I say as I dry my hands on my apron.

We walk. I study her face. Her expression is drawn. She looks older than usual. Her hair is pulled back. Her trademark lipstick is absent.

We reach the river. She's quiet for a spell.

"You reckon it's going to rain?" I ask, looking up at the overcast sky.

"Soon enough, I suppose," she says.

The water is low and the banks parched as they wait for moisture. The trees' roots, normally covered by the gurgling wash, lie bare in cracked mud like the outstretched arms of a panhandler begging for a drink.

Margaret sits down on a rock. "So, little Eva Dunagan's going to have a baby," she says with a sigh. "Saint Eva. Dear, sweet Eva."

"Quit it, Margaret," I say. "Don't be awful."

"No, no, you've earned it," she insists, managing to sound sincere and bitter at the same time. "Everyone looks up to you, and rightfully so. You're so good. Such a model missionary. I only wish I could be as virtuous as you—"

"Now you're being ridiculous. I really hope you're joking. I mean, look at yourself, Margaret. You've given over your life to the church. You could've had a husband and a car and a nice big house back in New Hampshire, and instead you're doing the Lord's work out here, where you need a mosquito net around you at night to keep from catching some disease. That's not virtuous?"

She rolls her eyes. "You make everything sound so simple and right."

"Nothing's ever simple or right for more than an hour or a day, maybe. But you've got to find the rightness in the world around you, or there's no point."

"Eva . . ."

"Yes?"

Margaret looks around uncomfortably.

"I have to tell you something. I've been keeping a very bad secret."

"Okay." There's a long pause.

"You're not the only one who's going to have a baby," she says quietly.

Oh, dear Lord. "Wh . . . who did you . . . I mean, who's the . . ."

"I told you it's bad, Eva," Margaret says.

It must be dreadful, for she seems unable to look at me. "Well?"

Another long moment passes before she speaks again. "It's one of the boys from the school," she finally says, shaking her head. "Mboto Antoine."

"Margaret!"

"I don't know how it happened," she says, her eyes brimming with tears. "Loneliness is a damning thing. It just . . . I didn't think. It's as simple as that. I'm stupid. I'm so stupid, Eva. I try so hard to uphold some sort of standard, you know? Like, when I was growing up. My family lived in the same little town for two hundred years. Everyone expected us to have a certain kind of life. I just couldn't fit into that mold, all about being proper and such. It would've driven me mad. So I came here on short-term assignment.

"It was a lonely decision," she says ruefully, wiping away tears with the back of her hand. "My father cut me out of the will—thought I'd lost my mind going off to Africa. Then I got here, and from the very first I knew I didn't fit in any more than back home.

See, I was raised to be an aristocrat. It's hard to just put all of that aside. The other missionaries saw it right away. My short stay turned into ten years, and the only real friendships I've made have been for the purpose of doing business, like with you, getting the houseboy and sending you to Ekebe Jacques. That's the only time I feel like I have a purpose. Can you understand?"

"I . . ." I struggle.

"I have nothing to hold onto, Eva. When I became a missionary, my family wrote me off. When my mother died, I heard about it in a letter from the executor of her will. From the time I got here, my compassionate colleagues have treated me like a black sheep. And now, with an illegitimate . . . oh, Eva. What's the Missions board going to say? The Church is the one thing I have in this life, if you can believe that. The moment they hear about this, they'll cut me loose."

"What about the boy?" I ask.

"I don't know. I haven't told him yet," Margaret says, her voice faltering.

"Jean?"

"I haven't told anyone, Eva! I've been walking around in a daze ever since I realized what was going on."

"Oh, Margaret," I say, reaching in her direction. She stiffens, turning away. Neither of us speaks for a little while.

"I guess I need Saint Eva's help," Margaret says at last, looking out at the river.

"I'll do what I can."

"I need to go away," she says quietly. "This has to stay a secret."

"You don't mean—"

"No, no. I mean I need to have my baby. I thought about getting rid of it, but I . . . this might be my only time around the block, as they say. I'm going to be forty-two, Eva. Do you know what that means? It's no lovely thing, I assure you. It means a great deal of longing right here." Margaret's hands become clenched fists that she presses tight against the center of her chest. She leans forward and closes her eyes.

Awkwardly, I reach out and lay my hand on her shoulder. This time, Margaret doesn't resist the comfort I offer. I hold her while she lets out all the heartbreaking torment she can, wailing and shaking.

Once her throes have stilled to mere hiccups, we sit cross-legged in the pale late-afternoon light, working out the plans for her deception:

She'll write a letter to the Missions board, telling of a family emergency but sparing excessive detail. She will request immediate travel leave at her own expense. But she won't go to America. Instead, she'll take an airplane to Cairo, where some hotels and clinics are prepared for such an eventuality as hers. Once the child is born, Margaret will leave it in a Catholic orphanage, return to Bolenge, and no one will be the wiser.

Margaret's lodging and medical care will take a heap of money, particularly as she becomes great with child, but I think that if Richard and I pool our savings with hers, there will be enough to cover it. Margaret will pay us back someday, if she's able. She doesn't ask me for this charity directly, nor do I, in so many words, offer it. Words aren't necessary. We both understand what must be done.

If it had been suggested to me, a week or a year ago, that I might engage in so ungodly a scheme as this, I would've scoffed at the idea. I realize now that I've learned an important lesson this afternoon—sometimes the path that is ultimately most beneficial isn't the most honest.

THE RAIN ARRIVES IN THE MIDDLE OF THE NIGHT, rolling in across the wide river while all the missionaries and villagers slumber, their heads full of sweet dreams of Jesus and wealth and billy goats and pots of palm wine.

Richard and I are awake to hear the raindrops begin their gentle tapping upon the roof overhead. I suspect there actually isn't one but two bedrooms in the mission bathed in golden lamplight this early morning. Like us, Margaret's surely sitting up, dressed in clothes meant for sleeping but unused for this purpose, listening to the rain, trying to make sense of a great predicament.

"You told her we'd pay for it?" Richard asks, a little incredulous. "That's the part I can't understand—"

"And the reason why you can't is simple," I tell him.

"Eva—"

"No, listen to me. You're a man. You're used to having options that we'll never have as long as we live. It's a lamentable thing, but that's just how it is. If you had a womb, Richard, my dear, if you knew what it was like to have a baby inside of you, you'd be falling all over yourself to help her."

Richard stews.

"I'm willing to entertain that possibility," he finally concedes. "But barely."

Thus, Richard joins my pact to sponsor Margaret's misbegotten pregnancy. Tomorrow after school, he'll clean out the cashbox we keep hidden in a gap in the wall and send a messenger to Coquilhatville to buy Margaret an airplane ticket to Cairo.

"Good night," I tell Richard. "Sleep well, my love."

"Not likely," he grumbles.

There's a flash of light outside and, after a moment, the slow, foundation-shaking rumble of jungle thunder. Mother Nature isn't a humorless woman.

LIFE GOES ON. The rains continue, never tiring of their task.

After school on Monday, I walk home to find Liyanza waiting on my front porch.

"Bonjour," I greet him.

"*Mama Boenga* is going to have a baby," he announces, as if I might need reminding. I don't. Drenched as I am, I feel like a sea mammal.

"Yes, I am," I say, shifting the weight of my backpack.

Liyanza follows me inside.

He and Ta Pierre greet each other as I go about the ungraceful business of sitting down on the sofa. It's not that I'm terribly large yet, but the balance of my weight has changed, and I find simple tasks suddenly awkward.

Liyanza stands at a distance and points at my stomach. "I can see it," he says seriously. "Baby in you."

"You can touch it, too, if you'd like. Come here," I tell him.

He advances hesitantly, holding out his hand and placing it on my stomach. "Can I listen? Maybe the baby have something to tell me?"

I laugh. Liyanza gingerly lays his ear against my stomach.

"What do you hear?"

His eyes are wide. "Strange sound, like water and stepping on a floor that squeaks."

"I suspect that what you're hearing is my lunch."

"Hmm." He's fascinated.

"Madame, I have a question for you," he says, sitting up once he's finished the examination.

"Go ahead."

"Don't laugh at me for asking."

"Of course not," I assure him.

"Could you tell me—I don't know about how it comes to be like this."

"Comes to be like what?"

"A baby. How does it . . . ?"

"It's very simple, really."

I consider how to explain the facts of life to a pubescent Nkundo. Despite his request, I feel inclined to laugh anyhow, not at his ignorance but in delight at his gentle curiosity.

"So, how does it happen, then?" he prompts me.

"Well, it begins by two people loving each other," I say.

"I thought it begins by two people being naked," he interjects.

"Well, yes," I say, flustered, "that too, but I'm trying to explain things in the proper order."

"Sorry," he says.

"That's all right. As I was saying, the man and woman, they're naked together, and the man goes inside her in a very special way, and when it's done, she has the seed of a baby left in her womb."

"Is that how the father's spirit gets into the baby?"

"Something like that."

"Does it hurt?" He draws his feet up onto the sofa so that he is sitting cross-legged.

"Not too much, not if they love each other."

"How long does it take?"

"Well, that all depends on—" I say, then feel my face flush with embarrassment as I realize I have misunderstood his question. "Nine months, I mean."

"Then it comes out?"

"Yes. The woman pushes and pushes, and the baby comes out."

"Does this not hurt also? I see a woman going to have a baby one time and her face was so . . ." His expression contorts.

"Well, now, I'm told that giving birth hurts a whole lot. I suppose I'll find out for myself soon enough."

"Yes," he says gravely.

"Listen, I've an idea." I go to the shelf where Richard keeps his catalog of educational books.

"What you got, Mama?"

I open the catalog and flip to the section of medical texts.

"You're old enough now. I'm going to order you a book about biology. What do you think of that?"

"Bi-lo-gee?" he says, making another face.

"It's the science of everything that lives. It's about how things get born and how they grow and eventually die."

Liyanza nods slowly. "So, then, I will read your book of bi-lo-gee," he says, getting up. "I will know all there is to know about making things live and die."

"Brilliant!" I exclaim.

"But I don't have the money to pay for the book, *Mama Boenga*," he laments, his expression growing long.

"How much have you got?"

"I have only twenty francs. I'm having had to buy food."

I pick the catalog up from the tabletop where I've set it. The *Biologie Comprehensive* text is listed at a hundred francs.

"What do you know," I say, closing the catalog quickly. "Twenty is just what the book costs."

THE COQUILHATVILLE POLICE COMMISSIONER came this week to arrest a man from the village who'd supposedly killed his wife during a native ceremony.

The events occurred while we were in the backcountry, so it's not until Dr. Baker recounts them for us that Richard and I get the full story. We sit in the Bakers' living room late in the evening, and the doctor tells his tale with a calm that, despite his best intentions, begins to unravel.

There are rumors that the murdered woman was unfaithful to her husband, a log-canoe builder named Lokutu. Apparently, when confronted, the wife flatly denied the accusations. Lokutu, distraught, sought the council of a witch doctor from a neighboring village. The shaman handed Lokutu a dose of poison to administer to his wife as a sort of test.

"If she is lying about her infidelity," the witch doctor said, "she will come to a swift and pitiful end. If she speaks the truth, the poison will leave her unharmed. This is how it's been done for as many generations as anyone can recall."

Lokutu paid the witch doctor, thanking him and taking the phial of poison home to mix with his wife's supper that evening. Sure enough, the woman was dead before bedtime. When the neighbors found her, she was lying still on the floor in the middle of the house, lips blue, clutching her gut. Lokutu sat by numbly, holding their small children on his lap. To him, the matter was finished and done. His wife had committed a crime and paid for it justly.

To the Belgian government, however, things looked different. It didn't take long for the Coquilhatville police to hear of the events and announce an investigation. It's at this point that the tragedy of Dr. Baker's story deepens.

The Coquilhatville police took quite a bit of time putting together their arrest papers for Lokutu. In the intervening weeks, the new widower was seen standing in the milk line each morning outside Jean's rain-soaked nurses station, the only man among a dozen unmarried mothers. For this act, the villagers treated Lokutu to scorn and jeers, both of which he bore with dignity and silence. He was a father. His babies were innocent of the wrong that had come to him. He couldn't let them go hungry. It was as simple as that.

At last the commissioner came to call on Dr. Baker, who was the only white man on the mission home to come to the door when the officer knocked; thus, it's he who has the story to tell.

"I'm looking for a man named Lokutu," the commissioner said as he stood before Dr. Baker's door, fingering the top of his ivory walking cane. The rain fell hard, and the officer looked displeased to have to travel during such a storm.

"The man with the babies, yes, I know him," Dr. Baker said, stepping out onto the porch curiously.

"I'm here to arrest him for the murder of his wife," the commissioner said.

"I heard there was some sort of disturbance about all that," Dr. Baker said. "I didn't know he murdered her, though. I thought it was an accident, some sort of native ceremony."

"There aren't accidents in matters such as this, Monsieur," the commissioner informed him, adjusting his black policeman's cape, which made him look a little like Mephistopheles.

"I suppose you can find him in the village," Dr. Baker said, "unless you want to come back in the morning when he walks in to get milk for his babies."

"I have no time to wait. There's business to which I must attend, and—"

"Then you'd better head on down to the village," Dr. Baker said with a shrug.

The commissioner nodded curtly and turned to leave.

"Say, there," Dr. Baker said.

The commissioner turned back around on the heels of his well-polished shoes, raising his eyebrows impatiently.

"What's going to happen to the children?" Dr. Baker asked.

"That isn't my concern," the commissioner said without any hesitation.

"I don't know what all went on with Lokutu and his wife, but ever since then, he's been the kind of father to those two little babies that any of us could only hope to have. I'd hate to think of what'll happen to them if you take away their only kin."

The commissioner cleared his throat. "Monsieur, you're a man of medicine, not a man of the law. And so, perhaps you're unaware of the current political climate in this region. Now is not a time for leniency or soft-heartedness. These native people must know they're subject to the laws of the government. A woman has died, and someone must pay. That's my only concern here."

"But if you take away those babies' father, then as I figure it, three people are going to pay."

"That is not my problem," the commissioner said and left without another word.

Dr. Baker knew better than to try to interfere with a police matter. Nonetheless, he found himself compelled to follow the commissioner to the village, where he witnessed the arrest. Lokutu had to be torn from his crying babies, for he wouldn't give them up of his own free will. It took a smart billy-clubbing by the commissioner's deputy to get him into the back of the police wagon.

The commissioner drove away. Lokutu looked out the back window of the police car as a neighbor woman carried off his baffled children. The fate of the babies has yet to be determined, but the prospects aren't bright. Perhaps there's a Catholic mission where the toddlers can be left alongside the result of Margaret's indiscretion. Long live the white man's system of justice.

MARGARET HEARS FROM THE MISSIONS BOARD. She comes by the house and shows me the letter giving her authorization to leave.

"This is it," she says grimly.

"This is it," I echo.

Neil Roberts volunteers to drive Margaret to Coquilhatville on Saturday morning to catch her plane, but she insists it will be best if only Richard and I accompany her. This will save having to explain why she's catching the flight to Cairo and not Léopoldville.

Richard loads Margaret's suitcases into the yellow van. She's packed lightly.

Margaret and I stand on the porch, sheltered from the rain, dressed for traveling. I have the luxury of donning maternity clothes, which I've stitched from mail-order patterns, but Margaret presently doesn't have such an option: she must continue to wear her regular clothes, even as they begin to bind in uncomfortable ways.

"It'll be over soon," Margaret says lifelessly, looking out at the storm.

I don't know whether she's talking about the rains or the deceit.

"Ready," Richard says, shutting the back door of the van. He slips in the mud and clutches the fender to steady himself.

The trip to Coquilhatville is a difficult one. It's been raining steadily for many days, and the road conditions are unfavorable. Our tires slip in the mire. We get stuck once, and Richard has to climb from behind the wheel in order to push the van out of a rut.

When we get to the airport, Margaret's plane is waiting on the runway. Richard takes her bags to a porter on the other side of the room, while Margaret and I sit on a long, polished bench.

"You've been good to me," Margaret says softly. "I . . . the way I feel toward you, you're like a sister," she says, her lips quivering.

"My mother used to call me that—'sister,' I mean."

Margaret nods and smiles sadly.

Overhead, the public-address speaker announces her flight.

"You'd better go," I say.

Margaret nods, gathering her gloves and her hat. We walk through swinging doors and out to the tarmac, where Richard is waiting. I stop below the eaves of the building, as the rain's gotten heavier. Margaret keeps walking.

Richard lays his hands on my shoulders.

The native ground crew pushes a rolling stairway into place and starts the airplane propellers. The engines are noisy, and the propellers create a wind that throws heavy raindrops in every direction. Margaret keeps walking.

I look to the side and notice a lanky African boy standing a few yards away. He's soaking wet, his white shirt clinging to his frame, and his trousers flap in the wind. Margaret reaches the airplane.

I turn and look at the boy again. My heart skips a beat as I realize that it's Mboto Antoine. Margaret begins to climb the stairs.

Tears stream down Mboto Antoine's face. Still, Margaret doesn't turn around.

Mboto Antoine calls out to her, but his voice is lost in the roar of the storm and the engines. Margaret is inside the airplane.

Mboto Antoine drops to his knees.

The other passengers hurry through the squall to board the plane, and the ground crew wheels away the stairs. The craft begins to taxi toward the runway.

Mboto Antoine waves goodbye, his face twisted with grief.

The plane takes to the air.

Mboto Antoine is awash in pain. His head's tipped back, and the rain falls hard against his face. He continues to wave toward the heavens as the airplane rises into the clouds. The boy looks like a new Christian testifying to the Lord at a tent revival.

I pray that Margaret is looking down on us and can see him.

Mboto keeps waving, now using both arms. It's a pitiful and stirring sight.

It's at this moment that I notice for the first time that Mboto Antoine's pinkie finger's been damaged in some sort of accident. Is it the left hand? Yes, it is.

Oh, dear God. I stumble backward.

"Are you all right?" Richard asks, catching me.

"I'm fine," I lie. I lean against a post and continue to stare at Mboto.

My thoughts race—weak left pinkie finger. The letter Q. Margaret's American typewriter. Saturday afternoons in the print shop. Revolutionary letters assailing a white government. A young man's abhorrence of his own interracial longings.

I look up at the airplane for a moment, wondering whether Margaret knows it was Mboto Antoine who wrote the damning letters. I glance back to the spot where the boy was kneeling.

He's disappeared.

Nineteen

December 18, 1958

To Our Sponsoring Churches:

Season's greetings to one and all! We are reminded of our place in your thoughts by the beautiful variety of Christmas cards we have received.

Christmas time in Congo means it is time for a pageant, the thing I sometimes suspect Nkundo converts like best about Christianity. This year, Richard had the idea to photograph the pageant, so you folks back home could get a look at our Bible study in action. The slides you will find included with this letter represent not just the Christmas story, but a variety of memorable scenes from Christ's life.

We had a hoot making the pictures—colored bed sheets do well in the place of Biblical robes, and doesn't my kitchen table propped on the stairs of the church look just like it has been thrown out of the money-changers' temple? We found, of course, no shortage of rustic locales in which to set the scenes, and the goats wandering through several of the shots came free of charge.

The École Moyenne student who got the role of Jesus asked me, once we were done taking the pictures, whether his performance might secure him higher marks during the new term. I explained, as tactfully as possible, that the two issues were entirely separate.

"Think of the others," I said, "the ones playing shepherds or disciples. Would it be fair not to give them higher grades as well? What would the real Christ think?"

It is hard to know what to give someone as a holiday gift, what with limited funds and access to store-bought goods. I have made Richard a bright-blue sport shirt, with mother-of-pearl buttons that

I found at the market in Coquilhatville. It looks very smart, I think.

Many of you have written asking what you might contribute in this holiday season to help make our ministry more effective. The greatest gift you can send us right now is your prayers.

My pregnancy is coming along well. I am large and slow, my profile beginning to resemble that of Alfred Hitchcock. But Nurse Jean Matthews does not seem worried by it, and the natives are delighted, telling me that I am bound to have a fat and healthy baby in the spring.

On a more serious note, we have received letters from several of you after reading articles in your local papers about rumblings of unrest in Congo. I wish I could give you greater insight into the political situation, but I cannot. We are isolated here, and the reports we get from Léopoldville are probably no more comprehensive than those you are already reading.

Rest assured that we remain busy, each and every day, doing the work you have sent us to do.

In Christ's service,

Mrs. Richard Dunagan
Bolenge CCM, via Coquilhatville
Congo Belge, Afrique

I take the letter from the carriage of my typewriter and lay it flat on the desktop to sign it, but I can't stop my hand from shaking. Why must I lie to them?

I'm frightened. The truth is that I've begun to see signs of the unrest everywhere I look.

AS I WALK THROUGH THE MISSION on my way to school early each morning, I go out of my way to avoid passing the print shop or, worse yet, Margaret's house. I don't want to see her idle presses. I don't want to see the flour-sack curtains drawn across her windows. I don't want to see the weeds growing tall in her front yard or the spots of rust where her roof will soon need patching.

I'm uncomfortable with Mboto Antoine sitting in my class every day. I try not to stare at him. I'm excessively aware of how often I call on him to answer a question, making sure it's not any more or less frequent than the other students. I haven't spoken one word to him about the revolutionary letters or his appearance on the tarmac in Coquilhatville. There's no benefit I can see in broaching either subject.

I do my work, study my Bible lessons, and wait for my baby to come.

On Christmas Eve, the mail carrier visits on his bicycle with a package for me. I can tell even before I untie the twine that it contains Liyanza's biology textbook, sent from Brussels. I can't wait to watch Liyanza leaf through the pages of color pictures. The timing's perfect. The arrival of the package is a fine Christmas present.

I tuck the parcel under my arm and go out through the mission, looking for Liyanza, but he's disappeared. Dr. Baker's been busy all day and hasn't seen him. Neil Roberts says Liyanza was missing from Bible study this morning, though this isn't surprising, as attendance during the holiday week is optional. Jean, sitting on her porch rewriting medical reports, suggests I send for him in the village if it's really important to me.

I take a coin from my pocket and give it to one of the little boys who are perennially scampering about.

"What's your name?" I ask him.

"Looko," he says shyly.

"Do you know Liyanza?" I ask.

He nods.

"Good. Then you may keep this coin if you'll walk to the village and bring Liyanza back with you."

"Yes, Mama," he says and dashes off.

Richard and I eat a dinner of canned ham and applesauce, talking about the set of mahogany building blocks we want to give our baby for Christmas. I offer to take the wood to the shop to be sawed into squares if Richard will later smooth them with sandpaper. We laugh at the notion of children receiving presents before they're even born. Richard says I'm going to spoil the child. I assure him that no such thing will come to pass.

The sun goes down. The little boy I sent to the village hasn't returned. Ta Pierre tidies up and leaves for the evening. Richard and I play Scrabble.

It's eight o'clock. Looko still hasn't returned from the village. I begin to worry. Perhaps the boy has gotten waylaid or simply forgotten his duties. Yes, that must be the case. I will try not to be cross with him. After all, it's Christmas.

Richard and I change into our good clothes. Dr. and Mrs. Baker bring their son Maurice by our house to sip powdered-milk eggnog and sing carols before the midnight candlelight service at church.

Just before twelve, the lokolé sounds to summon us. It doesn't quite inspire the same feeling of cheer as jingle bells, but it will do.

We've agreed to light the mission for Christmas Eve this year. In every window and beneath the eaves of every porch there are candles and lamps aglow. Several missionaries have put little votives in paper bags and lined the church path with these Chinese lanterns.

Every step of the way, we're bathed in lovely radiance. The only darkened door we pass is Margaret's, and I look down as we near her gate.

"Merry Christmas, sister," I tell her under my breath.

As we reach the churchyard, I finally catch sight of the little boy I sent to the village. He's running toward us, his arms swinging with each step like those of a marionette with snipped strings.

"*Jikambo, jikambo,*" Looko calls to me anxiously. "Liyanza finds himself much trouble this day."

"What do you mean?"

Looko's excited and breathless, and therefore difficult to understand. The gist of his story's that Liyanza's in a Coquilhatville jail. Looko doesn't know the conditions of Liyanza's detention or the reason.

"What's the matter?" Richard asks, joining me.

"Liyanza's in trouble," I say. "They've got him locked up in jail in Coquilhatville. We've got to go and get him out before—"

"It's the middle of the night on Christmas Eve," Richard reminds me. "There's nothing we can do for him now. C'mon. Let's enjoy the service."

I don't enjoy the service, nor do I sleep very well.

As soon as the sun comes up, I'm ready to go to Coquilhatville.

"Merry Christmas to you, too," Richard grumbles when I wake him unmercifully early.

"C'mon! We have to go," I say, rolling him over in bed. I'm already dressed.

"All right, all right," Richard concedes, stumbling to his feet.

We borrow Neil's van to drive to town. Once we leave the mission, we see no indications that it's Christmas morning. The trees are green from the recent rains, the air temperate. One would not know, without a calendar, that this is December.

All the way, I picture Liyanza spending his Christmas locked up. I can't imagine what he's charged with. I look over at Richard. I know that he, too, is anxious. He's just more reluctant to admit it than I.

When we reach the outskirts of Coquilhatville, we head straight for the district jail, a small, neglected building whose roof rains rust stains down the walls.

"I'm looking for Liyanza," Richard tells the bailiff, whom we find sitting on a wooden chair outside the front door.

"A native?" the old man asks in French.

"Yes, yes," Richard says impatiently, "a boy."

"About so big?" the bailiff asks, holding out his hand at shoulder height.

Richard nods.

"Come with me," the man says, getting up.

I begin to follow, but the bailiff shakes his head.

"You can't go inside, Madame," he says. "It is a men's jail."

"But—"

"I'm sorry," the bailiff insists, crossing his arms. He sorts through the keys on his giant ring and opens the iron door, showing Richard inside. I walk along the perimeter of the wall, waiting. It seems to take many minutes for them to return.

"Well?" I ask Richard eagerly.

"I talked to the government clerk," he says. "Liyanza's getting his things. He'll be out in a minute or two. I can't believe they keep children locked up with robbers and thieves."

"What kind of trouble is he in?"

"He got himself a job during Christmas week hauling cement for some Belgian. But the bags were heavy and the man made him work so hard in the hot sun that he collapsed. When the man tried to make him get right up and start working, Liyanza refused—said it was wrong to be working so hard in that kind of heat. That's when the man turned him over to the police for insubordination."

Through the barred doors of the jail building, I see Liyanza walking toward us. He wears a soiled, slept-in work shirt and old trousers that are too big for him.

"How'd you get them to let him go?" I ask Richard.

"It wasn't too tough," he says. "I just told the clerk that he has good character and isn't some sort of rabble-rouser."

"For a man of God, you sure are a sweet talker."

"If you say so," Richard smirks.

Liyanza steps outside, squinting in the sunlight.

"Merry Christmas," I greet him.

Liyanza doesn't answer right away.

"It's good to see you safe and sound," Richard says.

"Can we go now?" Liyanza asks a little sullenly, walking toward the van.

We stand and watch him for a moment.

The ride back to Bolenge is tense. Liyanza sits between us on the van's bench seat, contributing nothing but one-word answers to our questions.

Finally, as we near the mission, he relaxes a bit. "You didn't have to come and get me. I thank you very much, but it wasn't necessary."

"It's Christmas, for goodness sake and—"

"And yesterday was Christmas Eve," Liyanza says. "That man I get a job working for has nothing in his heart but the cement. That's all he can see. He cares nothing, because I'm African. He thinks it's so fine to have the police come and arrest me on the holiday because I've slowed his making a building. I sit in the little jail room last night; I wonder how many days they keep a man locked up just for being tired. I decide to find out. You know? It isn't right. And I'm a hardworking man, too."

"You're not a man, Liyanza. Not yet, anyhow," Richard says, looking away from the road for a moment. "That's part of the problem here. You're still a boy, and you've got a lot to learn. See, if you wanna show someone what you're made of, you do it by working hard, by being the best you possibly can every day from the minute you wake up until the time you go to bed. If you can do that, then you've truly won. There's no Belgian builder who can take away the satisfaction you feel."

"I understand you being sore about this," I tell Liyanza, "but sitting all stubborn in a jail cell just to prove your point isn't going to accomplish a whole lot of anything in this case."

"It would show that stupid Belgian that—"

"It would show him nothing," Richard says succinctly.

Liyanza snorts.

We pull up in front of our house. "Have you eaten?" I ask.

Liyanza shakes his head.

"For Pete's sake, they didn't even feed you?" Richard asks, suddenly incensed.

Liyanza's silent as we get out of the van.

"Come on. We haven't eaten either," I say. "I'll fix up some breakfast, then you can open your Christmas present."

Liyanza looks down at the ground in an attempt to remain stern faced, but a hint of a smile forces its way through his gloom.

"Christmas present?" he asks quietly.

I put my arm around Liyanza's shoulder. We walk up the front steps together.

DURING MY TIME HERE, I have learned a lesson. When someone comes knocking on your door in the middle of the night in the middle of Africa, they're coming to you with news of misfortune. So when I'm awakened late on a chilly Sunday by the sound of anxious pounding, I know that something must be amiss.

"Eva? Richard?" a woman's voice calls.

I rise with a sense of foreboding. Quickly, I gather my nightgown around me. When I throw open the door and switch on my flashlight, I find Jean Matthews in her night clothes, a look of distress upon her face.

"What's the matter?" I ask, drawing my hair back into a ponytail.

"Someone down at the dispensary has a shortwave radio," Jean says breathlessly. "They started picking up a broadcast earlier— said there's all kinds of trouble down in Léopoldville. The natives are rioting. The man talking on the radio says they're burning the Catholic mission."

"Oh, dear God."

I go to rouse Richard.

We all pile into Neil's van and ride south to the dispensary, where we find an operating room full of nurses and African orderlies gathered around the radio receiver. They've strung an aerial from one corner of the room to the other, but the signal's still weak. I have to strain to make out exactly what the newsman is saying.

"The city is in a state of siege," he keeps repeating. "It is a race riot, a free-for-all. The Belgian police corps are totally unprepared for this."

I stare at the glowing radio dial.

"They're telling me at least twenty Africans have been killed or injured, and things are only getting worse," a different reporter announces. "The sky is lit up bright with flames and the air is full of smoke. It gets in your lungs. I'm watching, from where I stand, a gang of three of four men, Africans, and they've started beating up a priest here in the European section of the capital city. They're beating him up. Dear God. He's on the ground and they're kicking him. He's quit moving. There's blood all over the place. I . . . I think the priest is dead. They've killed him. It's the most terrible thing I've seen."

Jean shakes her head in disbelief. One of the nurses cries quietly, whispering a prayer. Neil Roberts begins to say something, but several nurses turn around to still him.

The mayhem continues. It's January 4, 1959, and our new school term's scheduled to begin in the morning. Now Richard will have to cancel classes. I'm sure that at sunrise, the lokolé will tell the village of the unsavory goings-on, and none of the students will want to come anyway.

We stay through the night at the dispensary. The situation in Léopoldville goes from bad to worse. A nurse sits me down in a chair, offering me water and a pillow to put behind my lower back. I thank her.

"Indépendance! Indépendance!" the rioters shout.

"So they want independence, do they?" one of the better-educated nurses aides asks with a sarcastic laugh. "From what? From not being able to loot and kill whenever they feel like it?"

There are a variety of nods and mumbled agreement in the room. This leaves me with an uneasy feeling, as though my presence here associates me with their sentiments.

"Take me home," I tell Richard quietly.

When we walk outside the clinic building, dawn's only a slight pinking on the eastern horizon. The air's full of dew. The lokolé hasn't yet roused the village and mission from slumber.

Though dusk brings certain tranquility to the world, it's at the break of day that everything's at its most still—blackbirds and lemurs have finished their toils and sought repose, while the sunrise hasn't yet roused the sparrows and leopards with its warmth. There's something most unsettling about standing here, amid great calm, knowing that blood's spilling on the streets a few hundred miles away.

From inside the building, there comes the muffled sound of group cheer. Perhaps the military policemen have slain another looter.

I feel a sharp, sudden shift in my stomach. My baby is kicking.

THE RIOTS GO ON FOR DAYS. Before they're put down, thirty-four Africans are dead and a hundred wounded, most left wandering the streets, dazed and bleeding. The police advise Europeans in Léopoldville to carry guns for their own protection. Barbed-wire roadblocks stop natives from leaving their neighborhoods. We hear all this from Ta Pierre, who cocks his ear to hear the lokolé, which seems to be sounding all day long now.

Richard decides that we will reopen the school on Thursday, with the flag flown at half-staff in acknowledgment of the loss of life in Léopoldville. The boys in the dormitory seem anxious to get back to class, and the teachers are falling behind with their lesson plans.

Thursday morning arrives, and so do we, but we find only a few dozen white-shirted boys waiting for the ceremonial flag raising and singing of the anthem with which we begin each new term. I'm pleased to see Liyanza among the students for the very first time, but the sparseness of the company in which he stands steals the joy of this sight.

"What's going on?" I whisper to M. Boale during Richard's halfhearted morning address.

My question is met with silence.

For my first-period class, only four students are present. "Where is everyone?" I ask them, once I winch myself into the teachers chair, which is suddenly too small for my increasing girth.

"Everyone in the village is talking," one of the boys says. "We hear that soldiers are coming from Léopoldville to kill all the people. I hear many peoples say they're going to hide in their house with machetes. Everyone's so afraid."

Another boy exclaims, "And they're afraid that the Negroes are going to come over from America and take the colony for their own. The Nkundo must be ready to fight all strange people, no matter if they are black or white."

"So then why are *you* here?" I ask them.

There's a moment of silence.

"We're brave men. We don't believe in rumors," the first boy says.

After class, I go talk to Richard in his office.

"Can you believe this?" he asks, shutting the door.

"I'm getting to a point where I can believe anything. You know what's going on, don't you?"

"Please fill me in." Richard helps me into a chair.

"There's a rumor going around that troops are coming up from Léopoldville to kill Negroes."

"I've got to do something," he says. "I mean, the boys have got to know that it's safe to come to school. I just . . . I better go into the village and talk to them. That's what I should do."

261

I watch as Richard rises, locking his file cabinet and gathering his papers.

"You'll be okay while I'm gone?" he asks.

"I'll try," I say a little warily.

WHEN RICHARD RETURNS FROM THE VILLAGE, it's suppertime, and I'm sitting in the living room sewing buttons on baby clothes.

He looks spent, the color drained from his cheeks. "Where's Ta Pierre?" he asks.

"He didn't show up today."

"It figures," Richard says, sitting down beside me with a great sigh. "I've never seen anything like it. Even before I got there, I saw women walking up and down the village path with their hands in the air, crying and carrying on about heaven only knows what. One of them, M. Mbendeke's wife, begged me not to kill her! Can you believe that? Oh, and she called me 'white man.' 'Don't kill me, white man,' she said, as if she's never seen me before in her life, as if she didn't know my name perfectly well."

"And then?" I ask, putting my sewing back in its basket.

"Well, so I got to the village, and it's a ghost town. I went to Ekebe Jacques's house 'cause I figured that if anybody will be out, it'd be him. But no, he was inside, too. So I knocked on his door, and he was real suspicious when he answered it—said the people were told that if they go out into their gardens, they're going to die."

"Honestly," I whisper, shaking my head.

"So I stood in the middle of the square and it was all deserted, and I started calling out '*Nko polisi, nko mbwa,*' over and over, as loudly as I could, hoping they'd believe there's no danger. After a while, one man came out of his house and marched right up to me and accused me of trying to trick them. His eyes were all red, and he was breathing hard. I asked why on earth he would think that of me—tricking the people I was sent here to help. He said right to my face that all white men are alike. When things get bad, every-one sticks with his own clan, and the white man's clan has guns and bullets and evil medicine, and we can't be trusted. That's it!"

Richard gets up and paces. His wavy hair hangs in his eyes and sways as he gestures.

"I . . . I . . . I ran out of patience," he says, "and I turned around to go. Thank goodness I saw a couple of our boys from school walking toward me, you know, because I was leaving. I really was.

The boys came up, and I could tell they were scared, but they asked if everything's going to be okay. And I say, 'Yes, of course it is.' So then more of the boys came out of their houses, and a woman or two, and finally, a few of the men, and they were fine. Everyone was fine. No army came out of the bushes to massacre them. It just . . . I realized something, standing there in the middle of the square. We're white, you know? And therefore, we're the enemy—end of story. When someone is scared or mad, anyone who looks like the enemy becomes the enemy. It's not that much of a stretch, even if the person is someone they know. He just falls into a category, and that's it. It's frightening, Eva." There are tears in Richard's eyes.

"Shh," I say, getting up awkwardly and putting my arms around him.

I rock him gently. It's a slow dance with no music. After a bit, he calms down.

"C'mon," I whisper, taking him by the hand and leading him into the bedroom. I lie down and lift my blouse up over my belly. Richard climbs in beside me.

"Come closer. It's family time," I say quietly.

I take Richard's hands and put them over the baby. He touches me gently as he would a fragile china doll.

"Go ahead, I won't break," I giggle.

Richard presses the side of his head against my stomach.

"What are you doing?" I ask.

"Shh," he says with a cross face. "The baby's talking to me. He says I should kiss you right now. He says it's very important." Richard places his lips against mine.

"Smart kid," I say. "Guess he must really be yours after all."

We lie still and listen to the evening. It sounds as sweet and simple as any I have heard in Congo. Man can do what he will, but nature proceeds undaunted. The same phenomenon that put me on edge a few days ago now offers me comfort.

"You want some dinner?" I ask, sitting up.

"In a bit. You know, there's something I've been meaning to mention about all that," Richard says. "I mean, the baby's being my son and all. I was fixin' on what we might want to name him, and I was thinking, how about my father's name?"

"Wesley Dunagan," I say slowly, trying it out. "Wesley James Dunagan. I like it. Yeah, it's good. Wesley James. But there's one small problem. I think I'm going to have a girl."

"Na-ah."

"I'm telling you, Richard, I feel it. It's a thing a mother knows—don't ask me how. One of the women in the village said so, too. It's how I'm carrying, see?" I demonstrate. "And I'm big. They say you gain more weight with girls than boys."

Just then, the baby starts to kick. I take Richard's hands and lay them back on my belly. Everything's still for a moment, then a good sharp thump stills my breath.

Richard lets out a Tennessee yelp. "That's a boy, all right," he says triumphantly. "You can tell a Dunagan man by his pigheadedness, and that boy in you is gonna have one doozy of a temper."

Our laughter feeds on itself for a delightful few moments. When we calm down, Richard nuzzles up against me. "How did you know to do this?" he asks.

"Do what?"

"This—bringing me in here and making me lie down. Family time. When I was just about ready to—"

"It's not a question of knowing, exactly," I say. "It's a question of . . . if I didn't do something quick, I was liable to lose my own mind. And that's not something any of us ought to endure."

Richard starts to snicker again and is soon kissing me in so many places I have to order him to stop because of how much it tickles. We don't get around to dinner until almost ten o'clock, at which time our ravenous hunger dictates that it come straight from a can.

Twenty

N o . . . NO!" RICHARD SAYS, his voice shaking. "They must be joking!"

In one hand he holds an envelope, in the other a telegram. The fragile paper trembles in his grip. We stand in my classroom, me behind the teachers table and Richard in the doorway. It's a gray afternoon, a few minutes after my last class. I walk to the doorway, take the telegram from him, and read it.

The message doesn't seem to be a joke. It concerns Dr. Roger Ballard, the elementary-school principal at the Lotumbe mission, fifty kilometers upriver. Several months ago, Dr. Ballard traveled to Léopoldville with his wife. It was a trip to celebrate the arrival of the New Year, but their excursion was tragically ill timed. On the night of January 4, Dr. Ballard was caught in the crossfire of the rioting, beaten, and left for dead by angry natives. He's confined to an indefinite convalescence in Léopoldville while his lacerations and broken legs heal. In his absence, his school has begun to list off course, like a ship without its captain. The building's fallen into a state of neglect, teachers haven't been paid, and furniture and books are being stolen in the night.

It's the opinion of the Missions board that l'École Moyenne can do without Richard for a few weeks, so he's directed to travel upriver to put things right at the Lotumbe school.

"Did they even stop to consider the fact that I'm due in two weeks?" I ask, handing him the telegram. "What am I supposed to do? Cross my legs and hold the baby in until you get back?"

Richard sits down in one of the student desks.

"So this is what they mean," I mutter.

"What's that?" he asks, looking up without enthusiasm.

"They say you get punished for being too good at something," I explain. "The board wants things straightened out at Lotumbe, right? And they think you're the best man for the job."

"Well—"

"Listen to me now," I say, walking over to him. "If I were pregnant and you were just kind of average, they wouldn't think of making you leave. But the point is, you're nowhere near average. And to them, that outweighs your obligations at home."

Richard shakes his head and sighs.

We gather our things and hurry home through the rain. When we get there, Ta Pierre fixes us cups of warm KLIM instant milk as a countermeasure against the chill of the storm.

Richard and I sit at the kitchen table and discuss our options.

On one hand, Richard could refuse to go to Lotumbe. But a denial of the Missions board's bidding would be disrespectful. Furthermore, it would leave the Lotumbe school in its present state of upheaval.

On the other hand, Richard could go to Lotumbe without me. But then he wouldn't be here for my delivery. Neil Roberts or Jean would need to drive me to the European hospital at Coquilhatville when I went into labor, and Richard would be left to read the news of his baby's birth in a letter.

The third option, the one that most piques my sense of adventure, is for Richard and me to go to Lotumbe together. It is a gamble. There is no hospital anywhere nearby for me to have my baby, but Dr. John Ross, a charismatic American physician of renown, is stationed on the mission. I could deliver in his infirmary, many miles from the big-hatted Belgian nurses and the sickening jaundice I remember from my last visit to the Coquilhatville hospital.

As I muse over the decision, my hand traces the lumpy outline of the scar with which the Belgians left me. I think of all I've heard of Dr. Ross's reputation. It would do my heart good to know that I was taken care of by a mission doctor, someone who laughs as I do and has heard of my hometown.

When I first approach him with the notion, Richard shakes his head.

"I will be party to no such thing," he says adamantly.

"I—"

"Eva, listen to me. You think you're invincible, but you're not."

"Just a minute, now—"

"No."

I take a deep breath and set my jaw. Then I remind him of Dr. Ross's sterling reputation and of how, even on a mission, house burglars come a-prowling when they know women are all by themselves.

"But more than anything else," I tell him, grabbing his hands across the tabletop, "I want you beside me when it's time."

Richard looks into my eyes and sighs with resignation. "Oh, all right," he says. "I'm probably a fool, but we'll go to Lotumbe together and have the baby there. I should go send word for them to expect both of us."

He slips on his jacket and heads for the front door.

"You'd better pack lightly," he calls over his shoulder.

"You'd better be joking," I say quietly.

IN THE MORNING, we prepare to leave.

The rain has let up for a bit, though gray clouds hover low on the horizon, ready to loose a downpour if it should strike Nature's fancy.

I'm standing in front of the house, having a good, deep smell of the air, when I see someone walk toward me up the path: a Nkundo man I used to see working at Margaret's print shop before she barred the doors and went away. He's a short, jocular native with a wide face and nose. A spark of sweet innocence in his eyes leads one to believe he's smiling, even when he wears no expression at all.

"Nkoko Bongongolo la Mam'Oenga," he says with a respectful nod.

I look down as he presses his palms together, and I notice that his shirt cuffs are soiled and ragged.

"I'm known by Abraham Bitoko," the Nkundo says. "It's good to have seeing you again. It's been many weeks since I don't have my job at the printing shop."

"Are you getting by okay?" I ask.

He nods in such a manner that I know it's a lie.

"I have a favor to ask of you, if not making too much trouble," Abraham says, reaching into his pocket and taking out some crumpled bills. "I hear talk that you're going to Coquilhatville today."

"Yes, to catch the boat to Lotumbe," I tell him.

"So when will you return?"

"Several weeks. A month maybe," Richard says, hoisting a battered suitcase into the van.

"Ah," Abraham Bitoko says, looking down at the path and shuffling his feet. "Very well, then. Never mind."

"What was the favor?" I ask.

"I suppose that it isn't possible now," Abraham says, shaking his head. "If you were going to return right away, I . . ." He offers a smile that disappears as quickly as it arrives, then turns away as if to leave.

"Yes?" I encourage him. "What is it?"

"I need someone to go to the butcher shop for me and buy meat," he says reluctantly. "I would take any kind you brought me."

"Why can't you go into Coquilhatville and get it yourself?" I ask. "If it's a matter of road papers, I'm sure someone around here would be willing to write some up so that you—"

"No, no. I have papers," Abraham says patiently, "and I have the money to buy meat for my wife and children—at least until the francs I save from my job are gone. That isn't the problem. You see, in these days, things become bad in Coquilhatville like everywhere, and the men in the stores do not want to give business with natives. I wait on the line in a butcher store for an hour last week, and all the time a white person come in and the butcher man helps them and takes their money, but all the time he makes it as if I am not even in the shop. It's as though I'm a *jijijingi*, as though I am nothing but a shadow cast against his wall. Finally, I can't take it any more, and I go. I come home with money in my pocket and empty hands with no package of meat."

I stare at him.

"Put away your money. I have an idea."

I have to see if this phenomenon's really as he presents it.

The Nkundo folds his stack of five- and ten-franc bank notes and puts it into his front pocket.

"Now get in the van," I tell him. "We're going for a little trip."

Abraham squeezes in between boxes and twine-wrapped suitcases.

Richard finishes packing and fastens the shiny new padlock on the front door of our house. I watch him put the key into the tumbler and turn it. The process saddens me.

The trip to Coquilhatville is slow, in light of the recent rains. But at least the sky has been dry today, so there are no great mud patches to encumber our progress. Once in town, we head for the first Belgian butcher shop we see. I have Richard park around the corner.

"Go on into the shop," I tell Abraham once the motor is stilled. "Buy your meat."

"But, *Mam'Oenga,* they are sure to ignore—"

"That very well may be. But just do as I say, please. I'll be there in a moment."

I watch as Abraham opens the butcher shop's framed-glass door and goes inside, his normally rigid posture caving into to a slight slouch. A little bell clatters against the doorframe to announce a customer's arrival. When it rings, I begin to count. *One Mississippi, two Mississippi, three Mississippi.* I let a full minute pass before I follow him.

As I get to the front of the shop, I see Abraham waiting patiently before the counter. The shop is modest but clean, with white-washed walls and a glass display case. On the far side of the counter, the butcher leans over a big stainless steel slicing machine, seemingly oblivious to Abraham's presence.

I pull open the door. The bell clatters. The butcher looks up.

"Bonjour, Madame," he greets me with a plump-cheeked smile, adjusting his paper hat.

"Bonjour," I say coolly.

"How may I help you today? Our lamb is fresh, just an hour ago," the butcher says, wiping his bloody hands on his apron.

"Help him," I say, gesturing coarsely toward Abraham without looking in his direction. "He was here before me."

"*Mais, non,* Madame! He can wait. After all, you're eating for two," he chuckles.

"No, really." My tone flattens. "I insist you help this man first. To take me ahead of him, that would be exceptionally rude of you."

"Madame, I . . ." the butcher stammers.

"Go on, then, tell the butcher what you want," I say to Abraham.

The Nkundo walks tentatively to the counter.

"I would like seventy-francs' worth of whatever you've got today," he says quietly.

The butcher purses his lips and stares at Abraham, blinking several times.

"We haven't much of anything for you," the butcher.

"I thought you just got in some fresh lamb an hour ago," I interject.

There's a pause. The shop's silent enough that even with the door closed, I can hear the conversations of passersby on the street.

The butcher clears his throat. "How much lamb do you want?" he asks acerbically.

"Seventy-francs' worth, if you please," Abraham says with great dignity.

The butcher silently weighs the meat and begins to wrap it up.

"Ah-ah-ah. Don't shortchange him," I say, leaning over the counter for a look at the package.

The butcher hesitates, then drops another lamb chop onto the pile. When he's finished, he ties the white paper package up with string and tosses it disdainfully onto the counter. Abraham picks up the meat and lays a neat stack of bills in its place.

"Thank you," he says succinctly and leaves the shop.

When he's left, the butcher turns to me.

"Now that that's all finished, what can I get you, Madame?" he asks in a tone much less friendly than his first greeting.

I pause to consider how I wish to respond. "Nothing," I say at last. "You can get me nothing. I don't think you're the kind of man with whom a woman of conscience should be conducting business."

"Madame, truly—" the butcher says, as if someone were choking him.

"Good day, sir," I say, turning and pulling open the door.

The bell tinkles to announce my departure. Abraham Bitoko is waiting outside. As we walk together toward the van, he's quiet.

"I'm sorry that was so difficult," I say.

"I tell you what makes me the most angry about this. I thank you very much. I want you to know this. But I cannot believe that I need the help of a *mondele* woman to buy meat. I'm a good man who knows how to carry himself and how to talk to people. I have money that's just as good as anybody's. There's a great wrongness to all this."

We reach the van.

"Go on home," I tell him. "Get a ride home from somebody heading back in that direction. You gotta get that meat out of the sun before it spoils."

Abraham and I look into each other's eyes.

"It's already spoiled," he says softly and walks away.

WHEN WE GET TO LOTUMBE, I find the mission smaller and more rustic than at Bolenge. There's only one school and, true to the telegram from the Missions board, the building looks as though it's ready to be demolished. The church, too, has seen better days; its floorboards sag, and vermin make their home in the thatched roof.

The only public building that we find in good repair is Dr. Ross's two-room cinder-block clinic, its well-lit operating room out of place so many miles from civilization.

Richard and I will stay in the home of Dr. Ballard, the absent principal. The house has gentility about it and is full of finery I would not expect in so bucolic a climate. Dr. Ballard and his wife must come from money. They have paper shades for their lamps and prints of famous paintings hung on their walls. The china in the kitchen cabinet is thin enough to let the glow of light through when I hold a saucer up against the window, and there's a drawer full of good table linens next to the kerosene-powered icebox.

"Will it do?" Richard asks, watching me poke around the house.

"It'll do," I say with contentment, waddling out to the front porch and lowering myself onto the Ballards' wicker settee.

I look out at the mission. It's late afternoon. As a result of the solitude in which his employer's prolonged absence has left him, Dr. Ballard's houseboy seems delighted to have someone with whom he can converse. He offers me some tea. I accept, and we sit for a spell, watching village children play in the mud. The house-boy is thin and wiry, possessed of a constant need to apologize for his own awkwardness.

"You went to Dr. Ballard's school?" I ask.

"For three and some years, yes," he says, switching back and forth between French and Lonkundo. "Then I have doing the wash and some cooking for *Nkoko* Ballard and his wife. I'm not such a good student that makes more schooling in another village. Only the smart ones can study in the high school. This is ten years now I have do working in the house for *Nkoko* Ballard."

"Do you have a wife at home to bring you children?" I ask.

"No," he says, smiling and blushing. "They laugh at me, all of the womens of Lotumbe. They say I'm not fully a man. I have no *mpifo* and do not know how to talk to Nkundo womens."

"But you're talking to me," I counter.

"Ah, that is different," he says. "You are *mondele*. When I have talking to you or Mama Ballard, it would be as if talking to my mother. You understand?"

"Yes," I assure him. He's accustomed to being treated as a child by white women. There's no expectation that he might be their paramour and thereby, no pressure for him to fit a role for which he seems intrinsically unsuited.

Something in his manner reminds me of a man who lived in the apartment below us growing up. Like this houseboy, he led a solitary existence, playing songs from Broadway shows on an out-of-tune violin and cooking for himself every evening. I never understood why he wouldn't take a wife.

Richard appears on the porch to scold me for overexerting myself.

"You ought to get yourself into bed right this minute," he says.

Reluctantly, I heed his advice.

OVER THE NEXT FEW DAYS, with Richard busy at the Lotumbe school, I come to appreciate what a good idea it was for me to get away from Bolenge. Though gravity keeps my steps heavy, as a constant reminder of my happy burden, I feel as though I am on vacation. I'm accountable to no classroom full of rollicking teens, no boxes full of soiled communion cups, no circle of semiliterate village women. My attentions are entirely focused upon the process of having a baby.

I mark off days in my pocket calendar with a red pencil. My due date arrives and passes unceremoniously. What was once the focus of great anticipation is now just another little box with a waxy red X through it.

It becomes more and more difficult to walk. I'm bigger than any pregnant woman I ever remember having seen, and now I feel as though my thighs and legs have begun to swell in deference to my belly—as though, if I'm not careful to take tiny steps, something inside me is going to rip open. Therefore, I am content to pass much of my time sitting between the linen sheets of Dr. Ballard's bed, perusing his bedside reading, a book of verse and a folio of essays by Albert Schweitzer.

Dr. John Ross comes by each morning after breakfast, pulling up a chair and checking on me with the chit-chatty bedside manner of a Fuller Brush salesman. He's a short, sandy-haired man with a wide grin and a lot of stories to share.

Over the course of several days, he tells how, at the age of thirty-five, he gave up his job as a small-town minister to attend medical school. He and his wife had lost four children, each in the first year of life, each claimed by various ills, though physicians could never quite figure out what went wrong. Thus, Dr. Ross became a man obsessed with the preservation of human life, especially babies' and small children's.

During his tenure in Africa, he has delivered a thousand babies and saved countless more from the cruel ravage of diseases eager to steal them. This could never make up for the loss of his own children, left buried in a tidy row in a California-desert cemetery, but it helps.

It occurs to me that a preponderance of the sorrow I've seen in Africa has to do with the loss of children. The bearers of that grief, be they native or European, lament alike, despite the broad chasm, measurable not only in miles but in centuries, that divides our cultures. Who would have thought it most readily bridged not by God-given joy but by one particular woe?

Each afternoon, Richard comes in from school with a look of defeat on his face, sitting down next to me and shaking his head.

"What today?" I ask him.

"There's just so much to do, so much. One man can accomplish only a limited number of miracles, no matter how devoted to the cause he may be. The teachers at the school, Eva . . ."

"Yes?"

"There's always a crisis, always. Can you think of a month that has gone by since we got to Congo that one missionary hasn't had to fill in for another missionary's job, or . . . or that we've actually had a full-night's sleep for a two days in a row? They push us till we drop then tell us it's God's will. They want us to get higher and higher marks from our students in school. But they won't send more teachers. How short sighted is that? Do they think everyone out here was just lounging around up till now, and this'll somehow get more results out of us?"

"Richard, I—"

"It's like paint. No matter how vibrant the color might be, I reckon you can only spread the stuff so thin. After a while, I get beaten up enough that I don't even want to be creative. I don't think the Missions board's ever heard of the concept of diminishing returns."

He paces. "And . . . and the teachers at the school here? Only one of them can read, I think. It's amazing, it really is. I suppose it's no wonder that so many of the students end up repeating a grade. Still, we gotta follow the Belgian academic program to get our subsidy each term. It's just memorize, memorize—sit still, sit still—copy off the blackboard and parrot back. But that's the only way to reproduce the material and pass the exams so we can get their blasted money. It's not right. It's just not right."

"So . . . tough day, huh?" I ask gently.

"This is not what I came to Africa to do," Richard whispers and goes to wash up. He's quiet the rest of the evening.

The next morning, as soon as I'm up reading, Dr. Ballard's houseboy brings in a tray of tea. In the process of pouring me a cup, he spills the contents of the pot across the bed sheets.

"Must you be so clumsy?" I ask him sharply, surprised at my own tone.

He begins to stammer an apology, backing toward the bedroom door. I try a retraction, but before I can figure out what to say, he's gone.

I put down my teacup and dab at the dampened sheet.

When I look up, Dr. Ross has arrived at my bedside with a flower. "For the pretty lady," he says, laying the bud in my hands.

I smile at him, but I don't feel like a pretty lady, inside or out. I feel like an angry, engorged tick fit to burst.

"Any contractions today?" he asks, as he does every day.

I shake my head.

"How's about that swelling in your legs?" he says.

I let him take a look. When he's finished, he takes a bottle from the black physicians' bag he carries.

"With your permission, I think it's time we do what's necessary to get things on the road, so to speak. You're overdue and have gained almost sixty pounds."

"Fine," I say, too tired of waiting to begin even a cursory debate.

"All right, then—this is quinine," he says, shaking the bottle. "I'll give you a teaspoonful now, and you can take some more a bit later. Sometimes it gives a baby just the encouragement it needs to begin the process."

I wince as I swallow the medicine, then lick the last of its bitterness off my lips as if it were candy.

The doctor leaves. I wait. I hear thunder, and the wind blows hard. I think we're in for a storm. In an hour, I take more quinine. I finish my book. Richard comes home from school.

In two hours, Dr. Ross returns. "Anything?" he asks.

I shake my head.

"Well, then," he says with a chuckle. "I guess the baby's playing hard to get. I'm going to put you on a pituitary drip. That ought to get things moving."

The contractions still don't come. Three hours later, nothing so profound as a sneeze has disturbed my body's composure.

"All right," says Dr. Ross, standing again at the foot of my bed, this time with a look of consternation on his face. "If you're going to be difficult, Eva, I suppose this means we'll have to bully you a bit."

I smile.

"If we break your water," he says, "the baby will have no choice but to pay us a visit."

I've grown too large and unbalanced to walk the hundred yards to the clinic on my own, so Dr. Ross fetches two native assistants. He and Richard hoist me onto a canvas stretcher and, along with the natives, carry me out the front door.

"*Yalema bolotsi*. Be well," the houseboy says quietly as we pass him on the path.

Once again, I try to apologize to him, and once again, I'm too slow to summon the right words before he is gone. I lie on my back, looking up at Richard's face. The sky above him is dark gray. The coachmen of my chariot are of such disparate height and the path underfoot so mud slicked, that with every step the stretcher bobs and weaves like a camel on arthritic knees.

I start to laugh.

Dr. Ross looks down at me as though I were delirious. Then he sees my head wobbling—flop, flop—from side to side and understands what I find so funny. He begins to sing a marching song.

The rain comes. Big, sloppy drops fall on my face. The men carrying me hurry, and the lopsided, lumbering procession becomes comical in its indubitable absurdity.

At last, we arrive at the clinic. Dr. Ross has requested the assistance of his colleague George Johnson, a mission doctor from Illinois doing his orientation. Also in attendance is a nervous nurse from a neighboring mission, who stammers hello and giggles.

I'm laid atop a table in the tiny tin-walled operating room. The air smells like ether and Lysol. I raise my head to look around. The nurse has laid out a bassinet for the baby, and beside it, a little cotton stocking cap.

Dr. Ross conducts his operating room business like a vaudevillian magician. Everything worth doing, it seems, is worth doing with a degree of flourish and showmanship: He whistles. He puns. He boasts.

The doctors spread my legs and poke up inside me with their shiny instruments in order to break the water. This invasion of my womb is not painless. I grab hold of the sides of the table and suck in a sharp breath. *Easy now,* I tell myself.

Once they have undammed me, it doesn't take very many minutes for the contractions to begin. Eva's having a baby. It's for real. I laugh a little deliriously. Rain falls on the tin roof. Richard paces, looking every bit the nervous expectant father.

By suppertime, my labor has grown heavy, and the contractions are coming at short intervals. In the midst of it, I coax Richard into playing a game of cards with me. He laughs in disbelief but goes along with it. I win.

At last my contractions are so close together that I don't have time to recover in between.

"Push, that's right," Dr. Ross says gently, kneeling between my legs.

I raise my head to look at him, but the nurse eases it back against the pillow, mopping my sweaty brow with a towel.

I pant. I push and push. I squeeze my eyes shut and arch my back. The pain becomes impossibly intense, but it's wonderful. *Just a little longer. Just a little longer.*

"Give me a good one," Dr. Ross says.

I squeeze every muscle in my abdomen as tightly as I can and let out a most unladylike shout. My nether regions feel as though they're being turned inside out.

There's the sound of a tiny, piercing wail. Richard gasps joyously.

"A girl! A girl!" Richard says over and over, rushing to my side and kissing me on the cheeks and forehead.

"We have a daughter," I whisper.

The doctors applaud as the nurse holds up the baby for all to see. My sweet, sweet baby girl trembles and looks terrified, the little patch of blond hair plastered on her scalp.

"What will you call her?" the nurse asks.

"Ellen," I say, the name coming to me spontaneously. We have a whole list of boys names picked out, but none of them will do at present.

I turn my head and look at Richard for approval.

"Ellen," he says, nodding. "Ellen Dunagan, that's what your Mama's gone and named you. Welcome to the world!"

The nurse wraps the baby in white towels and hands her to me. I stare at her little body. My angel cries, and I shake her gently to still her.

This is a true wonder, the most remarkable thing I can imagine. My baby, this red-face, yawning, balled-fist miracle—she came out of me. For most of a year she's existed as part of my body, dependent upon my heart and lungs for the very continuance of her being. Now, with a few contractions that were more nature than will, I have sent her forth and everything's changed. I'm no longer her Alpha and Omega, her sole link to all that's actual.

Now, my baby daughter draws breath and caterwauls of her own volition. She opens her eyes to the world and begins to make her own decisions about what she sees before her. My angelic Ellen is tiny and vulnerable, and I don't want to let the nurse take her away from me, but everyone insists.

"Shh," Richard calms me, taking my hands in his when I protest.

Dr. Ross hangs his white operating gown by the door and congratulates everyone one more time. Meanwhile, Dr. Johnson begins cleaning up from the delivery. He kneels between my legs, sterilized needle and thread in hand. All of a sudden, Dr. Johnson's eyes widen and the utensils slip from his hands, clattering noisily to the floor.

"John, take a look at this," he says, an edge in his voice.

"What's the matter?" I ask anxiously.

Dr. Ross kneels, pokes around for a bit, makes a face, then stands up.

"It seems we're not quite done for the day," he says calmly. "There's another baby in there."

"What?" I ask, shocked. It can't be true. Perhaps I haven't understood correctly. I stare at Dr. Ross, waiting for him to begin laughing. It's another of his jovial jests. Ha-ha! Everyone have a good chuckle.

Only he doesn't laugh this time. Instead, he turns to wash his hands.

"Come on, then, let's do it."

Richard is dumbstruck.

"I'm having twins," I whisper to no one in particular, as though saying it out loud will make some sense of the notion. Lord in heaven! I'm having twins! All of a sudden, I understand why I've been so dauntingly large these last few months.

The nurse, nervous in her calmest moments, is presently in a dither.

"It . . . it can't be," she sputters, gesturing randomly about the room. "It just can't be. I've only made preparations for one."

"Well, I'm afraid we don't have a great deal of choice in the matter," Dr. Ross says, kneeling to begin the birthing process anew.

The second baby doesn't require as much persuasion to make an appearance. It's another girl. We decide in short order to call her Laura, after the sweet love song Dr. Ross has been whistling all afternoon. It turns out to have been a good thing to carry my babies past term, as even now, they weigh just four and five pounds, respectively. If they'd come much earlier, they would've needed incubation before being ready for the rigors of postpartum existence.

My head begins to hurt. The doctors bed me down for the night on the operating table, as there are no private rooms in this native clinic. Richard and the nurse will stay with me, sleeping on cots. If the rains let up, we can go home tomorrow.

The headache worsens. It feels as though my skull is being squeezed, each beat of my heart arriving like a sharp, flat-palm smack on the back of my cranium.

The doctors gather their things and leave. Richard and the nurse are beside me, one on either side. My babies are against the wall, Ellen in her bassinet and Laura in a galvanized washtub. *Two babies. I have two babies.* I would laugh at this, were I not in such pain.

My stomach pays its respects to my headache by turning woozy. Pain and nausea jockey for my attention. My skull feels as if it's going to explode, really and truly, emptying its contents all about the room.

I moan. It becomes difficult for me to keep my eyes open. I tell the nurse I have to vomit, and she fetches me a bedpan. Richard strokes my hair until it hurts too much and I have to tell him to stop. I begin to feel as though I would be better off dead. Once I've vomited half a dozen times, all that comes up is the brownish juice from my intestines. I'm cold. The slightest sound or sensation of light makes me shudder with pain and causes the table to rattle against Richard's cot.

My head is going to blow up. I know it is. This is wrong, very wrong. I'm not supposed to feel like this after having a baby, even two babies. I whimper to Richard to do something, please, something, anything, dear God, oh, please make this stop. I can't stand it—this is more than I can bear, and the nurse is saying something to me about fever, and Richard isn't in the room anymore, and I hear my babies crying and I can't go to them because I can't open my eyes and move my arms, and the babies are crying, and the walls of the room are falling away, and my head is splitting, and I hear the sound of Richard's voice so I know that he's returned.

"I have some ice." He lays some of it against my forehead, and it's like water to a man in the desert.

"More," I beg him, crying. "More!"

Richard puts a cube of ice against my lips, running it back and forth.

I lick desperately at the melting ice.

The babies are still crying. I can't understand why the nurse isn't attending to them. I close my eyes and see the room as though I'm looking down from a high branch of a tree in the clinic courtyard. I see myself lying, tortured, on the narrow bed. Richard and the nurse pace, not knowing what to do. I look out beyond the clinic to the ramshackle church with a graveyard beside it. Rain-soaked wooden crosses poke up from the soil, tilting this way and that. With great clarity I can see the missionaries' names on the crosses, all of them familiar, like the words to the Lord's Prayer or a nursery-school rhyme. I try to reach out and touch the grave markers but find my arms paralyzed.

When I open my eyes, I'm back in bed. It isn't a true waking, but a sort of bleary, nightmarish awareness of my surroundings, of the room in which I lie, of Richard and the nurse leaning over me, of something filling my mouth. Then the colors in the room go drab, and I'm lost in darkness.

WHEN I AGAIN COME 'ROUND, it's deep in the night. I try to raise my arms but find that they're bound to the iron rails of the bed. Richard and the nurse have switched positions, but now their heads are nodded in sleep. I see, in the shadows, Dr. Ross standing near the door with his arms crossed.

"Please . . ." I whisper but am too hoarse to produce any more sound. The world slips away from me.

IT'S DAYTIME WHEN I WAKE AGAIN. I am no longer at the clinic. I study my surroundings and slowly realize that I'm back in Dr. Ballard's bed.

Then I notice Richard sitting beside me. His clothes are wrinkled, and he could use a shave.

He holds a glass of juice to my lips so that I may take a sip.

"What time is it? Am I awake? " I ask feebly.

"You're awake," Richard says. "Just relax now."

"How did I—?" I wheeze.

He stills me and makes me finish the juice.

Then he tells me of how the sound of my hospital bed frame banging against the floor awakened him. He sat up in the half-light and saw me convulsing violently, gagging, unseeing. It took both him and the nurse to restrain me and force a stick wrapped with cotton into my mouth to keep me from biting off my tongue.

Then Richard got on his borrowed bicycle to summon Dr. Ross on the far side of the mission. It rained hard that night, harder than it had the entire season. Richard pedaled desperately, full of fear, shoulders hunched against the downpour.

Halfway to the Ross house, the bicycle's narrow tires became so jammed in the mud that Richard had to abandon the contraption and make the rest of the trip on foot. He stumbled on the muddy, uneven ground, dropping his flashlight and cursing. The rain became so heavy that he couldn't see the path.

All was dark and wet. Richard fell again and rose, having lost track of which direction he was headed and from which he'd come. He went forth blindly. Just when he was ready to give himself up for lost, he tripped and fell forward onto one knee. When he regained his wits, he shined the flashlight around and realized he'd happened onto the first flagstone of Dr. Ross's front walk. With a prayer of thanks half-shouted and half-sung, Richard made his way up to the porch and pounded on the door.

Dr. Ross, half-asleep, hurried to answer. When he threw the door open, he found Richard utterly drenched and ready to collapse. Richard's trousers were ripped, and there was an ugly gash across his knee. With great desperation, Richard explained my condition.

Dr. Ross's trademark calm left him. He grabbed his black bag and, with Richard at his side, ran out into the night to save me. For thirty-six hours I tiptoed in and out of consciousness. I filled the room with incoherent rambling, aided by sedatives Dr. Ross administered to still my seizures.

I try to listen to Richard's story, but a troubling notion consumes my attention—no one thought I was going to pull through. Richard won't acknowledge this in so many words, but I can tell it's so. Twice in two years I've faced the Almighty, and those I would have left behind quickly resigned themselves to my departure. I'm horrified that my life would be so readily forsaken. What of hope? What of Providence?

"What's wrong with me?" I ask, interrupting Richard's story.

"Oh . . . it's toxemia," he says, missing the rhetorical nature of the question. "Dr. Ross thinks there was something growing in your uterus along with the babies, a lump of something poisonous. When you delivered, it broke open and got in your blood. Toxemia, they call it."

"I see," I say.

Why me? For the second time in my tenure in Africa, I must ask what I have done to deserve this.

Is this a punishment, Lord? If so, tell me what great crime I have committed, for I don't know what I've done to warrant this castigation.

Perhaps the trespass is my very presence here.

OVER THE COURSE OF HOURS AND DAYS, many things come into my head, bad things, mostly. I feel no benevolence toward people or events. Each night, as I lie in bed, I try to say a prayer, but the words that find my lips are choleric and uncivil.

The missionary couple taking care of the twins 'round the clock brings them by for a few precious minutes every day. It will be weeks before I can nurse them. If I try it too soon, the doctors warn, I might poison the girls with tainted milk. The inability to offer them sustenance only worsens my mood, leaving me without a sense of purpose.

The nurse comes by each day to pump my breasts. Afterward, I curl up in bed and cover my head with a pillow, so I don't have to listen to the horrible sound of her emptying the milk down the drain.

I cry often. Richard comes to console me but I send him away. "If you don't mind, I'd like to take a nap," I say in a voice not my own.

He stands in the doorway for a moment, looking at me, then shakes his head and shuts the door, leaving me in solitude. I try to read books but can find no interest in the words on the page.

After a time, Dr. Ballard's houseboy quits speaking to me. I think he's frightened of my temper. He's supposed to bring me glasses of fruit juice, prescribed by the doctor, but takes to leaving a tray outside my door and coming back later to retrieve it.

I sleep. I stare out the window. I cry. I sleep some more.

I take up pen and paper and write a letter:

Mr. Wallace P. Hinton
Missions Building
Cleveland, Ohio
USA

Dear Mr. Hinton,

I am writing to you because I am at wit's end. I am not a quitter; this you must know by now. But never in the course of our missionary training did I imagine I might encounter such adversity as I have in Congo. I do not need to catalog for you the trials Richard and I have endured.

Our hands are overworked and we are undernourished of spirit. We were prepared to contend with the Nkundos' poverty and greed, their spiritual waywardness. We figured we'd adjust to their culture—after all, we've studied anthropology.

That might have worked in the past, but now the challenge is much greater. More and more, I get the sense that I am unwelcome here. It is hard to teach someone who does not want to listen.

As I write to you, I lie in my sickbed, recovering from a bout of illness that almost took my life. What if I had succumbed? Richard would be left to raise our children alone in this ever-threatening realm.

You expect miracles of us. You taught us to rely on each other, and to keep our eyes on Jesus. I tell you now—the view is not so clear.

In Christ's service,

Mrs. Richard Dunagan
CCM Lotumbe, via Coquilhatville
Congo Belge, Afrique

WEEKS PASS. At last they let me feed my own babies. The next day, we leave Lotumbe. I hold my dear daughters close, and I don't look back.

Twenty-one

April 1959

Iᴛ's ʟᴀᴛᴇ ᴀғᴛᴇʀɴᴏᴏɴ when we pull into the docks at Coquil-hatville. Our log canoe is buffeted in the wake stirred by larger tugs and steamboats mooring on either side. Native dockworkers stand about, coiling rope, smoking cigarettes, and telling lewd jokes in Lingala and the Mongo dialects I struggle to understand.

Neil Roberts waits for us. As we approach, I see that he's wearing a long face. He slouches slightly and holds his felt cap in his hands, fiddling with the brim.

"Welcome back," he says, managing a weak smile.

I stand with a baby in the crook of each arm, the traffic of the riverboat landing bustling around me. Ellen begins to cry. Laura, encouraged, joins in. I shift my weight from side to side and coo at them.

"What's the matter?" I ask Neil.

"It's good to see you looking so well," he says without actually looking me in the eye. "I hope the trip wasn't too hard. What with the babies and all, I mean."

"We survived. How about you? You seem a little iffy."

"Oh, it's nothing, Eva. Really, I don't even think we should make a big fuss—"

"Neil . . ."

"Well, I just . . . there's been more trouble. I don't figure the news made it up to Lotumbe."

"No," I say, my calm leaving me. "There's not a lot of communication with the outside, up there, I mean."

"Well, we've been hearing plenty about it on the radio at the dispensary. There's been more rioting, Eva. This time it's among tribes."

"Where?" Richard asks, dusting his hands on his trousers after loading the last of our things into Neil's van.

"It's moving north—Stanleyville and East Katanga this time—but all over, really. The natives are excited over the idea of independence, and, the way they talk, it's like a gift they can hold in their hands and unwrap. And now they're starting to figure out that if it comes, somebody's going to have to be in charge. They all think their particular tribe should be on top."

"Does that mean what I think it means?" I wonder aloud, easing into the back seat of the van.

"What? Civil war?" Neil asks with uncharacteristic hardness. He gets behind the steering wheel and slams the door. "I'm not even going to go near that notion."

He starts up the motor and pulls out into traffic.

"Welcome home, Eva" I say, staring out the window at a world that seems to have resigned itself to unending strife.

THE THIN LAYER OF DUST on everything in the house and the musty air reminds me of books that have been closed up in a basement.

I lie down on the bed with Ellen and Laura beside me, while Richard unpacks. My babies' innocent eyes stare up at the world.

"This is Mama and Daddy's room," I tell them. "And that's Daddy right over there."

Richard shuts a drawer and waves gamely.

"You see that tree outside the window?" I ask, though I know neither baby will know to turn and look. "When you get a little bigger, we'll get mangoes out of that tree and you can eat 'em. You like that idea?"

Ellen burps. Laura gurgles, and her head lolls from side to side.

DAYS PASS. Vigor returns. My body begins to remember how it's supposed to be shaped, though most of my clothes still don't fit right.

Ellen and Laura are ferocious little machines who seem intent upon three particular activities—eating, crying, and elimination. I think I would find the condition of motherhood more endearing if even one of their exploits could be completed without my participation, but such isn't the case. I nurse. I burp them. I console. I change one diaper; I change another. I put one baby down; I console her sister. I change a diaper anew. The first baby wakes; the other is ready to sleep. Then the process repeats itself. This goes on twenty-four hours a day.

As vexed as I was to have the girls kept from me in the days after their birth, I would give most anything to be relieved of them to sleep for more than a half hour at a stretch. I suppose, if Richard and I had any spare savings, we could hire one of the village women to spell me now and again. But with extra mouths to feed and chubby little bodies to clothe, we barely have enough to pay Ta Pierre for his housework.

I try teaching one hour a day. The boys in my class are beside themselves with excitement over my return. I sit with the babies on my lap and answer their questions: No, I did not know I was having twins. Yes, I'm glad I did, for it's a blessing from Jesus. No, the babies don't yet eat the white man's food, just mother's milk, as all infants do.

After class, Liyanza is animated and ripe with comments about every conceivable subject. He walks me home, carrying my books so that I may fully attend the babies. Over the next few days, he makes himself a constant companion, at once full of youthful questions and greatly determined to demonstrate knowledge he's gathered from his biology textbook. When the babies need changing, he's my assistant, juggling bottles and safety pins and manning the can of talcum powder.

"You must be careful for the babies to be getting bacterias," he warns one afternoon as he and I sit on the front porch. I'm busy going over my students' assignments, and he's busy bouncing up and down in his chair and looking out at the world.

"Thank you," I say, having had just about enough of his assistance for one afternoon.

"I'm going to go to the University and be a doctor," he announces.

"Oh, are you?"

"Oui, Mama. And I'll cure all the diseases, and people will remember my name for their grandchildren's grandchildren. It will be so. I'll be a great man. You will see."

On Saturday, I can bear my duties no more. Richard takes care of the babies, so that I may have just a bit of a break. I wash my hair and put on sweet-smelling powder and try to make myself look presentable.

Then I indulge myself in a trip to the village.

Ekebe Jacques greets me with a broad smile, though he looks thinner. He confesses that he's not been in the best of health.

"Did you see Nurse Matthews for a checkup?" I ask.

He coughs and shakes his head.

"The white man's medicine has many miracles. But I haven't yet seen it can take the old man's tired bones and make them dance again. That is the work of the gods."

"Maybe," I say, "but if you hurt or you're coughing like that, Nurse Matthews might have medicine to make you feel better."

"You have your way, and I have mine."

"But you said before how wonderful you thought it was that we can come here and save babies' lives. Is there some difference?"

"I said it, true. And I meant it. But with all the times that change, a man can change what he thinks in his head. I still believe it's more good than bad, the white man's medicine. But when we talked of it before, I didn't have an evil spirit in me. Now it's here." He taps on his chest and sticks out his tongue to show me.

"Witch doctor have kept me alive for many years, more years than your life and *Nkoko Bongongolo* put together. I'll do as witch doctor tells. It's best."

The stubborn part of me wants to insist that he simply must go to Jean and get some antibiotics. But the wiser part of me, the part that grows more active the older I get, knows that a man who's lived as long as Ekebe Jacques hasn't persevered by bending to the will of another.

"Very well," I say, and Ekebe Jacques nods his appreciation for my leaving the subject alone.

I ask of the news in the village, and he's full of stories of the strange family from Nigeria who came to visit and have yet to leave.

"It's been one rain and now another and they're still here. They keep all quiet to themselves, which suits everyone. It's foreign, these people's ways. They cook foods with different smells and do strange *woso woso* dances different from ours. Nobody wants to go by the house where they're living." He coughs some more. He has to stop and catch his breath.

"Where do they live?" I ask.

"That way." He points toward the far end of the village.

"Why did they come here? I mean, so far away from their home?"

"They moved in because one of the cousins married an Nkundo from Bolenge years and years ago. So now that makes him a far member of our tribe. They pay in grains and metals for using the house. There's much talk of this in the village. Many stories want to be told. The one that's most believed is someone in the family has made great crime, a killing or taking of the tribe's honor, so the elder in their village sent them away for seven years. That's how it is with their people."

"So they're banished? They're here for asylum, all of them?" I ask.

"Four and ten of them, yes. Six young men and one old like me, and seven women and children. One of the men has a bad fever in the head from when he was a baby, I think. He's in the body of a man but talks like a child. I watch them walking by as they go to the river for fishing. It's that fever man who did the crime that makes them have to go away."

The notion of a retarded man's family sequestrated for an unspeakable crime sends a chill through me. I wish Ekebe Jacques well and excuse myself.

All the way home, I think of Ekebe Jacques's darkened eyes and the raspy cough with which he greeted me. Would it be so wrong to suggest that Jean find herself in the village in order to pay him a visit? Yes. I must honor the old man's wishes. This is the only course of action that affords him the dignity of self-determination and the respect he's so thoroughly earned.

A PLAIN POST CARD arrives addressed to me. I recognize Margaret's handwriting:

Sister,

We've been walking parallel lines, you and I. I've been a few steps behind, many miles removed. But the day before yesterday, I caught up. There is eight pounds of new life in the world! What a strange time for this, and what a strange setting.

I will never forget what you did for me. I greeted you with suspicion and you met me with kindness I hadn't earned. I made fun of your sincerity, and, rather than retaliating, you extended yourself. I don't deserve a friend like you. But I'm glad to call you that nonetheless—friend. God bless you.

The woman from the orphanage will be coming tomorrow. I'm reluctant to give the baby up. But I know I must follow our plan.

I must go nurse now.

Yours,
M. H.

SUNDAY MORNING AT CHURCH, Neil and the native pastor introduce my babies amid a flurry of merry-making from comers of both races. There's singing and clapping, and the girls are kissed so many times that it's a wonder they are not left chapped.

After the service, Richard and I walk by the river, still in our best clothes, pushing the twins in a baby carriage Richard rescued from the mission junk heap then cleaned and repainted. I look down at the girls' faces. Everything about them is soft—their skin, their cherry lips. It's only the crowns of wispy hair, one blond and one brunette, that let us discern one little angel kiss from the other. After a bit of time in the sun, their skin has turned the golden hue of ripe Braeburn apples. The girls seem at once utterly vulnerable and impressively stout of health. At night, I like to hold them close and smell their sweetness. How is it that babies smell so good? We must be told, at birth, the secret of achieving this sweetness. Then, somewhere along the way, we get distracted and forget the recipe.

I look down at them and make a face, wrinkling my nose. Ellen smiles gently and gurgles.

"I needed this," I tell Richard.

"What's that?"

"In my heart I needed this, all of it—the dedication, the way everyone's acting today. It's an affirmation. Like there've been these questions in my mind, you know? Things I don't want to think about."

"Like why we're here?" Richard asks dryly.

"Well, yeah, something like that. I just . . . it was hard enough to think about bringing one child into a world, as jumbled as Congo's becoming, and now look at us—we've got two. It's been eating at me."

"Well, it's obvious something has," he says with a smirk.

"What's that supposed to mean?" I ask, slightly put off.

"Please, Eva," Richard says with a laugh of dismay. "You've been on another planet. I haven't known what to say to you. Nobody has. They whisper behind your back and ask me questions about whether you're going to be okay and whether this is just some kind of a phase—"

"You tell them it's none of their cotton-pickin' business," I snap, thinking of the evils of gossip, angered to imagine myself its target.

"Eva . . ." Richard says reproachfully.

"I'm sorry," I sigh, trying to temper my reaction. "I know. I've been awful. I was just so heartsick when they wouldn't let me nurse the babies that I . . . but things are better now, I promise you."

I hope I can keep this promise.

WHEN RICHARD AND I WALK TO SCHOOL on Monday morning, burdened with books and babies, he notices that I'm quiet.

"What's the matter?" he asks.

"I've got a strange feeling and I can't shake it," I tell him, moving Ellen from my shoulder to a position more suited for travel. "It's as if everything's about to go terribly wrong. Like I'm in a little boat drifting on a lake of gasoline, and someone is holding a match just above the surface. It's—"

"Sweetheart, you're tired," he says, putting his hand around my waist. "You've been through a lot. But the worst is behind us. Why, any day now the girls'll be sleeping through the night, then we'll be back to normal."

"You think so?" I ask, not calmed by his words.

As we get to the corner of the building, I see M. Boale standing outside Richard's office with his arms crossed.

"Good morning," Richard calls to him with more cheer than is warranted.

M. Boale nods, a grave expression on his face. As we approach, he steps in front of the office door, barring Richard's entrance.

"Is there something you need?" Richard asks hesitantly.

"There is something very much that I need."

The babies fuss, and I quiet them.

"Well, I, uh . . . do you want to come in and talk about it?" Richard asks, gesturing toward the door, which M. Boale still blocks.

"It is something for everyone to talk about together, however much talking there's to do. We're waiting in Madame Dunagan's classroom."

"We?" Richard asks dourly, beginning to lose his patience.

"The teachers," M. Boale explains.

"Where are the students?"

"I've sent them back to the dormitory. There are things we must settle before any more teaching will happen."

"You're overstepping the bounds of your position, Monsieur Boale," Richard warns. "Whatever it is that's eating at you could surely wait until after—"

"My position is one of *mpifo*, white man," M. Boale says sharply. "I have taken your orders for two years now—"

"Orders? What orders? All I ask is that you show up on time and give the students a basic education."

"And do everything you say because you come over here from many, many miles away and decide that you're in charge. Well, soon enough the Congolese will be in charge of our own country again, and you can work for us. That's how it should be."

"So you sent the students back to the dormitory? You wasted valuable hours of the school day to tell me this?"

"No," M. Boale says, almost shouting. "I sent the students home because I've talked to the other teachers, and we all agree that you're being too stingy with the money. We won't work unless you pay us more. I wanted to tell you in front of the others so that everyone could see your face, but you've forced me to say it now."

"You're striking?" Richard asks, incredulous.

M. Boale smiles and nods condescendingly.

I can't believe he would do such a thing. He's a greedy, godless man. I don't feel guilty about the rancor that wells in my heart when I look at his face.

"It's been time for more money since a long while. But you were away at Lotumbe then came back with new babies. Now, there are no more excuses. I see those fancy clothes you buy for your babies—"

"I made almost all them myself," I interrupt angrily, appalled that M. Boale should stoop so low. "What would *you* know about it?"

"I see the way you lord your wealth over the Nkundo peoples."

"You've got to be joking," I snarl, spitting out the words as if they are thorns I must get out of my mouth.

"Please, now, both of you," Richard says, stepping between us, "I'm sure we can find some way to work this out that doesn't take us away from our reason for being here. Have we forgotten that? We are here for the boys."

I glare at M. Boale, shifting the weight of my babies from one hip to the other.

"You're here for yourself," M. Boale says. "To take what is ours."

Richard looks at the ground, making a little pattern in the dirt with the toe of his shoe. "Do you really believe that?" he asks quietly. "I mean, really and truly? Do the others believe that as well?"

M. Boale is sullenly silent.

"Come on, let's go talk to them," Richard says, looking up.

He walks briskly toward my classroom. M. Boale and I follow without acknowledging each other.

Inside my schoolroom, the mood is unsettled. The teachers sit at the desks, filling the front two rows. They grumble and gesture among themselves but turn silent when Richard and I walk into the room. The only sound left is Ellen babbling gummy infant talk.

"I have informed the *mondele* of our demand," M. Boale says to the group, calling his kangaroo court to order.

"And what does he say for himself, eh?" one of the older teachers asks, looking at Richard.

"There's no more money," Richard tells him bluntly.

"No more money where?" Joseph Boale asks.

"I'm not playing games with you," Richard says coolly. "There's no more money. The district gives me a certain amount at the beginning of the term. We paint the school, we buy notebooks, and the rest is divided up for salaries. It's as simple as that."

"Liar!" one of the teachers calls out. "You have so many things, and food, like your breakfast flakes that come in a box with pictures, and you take trips far away—"

"The Missions board sent us away," Richard interrupts. "I was working. I had no extra salary for those weeks either, just so you know."

I study the mistrustful expressions on the faces before me. These are the faces of my colleagues, of people who I thought were my friends. The word "betrayal" suddenly takes on new resonance. We stand accused of a crime at once absurd and indefensible.

"You're not telling us everything," Joseph Boale insists. "You would be wise to hide your stash of money, 'less someone comes in the night to help you count all that you've stolen from our people."

"You really need to get that notion out of your head right now," Richard says. "It's insulting to both of us."

M. Boale snorts. "Even if we believed what you are saying, we would still refuse to submit. Ask the district for more money."

"Impossible," Richard says flatly, shaking his head.

"And why's that?" M. Boale asks.

"Maybe you'd like to write to King Baudouin yourself, eh? He's up in Brussels. I can get the address, if you'd like. Tell him you want more money. Tell him you can't buy every single thing you hear exists, and, therefore, you're unwilling to work in his service.

Maybe he can cough up the extra francs—and by the way, just how much are you demanding? Have you figured that part out?"

"You must pay us two times what we're receiving now. That's fair."

"Fair?" Richard asks, the pitch of his voice rising a half octave. "This isn't about fair; this is about greed and you know it. Look at you, all of you. You have roofs over your heads. You have food in your bellies. Think about how you got to where you are today, with respectable jobs as teachers. It was in the white man's schools, where you were taught by missionaries or a native teacher who made less than you make now."

"This defiling of our people has gone on for a long time, yes?"

"No, you're missing my point! I was talking about what's fair. Think of the boys in your classes. What do they deserve? There's no more money that can come from the district. I could ask, but they would only laugh at me, and I know it would end up hurting us all down the road."

Upset by all the carrying on, baby Laura begins to cry.

I get up and walk her around the room, whispering to her gently. Should not the sight of this soften their hearts and remind them of their purpose?

"Monsieur le Directeur," M. Boale says, "Our demands are very clear."

"What are you going to tell the boys sitting out in their dormitory building right now?" Richard asks. "Huh? What are you going to tell them? That they won't be allowed to learn to read and write and get ahead in the world because their teachers are too busy being greedy to put the good of the next generation in front of their own petty materialism? These boys are Congo's great hope. Without an education, their future is just as dark as your past. It isn't right. You know that in your heart."

"Do not let the white man shame you with fancy words," M. Boale says to the group. "Remember what we talked about. You must walk out that door in order to have the things you want. Otherwise, the white man will continue to eat you alive."

Richard and M. Boale stare at one another. I hold my breath. There's a terrible, electric tension in the air.

"Come, then. Let us go," M. Boale whispers.

No one moves. Then, ever so slowly, one of the teachers rises. He walks to the door without a trace of emotion on his face.

The room's still again.

Another teacher rises, then another and another.

I swallow hard.

"Now you know what it means to be a man of *mpifo*," M. Boale says to Richard, once all the other teachers have left. Then he turns and walks stiffly from the room.

I look at Richard, who's gone pale. Oh, Lord, would that he could be comforted as readily as my wide-eyed, wriggling babies.

"DID THEY THREATEN VIOLENCE?" Dr. Baker asks. His wife holds their son Maurice close and strokes his hair, as if this will protect him from the dangers we all perceive.

It's after dinner, and Richard's called an emergency meeting of the Missions council. We fill the pews of the church, two dozen white people, sweaty and soiled from a day's labors beneath the African sun.

"I hesitate to say that I've lost control of my own school," Richard says, pacing back and forth in front of the pulpit, "but I'm sure by now all of you've heard what happened today. It was nothing like violence. It's just a labor strike."

"Did you tell them there's not a thing to be done about it? Their demands, I mean?" Neil Roberts asks.

"I did."

"Then you should have them arrested," Jean says resolutely.

"What?" I exclaim.

"You heard me, Eva. Sometimes you have to teach people a lesson."

"Arrest them for what?" I ask, amazed.

"Well, they have contracts, don't they?"

Richard nods.

"And they got their money at the beginning of the term, the full amount that the contract says they're due?"

"We pay all the teachers in the first week of the term. Yes, that's right," Richard confirms.

"Then it sounds to me like they've broken their contracts," Jean says. "In Congo, that's against the law. You can send them to jail in Coquilhatville. Let them think about it for a few days. See how they feel about things then."

There is a general chorus of agreement for Jean's suggestion.

"That's fine, just fine," I say. "Listen to all of you, hungry for blood. Y'ought to be ashamed of yourselves. Is this a Christian response to the situation?"

"Christ never had to deal with this kind of insolence," Dr. Baker suggests.

"Oh, really?" I ask. "What about the night before his death? Each of Christ's disciples betrayed and forsook him. You should remember that from first-year Bible study. What was his response then?"

"He forgave them," Richard offers.

"Exactly," I say tersely.

"Spare the rod and spoil the child," Dr. Baker warns.

"And what good will it accomplish?" I ask, struck by the irony of standing in the defense of those I was ready to condemn a few hours ago. "If we call in the police and have them taken to jail, they're bound to give in after a few days, right? They have families, for heaven's sakes. So they come back to class and everything returns to normal, more or less. But what happens at the end of the term? It's the same all over again, only this time we don't have a leg to stand on. Don't you see? If we can't find common understanding, we're in deep trouble. As ignorant as these teachers seem, I would remind you that there aren't exactly a bunch of other natives waiting in the thicket behind the school, educated and ready to take their jobs. We need those teachers just as much as they need us."

"She's got a point," Mrs. Baker says.

It's then that Liyanza appears in the sanctuary doorway.

"*Mam'Oenga,* you must come," he calls to me.

"I'm busy now. Don't interrupt," I scold. "Come and talk to me tomorrow."

"No, you must come right away," he insists, shaking his hands at his sides, "and *Nkoko Bongongolo,* too. I've been sent to get you."

"Whatever is the matter?" Jean asks Liyanza.

"Someone in the village, they ask for Mama *la Nkoko,* and the person not going to wait long time for them," Liyanza says, looking as though he might start to cry at any moment. "Please be coming now."

"Let's go," Richard says, rising.

"All right," I agree and begin wrapping Ellen and Laura in their blankets against the perils that come along with dusk.

"Shall we take a vote on the strike?" Richard asks everyone.

"Maybe the best thing to do is nothing at all," Jean Matthews suggests. "Let 'em think about it for a few days. Let 'em feel what it's like not to have a job. We may need them, like you say, Eva. But those teachers better figure out they need us, too!"

"Fine," Richard says dismissively, walking down from the pulpit to where I stand. "Since I have the final say anyhow, y'all talk about it some more and let me know tomorrow if that's what everyone agrees on."

"Go to the house and get the stroller and the flashlights," I say, handing my key to Liyanza. "We'll meet you halfway back. Oh, and you know where I keep the extra diapers."

"Oui, Mama," he says, running off.

It's no later than seven o'clock, but the warmth and light have gone west to Spanish Guinea, to the ocean, to the New World. The ground is soft from the rains this afternoon, and the moisture clings to all the world that will have it. For the first time since coming to Africa, I can see my breath in the night air.

Tonight is a night of little moon, so our passage is lit by the flashlights Liyanza has brought from the house. I've never been to the village at night. I don't know what to expect, nor even why I'm going. I don't need to feel any more dread on this day, but as we walk along, it fills me. I soak it up from the air like a wick.

"Who is it that wants to see us? I can't imagine anyone leaving in the middle of the night. It makes no sense," I say, and the moment the words are formed of thin steam and left me, the rest of my breath catches in my chest. I know the answer to the question. It took saying the question out loud to realize it.

"It's your old friend," Liyanza tells me solemnly.

He guides us along a path that is familiar to all by day. Yet at night the path has been known to disappear, leaving white men wandering out into the part of the forest where the natives lay their dead.

I can see and smell the village before we get there. A trail of wet smoke drifts toward the clouds, lit from below by the fire from which it issues. I can hear much dancing and carrying on.

Soon enough, we arrive. In the middle of the square, the villagers have built a bonfire. It crackles and roars, the wood damp from rain. All around in a ring, drummers drum and dancers dance, near naked, wild, and impassioned. An old witch doctor wanders about, hands shaking in the air, his leopard-tooth necklace rattling with each step. The man speaks rapidly with his eyes closed, rambling in a tongue I can't understand. Women and children sit in their doorways, watching the proceedings in reverent silence.

I've been here long enough to know what's going on—they are sending forth a much-honored man.

Richard pushes the baby carriage down the row of houses. When we reach our destination, Ekebe Jacques's niece is waiting outside.

"I bring them," Liyanza tells her.

She nods. He turns and leaves.

"Come inside," the niece says gently, her asperity held in check for once. "It's almost time, and he wants to see you. I will watch after your babies."

I hesitate for a moment, not sure that I want to leave Ellen and Laura in her charge. Then I look in her eyes and see no malice there. I roll the carriage over to her and hold out my flashlight.

Ekebe Jacques's house smells of death. I remember this miasma from my visit to the Mondombe leper colony when we first arrived in Africa. Palm-oil lamps light Ekebe Jacques's room. Ceremonial fetishes hang on the walls and dangle from the rafters. The old man lies on a straw mat in the corner. He doesn't stir to acknowledge our presence.

Richard and I look at each other, then cross the room cautiously.

"Ekebe," I whisper, and he opens his eyes.

"Mam'Oenga," he says with a trace of a smile. His voice is faint and his eyes dim. There's no strength in him to lift his head. "I'm so glad that you are come, and *Nkoko,* too. The people of the village, they have a great party for me. Did you see?"

"It's very fine," I say, kneeling beside him and taking his hand.

Ekebe Jacques coughs and winces.

"They're making ready to send me on to heaven. I'm the oldest man in the village now, so it's of great importance. The witch doctor, he says tonight is the night that I will leave."

"If you would just . . . Richard can go back right now and get Dr. Baker or Nurse Matthews," I say anxiously. "Surely there's something they can do to help get you better."

"No, no. I'm better already. I am well," Ekebe Jacques says gently, taking both my hands in his. The old man's gnarled knuckles are rough against my skin.

"I worry sometimes," he says. "I worry that I have taught you nothing. My two students, look at you. I spend many afternoons to tell you of how it's been in Congo in the days long ago. Remember well the things I have told you, children. I'm afraid that my own people want to hurry and forget. They have no use for proverbs and the knowledge of their grandfathers. All they want to talk about is guns and automobiles. Many people will die for this. You must listen to me well now."

I open my mouth to speak, but he stills me.

"Every season, anger grows. It grows like the vines and the trees. The rains wash our spirits clean. But if the rains don't cleanse . . ." His breathing is shallow. His time is near.

"I must go," he says, once he's caught his breath. "I don't want to live to see my people spill one another's blood in greed for the white man's bunk-bunk."

The old man falters. I wait.

"There is much carrying on outside—listen to them," he says, looking out the door at the dancers. There should be some music inside as well. Give me this gift now. Sing to me one of the church songs from your Jesus man. I will rest and listen."

I look at Richard. His eyes well with tears. He comes up alongside Ekebe and begins to sing, softly and sweetly, his voice trembling with emotion:

Swing low, sweet chariot,
comin' for to carry me home . . .

Ekebe Jacques's niece appears in the doorway with my babies, curious about what's going on inside. She balances the twins on her ample hips.

I join Richard for the verse of the song:

I look over Jordan and what do I see
comin' for to carry me home.
A band of angels is comin' after me
comin' for to carry me home.

When we finish, Ekebe Jacques is very still.

This moment changes history. The last memories of life before the disruptions of the white man are now gone, floating up toward heaven with the sparks and embers of the fire outside the door.

Though there is sound all around us, I can hear nothing but the breath of Ekebe Jacques's niece. It comes to my ears now in little gasps.

She steps forward clumsily, as if she has just learned to walk. Her face reddens and twists. A thin, miserable wail begins in her throat. Her hands rise up in the air and shake like the leaves of a tree, and she throws herself upon Ekebe Jacques's body.

"Nkokonyango, Nkokonyango," she weeps, burying her face in the blanket and writhing.

Richard puts his arms around her shoulders, but she throws him off.

"No, let me alone," she begs, her eyes flashing wildly. "I must have this."

Hours pass. I mind the babies. Eventually, the men from the village look in and see that Ekebe Jacques has passed on. This seems to spur them to even greater frenzy in their dancing and drumming.

Eventually, Ekebe Jacques's niece calms down. I put a blanket around her shoulders and sit with her against the wall by the fire. We stay with her until the men from the village come to get the body and the morning sky has grown light enough for us to return to the mission safely on our own.

THE MAIL ARRIVES FROM COQUILHATVILLE.

I receive one item: a single-spaced typewritten letter from Wallace Hinton, sent via airmail from Cleveland.

> *Dear Eva,*
>
> *Congratulations on the arrival of the twins! You and Richard must be very proud. I cannot think of two more loving and compassionate people than you, or any better suited to receive the gift of family in such abundance.*
>
> *We at the Missions board are all aware that Congo is going through a period of upheaval right now. We have received reports from various mission stations across the Equateur province that native sentiments are stirred up.*
>
> *You will recall that I, myself, have been in the field. For ten years I was the minister of a small flock of converts in Jamaica. I remember coming home from a central committee meeting one day with a sense of frustration that knew no bounds. It seemed that the tone of the whole meeting could have been expressed in the words "What's in it for me?" The pastors wanted more salary. The laymen wanted more money for meetings and expenses, though most of them were not out of pocket a farthing. The wife of one pastor was trying to manipulate the planning of an annual conference so that her church*

would be host, and all present knew she would bleed the treasury of its last penny when she arranged for the meals. I sat down and wrote a letter of resignation, but I had the good sense not to mail it.

If you give up now, you will not only be letting yourself down, you will be letting down your church family.

Yes, we at the Disciples of Christ think of ourselves as a family. You, the missionaries in the field, are our children moved far away from home. We care about you deeply. My heart goes out to you and Richard in this present struggle of your souls.

Sincerely,

Wally P. Hinton

When I have finished reading the letter, I crumple the piece of paper and throw it at the living room wall.

The girls are crying in the bedroom and need my attention. They've been carrying on almost constantly since this early morning, when I had to call Jean over to dig insect eggs out of their backs.

I don't believe that Wallace Hinton, for all his hallowed years of Christian service, knows what it's like listen to his babies scream with pain because someone's troweling beneath their tender skin with the point of a scalpel.

I shall not write any more plaintive letters to Wallace P. Hinton.

BY FRIDAY, Richard has not bent to the teachers' demands. The boys wait patiently in their dormitory for a resolution. I suggested that Richard at least unlock the typing room and let them practice their lessons, but he's declined, fearing reprisal from the striking native teachers. Richard and I've discussed a plan for dealing with M. Boale, and on Saturday morning, we go to the village to give it a try.

"What's it feel like, being without your little dirty-diaper machines for a couple of hours?" Richard asks as we roll along on our bicycles.

"Good," I say hesitantly. "Except I hope I left Jean enough milk, and—Oh! Did I take both blankets over to her house? 'Cause I only remember packing the one and—"

"Cool it, Eva. Save your fretting for Monsieur Boale—"

"I don't see why you just can't fire him."

"Great," Richard says sarcastically. "Then who knows what the others would do. I don't even want to think about—"

"You know what I mean," I tell him, growing annoyed.

"Yeah, well, it's a bad idea."

"Says you," I retort.

We fall into silence. When we reach the village, the natives treat us coolly, more so than I can ever remember. I look around for a familiar face. When I at last see one, it is that of M. Boale's wife. She sits outside her door, pounding banganju greens with chilis.

"Are you ready for this?" I ask Richard quietly.

"No," he says. "Should I be?"

We reach M. Boale's house.

"Mama Boenga," his wife says, nodding respectfully as she lifts the ends of her apron to wipe the grain from her hands. "What brings you to this door today?"

"We're here to see your husband," Richard tells her.

"Today isn't a good time for talking," she says. "You come back another day. It will be better for all."

"No. I need to talk to him now," Richard says. "Is he inside?"

"Yes, but—"

"Monsieur Boale," Richard calls out loud enough for several households to hear him. Then he clears his throat and repeats the name. "Monsieur Boale!"

It is a few moments before M. Boale appears in the door of his house, squinting and blinking in the bright sun. He wears a simple piece of native fabric.

"What do you come here for?" he asks. It's when I hear M. Boale's voice that I realize Richard has woken him.

"We've come to talk about your strike," Richard says, crossing his arms in the same affected manner that M. Boale typically exhibits. "I've had many conversations with the government district and the Christian Missions board."

"Yes?" M. Boale says, suddenly excited. "And?"

"You and your striking teachers are all fired," Richard says.

M. Boale gasps. A look of horror plays across his face before he's able to contain it.

"Wha . . . what do you mean? You can't do that," he sputters.

"I can, and I have," Richard says matter of factly. "The Missions board is sending Americans down from Boende and Mondombe to take your jobs. They should be here in a week."

This isn't a mere distortion; it's a bald-faced lie, the kind of gamble one makes when there is nothing further to lose. But like the creative truths I told as Margaret was getting ready for her disappearing act, Richard's lie is offered in the interest of ultimate good, not for temporary personal gain.

"No!" M. Boale blusters like a little boy robbed of his toy train the day after Christmas.

"I'm afraid so," Richard says. "If you would be kind enough to have your desk cleared out by tomorrow morning, we can spare you the embarrassment of having one of the boys bring your things here in a box."

"This is a very bad idea," M. Boale says, his voice shaking. "You should know better than to fool with me like this. I'm a man of—"

"*Mpifo*, yes, I know," Richard says blandly. "Although that won't be the case for long. Being a teacher is what gives you your prominence. Without a job, you're pretty much out of luck in that department."

Suddenly, M. Boale turns to me, clasping his hands together.

"Tell your husband this is unwise," he begs miserably.

"It seems pretty sensible to me," I inform him.

"A curse on both of you," Joseph Boale says, anger flashing in his eyes.

"That would pretty well describe the last week," Richard tells him. "Now go talk to your teachers and see what they think. I'll tell you this—if you're all willing to come back to work and do the job of teaching that you've already been paid for, I might be willing to do the Christian thing and forget about all of this."

M. Boale draws a deep breath and presses his lips tightly together. He stares out at the village.

Richard waits patiently. I've no idea how he can keep his cool.

I look back and forth from one man to the other, then steal a glance at Mme standing frozen before us, bits of grain mash dripping from her forearms and apron onto the ground.

"I don't need to talk to them before I make the decision," M. Boale says at last. "They will do as I say."

"And what is it that you say?" Richard asks.

"Monday," M. Boale spits.

"What's that?" I ask.

"We will return Monday, all of us, you insolent woman," he says. "A curse on both of you."

"I think we've already covered that," Richard says blandly. "If there's nothing else, then congratulations—you've got your job back. See you Monday morning. Be on time, and I'd appreciate no trouble, if you don't mind."

"Goodbye," I say to Mme Boale.

"Goodbye," M. Boale mumbles.

Richard waits until we have reached the edge of the village before he drops to the ground, letting his legs collapse under him.

"You were amazing!" I say.

He looks up at me and squints.

"I think I'm gonna throw up," he whispers.

Twenty-two

December 1959

MY BABIES ARE GROWING.

With the passing days, their personalities become more and more distinct. Though they're twins, each is becoming her own little woman. Blonde, bright-eye Ellen is a talker. She has mastered "Mama," refers to her sister as "Lala," and garbles a range of other words that are her private domain. She's constantly pointing at the world and making comments in a vernacular I've yet to decipher. It's a curious tongue, one that I imagine she will soon abandon in favor of more practical options such as English and Lonkundo.

Laura, with her dark curls and similarly toned moods, is more meditative. Where Ellen will have an immediate comment on the flavor of her breakfast or a native witch doctor's garish headdress, Laura will sit very still, silently observing as the world muddles through its travails. I wonder what secrets she's learned about the order of man and nature, busy as she is, watching and listening.

Both girls seem intent on walking upright well before the books say they're supposed to. Unfortunately, neither has the necessary certainty on her feet to get very far without crashing into the corner of a table, the edge of a door, or the flank of a goat that seems to have taken up residence in our yard.

One thing the girls share is the love of getting dressed up. They offered little resistance to being costumed as reindeer for pictures to send to the congregations back home. After that getup, I fitted their bare bellies with matching sashes upon which I painted "1960" in bold white numerals.

I'll raise my babies in a new decade. Simple as it is to say, it's a difficult notion to fully digest. The implications are awesome—for as different as the 1950s were from the war years of the 1940s, and the decade of Depression before that, what new threats and opportunities will my girls encounter in the years ahead? I stare at their New Year's snapshot, smiling for the era to come. I take a copy of the picture and post it beside my bed.

The school term's drawing to its close. As summer passed, with its spirit-withering dry season and then rain again, M. Boale and I actively avoided each other. We've found no occasion to exchange more than a few words since our square off in front of his house, and the times we've needed to speak, the exchanges have been stilted in the distant manner children assume after a playground scrap.

Five days before Christmas, one of those necessary conversations arises. I have to go to M. Boale's room to collect the grades of the students for whose records I'm responsible.

"Take them," he says, tossing a folder on his desk and turning his back to me officiously. The impact of the folder against the table-top causes the manila cover to open and several sheets to slide out.

"Thank you very much," I say tersely, tidying the pages and looking through their contents. Everything seems to be in order.

"You're very welcome," he tells me, back still turned. "Good day."

"Good day," I say and turn to leave.

"Oh, Madame Dunagan?" He says from behind me.

"Yes?"

"Merry Christmas to you."

I stop, surprised by his graciousness.

"Well, Merry Christmas to you, too," I tell him. "I hope the holidays bring you joy and surprises."

"Oh, they shall," he says with a Machiavellian laugh. "And I'm sure there will be surprises for you. *Tomboofomana.*"

I ponder what he means by invoking Richard's proverb: "We shall meet again."

I hold the folder tight against me and hurry from the room.

AFTER DINNER, Richard and I put on our good clothes, dress the girls, and ride in Neil Roberts's van down to the dispensary. Tonight, the BBC worldwide service is broadcasting a performance of the *Nutcracker* ballet from the Royal Albert Hall in London.

The staff at the dispensary has strung up a special aerial so that we can tune in the program from a transmitter boat off the coast of Madagascar.

Twenty of us have gathered to hear Russians and sugarplum fairies dance. We occupy the same chairs in the same operating room that we did one year ago, when we gathered in a state of shock to listen to the riots in Léopoldville. Tonight, our dress is different. Our humor's different. The furrows in our brows are lax, though perhaps only temporarily so.

One of the nurses has made up some eggnog punch from powdered milk and, as the evening progresses, we toast every conceivable thing.

Richard walks the girls around the perimeter of the room. I close my eyes and listen to the music, which is faint at times. The violins sound scratchy, and at one point a sort of electrical hissing drowns out the music for a few minutes, but the ballet's glorious nonetheless. I sway with the music and imagine the audience, bedecked in furs and jewels, thrilling to the pliés and pirouettes on stage.

My life is utterly different from theirs. But when they applaud, so do I, and it feels as though I'm among them. I take care to remember this feeling of lightness. It's a lull in a great, threatening storm that rages within and without.

CHRISTMAS IS BLESSEDLY QUIET.

Richard loves the striped seersucker pants I made him from a Singer pattern, and I shall enjoy using the sheets of fine-milled linen stationery he bought me in Coquilhatville.

Mother's mailed us red candles scented like pine trees. They arrived partly melted, but I was able to prop them in a drinking glass to create a gay holiday centerpiece. The smell the burning candles make brings up Christmas memories from my girlhood: a bittersweet reminder that, although Africa is where we live, there's indeed another home we've left behind.

LATE AT NIGHT, a sound awakens me.

At first, I can't tell what the noise is—perhaps an animal's prowling in the garden—but then I hear the unmistakable twig-snap and squeak of shoe leather that tells me the visitor is human.

I sit up in bed, easing aside the mosquito netting.

There's just enough moonlight to render the edges and corners of the room visible. Ellen and Laura sleep silently in their bassinet and washtub. Richard lies beside me with the sheets twisted around his legs.

The sound from the garden has stopped. I hold my breath, not knowing whether to be terrified for my safety or go straight outside with a flashlight to remedy whatever trouble is come.

There is sound again. This time the footfalls come from the front porch.

"*Mam'Oenga*," a man says in a deep, hoarse whisper. It's an African voice, but not one I recognize.

"Yes?" I call back.

Richard stirs.

"Come to the door," the man says. He speaks in a strange accent, one I have heard before, though I can't remember where and when.

I take my flashlight from beneath the pillow and stumble toward the living room with Richard quick on my heels. When I get to the screen door and shine the light around, there's no one to be seen.

"Where are you?" I ask.

"Here," the man says, and this time the voice comes from nearby. "Come outside. I must talk to you."

I look at Richard. He shrugs. I open the door, and we walk out onto the porch.

"Over here," the voice insists.

I shine my flashlight to the corner of the house, but still can't see who's come to call at such a late hour. I sense that something's amiss in the whole transaction, but I walk toward the end of the porch.

"Who is it?" I ask.

"Must talk to you and *Nkoko,* too. Come," is all the man will say.

I point the beam of my flashlight around the garden. There's no one here. It feels as though a ghost is addressing us. I get chills.

It's then I realize that the man's gone inside the house. The intruder has run into a piece of furniture, or a wall, perhaps, for a thud and the tearing of fabric is followed by what is unmistakably cursing in an African tongue.

Time slows down.

As my feet get me to the front door, I hear Laura screaming. As I'm able to pull the door open and step inside, the screaming no longer comes from the bedroom but from the kitchen. As I shine my flashlight beam wildly around the room and run toward my daughter's voice, the back door swings shut with a sharp spring-smack.

"No!" I wail, running through the kitchen and throwing my weight against the door.

The latch has been broken, pried clean off its hinges.

I trip down the back steps and out into the yard, but the man's gone.

"Come back! Come back!" Richard pleads desperately, running past me and out toward the brush at the perimeter of our yard. He stumbles in the darkness.

Ellen cries from the bedroom. I can't move.

Richard returns, limping up the steps. He's drenched in sweat, the legs of his pajama bottoms shredded by razor grass, his feet nicked by roots and stones.

"No! No! Go get Laura!" I cry hysterically and push him back outside.

Richard stands and looks at me for a split second before turning and disappearing into the brush, the beam of his flashlight less and less distinct as he gets farther away.

This isn't happening . . . this isn't happening. This is a bad dream from which I will wake and everything will be fine. Where's my baby? Please, Jesus. When I go look, Laura will be back in her galvanized washtub, right where she belongs, okay? I'm going to go look now, okay?

No! My baby's gone. She's gone.

My heart's breaking, right this minute. *Oh, God, take me instead. Put my baby back where she belongs, and let it be me who's stolen off in the night by unfriendly hands, wrenched from my bed for what purpose I don't even want to imagine.*

I dash back out to the yard, Ellen bouncing on my hip. The lights in the Bakers' house are glowing.

"Bring her back!" I wail hysterically, running out onto the path. "Bring my baby back!"

Wake me . . . wake me. This is the worst nightmare I can imagine. May I open my eyes now and have it all be put right? Please, make this be a dream and nothing more. The African night's swallowed up that which is precious to me. My baby is gone, and my husband, too, out searching blindly for her through the snake-riddled brush.

Everything that impedes me is an enemy—the darkness, the brambles and burrs that scratch at my flesh, the night air, humid and no good for breathing.

I near the river. Due not so much to the sniveling tears that obscure my view but the panic that now fuels me with greater purpose than my own heartbeat, I lose sight of the path and trip over a vine. As I fall, I clutch Ellen close to my chest so that I don't crush her.

I get back on my feet and start walking again, but someone has got hold of my arms. I try to throw them off, but I can't. When I realize that it's Dr. Baker and Jean who are holding me, I quit fighting. Still, it takes their combined efforts to calm me.

Dr. Baker goes to wake the other missionaries.

Fifteen minutes later, everyone's gathered at our house, pacing and speculating in hushed tones. It's decided that if Richard's manhunt is fruitless, a search party will be organized. Should the larger effort produce no results, we shall summon the police commissioner.

"Forgive the indelicacy of my asking this, but do you have any enemies? Anyone who'd do something like this?" Neil Roberts asks.

"No," I say dully.

"Think, Eva," he says.

I can't think. I'm out of my mind. Yet suddenly I'm confronted by the memory of M. Boale, standing with his back to me on the last day of the school term.

"I'm sure there will be surprises for you before we meet again," he said. I wondered what he meant by that. Surely, despite all his pettiness and venality, he couldn't be responsible for something this wicked.

As cocks crow and the lokolé sounds, dawn creeps across the open threshold, bearing Richard in tow. He's stoop shouldered and disheveled.

"Anything?" I ask anxiously.

Richard fights back tears and can't speak. Wearily, he shakes his head.

I COUNT THE HOURS THAT LAURA HAS BEEN GONE as anxiously as if she were underwater without oxygen. Indeed, the analogy is apt. Laura isn't so sturdy as to survive an extended ordeal without the care and attention only a mother can provide her.

I'm stupid. I shouldn't have gone outside to try to talk with the stranger. If I had any sense in my head, I would've seen this coming. What kind of a mother am I?

I begin to wonder why it couldn't have been Ellen who was taken instead of Laura. She's hardier, better suited for such an ordeal. But no, this kind of thought is madness. I'm optioning one baby in favor of the other. I must quit thinking of this right now. Would that I myself were stolen instead of either of them. That would be just.

By nine o'clock in the morning, nothing's been found—no shoe print, no torn bit of fabric, no native houseboy who's heard anything. Nor has any sort of ransom note materialized.

The police commissioner has come from Coquilhatville.

"What was the sound of the man's voice?" he asks, taking notes on a little pad.

"Foreign," Richard says.

We sit on the sofa. On the table before us is oatmeal, which Mrs. Baker fixed, but I haven't the appetite to eat.

"Foreign?" the commissioner asks skeptically.

"African," I insist. "He was talking Lonkundo, but he didn't sound as if he was from around here. And he was really anxious, whispery and hurried."

"And you saw what of him?"

"Only his back," I say.

"What did that look like?" the commissioner asks.

"I can't really remember," I say remorsefully. "It was all over and done so quickly."

"Very well," the commissioner says, closing his note pad. "I thank you for your time, and if I hear anything I'll be certain to let you know right away."

"That's it?" I ask, looking up with surprise.

"Madame, I'm very sorry for what's happened to you. But there's much trouble in the region at present. The dockworkers in Coquilhatville threaten a strike, you know? There are revolutionaries that break into the newspaper and try to ruin the press. I wish I'd the resources to send my whole squad of detectives here to Bolenge to look for your little girl—"

"Baby," I correct him, standing up. "She's not a girl; she's a baby. And every hour that passes, I'm just so afraid that . . . this is a human life. I can't believe you'd just put her in the same category as—"

"Madame, please," the commissioner says, picking up his cane and notebook. "I understand your suffering. I've children of my own. I tell you what I'll do. I'll send a native constable down from

Coquilhatville this afternoon to ask around the village and see if any of them knows anything."

"Oh, for goodness sakes! We've already done that," I say brusquely.

"Ah, but have you had a native do the questioning?"

"What difference would it make?" Richard asks, irritated.

"The difference between lies and truth. The kindly natives you've thought are your friends may not be so any longer. Everything changes."

The commissioner rises. "Messieurs, Mesdames," he says, nodding and walking toward the porch.

"Have your constable inquire about a man named Monsieur Joseph Boale," I say.

"What's that?" the commissioner asks, turning around.

"Joseph Boale," I repeat the name succinctly. "He's a teacher at the mission school. Find out where he was last night."

"*D'accord,*" the commissioner says. Then he's gone, out the door and off to the city in a cloud of road dust.

I follow him.

"Eva!" Richard calls after me, but I don't listen.

I wander through the mission with greater and greater abandon, looking for any clue to Laura's whereabouts that the search party might have missed. Part of me expects to find her cooing, diapered and unharmed, by the side of the road. I let this hope fill me in an attempt to block out the insidious image of my baby crying pitifully from hunger and dehydration.

"Laura!" I wail, imagining her crushed under a rock or drowned in the river. I look around and realize I've been walking in a circle.

Mrs. Baker comes out from her house and takes me by the shoulders, leading me home.

"Shh, Eva," she whispers in the way one would speak to someone who'd genuinely lost her mind. "Take a deep breath now. Get a hold of yourself. Where are your shoes?"

I look down at my feet.

My shoes are back at home in my closet.

Don't they understand? Can no one around me appreciate the horror of this day? If it were happening to them, they would behave differently; that's for sure. They've never had their child ripped from its bed, a child they almost died to have. Perhaps what makes my girls so precious to me is that I nearly lost my own life to give them theirs. In any case, being without Laura is like being without a limb. I keep reaching for her, and each time I don't find her I grow more and more agitated.

We reach the house and climb the stairs.

I grasp at the doorframe for support.

"She just needs some rest," Mrs. Baker tells Richard.

"She just needs our baby," Richard replies.

LATE IN THE AFTERNOON, the native constable comes by the house. His drab olive uniform is smart, and his manner characteristically stiff.

"Madame, I regret to inform you that I've turned up nothing in my search. The Monsieur Boale you inquire about is in Boende on business, gone three days now. His wife sends regrets on your loss."

M. Boale is probably visiting one of his girlfriends. I wonder whether his wife knows this.

"Come. Sit down," I say, ushering in the constable.

I've just returned, wet and muddy footed, from walking through the shallow water at the river's edge, searching fearfully among the reeds and rushes. I must look a fright. I suppose, too, that I should be hungry and tired from the many hours of duress. Yet all normal functions of living seem greatly unimportant. All that matters is Laura's safety.

"And your husband? Where is he?" the constable asks, looking around for Richard.

"He's in Coquilhatville, sending a telegram to the States," I say. "That way, maybe the CIA or the FBI or somebody American can help us out."

"I see," the constable says. "Well, you can tell him when he returns that since there's been no letter of ransom offered, we're assuming the motivation for the kidnapping is political."

"Polit—what on earth makes you jump to that conclusion?"

"Madame, please be calm," he says, shaking his head. "It's sad to say, there's much anger among the tribes, and even more for the Belgian people."

"But we're not even Belgian!" I shout. "Besides, we're here to help, to teach, to . . . to . . . ."

"When a man's angry, all he sees is your skin."

"But why take only one of the babies, then?" I ask.

The constable looks down at the floor and doesn't answer.

"Eh, Monsieur?" I prompt him. "Why just one?"

"I can't speculate," he says reluctantly, "except that it's easier to dispose of one body than two."

These are the words that at last undo me.

Standing in the middle of my living room, I feel as though a part of my spirit has suddenly died. This must be what it's like when someone's heart stops and she can sense that blood's no longer moving through her veins—an impending nothingness. The difference is that what has just been stilled isn't my heart; it's my faith.

"Go away," I tell the constable.

I walk into the bedroom without showing him out.

My baby's dead. My baby's dead. My baby's dead.

I fall face forward onto the bed and pull a pillow over my head.

God, if You are actual and omnipresent, then why do You let someone who's devoted her life to Your service endure such suffering? Is it perhaps that You're not truly benevolent and all loving, but rather, cruel and divisive? No, I can't believe it. I'm more prepared to look into my heart and refute Your existence than to believe the Creator of all things is so sinister.

I lie still for many minutes.

When I take my head out from beneath the pillow, it's dark.

Ellen cries. I must feed her and change her diaper. I wonder if she misses Lala. If so, she keeps it to herself.

I suppose it would be comforting, in a way, if all life on the mission would grind to a halt in light of the tragedy. But such isn't the case, for each missionary's overburdened with duties, and every day seems to present a new crisis. Our nerves become dulled to trouble's arrival, and what would once be looked upon with horror is now met with a mere sigh of fatigue. It's the day after Christmas, and the work of the Disciples of Christ mission at Bolenge must continue, with or without little Laura Dunagan.

I agonize alone.

RICHARD RETURNS FROM COQUILHATVILLE.

I'm standing in the kitchen, beneath the bare light bulb, rearranging dishes for no good reason.

It is just past dusk.

I've never seen him worse for wear.

"Don't ask," he says as he comes in from the darkness.

"What do you mean, don't ask? Tell me everything," I demand.

"I'm just too exhausted, Eva."

"Like I'm not? What happened? Were you able to get through to America?"

"All right, calm down," he snaps. "I sent a telegram to Wallace Hinton in Cleveland. Then someone at the police station suggested I go down to the docks and see if I could get a Morse code relay to New York through Portugal or Iceland."

"And?"

"It took a while, but I got through. I had to buy the radio operator a bottle of liquor in order to use his rig, but I reckon it was a small sin. Anyhow, he got through to New York. It was first thing in the morning there. I had the operator on that end make phone calls to the FBI and Senator Wilkerson's office to let them know that an Oklahoma couple had their baby kidnapped. I'd been waiting about an hour there at the docks when the radio man came running out and told me that he's got a transmission from New York. Senator Wilkerson's on a Christmas vacation, and the FBI says Africa is a little ways outside their jurisdiction."

"What about the CIA? Why didn't you radio them?"

"Can you hold on just one second before you jump all over me?" Richard snaps. "For God's sake, Eva! That was the very next thing I did. But I guess the CIA doesn't take calls from ordinary citizens because the best they would do is offer to take down a telephone message. As for Wallace Hinton, I reckon it'll be several days probably before we hear back from him, though I don't know what lot of help he's going to be."

"Fine," I offer with a snort. "Wonderful."

"Eva, I did everything I could."

"So now it's my turn, I suppose," I say dully, getting up and walking toward the bedroom.

"What do you mean?" Richard asks, following me.

I sit down on the edge of the bed and put on a pair of long socks.

"Eva, what are you doing?"

I take my sturdy shoes from the closet and slip my feet into them.

I OPEN THE TOP DRESSER DRAWER, take out a rayon scarf, fold it in two, and set it on top of my head, knotting the corners beneath my chin.

"Where's my flashlight," I ask at last.

"You're not seriously thinking of going out there."

"Dead serious," I say sardonically. "Where is it?"

"So what? You're just going to wander around in the dark looking for Laura? I thought you already did that this afternoon. It's been almost twenty-four hours, Eva. She could be anywhere by now."

A vision of Laura lying in a patch of grass has come to me. It is clearer and more vivid than any imagining I have had since her disappearance.

"She's in the village," I say with assurance.

"So you're going to Bolenge in the middle of the night? Why don't you just lie down, Eva. What you need is some sleep. In the morning, I'll get Neil to drive us to—"

"In the morning, she'll be dead." I don't why I'm so sure of this. I just am.

I find my flashlight under my pillow.

"Take care of Ellen while I'm gone," I tell him and run my hand along the sleeve of his shirt in an awkward goodbye. He knows better than to try to stop me.

I jog along the path to the village, running the beam of my flashlight back and forth across the rocks and vines. Tonight the sky's clear, prickled with stars, and the crescent moon throws a thin, milky cast across the high treetops. In the chill, a thin layer of fog blankets the forest and grass beside the path.

I have to stop once and rest on my way to the village because my side cramps. But I don't lose the path, as we whites are known to. I don't go wandering off into the forest. I've a destination and a purpose, and I will see these to their completion. I will find my daughter, dead or alive, before I sleep.

When at last I smell the smoke from the Bolenge cooking fires and my flashlight beam catches the geometric regularity that must be a house, I let out a whoop and announce my arrival to no one and everyone.

I am not running on the fuel of reason now; I'm running on need.

There are two people who can assist me tonight, two natives I can trust. When I get to the middle of the village, I seek them out. Everyone has gone to sleep, and the cooking fires are reduced to glowing embers. The paths seem unfamiliar in the darkness, but at last I find my first stop.

Ekebe Jacques's house is untouched since his passing. I shine my flashlight around and see the curtains I sewed for his birthday still hanging in the windows. Then I swing the light to his niece's house and walk toward her door.

"Bonkune-o," I whisper loudly.

In a moment, she appears at the window, yawning and shading her eyes from the glare of my flashlight.

"Who is it?" she asks, startled.

"Eva," I say, switching off the beam.

"Why do you come here in the middle of the night? I've heard of your troubles, and I'm sorry—"

"What I carry in my heart tonight is large, yes," I tell her. "I come because I need your help. Do you have good shoes?"

She squints at me for a moment, then nods. "Wait a minute."

She brings a lantern with her, and we go to find Liyanza.

"Why do you think the baby is here in the village?" she asks.

"I just feel it in my heart," I say. "I don't know how to explain it. Laura's here—or somewhere near, anyhow."

I've never been to Liyanza's house, so Ekebe Jacques's niece has to show me the way. We cough to announce ourselves, and Liyanza's aunt comes to the door. We ask the woman to let Liyanza come with us, but she's reluctant to let him go.

"He gets in much trouble out in the night," she says warily.

"This is different," Ekebe Jacques's niece urges her. "The white woman's a friend. She's the one who gives him the book for learning. She's his teacher in school."

Liyanza appears in the doorway behind her, yawning and stretching.

"She's good, Auntie," he says. *"Mam'Oenga* is my friend."

The woman rolls her eyes and swats the air in dismissal, then turns and goes back to her bed, handing Liyanza a walking stick as she passes.

"Take this," she says, "to kill the snakes that will want to eat you in the night."

We wait for Liyanza to lace his shoes. Ekebe Jacques's niece rubs her hands together above the cooking fire's embers to ward off the deep chill that's settling along with the fog. At last, Liyanza's ready to join us.

"What do you need so late, Mama?" he asks. "Is it about Laura?"

I explain it to him as we walk across the village, and he shakes his head.

"So you're completely sure neither of you have heard or seen anything strange?" I ask.

"No," Liyanza says. "I mean, yes, I'm sure. The missionaries come around this morning and the black policeman later, and we tell them the same thing. No one seen any white baby here today. No one seen anything out of normal in the village."

"There's something I have been thinking about since I heard all of this," Ekebe Jacques's niece says.

"What is it?" I ask.

"It's nothing, I'm sure. It could not be the same—"

"Tell me!" I insist.

"I remember stories my *Nkoko* Ekebe used to tell from when I was very small. All kinds of things about how it used to be before the missionaries come. As I grow up, I don't want to hear about his stories so much, but all the things he said when I was small, they stay, like a song I learn. When I hear of one of your babies being taken, I think of an old proverb Ekebe taught me. It says: 'The egg falls from the nest.'"

"Which means?" I ask anxiously, for I don't like the sound of it.

"If a mother chicken has too many eggs all at once, one may fall from the nest. This is a very bad omen. We do her a favor by taking the eggs from her."

"So what you're saying is—"

"A woman who has two babies at the same time must hurry to kill the one of them that's weaker. If not, the runt may die on its own and become an *ogbanje*, Ekebe called it, an evil spirit. Then it can bring much trouble for all the peoples who live near."

"You believe this?"

"Oh, no!" she says in saucy disgust. "It's a very old story and not from here or any of the villages around here. My *Nkoko* Ekebe says it comes from the tribes that live far on the other side of the great river, off in the direction of the setting sun."

"Nigeria," I whisper.

"What?"

"It could be Nigerians who believe that proverb, like the family that's come to stay," I say grimly, the puzzle pieces beginning to fit.

"In practice, what do they do with the body of the baby?"

"They put it out into an evil forest with the bodies of man and woman not fit for burial. It's bodies with bad diseases or men who made great crimes, like killings. The mother must hurry away so the spirit won't be able to find its way back to the village."

"Is there an evil forest around here?" I ask.

"No, no," Ekebe Jacques's niece insists. "I told you one time already, it's an old practice from a tribe far away. They had different words and gods than Nkundo, I think. We don't believe in silly—"

"Oh! Oh!" Liyanza interjects excitedly, then turns to Ekebe Jacques's niece and says a few sentences in rapid-fire Lonkundo.

"What?" I ask.

"The old burying grounds, Mama," he says. "It's where the Bolenge used to put their dead people before we had cemeteries like now. Sometimes children want to play there, but the old people get very angry and say we must stay far."

"Where is it?"

Liyanza points to a broad grove of trees a few hundred yards in the distance. I can just make out where it begins in the pale moonlight. The forest, if that's what one were to call the mangy grove, is at least a hundred yards across and extends a like distance up the rolling hillside.

"If we were to search across all that land ourselves, it would take a day, two days, maybe more," I say. "We will need help."

I turn around and look at the slumbering village, hoping for inspiration. It's dark and silent, save for an occasional loud snore or the yap of a dog.

Then I see M. Boale's house.

"Go and wake my women," I say to Ekebe Jacques's niece.

She shakes her head, not understanding.

"The ones whom I have taught," I say. "Can't you remember? The women I taught to read?"

"Ah!" she says with a nod and dashes off down the path. With one hand, she holds her bosom down flat so that it won't bounce too much as she runs. In her other hand swings the lantern, flame turned up bright to light her way.

"Let's go talk to the Nigerians," I tell Liyanza.

When we get to the visitors' house, Liyanza takes his walking stick and knocks it soundly against the door like a true man of *mpifo*.

A wrinkled, bare-breasted old woman comes and undoes the latch, pulling the door open cautiously, peering out at us.

"We're sorry to bother you so late in the night," I say in slow, studied Lonkundo. "But a terrible thing's happened, and we need to ask some questions of your family."

The woman shakes her head. At first I think she is refusing to talk to us, but then I realize it's because she does not understand me.

I look at Liyanza.

"Mama," he says slowly. "A baby is missing."

She nods at his words, though I'm not sure she has understood Liyanza any more clearly than she did me. She turns around and speaks some foreign words into the house. Her voice is harsh, like a crow's.

Soon the men of the family assemble in the doorway. Though we have no common language, it seems clear they are not happy Liyanza and I have disturbed their sleep. They talk at us all at once, their voices loud and agitated.

I begin to offer apologies, though I know it can do no good. Six men stand before me, each of them trying to outdo the last in how much indignation he can communicate. Yet I seem to recall Ekebe Jacques telling me there was a seventh man in the family.

I look behind the row of Nigerians and through the open doorway. Palm-oil lamps illuminate their house. There, against the back wall, another man crouches on a low stool with his head against the wall. He's dressed in rags.

When the seventh man sees me staring at him, his eyes grow wide with horror. Then he begins to cackle.

One of the women quickly shuts the door.

"It was him," I whisper to Liyanza.

"What?" he asks.

"There was a man in the house. He's the one who took Laura."

"Do you think that he will show us where he's put her?"

"If the proverb is as it has been told, then there's no chance."

From across the village, I see a lantern bobbing and weaving above the path, like a leaf floating on a stream.

"Come on," I say. "I think the search party is ready."

We were three and now are a dozen and a half. The women of Bolenge gather round me, clucking and whispering words of consolation deep in the dewy darkness.

"We don't want to go to the old burying ground," one of them says. "But if it was our own baby missing, that would be different. So we will go for you, teacher."

"It's very sad," another agrees. "You've waited almost your whole year to find whether your baby shall live. Now, as you begin to love true, a bad man comes to take it away."

We cross a grassy meadow in a long line. Our pace is slow, since several of the women are old and can't walk quickly. The night around us is alive with the eerie mischief of untold jungle insects.

As we progress I think of the commissioner's admonition about believing certain Nkundo are my friends when they are, in fact, enemies. Here, in the midst of a crisis, I have found the opposite—a whole squadron of Africans I never thought of as friends, willing to rise from their beds and comb a cemetery for this American woman's lost baby.

Soon the edge of the grove's upon us. The women have fanned out so there are several arms-length of space between each of them. As we step among the trees, the women call tentative reassurances back and forth to one another, frightened to be treading on forbidden ground. When—after several minutes of tromping through the fog over peaty leaves and vines—no catastrophic ghost-summoning has occurred, the women relax, allowing us to begin the search in earnest.

Each time my foot strikes against something solid, I dig through the mulch and brambles to discover what it is. My fingers grasp at the rot, not knowing if they will find the battered body of my baby, the root of a tree, or a skeleton laid here generations ago.

I laugh to myself. I am losing my mind. *Ophelia, mistress of water and madness, you're my kin.* I want to climb into the decay around my ankles and bury myself in it, in the pungency and mildew. That's where Laura is. I want to be with my baby. Damn everything.

I shake myself. I regain my wits.

Minutes become hours. The sky lightens. The footfalls of the women begin to sound like the dull music of a heavy rainstorm. I stumble along, blinking my eyes hard to fight the fatigue that clings to me along with the dampness and cool of early morning.

Laura's nowhere to be found. My pulse quickens, now and again, as I think I see her in a gully or between the hollows of tree roots where they grasp at the soil. Then, as I get closer, I realize they're only a pile of leaves, or a rock, or a patch of soft morning light that's penetrated the treetops. Maybe this whole pursuit's an exercise in foolishness.

Then, from a fair distance, a woman screams. I run toward the sound, and the other women chase after me. When we reach the source of the hysteria, it is Mme Boale. She stands, shaking and weeping, her hands covering her face.

At her feet lies Laura's naked body, dirty and bruised. My baby's skin is gray and her lips have no color. One leg is twisted oddly. Laura's eyes stare up at the sky but see nothing.

My baby's dead. My baby's dead. My baby's dead.

I drop to my knees and wail.

Several women reach out simultaneously to hold me, but I don't want them near. I let out a bloodcurdling scream, and they step back, cautiously forming a circle around me. I bury my face in the leaves and slap my palms flat against the ground again and again.

Oh, God. Oh, God. Oh, God.

Lord, take me now. I can't live after this sight. It will be burning into me, making me ugly, too ugly to go on. You have cursed me with this vision, all horror, all torment. Take me now. Stop my breathing. Have You no mercy?

"Mama, no!" I hear Liyanza's voice crying. "Wait!"

I look up at him.

"Baby Laura, she isn't dead," he insists.

"Look at her, Liyanza!" I moan. "Get away from me. Go away! Leave me with her body. "

"Mama, I tell you. You must listen to me. You give me all the medicine and biology books, and I read them. Baby Laura has *l'hypothermie*."

He walks over to her body and kneels beside it, gently brushing leaves from her chest. I don't know whether to believe him. It's horrible, horrible.

"She's still warm," he says, laying his hand across her forehead. "You see? And if you feel very close, there are little breathings. I feel it now. We must warm her or she will die for sure."

"Put her against her mother's breast," one of the women suggests excitedly, dancing her way around behind me.

"No! That would be very bad," Liyanza says. "If the baby's arms and legs warm up before her insides do, the slow blood that has been staying in her hands and feets will go to her insides and

320

kill her. She must have milk in her and wrap up good so she can warm her own body.

"My breasts are already dry!" I wail.

One of the women whose baby is still small opens her sleeping cloth.

"You can use my milk," she says.

Another woman gives up her robe so we can wrap Laura tightly. I sit down on a big rock and take off my socks, slipping one of them over my baby's head as little hat.

"Give her breathing," Liyanza instructs.

I pick Laura up and take a deep breath, exhaling into her nose and mouth. It is hard to complete the process with any composure, but somehow I manage. When I've finished, l look up at Liyanza.

"Keep going," he says. "Give her and give her until she has her own breath. And get the milk into her, but make careful not to let her choke."

In a desperate act of faith, we follow his instructions.

After what seems like twenty minutes, I fear it's a lost cause. I stop breathing into her. It's then that I realize she's, indeed, begun to draw shallow breath on her own. She's alive.

Good God, she's alive!

"Give her milk!" I say, and the young mother complies.

Laura coughs and sputters. It's the most beautiful sound in the world. I weep again, but this time for joy. A miracle, a genuine miracle. The women raise their arms to the sky and shake their hands like leaves, doing a dance of thanksgiving.

"She is not all good yet," Liyanza warns. "You must take her quickly to Nurse Matthews and Dr. Baker for more medicines."

"Thank you, Liyanza," I whisper, pulling him close and squeezing him. "Thank you."

I SLEEP FOR FOURTEEN HOURS WITHOUT STIRRING.

It will be many days before Laura regains her strength. She had a concussion, bruises dot her body, and Dr. Baker has tied her leg in a splint. She coughs all day and runs a fever at night. This, Dr. Baker says, is to be expected after such a trauma.

"Who would do something like this?" he asks as he warms a stethoscope. He's come by the house for a daily examination.

"I don't know," I say. "All I can think about is how glad I'm to have her back. I mean, yes, I care who did it, but—"

"I'll tell you one thing," Dr. Baker says, finishing his exam. "She certainly takes after her mother. You're both stubborn as mules when it comes to dying."

"Yeah, you can't get rid of us Dunagan women," I joke feebly.

"Speaking of which," he says, "you can thank that boy for saving her life. That was some sound medical advice he gave you."

"He says he wants to be a doctor."

"Well, good. It'd be an honor to have him in the profession."

ON THE SECOND EVENING after Laura's miraculous recovery, there's a knock on the door. At the time, I'm sitting, talking to the girls about the pictures in a Dr. Seuss book.

Richard goes to see who's come to the house. There's been a steady parade of well-wishers bearing baked goods and prayers, but it's surprising that anyone should come at such a late hour.

"Eva," Richard says as he opens the door. His voice rises in such a cautious way that I know I must put down my book and join him right away.

When I get to the door, I look out onto the porch and see Mme Boale. She's bloodied and beaten. One eye is swollen shut, and an arm hangs limply at her side. Her feet are bare and dusty.

"Come in," I say, but she doesn't respond.

I realize that she's in shock. I step out onto the porch and gingerly walk her inside.

Richard goes to the kitchen to pour her a glass of water.

"Sit down," he says. "I'm going to go get Jean."

I look over her wounds. There are no claw or tooth marks to indicate a wild animal has mauled her.

"How did this happen?" I ask.

"It was he," she whispers, staring straight ahead as anguish twists her face.

"Joseph Boale?" I ask, already knowing it's true.

"It was him who did all of it. I thought so when I first heard your sad news, but now it's sure."

"I . . . I thought he was away, out of the region. The police said—"

"It wasn't his hands that took your baby. It was his words. He's a powerful man with the words. He whispers in the ear of the crazy Nigerian man many things. He reminds him of the bad luck twins can bring. He tells the Nigerian that you're too stupid to know to kill your own baby, so the Nigerian must do it for you. Then he goes away."

Mme Boale takes a sip of water and winces in pain.

I'm speechless.

"When Joseph came back from his trip, he heard all the village talking of how I found your baby out in the burial ground. He smiled and congratulated me in front of everyone. Then, when we were alone back at the house, he took me by the neck and squeezed it until I could not breathe. He's so angry that I have ruined his plans. He tells me all about his cleverness while he beats me. Then when he's gone to urinate, I run away. I come to your house now. It takes me much time because I'm hurting and have no shoes."

Richard returns with Jean and Dr. Baker, who examines Mme Boale and finds that her injuries may be more than superficial. It's impossible to know for certain without an X-ray, but her skull may be fractured.

In between the doctor's poking and prodding, Mme Boale repeats her account of how she came to be in such battered condition.

"We need to get her to the hospital in Coquilhatville tomorrow," Dr. Baker says, slipping off his stethoscope. "Meanwhile, she shouldn't be moved too far."

"She can stay here," I say.

"At Dunagan Memorial Hospital, you mean?" Dr. Baker asks, looking in at Laura asleep on our bed.

"Yes," I say.

The doctor gives Mme Boale a bit of morphine as a hedge against the insult of advancing aches and pains. She falls asleep on the couch, and I lay our spare blanket gently over her.

"I'm not sure it's best that she stay here any longer than necessary," Dr. Baker whispers. "I mean, this has to be the first place her husband will come looking for her, and I hate to think of what kind of mood he'll be in when he finds her."

"That won't be a problem," Richard says. "I'll get a ride up to Coquilhatville at first light to talk with the police commissioner. I reckon Monsieur Boale will have other things on his mind besides visiting our house."

Richard and I thank the doctor and tell him good night, then go to bed.

The girls, still exhausted from our ordeal, sleep soundly. I lie awake for hours, staring at the ceiling and listening to my family breathe. If I can hear them, I know they are still alive. I match my respiration to Richard's. He breathes in; I breathe in. He breathes out, and so do I. I play this game sometimes when I need to feel close to him, in agreement, but I don't want to wake him. In and out, our breath travels in tandem.

Then I hear the sounds the village makes in the morning—the lokolé, the crowing of cocks, the bleating of goats, the tall tale–telling of houseboys walking to the river for water. I open my eyes. The sky's growing bright. I realize I've been sleeping.

I rise and go to check on Laura. She is wide eyed and well.

I open the bedroom door to have a look at Mme Boale. On the couch, where I left her, there is nothing but a bit of dried blood and the rumpled impression her weight left on the cushions. The blanket I laid over her is folded neatly on the floor.

"Madame?" I say quietly, looking in the kitchen.

I see a note on the table. The words are in Lonkundo, and the handwriting resembles a child's rough scrawl:

Mama Boenga,

You take care of me, and I thank you. I must go now before the sun comes and walk many miles to return to the village where I was born. Only there can I be safe.

When Joseph hears that I have told his secrets, he'll find me and kill me if I am not far away. Putting him in jail will not stop the trouble, for he has many brothers to do the killing for him while he's locked up.

Please do not worry for me, as you've enough troubles already. Thank you for teaching me to read and write so that I could leave these words on the paper.

Mme Boale didn't sign her letter. I guess we never got to that lesson.

"IS THIS THE MAN?" the native constable asks, poking his nightstick into the small of M. Boale's back so that he makes a face and stands up straight.

It's New Year's Day, 1960. I stand on my porch with my babies balanced on my hips. I nod at the constable.

At the end of our garden path stands M. Boale, handcuffed and dirty. There are large circles of sweat beneath the arms of his shirt and a look of deep umbrage from head to toe. Behind him, handcuffed and ankle bound in the constable's car, is the wild-eyed Nigerian man.

"Independence for my people will come," M. Boale says. "It will be a great day. And you'll be made a slave, along with the rest of your meddlesome *confrères*. When I pass you, working in a field, I'll spit on you."

"Take him away," I whisper.

Twenty-three

March 1960

A CONVEX, impossible-looking bit of water balances atop a drinking glass even as it seems it's already filled to capacity. This extra volume is called the meniscus. If one disturbs the glass in any way, the meniscus splashes off to one side and makes a great mess.

"Meniscus" is the answer to the extra-credit bonus question on tomorrow's science exam. I sit alone in my classroom, drawing up an exam. Of late, natives avoid looking Richard and me in the eye. Houseboys are quarrelsome. There's an eeriness to the fishermen's whistling as they walk through the mission.

Revolution is upon us. It's no longer a question of if, but when. Every element of nature seems aware of it. I imagine if I were to lay the side of my head against the soil, I would be able to hear a rumbling freight train sound, as I used to in Oklahoma just before a tornado hit. Yet the Missions board instructs us to proceed blindly forward. Actually, "Let your prayers guide you" was the way Wallace Hinton's telegram, following Laura's disappearance, was worded:

LET THE AUTHORITIES HANDLE THEIR JOB AND YOU HANDLE YOURS STOP LET YOUR PRAYERS GUIDE YOU THROUGH THIS DIFFICULT TIME STOP I HAVE PUT IN A CALL TO THE EMBASSY IN LEOPOLDVILLE STOP WILL WIRE AGAIN WHEN I KNOW MORE

AS THE RAINY SEASON BEGINS, Richard and I find business at l'École Moyenne taxing our energies. M. Boale's gone. Richard's duties have grown. There are many days when he doesn't return from school until well after dark. I've picked up an extra class and no longer have the luxury of an hour of preparation during the day. My test correction and lesson planning now come after classes and once my boys have finished their extracurricular activities.

There's little peace in my classroom. I keep Ellen and Laura in a homemade playpen in the corner while I go through the lessons. My students are restless and make great demands of my already dwindling patience. Their attention seems to be anywhere but on their studies.

I administer a language test on which the class as a whole performs poorly. After I hand back their papers, one of the boys walks to my teacher's table with a look of disgust upon his face. He holds his exam out as though it's soiled.

"You must not give me such a low mark," he insists.

"But a low mark's what you earned," I tell him plainly.

He complains further. The test was too hard. I did not give the students enough time to prepare. The material was tricky to learn when it's so hot and humid just before the rains.

"Fine," I say sharply when I've had enough of his grousing.

I rise to address the class. "Would everyone please bring his test paper up to the front of the room? It seems I've made a mistake in grading them."

The boys line up and, one by one, I cross out their Cs and Ds and give every student an A.

The boys exchange troubled looks as they take their seats.

"Does that grade suit you more?" I ask the first boy.

"*Non*, Madame," he pouts. "You give me an A, but now it's no better than the others."

"If you want a better mark, study harder next time," I tell him.

The next day, the students come to me after class, wanting me to stay late and allow them to do an extra art project. When I tell them I've been up since five in the morning with sick babies, they sulk.

"Please, Madame, we want to make pictures," they beg.

"I'm sorry," I say. "Not today."

"You are so selfish and stingy," one of them grumbles. "You can't give us just one little bit of your time?"

"Selfish?" I shout angrily. "How dare you! I've given you my very life and you have the audacity to make like I owe you something. Get out, all of you. Get out!"

The boys scamper from the room, startled.

I'm startled to sound like an Eva I don't know.

STORMS RAGE ACROSS CONGO, and I am haunted by clouds of my own, filled with a terrible sense of being in limbo. All the advice I've been given about keeping bad news from sponsoring churches and family is catching up with me.

There are doubts in my mind, and I have no one I can tell—doubts about my purpose here, doubts about the existence of God. There are too many trials with the natives, too many contradictions meeting me at every turn, too much hypocrisy piled on the church steps.

I try talking to Richard, but we don't have the luxury of idle hours for conversation. It is a humiliating thing to open my heart to someone and get the sense that I'm an inconvenience to his tired ears.

It's not as though I have been shunned. The missionaries around me are truly kind and loving people. But each is too occupied with his own condition amid the growing ugliness to notice how Eva's discomfiture grows.

My spirit is left to wander.

I try to find empathy in the women of the village. But the more Lonkundo I learn, the more I realize how little there is for us to talk about. We teach them rudimentary home economics, but not economy of language in forensics. Girls here aren't raised to philosophize, ask questions, or deliberate, and by the time they reach adulthood, even the lowest hanging of these fruit are beyond their reach.

Like the missionaries, the Nkundo women are great of heart, yet they have grown to seem best suited for having babies, carrying loads, and weeding fields. In their company, my ruminations are dismissed with a cluck of the tongue and a shake of the head.

Something has to give.

A PECULIAR SOUND AWAKENS ME FROM A NIGHTMARE, deep in the darkness: a sharp percussion of hits that seems to come from overhead. Richard's heard it, too, and he sits up.

Then there's a sturdier thwack from the roof, followed by the sound of something heavy rolling down the slope of the corrugated metal.

"What is that?" I whisper, aghast. I gather the sheets around me and cower in the hollow of Richard's arm. Instinctually, I look to where the twins lie still, undisturbed by the clatter overhead.

The noise comes again, several louder reverberant hits in rapid succession.

Now startled, the twins cry. I get up cautiously to comfort them.

"Sounds like rocks," Richard says.

He's right. Someone's pelting us.

"Who would be throwing rocks at our roof?" I ask, dismayed.

Then, as abruptly as the barrage began, it ceases.

I stand and hold the girls, fearful of another trauma like the last time we were disturbed in the wee hours.

All is silent for a bit, then there are some garbled words shouted in Lonkundo, and a man laughs. The rock throwing begins again. This time the impact's fainter, for *our* roof is no longer the target.

From the sound of it, the hooligans have moved on to Jean's house. Her monkey chatters angrily at the hubbub. There's nothing to be done about the trouble at present, so I climb back into bed uneasily and snuggle the girls between Richard's body and my own.

It takes a long time for me to fall back asleep.

IN THE MORNING, Neil Roberts calls a meeting at church.

"It seems our security has become a concern," he says, standing up in front of the group. "I'm sorry to have to say it, but after the incidents last night, I wondered if there was something afoot on a larger scale. I went down to the dispensary and heard a news broadcast saying that the natives had burned an evangelist's house outside of Boende. I don't know if the episodes are connected, but it raises the question of whether we ought to take certain measures—"

"I won't tolerate guns on this mission," I say, rising abruptly.

"I wasn't going to advise we keep guns, necessarily," Neil says, though his averted gaze tells me that's exactly what he was about to suggest.

"What then?" Jean asks both of us. "I thought all hell was breaking loose when they went after my roof last night. It's tough times, Eva."

"If they had told me in missionary training that I'd have to keep a gun ready to shoot a native, I wouldn't have come here," I say.

"If they had told you about a lot of what we go through on a daily basis, you wouldn't have come," Jean counters wryly.

Richard tugs at my wrist to make me sit back down in the pew.

"We can put a second sentry on at night, for pay," Neil Roberts suggests. "I think we ought to tell the Missions board we need the budget to hire two natives to sit out beside a fire and keep an eye on things."

"How about securing the houses?" Dr. Baker asks. "The Dunagans and us, we've got children to think about."

"I've been working on that one. too," Neil says. "I think we can get a mission builder to come and put expanded metal on the windows. That'll keep out the house burglars."

"Will it keep out revolution?" I ask.

Someone coughs, but everyone else is silent.

RAIN FALLS ON SATURDAY AFTERNOON. The weather prevents me from drying clothes in the backyard, so Ta Pierre and I have laid diapers out all across the back of the sofa, giving the living room a jumbled, messy appearance.

Richard's at school, preparing for the district inspector's midterm visit.

I sit on the floor in a cotton T-shirt and a pair of Richard's pajama pants and play with the girls. There are many games that bring them great delight, from patty-cake to airplane rides, but I fear I shall never be able to tolerate a round of hide-and-seek.

I hear someone approaching and look out the front window, newly crisscrossed with obtrusive steel bands, to see Neil Roberts coming up the front steps.

"Big news down in Léopoldville," he says as he gets to the door.

"You know better than to try to come into my house with that thing," I say, pointing at a gun he carries in a holster. It makes an odd companion to his ever-present Bible, and I don't find the juxtaposition amusing.

Neil takes out his gun and sets it beside the door.

"Uh-uh. Don't leave it on my porch, either," I tell him.

"Eva, come on," he says testily.

"It's my house," I insist, "and I don't want guns around my children. Put it off my porch, now."

He complies, laying his gun beneath the steps.

"Now what's your news," I ask, opening the lock and letting Neil in.

"It's finally coming," he says. "They heard it on the radio down at the dispensary. The Belgians are giving the country to the natives."

"What?"

"Whassa, Mama?" Ellen asks, seeing me go rigid.

"It's independence," Neil insists. "They're going to let them set up their own government. It'll take a while, but King Baudouin is coming down from Brussels in three months to hand over power."

"Th-this is . . ." I stammer.

"They didn't speculate on what it meant for people like us, up here in the provinces, but the news reports say that Belgians in Léopoldville are already flocking to the airport to get out."

"What else did they say?"

"Not a lot," Neil says. "It's just kind of happening spontaneously."

"Tell me something honestly. Do you think these people, the natives, I mean, do you think they're ready to run their own government?"

Neil hesitates, then clears his throat. "I've got to go tell everyone else the news," he says, stepping out onto the porch.

"That's what I thought."

"You and Richard really should get yourself one of these," he says, pulling his pistol from where he's left it. "It'd let you sleep better at night."

"Not a chance."

"You know, Eva, " he says, patting the weapon, "sometimes the straight-and-narrow is a crooked path."

THE NIGHTS ARE NO LONGER QUIET IN BOLENGE.

The natives know that independence is coming, and the mission hunters fire off their guns in the air, using up their season's ration of bullets. Richard and I lie awake and watch the flashes of light in the distance.

Some of the village men have decided that independence means they don't have to work their jobs anymore, so they sit around the central path, drinking palm wine until they soil themselves. Others see it as an invitation to steal from one another without fear of repercussion. Few natives come to church. One evening, several weeks after the announcement, Jean comes pounding on our door.

"Richard, Eva! Hurry!" she calls.

"What's the matter?" Richard asks, getting up from the table.

"Come to the clinic. The natives are talking crazy."

As we get to the door, I'm stunned to see that Jean's crying. She leads us across the mission to her little clinic. Outside, some native men argue hotly with Dr. Baker. They turn to us as we approach.

"These men," Dr. Baker says breathlessly. "They came and told the African nurses and aides to go home. They say it's the nurses' prerogative. Now they seem to want to shut us down."

I look at the men. They stare back sullenly. I recognize two of them from the village, but the others are strangers. All are dressed in peculiar, brightly colored clothes they seem to believe are congruous with their new role as revolutionaries.

"I told them it's foolishness," Jean says in a dither. "I said if they sent the nurses home, patients would surely die, mostly the natives we're treating for infections and such. But they won't listen, or they don't understand. I don't know."

One of the natives steps forward, speaking broken French.

"It's time for you to leave us alone," he says. "The independence comes, and you still want to control us."

"We're not the government," I plead with him. "You have to understand—"

"What I understand is that Nkundo women and men will work here no more," the man says bluntly. "We might let your *mondele* nurse keep to her medicines and essences to help one of our brothers. But beyond this, there will be no dealing with our peoples."

"They seem pretty sure about this," I tell Jean.

Richard takes his turn, making use of his diplomatic aptitude in dealing with the peevish men. In the end, he gets their pledge to let Nurse Matthews and Dr. Baker stay at their posts indefinitely, but without assistance. If patients die, they'll be casualties of a war that has not yet been declared.

The native aides are discharged and run back to the village. We nod feigned respects to their liberators and turn to go home. It's an uneasy truce.

RICHARD AND THE GIRLS HAVE GONE TO SLEEP. I stand before the bathroom mirror and stare at my own reflection by the light of a kerosene lantern. The woman who looks back at me is pale yet weather-beaten. Her hair is limp and needs a shampoo. Wrinkles are beginning to form at the corners of her eyes, and her posture's slack.

I do not like her.

The woman in the mirror is cynical. She laughs at irony. She often speaks before she thinks. She's lost her awareness of propriety and manners. She's moody and tired. She is a cultural elitist. She can't decide between frowning on her own upbringing or the

333

Africans', so she decries both. She believes herself, impossibly, both savior and victim. She's defeated, and she's the thing I found the most repugnant upon my arrival in Congo—she's hardened. She's lost her faith, unable to find the loving God she once thought she knew.

When I can't look at her any longer, I turn away from the mirror and walk to our little desk in the bedroom.

"What are you doing?" Richard asks groggily.

"There's a letter I have to write before I can rest," I tell him.

It takes hours for me to capture what I need to say. I begin several times and stop, discarding my first attempts as diffuse and fraught with affectation.

As dawn comes and Richard wakes, I'm finally satisfied with what I've written. I climb into bed beside him. As I read the letter aloud, he cries quietly.

"I've been waiting for this a long time," he says once I've finished. "But I haven't wanted to influence you—I mean, everyone has to make their own decision. But this is the best thing for both of us."

"Good. Add anything you like," I say, handing him the pages.

After breakfast, he writes several paragraphs of his own.

In the end, I type the following on airmail paper:

Dear Wallace P. Hinton,

You sent us here to do a job. We have done our best.

If we have failed, then let the record show that it was not for lack of diligent effort.

In your last letter, you advised us to have a constant prayer ready and to thank Jesus in our hearts. These are pretty words, Mr. Hinton, but they will only take us so far in the real world. Jesus may have been able to feed the multitudes with loaves and fish, but we cannot.

Please understand that we are not asking you for more money. We are not asking for more assistance. We know that is impossible. You have made that clear. We are merely trying to give you an understanding of why it is that we must leave Congo.

There are grave concerns that weigh on our consciences:

We feel uncomfortable with the degree of paternalism with which the mission and its officers treat the Nkundo people. We were advised to treat natives like children lest we find ourselves disappointed with their lack of conformity to our Western standards— standards that we arrogantly and unquestioningly assume to be bet-

ter than their own. Can this really do anything other than sap the natives' spirits?

There is a star pupil in Eva's class, a boy who has expressed an interest in medicine from a very young age. During our tenure in Congo, we have watched his mind mature and develop. We have gone above and beyond the call of duty to supply him with books and encouragement in his studies. When baby Laura was found half-dead in the woods, this boy was instrumental in saving her life.

It seems a great success story. But what happens in ten years? With any luck, the boy will have gone on to university and medical school in Brussels or Johannesburg. And then what? Will he return to Congo to treat infections and deliver babies? We think not.

The danger of this phenomenon, this skimming off the cream and leaving the rest, comes into play for our business students, as well— any of them who show a spark of promise or delight in the expectation that they will someday find an office job in Léopoldville or Brussels. They are all dying to get out, and we are helping them write their tickets.

So what happens after we have relieved Congo of its brightest young minds? Who will run the country then? As independence looms, this becomes a pointed question. Are we really doing the Congolese any service with all our noble efforts? We have watched as many Nkundo move from villages like Bolenge, heading off to cities where they are sure to lose the framework of their traditions.

When we were training to be missionaries, we were sold the prospect of fresh, young minds eager to learn. What we find, instead, is a native population ripe with resentment. Our very presence here is an imposition, a reminder of a government they have ousted. Now that they have seen the white man cannot solve their woes, and his pockets are shallow, they not only question but also resent his authority.

They do not want us here any more.

When we got to Congo in 1956, the biggest threat that confronted us was nature—the mosquitoes that carry malaria and the venomous snakes in our garden. Now we must contend with roving bands of marauders, stories of violence getting closer every day, and evangelists who carry firearms to church along with the communion sacraments.

We have a family now, as well. Three times since we have been in Congo has one of us nearly lost her life. We do not want to sit by and wait for the reaper to come knocking again.

Mr. Hinton, our work here is done. We do not like the people we have become, and we question the impact of our efforts.

We ask that you assist us in making arrangements to return to the United States. We do not know what we will do once we go home. Right now, we are taking things one day at a time.

Yours truly,

Richard Dunagan
Eva Dunagan

We sign the letter, each in turn, and I seal the envelope.

Twenty-four

June 1960

EVERY DAY I WAIT FOR A REPLY from the Missions board in Cleveland.

Weeks become months. The school term drags on.

Everyone is disheartened that we have resigned, though no one should be overly surprised. The other missionaries try to dissuade us, but their arguments only serve to deepen our resolution. I have decided not to tell my class until everything's settled. There's no need to add to the chaos that surrounds us now.

While the violence has not yet fallen on Bolenge, there's much trouble in Coquilhatville. Twisting in the wake of the discord, we struggle to stay true to our purpose. The Belgian police in town are relentless in their show of power, and the native workers take this as an invitation to remind the panicked Belgian business owners who will be assuming control in a matter of days. There are reports of arrests nearly every time someone comes by the mission with news.

At last we receive an airmail letter from Wallace Hinton. I'm home when the mail truck rumbles through the mission. I meet it at the end of the path, as I have every day for many days. It's difficult for me not to tear into the letter while waiting for Richard to get home. I put the envelope in the cupboard so I won't look at it and be tempted.

When at last Richard arrives, we open the letter together. I find its contents surprisingly terse:

Richard and Eva,

We at the Disciples of Christ Missions board feel your recent decision is a mistake. Still, we cannot live your lives for you. You have

337

made your choice, and we will respect it. Let us know when you want to come home, and we will arrange for a delegate at the airport in New York to meet you.

As far as the board is concerned, we are answering questions about your return by simply saying that because of your personal desires you are resigning from service to the Lord and returning to the States. We will protect you in every way from questions that have been asked and those which have not yet arisen.

I request you let us deal with the churches.

I think you are both intelligent enough to realize that your reactions now are probably nothing like those you will have in moments of serious reflection in the future. Sometimes our emotions are very closely tied up with our physical well being. The wise thing for you to do is to keep your disillusionment to yourself at this stage until you can look a bit more objectively at the experience. It would be unfortunate if you make statements now on the matter that you will regret later on.

According to the rules of the Missions board, your salaries are terminated, effective upon receipt of your resignation. But the Missions staff is deeply concerned that there be no undue hardship on your part. We have every confidence you will behave in accordance with the requests I have made in the preceding paragraphs, and therefore, the board is willing to pay you an additional four weeks' salary.

They are not, however, advancing travel expenses to bring you home. That will need to come from your own pockets.

Prayerfully yours,

Wallace P. Hinton

"If I didn't know better, I'd say they were scared of us," I tell Richard as I finish reading the letter. I hand it back to him and have a seat at the kitchen table.

"Wouldn't you be scared if a couple of malcontents were threatening to blow a gust of wind through your house of cards?" he asks.

"I suppose," I say. "Though they didn't seem to feel we're enough of a threat to try buying us off."

"What?"

"I mean, paying for our tickets home. How much will it cost us?"

"A lot," Richard says, pulling out the chair across from me and sitting down. "Four tickets from the middle of Africa to Oklahoma City? That's going to be—well, it'll be hundreds of dollars, I reckon."

"We don't have it, do we?" I ask darkly.

Richard is still for a moment, then shakes his head.

We're trapped. They've sent us here, and now they won't bring us home. I come back to the notion of the house of cards. The Disciples of Christ church knows, as surely as we do, that the house is on fire. It's just matter of time before it topples on its own.

"We gave every last bit of what we had saved to Margaret," Richard says. "I was just looking over the books a couple of days ago. We're broke, Eva. The way I was brought up, the man in the family is supposed to have all the answers. He's supposed to provide. Now, if I don't come up with something quickly—"

There are gunshots in the distance.

"We do whatever we have to," I say, stealing a glance out the window. As I turn back around, my gaze stops on the sewing machine in the corner. Then I look over at Richard's phonograph and the records he loves, and I think of my dresses hanging in the homemade armoire in the bedroom.

"We could sell our things," I say, trying to keep gloom from creeping into my voice. "You reckon we could get enough for all the stuff we've got? I hate to think of it, but if we took it up to Coquilhatville and sold it in the marketplace, you think that'd be enough for the tickets?"

Richard won't look at me.

"I don't know," he says with a sigh, shaking his head dejectedly.

"I'm sorry," I say. "I'm trying. I just can't wait to get out of here."

AFTER THE SERMON AT CHURCH ON SUNDAY EVENING—the service for missionaries only—Richard and I get up and announce that the letter from home's arrived and it's finally time for us to leave. Saying this out loud is harder than I imagined. As I look out at the beleaguered expressions of the missionaries before me, I can't help but think I'm letting them down. I stammer, unable to say things right. Richard has to finish sentences for me.

I'm glad when it's over and we can sit back down in the pew.

"We knew it would be soon," Dr. Baker says, once the recessional hymn is finished. "People have been talking."

339

"What have they been saying?"

My girls climb on me and pull at my hair.

"Africa's taken its toll on you, Eva. I guess there's no more polite way of putting it. Both of you, you're in over your heads," Dr. Baker says quietly, lifting Ellen from my shoulder before she can topple backward and land on the floor.

"Don't you think we all are in over our heads?" I counter, snatching Ellen from him with enough force that she begins to cry.

"Maybe so," Dr. Baker says, raising his hands in an attempt to appease me.

"Besides," I insist, "whose fault is it?"

"Shh. Lower your voice, Eva," Dr. Baker scolds in a whisper. "Have you forgotten you're in a church?"

"I'm reminded of it every day," I say as I turn to leave.

THE MISSION TAKES UP AN OFFERING, in the end raising twenty-seven francs to help us buy our tickets. It's a fraction of what we'll need, but every bit helps. I get out my set of watercolors and make greetings cards to thank everyone for their generosity. Then I begin to sort through the trappings of my life to prepare them for sale.

Early on the morning of June 30, Neil Roberts shuttles the entire mission staff to the dispensary in his van, so we may listen to the big radio broadcasts from Léopoldville. Today, Belgian Congo ceases to exist. As of this afternoon, our country is known simply as "Congo."

The BBC radio commentators have a fine time telling what ignorant Africans believe independence portends. They put microphones in the faces of back-bush natives who feel they've been deprived of extra wives by mission teaching. The natives eagerly tell how they will now have as many wives as they can afford. One native boy brags to a reporter that when independence comes, he will own a Chevrolet and a wireless radio and he'll be able to kick all his relatives out of the house without the fear of being poisoned.

In Léopoldville and Brazzaville, the reporter says, hucksters are selling independence tickets, spurious pasteboards that allegedly allow the buyer to take over any white homes or cars or anything else of European proprietorship that isn't nailed down. Brisk raffles are going on selected white women—except, of course, the ladies in question have no idea they have been bought and sold several times.

Much fanfare rattles the nation's capital. Bands play and the Belgian army fires guns into the air on cue. One might easily assume that what we're hearing is the celebration of a holiday, not the unconditional surrender of a monarchy's most-prized colony. Considering everything, the Belgians are putting on a brave face.

Young King Baudouin, upon whom much pressure has come to bear, arrives in full military dress. He rides through the city in a convertible car, saluting the natives. I think of the irony of Ekebe Jacques having prepared his humble shack for the King's visit. The crackling roar of the crowd loses none of its fervor as it makes its way through the ether to our radio set.

Ellen and Laura are restless, as has become their wont in recent months. They don't understand the significance of what the grown-ups are doing today, all of us quietly intent on the voices booming from the wooden box in the corner of the room. I try to still the girls, but they're rambunctious, climbing through the legs of chairs and looking up women's skirts.

"Bug," Laura announces, grinning proudly as she opens her hand to deposit a large dead roach on my lap. As I brush the insect onto the floor, Richard collars the twins and carries them, crowing in protest, from the room.

"Thank you," I mouth in his direction.

Jean makes her way among the rows of missionaries, handing out glasses of juice and sandwiches she's prepared for the historic occasion.

As the radio broadcast continues, I wonder again what I'll tell people back home in America about my experiences here. How can I talk about frustrations with Nkundo culture without sounding like a racist or furthering the sort of comic book imagery of lazy, moon-eye Negroes that has hindered the advancement of people of African descent on my own soil for hundreds of years? If I lay it all out before my audience, I fear they'll hear only racial aspersion and not understand the friendship and loving admiration I share with so many of the Nkundo.

Yet, I'm faced with a dilemma—if I keep it all to myself, I will remain lonely. Family and friends will sense I'm holding back and treat me queerly as a result. I can find common ground with neither Nkundo nor American audiences. Whatever wasted wisdom or insight I have accrued will see me to my grave.

In Léopoldville, the hoopla continues. M. Patrice Lumumba,

Congo's new prime minister, launches into an angry harangue against all that is Belgian. I wonder what he has to gain by his words. Hasn't he already won the war?

At last, the ceremonies finish. The radio announcer signs off and the signal goes dark. One of the doctors snaps off the receiver.

"There you have it," he says.

There you have it. I have struggled for four years to call this strange country my home, and now the country no longer exists. The irony of this makes me cackle out loud.

The doctor looks at me, puzzled.

WE GET WORD that the Missions house in Coquilhatville will be closing at the week's end. The letter from the board says something about "decentralization" but also makes mention of the thievery and looting that have plagued the house in recent months.

"It's a sign," I tell Richard.

We have agreed to stay at Bolenge through next week. This will see us to the end of l'École Moyenne's academic quarter. There's no sense in hiding our departure from the boys any longer, so at the end of the school day on Friday, I make the announcement. It's greeted by the kind of histrionics typical of the very young and the very old. There's much beseeching and wringing of hands. For all the angst and aggravation the boys have brought me, they now claim they'll be lost without my guidance. I must admit this warms my heart.

As the count of days I'm to remain in Bolenge dwindles, a new sadness overcomes me. I teach class, realizing that each lesson is one of my last on a given subject. The boys will go on without me. Some will excel; others will falter. Perhaps, if I had the perseverance of which Mr. Hinton spoke, I'd stay and right the courses of those who would otherwise drop out of school to take up fishing nets and hoes. Then again, perhaps I'd ultimately be doing them a disservice by hindering the natural course of their lives.

On the day before we're to leave, I give my class their last assignments and load my belongings into a box. As I linger in the doorway, I remember when I came here for the first time, nervous as anything. The boys stood for me.

"Asseyez-vous," I tell the empty classroom, with tears in my eyes.

Outside the door, Liyanza waits for me.

"Will you forget me in America?" he asks.

I smile gently.

"I could never forget you," I say. "If ever I miss you, all I'll have to do is look at Laura, and you'll be right there with me."

"I won't forget you, either," Liyanza says. "There will come a time for you to return to Congo. I will be a man of *mpifo* then. You will see."

"I'm sure you will," I tell him, knowing I shall never return to this soil. It's dead for me, and I for it.

"Goodbye, Mama," he says, turning and walking off toward the dormitory. I wait for him to disappear around the bend before I continue on my way.

When I reach the house, I find a letter jammed between the front door and its frame. It comes from Ohio. At first, I don't recognize the name atop the return address, for the handwriting's shaky and hard to read. Then I realize that it must be from Gloria Snead, the principal of l'École Moyenne whom Richard replaced upon our arrival. I open the envelope curiously. Within the first few sentences, it knocks the breath out of me:

Dear Eva and Richard,

I have just returned from a trip to Tulsa. Some of your good friends were asking about you on Sunday. I told them that you are coming home, and they marveled that you are returning so soon.

Really, it breaks my heart to think of your leaving God's service. Why, oh, why could you not keep your ears tuned to Jesus, your Lord and Master, and let the noises of man pass by unnoticed? Jesus sent you there to do His work. Couldn't you have spent your time telling the people of the love of Jesus, our King, instead of complaining?

Eva, I have heard of your growing family. How dear the twins must be. What an inspiration they would have been to the native people. Can you not get a fresh call from the Master and start all over again in the field of evangelism? The need is so very great! I wish I were starting fresh, but they tell me forty years is long enough. The people are wonderful and they need Jesus so badly. How my heart weeps for them and for you. I would love to know why you are coming home, resigning, abandoning the school I worked so hard to build up.

Anxiously waiting for your reply,

Gloria Snead

I drop the letter onto the kitchen table.

Surely others will share Gloria's sentiment. The churches back home, the same congregations whom I've been writing ingratiatingly sunny letters for years will now view me as a traitor to their cause. They'll greet us with wary skepticism, not the open arms we shall dearly need.

I have a good, long cry and try to resign myself to that which lies ahead. Laura comes to me in the middle of my muddle and puts her palm against my cheek.

"No more, Mama," she suggests with a concerned look.

I take her hand and kiss it, drawing her onto my lap.

"Okay," I whisper.

There's a sharp knock on the door. I look up and see several native men standing on the porch. Each has a rifle in his hands. They're all four strangers to me. My pulse quickens.

"What do you want?" I ask with trepidation.

"We're here for an inspection of your home," one of the men says. "Open up immediately."

I carry Laura to the front of the house and undo the hook on the screen door. Before I can pull the frame open, one of the men pushes it against me.

"Step aside," the first man says. He kneels beside one of our moving boxes and begins rifling through its contents.

"What is this about?" I ask anxiously, grabbing Ellen from her game of blocks and hugging both girls close to me. "My husband's *le Directeur* of the mission school, and he'll be home in a few minutes. I'm sure there's some kind of misunderstanding here. If you'll just sit down and wait for him, he can explain whatever you need—"

"Shut up," the second man says. "We're making an inspection."

"What are you looking for?" I ask, increasingly upset.

The leader shakes his head but doesn't answer. The men pull the sofa away from the wall. One of them takes the knife from his belt and slices open the cushions, sending straw and feathers flying through the room. Meanwhile, another man goes to the cabinet and helps himself to a mouthful of bread.

"What is this inspection about?" I ask again. "You're not looking for anything at all, are you? You're just here to put our home all *woso woso.*"

"I've told you to shut up," the first man sneers at me, cocking his rifle and pointing it in my direction.

I freeze. I have never before had a gun pointed at me. It's a cheerless and humbling thing to know that one's life could be over in a fraction of a second if someone willed it. I look into the man's eyes and find them compassionless. He sees my fright and smirks. Another man takes a tin of cocoa from the cabinet and opens it, tossing the dark brown powder at my face so that I recoil, coughing and sneezing chocolate. The girls begin to cry. My white blouse is ruined. The men laugh heartily at all this.

There are footsteps on the porch. Richard comes in.

My nose is burning from the powder. I sneeze. I'm so furious and frightened I can't shop shaking, though I will it otherwise.

"What in God's name is going on here?" he asks.

The men stop their harassment and turn to look at him.

"We are making an inspection of this house, *mondele*," the one with the full mouth announces. "This wife of yours has too much talking."

"Who's in charge here?" Richard asks angrily, stepping up to the man who has me cornered.

The natives look at one another curiously. It seems they've gone out for the day's pillaging without electing a leader.

"We're here from the new army," one of them says at last.

"*What* new army?" Richard persists.

"The new army of Congolese peoples," the man says. "We're independent now. We can do as we choose."

"That isn't how it works," Richard says, shaking his head in exasperation. "You can't just run around doing whatever you please, making up . . . I mean, if you're in the army, what are your ranks?"

Again, the men look at one another.

"We don't need ranks," the first man says snidely, pointing his gun at Richard. "Now get over by the wall with the woman. You are all alike, you missionary people. You talk too much."

Faced with the grim prospect of a bullet in the chest, Richard complies. We watch in dismay as the men continue the mockery of an inspection, upturning boxes, slicing through bed sheets, and squeezing toothpaste out of its tube. The men sweat amply as they maraud, giving rise to a smell I'll always associate with having a gun pointed at me.

Again and again, I steal glances at the door in the hopes that someone will come to our rescue. As much as I despise the pistol that Neil Roberts carries, I would now like to see it clear these men from our house.

At last, the natives grow bored and leave. They don't steal anything, as I had feared they might. Their visit today was to harass, not to poach. I suppose they were marking their territory, like a dog that marks the perimeter of his turf.

When we're sure they are gone, I let my weight fall against the wall. Things are still for a few moments. Then a gunshot sounds nearby.

I gasp.

We put the girls in their beds and go out onto the porch just in time to see Jean walking along the path, looking lost and disoriented.

"Jean!" I call.

"They shot Edgar dead," she says unsteadily.

Richard and I go to her. As she turns toward us, I see horror in her eyes.

"They . . . they came into my house and yelled at me then shot him as though it were for sport," Jean says, starting to cry.

It takes Richard some time to quiet her. I go back inside to get the girls, and as I walk through the kitchen, I see that Gloria Snead's letter is still on the table. Somehow, amid the cacophony, it's remained undisturbed. I think again of its contents. Gloria doesn't understand that the Africa we face is nothing like what she left four years ago.

I can't wait for morning to arrive.

Twenty-five

July 1960

RICHARD AND I DECIDE TO LEAVE our furniture behind. It won't fit well into the mail truck we've hired for our final ride to Coquilhatville, and the bed and sofa cushions are ruined from yesterday's looting. Also, I'm not sure just how much success two Americans would have trying to sell a slipcovered sofa in an African marketplace in the middle of a revolution.

I imagined, somehow, that there would be great fanfare when it was time for us to go, perhaps something on the order of that to which King Baudouin was treated in the capital last week. Yet no one seems to take any great notice of our departure. Jean, calmed somewhat since the murder of her pet, has packed up sandwiches in a paper box for our lunch. Beyond this, there's no hallowing of the event.

I stand on our front porch, smelling the mission's earthy smell and watching the parade to the river one last time. It can't be long before telephone wires are strung along the roads, making the sound of the lokolé a thing of memory. There's already talk of putting in a two-way radio at the dispensary. The roads will be paved, and industry will come in from Coquilhatville and Léopoldville and Stanleyville. No one will remember the time when it was Christianity and cannibalism, not communism and democracy, that squared off in Congo. The innocence of this place, if something so raw and brutally unforgiving may be called innocence, is leaving.

Perhaps we're the unwitting vanguards of its departure.

Richard and the mail-delivery man have nearly finished loading the truck with two steamer crates and half a dozen big wooden boxes, which we made with a borrowed saw and hammer. Their construction isn't nearly as solid as the crates in which our belongings arrived. Such safekeeping isn't necessary now, for the trappings of our lives will be traveling ten kilometers instead of thousands of miles.

Ta Pierre has finished his last cleaning up, and I bid him farewell.

"*Allons-y!*" Richard calls, leaning in the driver's side window of the truck and honking the horn.

I take a final walk through the house. When I first laid eyes upon these rooms, I felt despair. Now, I'm filled with quiet relief. The struggle's over. I've given the best years of my life—indeed, I've nearly given life itself—in pursuit of a noble abstraction. Have I achieved what I set out to do? I fear the answer is no, yet I believe that the very audacity of the undertaking ought to leave me with some sense of accomplishment.

Richard honks the horn again.

"All right, already," I call crossly, turning to lock the front door. Then I realize there's no reason to fasten the lock, so I leave it hanging in its mounting.

The bench seat is cramped. There are three grown-ups all in a row: the driver, Richard, and I. Ellen and Laura are squeezed in between.

As we roll toward Coquilhatville, I put my arm out the window, letting my skin drink in the amazing heat of the African sun one last time. The twins talk to each other, touch the lights on the dashboard, and laugh at the bumps in the road and the buttons on their traveling clothes.

"Look out the window," I want to tell them. "Breathe the air. Stare at the goats and big flying insects and palm trees. Listen closely to the drums beating and the sound of the giant truck tires going over rocks. Study these things as intently as you may, for they will soon be gone from your lives and you'll always wonder about them. You'll come to me and ask me questions, and I'll sigh as I tell you stories so fantastical that you will accept them only as make-believe. Yet if you could absorb all this now, you would know the stories must be true."

I don't say this to my children, for I know they're too young to appreciate my words. Instead, I hold them close and hum the melody of a simple song Ekebe Jacques taught me in pentatonic scale.

AS WE REACH COQUILHATVILLE, I sense that malevolence is afoot.

The town's warehouse district, adjacent to the river docks, boasts a number of two-story buildings, many with metal roofs. Smoke is pouring from one of the largest structures' windows.

"Is that from some industrial process they're using?" Richard asks the mail-truck driver.

"No. It's big trouble," the native says, pulling off his cap to wipe the sweat from his brow. "The workers in the factories, they say this morning that they going to have striking. I think they're not telling stories. The police, they say in the newspaper yesterday that if the men strike, they'll be fired."

"The Belgian police?" I ask.

"No, no," the driver says. "The new Bantu police. We all think it's so much better for the independence to come, but I guess a beating feels no good no matter who gives it." He chuckles at this, shaking his head.

We are nearing the heart of the warehouse district. The streets are unusually empty for late morning on a weekday.

"You want me to take you to the airport, yes?" the driver asks.

"No," Richard says. "We need to go to the marketplace, where people are buying and selling. We're not taking any of this with us."

"Oh," the driver says, taking a sharp turn. This puts us on the street directly behind the burning warehouse.

As we proceed, I see a worker stumble from the back door of the building. There's blood on his forehead, and his shirt's ripped. He wails and grasps at his arm as he weaves into the path of our truck. Our driver curses in Lonkundo and slams on the brakes so as not to hit him.

Instinctively, I put one hand on the dashboard to brace myself against the sudden stop, shielding the girls with my free arm. The truck engine dies. Behind us, our belongings shift violently forward and I hear the sound of glass breaking. For a quick moment, I wonder which of my wedding dishes are no more.

In front of us, the bloodied worker falls to the pavement. He clasps his hands together, looking up at us and weeping desperately. The man speaks, but the words that come from his mouth are a hysterical garble.

From the same door from which the man fled the warehouse, there now comes a uniformed African policeman, billy club in hand. The officer crosses to the worker cowering in the middle of the street and raises his club to strike a blow.

Through the dirty windshield, I see the whites of the officer's eyes and the flare of his nostrils. He exhales, and I'm sure I can feel his breath on me, stinking with anger. As the billy club reaches the top of its arc high over the policeman's head, I let out a bloodcurdling scream.

The policeman turns and looks at me in surprise, but his billy club already has begun to drop. In one downward swing, it completes its purpose. The movement is swift and economical. Blood splashes across the windshield.

The worker topples to the side, his body taken up with horrible trembling convulsions. "No!" The word I've screamed echoes through the street, drowning out all else.

Then there's silence. Richard's wristwatch ticks. I hear the crackling of the fire in the warehouse. The worker's body stops twitching. The policeman stoops to the grass beside the road, wipes the blood from his billy club, and looks up at us.

"Don't do anything; don't say anything; just keep your mouth shut," Richard warns me in a hoarse, measured whisper as he grabs my wrist.

I sit still, sweating and trembling.

I look down at the girls. I would expect them to be fussing and crying amid such dramatics, but they, too, are still. They stare at the blood on the windshield as it collects along the wiper blades.

The policeman begins a slow saunter toward us, swinging his billy club.

"Get us out of here, please," I say as calmly as possible.

Our driver starts the motor and puts the gears into reverse. We begin lurching backward up the street, blind to anything that might be in our path. When we reach the corner, the driver swings the truck around and pulls out onto the main boulevard.

I have just witnessed a murder. I'm dismayed, but there isn't time to dwell on the matter at present.

"That man, he deserves what he gets," the driver says calmly.

"H . . . how could you possibly . . . I mean—"

"The workers of the factory," the driver interrupts, "like the rest of the city, they go on a general strike. I left this morning before the starting of work time, but I heard talking, and I know it would come. Some men, they say they will burn the warehouses if they don't get a higher wage now that independence comes and Bantus take charge of their own region. This man's a greedy worker who gets it in his mind to destroy a business. He knows what the consequence may be. I believe it's just, but I'm sorry that you have to watch."

We pass the abandoned Missions house. The window panes are broken out and the curtains of the front sitting room move slightly in the breeze. It isn't long before our truck nears the Coquilhatville marketplace, which is one city block wide and three blocks long. Everything imaginable is for sale—batik clothing, elephant tusks, brass rings, and comestibles of every variety. The market entrance is flanked on one side by a display of milky-eyed boar and attended on the other by a cluster of flies swarming around fresh-slaughtered antelope. Some of the vendors shade themselves with palm fronds spread across rickety frames, while others, mostly the older men and women, tolerate the sun.

The jubilation I've come to associate with an African market is absent. In its place is a furtive desperation. No one speaks much. Eyes dart around. Everything moves with an uncomfortable briskness. I turn and notice, at the far end of it all, a squadron of African troopers standing watch. They wear berets, and rounds of ammunition crisscross their chests making them look like true revolutionaries. The young men watch the marketplace goings-on with stern expressions, as if the feeble peddlers before them might rise to their feet at any moment and begin rioting. The soldiers' guns rest lightly on their shoulders, but I see in their eyes the same readiness to turn against their own people as was evident in the policeman at the warehouse. It quickens my pulse and sickens my stomach.

As we pull in and park, several of the soldiers point to the truck and confer sharply with one another. I realize, after a moment of panic, that they're looking at the blood on the windshield. As I get out of the truck and walk around front with Laura on my hip, I see that the grill, too, got a grisly splattering during the warehouse dissident's braining. I shudder and turn away from the sight.

The soldiers begin walking toward us. As they near, I realize they're very young, eighteen or nineteen years old. They look as though they would not be out of place in a class at l'École Moyenne.

"Don't tell them that you're leaving," the driver warns. "Do not tell them anything or they will give you trouble."

"Bonjour, Messieurs, Madame," one of the soldiers says. His speech has an air of self-importance that borders on disdain.

"What have we here?" another asks.

"We are offering some extra things from our house for sale," Richard lies, stepping forward. "We're American church missionaries from the village of Bolenge, to the south. We're just in Coquilhatville for the day, then we will return home."

"And what is that on your truck?" the first soldier asks suspiciously, walking toward the bumper and sliding his finger along the metal so that the tip is wet and red.

"We had an accident on the way." Richard's lies slip from him with disconcerting ease. "We hit an animal on the road coming here. We're going to clean it up straight away."

The young man nods slowly. "All right," he says. "Sell your things then leave. It's foolish to be traveling the roads now. Get home with you!"

He turns and joins the other soldiers in their position against a wall.

Keeping a close eye on the twins, we begin to unload our belongings from the truck bed.

As we work, a silver-hull Sabena plane takes off from the Coquilhatville airport a few miles away. It rises and makes a gentle arc over the city. In unison, the African troops crane their necks to stare at the craft.

I nudge Richard and point in the direction of the young men. We watch together as they shield their eyes against the sun, remaining greatly intent upon the plane overhead. I hear them conferring about the letters and numbers painted on the belly of the hull.

Stories floated around the mission last week that the new government might inter all Belgians that remain in the country. When I heard this, I dismissed the notion as a hysterical response to the general state of duress. Yet now, as I see how intent the soldiers are on the workings of the airport timetable, I wonder whether there might be substance to the notion.

It'd seem a great irony—the Africans going to lengths to prevent the fleeing of those they were so eager to oust. The Europeans that remain no longer pose a threat to the Congolese. Nonetheless, they have a certain value. Most are businessmen and land barons, people of stature within the international European community. I fear that the new African regime sees these people not as human beings but as political pawns and insurance against any last-minute posturing by the departing Belgian rule.

I set down a box of dishes, some of them cracked during our sudden stop in the warehouse district. Before the box reaches the ground, hands thrust past me, pulling dishes out of the box for closer inspection. Old African women hold saucers up to the sun, sniff them, scratch them, and weigh them in their palms. As I stand up, they've already begun haggling over the price: Am I selling in sets, or can they buy dishes individually? Are the plates two for one if they're cracked? An older woman elbows me aside to get to a box of toiletries.

Richard comes to my aid, taking my arm and steadying me as the huddle of women digs through our hairbrushes and pillowcases.

For one franc, I sell a brush-and-mirror set that belonged to my mother in her teens.

A neck-tied and bushy-hair man buys Richard's collection of long-playing records for ten francs. Ten minutes later, he comes back to negotiate the price of the phonograph.

Through it all, I'm curiously numb, though I suppose there's an innate, self-preserving wisdom to this. For if I were to allow myself to react to the pillagers, I might come apart into bits. It's hard not to feel as though they're stealing from us. It's hard to resist the impulse to run after them shouting, "Give it back!" as they walk away with our tools and treasures. But I know I must have the presence of mind to keep still.

My dresses go for twenty francs apiece, which seems a good price, until I begin to think of all the time I put into sewing them, staying up late into the night, pinning patterns and taping hems.

Richard minds the money.

I look on with hope as I see the pile of currency grow.

Our good silverware sells as a set. Sixty francs is the take. The girls' toys fetch just five francs. My kitchen utensils earn us ten francs. Our steel flashlights go for three francs each.

A Belgian couple, likely a businessman and his wife, walk through the square, dressed in black. He relies upon a walking stick, while she's pulled by a poodle. They comport themselves in the peculiar manner of people who must maintain aristocratic decorum while in a state of true physical jeopardy.

"How much for that?" the woman asks me, pointing condescendingly at my box of jewelry and trinkets. She fiddles with the much-finer pearl necklace strung round her own neck.

"For all of it?" I ask, surprised.

"Oui, oui," she says dismissively.

"Four hundred francs," I say. I think this to be a fair price.

"Oh, là là," the woman balks, whistling theatrically and rolling her eyes. She turns to her husband, or lover, and they chuckle.

"Two hundred. That's all. Take it or leave it," the woman offers, suddenly serious.

I look down at the little velvet-lined box. It holds the earrings I got my freshman year at Phillips and a slender gold chain, the only piece of jewelry my mother ever bought me. My date-night pearls are coiled beneath these souvenirs. The end of the strand of pearls is twisted around my charm bracelet from junior high school.

Slowly, painfully, I close the box and hold it out to the woman. After she takes it, I realize that I have made her tug it from my hands.

The woman reaches into her purse and withdraws a money clip. She counts off several bills and hands them to me, then turns and leaves with my treasures. At the end of the transaction, I find I don't warrant so much as a *"merci"* or *"au revoir."*

BY TWO O'CLOCK OUR BELONGINGS ARE ALL GONE—a good thing, for the African troops at the market perimeter have grown restless and harass the vendors directly in front of them. Several women protest, with saucy mouths and hands akimbo, and the muzzle of a soldier's gun strikes one of them to the ground.

Richard and I hurry to clean up the last of our boxes. We have a stack of francs that will pay for our tickets to America and, if we are thrifty, dinner tonight.

It was suggested to me half a decade ago that I might trade material wealth for a sense of spiritual fullness that could not be bought at any price. This was something I could not refuse, but it was also a trick. After a period of inconceivable struggle, I find myself both financially destitute and spiritually bankrupt. It's a sad state of affairs. Shall I blame the Church and the Missions board? They're the easiest targets but not necessarily the most apt. How about the natives, with their seeming propensity for indiscipline? No, in the end I must shoulder the blame for my own failures. If not, how can I ever take part in any celebration of my successes?

Even as I think about it, there's a quiet comfort in this notion of personal accountability. For years, I've looked to Jesus or the government or the change of subtropical seasons as a cure for my unhappiness. In hindsight, this was nothing but wishful thinking.

How much time, then, have I wasted? What part of my life have I squandered trying to do good when all I was accomplishing was my own torment?

As we roll toward the airport, I recollect on my days in Congo and take inventory of all the people I may have affected. I think of Margaret, of my talks with Liyanza, of trying to teach the women in the village to write their alphabet. While these images, tender scenes from a life I'm leaving, ought to give me comfort, I find myself unable to see their benefit. I'm depressed.

I hold my girls close and look out the window at a regiment of Belgian soldiers marching beside us, cheeks ruddied by the heat and the burden of their heavy, woolen uniforms. I wonder how they feel, knowing they will soon be unemployed, shipped back to Antwerp or Ostend for reassignment. I can't image they're readily inclined to tolerate African troops in a jurisdiction that was for so long exclusively the Belgian military's.

At the airport, only two cars are parked in the gravel lot. The facility looks as deserted. We pay the mail driver his agreed-upon fee and carry the twins into the waiting room. Richard goes to the ticket window to book passage on the afternoon flight to Khartoum, the first stop on our journey.

There are green-painted benches lining each wall of the waiting room, and I have the choice of any of them. I wonder why no one's about. Besides the ticket seller and an old African man pushing a straw broom across the floor, Richard and I are the only ones here. I look out onto the runway, where a DC-4 airplane is parked, presumably the one we will fly, and a windsock moves gently in the breeze. If it were not for these two pieces of solid evidence, I might mistake the room in which I'm sitting for an unused warehouse with a incidental gravel strip beside it.

"That was strange," Richard says, putting away his wallet and walking toward me.

"What?" I ask. "Did you get the tickets?"

"Yeah," Richard says with a troubled look on his face. "But the agent was real cagey, as if he were nervous about something. He kept looking around, checking his watch, you know."

"Did you ask him what was the matter?"

"I asked him why there wasn't anybody here, and he said it's a bad time for traveling. He didn't want to say much of anything beyond that."

I hear a sound from the front door of the terminal and turn. I'm surprised to see the Belgian woman who bought my jewelry. She's accompanied by the same escort and yapping poodle as earlier, only now she's dressed in traveling clothes and her companion carries several suitcases. As if in imitation of Richard's and my own actions, the man walks to the ticket window, while the woman takes a seat on the bench opposite us. She plays with her dog and fiddles with her luggage, all the while working very hard to ignore me.

Laura begins to cry, upset by the dog. Richard takes her from me and walks her around the room to console her. I watch them, and the Belgian couple, with slow-moving eyes. What I see isn't the waiting room before me but the face of the rebellious factory worker as life left him. The expression he wore as he died was horrible and peculiar—eyes wide and blind, lips spread back over his teeth in a voiceless scream. It was quite different from the expression worn by Ekebe Jacques, the only other person I've seen return to our Maker. On the night of his passing, old Ekebe Jacques's air left me with a sense of contentment, of completion of purpose. In contrast, the face of the slaughtered worker in the street shall prove naught but fodder for nightmares.

The sound of automatic-rifle fire in the distance pulls my attention back to the waiting room. I shift my weight, uncomfortable in the afternoon heat.

The Belgian woman's dog stands in the corner with one leg raised, wetting the side of one of the benches. I look at the woman, appalled that she wouldn't do something.

It's then that I recognize she's preoccupied: She holds a fashion magazine and tries to read it but is clearly too distracted to give her attention to the articles on the pages. Her hands tremble and she keeps stealing glances at the front door.

"Madame," I say, pointing to the corner of the room when she looks over at me. "Your dog."

The woman scowls when she sees her dog relieving itself. "Auguste! Come here!" she calls sharply, and the little dog waddles back to her, having already finished its business.

I hear the distant sound of men's angry shouts. I can't understand what they're saying, but I'm sure I hear both French and

Lonkundo. I look at the Belgian woman. She's heard the shouting, too.

"Richard . . ." I say cautiously. I don't know what's going on, but indicators are not good. "Keep Laura close. I'm going to take Ellen to the bathroom with me. I'll be right back."

As I walk from the building to find the outhouse, I hear gunfire again. This time, it's followed by the sound of a woman's hysterical screams.

I shiver and hurry.

The mechanics are starting up the propellers of the plane. This seems strange to me, as our flight isn't scheduled to leave for another hour. Yet they open up the door of the craft, extend down the folding stairs, and go about their other duties with a sort of uncomfortable briskness, none of them talking or carrying on in the casual manner typical of Nkundo workers.

The outhouse is small and smells foul. I wrinkle my nose, uneager to set Ellen down on any bare surface. I end up balancing her on my knee. I can hear the engines of the plane revving up to what must surely be full speed.

Then someone bangs on the outhouse door.

"Eva!" Richard's voice calls, straining over the din. I pull up my underpants, drop my dress, grab Ellen around the midsection, and throw the door open.

"What?" I ask, looking around to see the Belgian couple walking hurriedly across the runway toward the plane.

"We've got to go," Richard shouts. "There was a phone call. The troops are coming. They're just up the road. They're going to shut the airport down and keep the flight from leaving. Everything in town's gone to hell."

I turn and look toward Coquilhatville. The squadron of African troops is several hundred yards away, marching in our direction. There are untidy plumes of black smoke on the horizon. I clutch Ellen close and take Richard's hand as we run toward the plane, stumbling in the cloud of dirt the propellers have raised. The African flight attendant leans from the door to the craft, shouting hysterically for us to hurry.

I turn and look over my shoulder at the troops. They've seen us and are in the process of abandoning their orderly march in favor of a mad scramble through the brush. They seem intent upon taking the airport by siege.

The engine roar's deafening. The plane begins to move.

Richard tosses his suitcase into the hull and helps me up the stairs. Once I have climbed into the craft and turned around, he hands me Laura.

The troops are swarming through the terminal building. The plane moves more quickly, cutting a grand arc through the dirt, so it will have a pass at the full length of the runway. Richard jogs alongside us, trying to get hold of the handrail, but the plane continues to outpace him.

"Come on!" I shout wildly, hugging the edge of the doorway and stretching my free arm in his direction.

The troops have reached the runway. They shout at us.

With a desperate burst of energy, Richard throws himself forward and grabs for my hand. I gasp and reach out to him. Our palms connect. I feel Richard's fingers lock around my wrist. We hang on for dear life.

Richard's feet drag on the ground until he's able to swing his body around and seize the rail. As he lifts his legs into the air, he loses one of his shoes. Grimacing, he pulls himself up onto the stairs.

The Belgian woman scoops up Ellen and Laura off the floor. The steward and I grab Richard by the arms and pull him into the aisle. Then we drag the heavy stairs up into the plane.

Richard lies on the floor, heaving and sweating.

I look up to see that the troops have dashed onto the runway and assembled themselves in a line across the runway in order to block our take-off. Their guns are trained on the plane's cockpit. The pilot sees them and unbuckles his seat belt, still minding the accelerator.

"*Dear God, Baby Jesus, protect us,*" the Belgian man mumbles, hands clasped in prayer. The woman crouches beside him and cries quietly. I reach over and take the twins from her. The pilot opens the throttle. We speed up, the plane vibrating and shaking as we haul forward along the runway.

Soon we near the troops.

The pilot eases out of his chair and kneels in the cockpit so that just the top of his head extends beyond the panel of levers and dials.

The troops open fire, and a hail of ammunition comes at us all at once.

The Belgian woman screams hysterically. The pilot hides himself beneath the control panel, throwing the throttle wide open.

Bullet holes pepper the glass of the windshield. There's a deafening metallic ping, and a dime-size puncture suddenly opens up on the left side of the hull, a few feet from where I crouch.

We reach the troops. They break ranks and dive out of our path.

The pilot scrambles into his seat, simultaneously pulling back on the controls. The nose of the plane rises. Suddenly we're airborne. Still on the floor, Richard slides backwards along the aisle until he bumps into me.

Another round of crackling gunfire. This time our right wing is hit. The plane rolls sharply to starboard, and Laura is tugged from my arms by gravity. Her head hits the hull of the plane.

We lurch violently through the air, hovering perhaps ten meters above the ground. Laura falls to the floor. There is no more runway beneath us, only brush and swamp.

"It's on fire!" I shout frantically to the pilot. "The wing is on fire!"

"D'accord!" he calls back to us. "Hold on tight!"

We reach the place where the swamp broadens out into the Congo River. The pilot takes us down low over the water, continuing his right-handed roll until we are parallel with the river's current.

I realize what the pilot's doing. If it works, he's a hero. If not, it will be the death of us. The fire on the wing burns. Any moment, the right engine will ignite. He must put the blaze out before this happens, or we will go down like a plane in a World War II dogfight.

It's a great blessing that the ardor of revolution has stilled boat traffic on the river, or a catastrophic collision might occur.

The pilot inches the plane downward until we are low enough over the surface that the force of the propellers begin to throw water up against the windows and obscure the view. The Belgian woman rocks back and forth in her seat, still weeping to herself. The pilot tips the plane ever so slightly to the right. I hold my breath and squeeze my eyes closed.

With a horrific shearing sound, the tip of the right wing grazes the surface of the water. We take an abrupt turn in that direction, then the plane teeters wildly from side to side. Ellen and I are thrown across the aisle and against the far wall. My shoulder smarts from the impact.

The pilot pulls back sharply on the controls, and the nose of the plane points up toward the sky. I look out the window as the world rapidly drops away below us. The right wing appears undamaged. Most important, the fire is out. We all cheer, spontaneously.

I pick up Laura, who is bleeding from a small cut on her head.

"Baby? Baby?" I say to her, but she doesn't respond. She's half-conscious. She looks up at me, too stunned to cry. I dab at the blood with my handkerchief so it doesn't run into her eyes.

We circle back over the airport. The soldiers have become ants, running around randomly, guns raised over their heads.

Then they're gone.

At last, Laura's face tightens up like a prune and she lets out a loud, indignant wail. I know this is a very good sign. I pick her up and kiss her, though she's shaking her arms and legs, furiously upset. I recall a poem from *Songs from the Slums* where Kagawa says the cry of an infant is beautiful when you've been trying to pull it back from the dead.

"Go on, let it out," I tell her joyously.

"The man at the ticket window," Richard says, "said he got a telephone call saying that natives and whites are attacking one another in the street. The police fired tear gas into the marketplace. It must've been just after we left. There are people dead, a lot of people."

We climb higher and higher, finally leveling off. I look down at the jungle below us. It seems so clean and unspoiled. Rivers meander about the terrain, fingers of deep, tea-color water weaving among the forest of green. The sun is hidden behind clouds that rise high from the western skyline.

This is how I want to remember Africa.

"Mesdames, Messieurs, welcome aboard Sabena airlines. We hope you have a safe flight," the Belgian pilot says in a shaky voice, finding his cap and squaring it atop his head.

"Where's your suitcase?" Richard asks, looking around.

"Huh?"

"Your suitcase," he says again.

I shake my head sadly, for I realize I left the little case sitting on the bench back in the terminal building, leaving me totally divested of material possessions.

IT TAKES THREE IMPOSSIBLY LONG DAYS to reach Idlewild Airport in New York City. The twins didn't take kindly to being fired upon, nor did they find the up-and-down pressure in their ears amusing. As a result, they cried and fussed their way across the Atlantic. Richard can now brag that he walked all the way home from

Africa, and it's true—for too many hours he marched up and down the aisles of several aircraft, trying to quiet our dearly disoriented children.

With all the distress, the twins have become terrors. The perils they faced on the mission are suddenly supplanted by what the civilized world promises. At the Athens airport, Ellen eats cigarette butts from an ashtray, refusing to cough them into my hand until I slap her on the back. When we change planes in the Canary Islands, Laura gets her arm stuck in a vending machine and we very nearly miss our connecting flight.

It's dawn in New York when we step off the tarmac and into the terminal building. I'm overwhelmed by all the people speaking English. I feel as though I should listen to all their conversations at once.

There are television sets in the waiting rooms, and padded chairs, and women wearing high heels and hats and perfume. Where a few days ago I was part of the elite class, I suddenly feel extraordinarily plain and poor.

True to their promise, the Missions board has sent a representative to meet us. A tall, dark-hair man from Brooklyn waves when he sees us come through the door.

We borrow five dollars from him so we can buy some breakfast.

"I'm supposed to tell you that Mr. Hinton's glad you made it out okay," the man says. I wonder what he means by this until we pass a newsstand in the hallway and I get a look at the headline across the front page of the *New York Times*: BELGIAN PARATROOPERS STORM CONGO: MURDER AND RAPE CLOSE AMERICAN MISSIONS.

Below this, they've printed a map of the *Equateur* provinces: Bolenge, Mondombe, and Longa are marked with black stars. I turn away from the newspaper. Without warning, the horror of the last week of my life, until now deferred, hits me.

I crumble to the floor.

MY NAME IS EVA MARIE DUNAGAN.

In two weeks, I will be thirty-one years old.

The Disciples of Christ Missions board sent me to Africa. I wanted to do what was right.

In my pocket are a handkerchief soiled with dirt and blood, a pair of scratched tortoiseshell sunglasses with no case, and the some leftover change from breakfast.

I'm a spectacle in the late-morning summer sun that fills a crowded waiting room. I have left the Dark Continent, poor of possessions but rich with truths about God and man, truths that have taken my innocence and forever changed my faith. Love has become my God; I want to be loving, when and where I can. I want to accept that sometimes I don't know the way, and not insist that I do. There may come other ways and other times. . . .

And for as many rains as I may survive, I will carry this truth in my heart.

LaVergne, TN USA
20 August 2009
155388LV00002B/15/P